FLANN O'BRIEN
A CRITICAL INTRODUCTION TO HIS WRITINGS

Anne Clissmann

FLANN O'BRIEN
A critical introduction
to his writings

The Story-Teller's Book-Web

GILL AND MACMILLAN • DUBLIN
BARNES & NOBLE BOOKS • NEW YORK
a division of Harper & Row Publishers, Inc.

First published in Ireland in 1975

Gill and Macmillan Ltd
15/17 Eden Quay
Dublin 1
and in London through association with the
Macmillan Publishers Group

Published in the USA in 1975 by
Harper and Row Publishers, Inc.
Barnes and Noble Import Division

Gill and Macmillan S B N 7171 0718 3
Barnes and Noble I S B N 0-06-491215-9

Printed and bound in Great Britain by
REDWOOD BURN LIMITED
Trowbridge & Esher

To Frank

Contents

Acknowledgments

Mrs Evelyn O'Nolan, Kevin O'Nolan and Ciaran O'Nolan helped me enormously by providing me with essential information and giving me access to press cuttings and book reviews. I am indebted to them for their willingness to help and to answer questions.

The staff of the Morris Library, University of Southern Illinois were always willing to photocopy material for my use. Without their help it would have been impossible to proceed. The staff of the National Library, Dublin were helpful in finding the early magazines and providing photocopies where necessary. Timothy O'Keefe and his secretary allowed me to see all the letters and drafts in their possession and sent me copies which proved to be invaluable. My publishers, through MacGibbon and Kee, made the manuscript of Patrick Power's translation of *An Béal Bocht* available to me in time for it to be discussed in this book.

Special thanks are due to David Powell of the University of Western New Mexico, who allowed me to see all the fruits of his labours, made innumerable copies of letters for me, and allowed me to read his thesis on Flann O'Brien. In particular, I am indebted to him for the account of the biography of Myles na gCopaleen.

Among the many others who helped me and to whom I extend my warmest thanks are Niall Sheridan, Niall Montgomery, Seamus Kelly, Brian Inglis, and Richard Watts, Jnr.

ABBREVIATIONS

AS2B	*At Swim-Two-Birds*
BM	*The Best of Myles*
BON	Brian O'Nolan
CL	*Cruiskeen Lawn*
HL	*The Hard Life*
SP	*Stories and Plays*
TOK	Timothy O'Keefe
TP	*The Third Policeman*
WLA	*A Weekly Look Around*

Note. Although Flann O'Brien was meticulously careful in his presentation of material in the Irish language, many of the newspapers and magazines to which he submitted his writing had no facilities for printing *fadas* (length-marks on vowels) or were careless in type-setting from his manuscripts. *Fadas* have therefore been inserted in all extracts in Irish quoted in this book.

The author and publishers acknowledge with thanks the permission of the following to quote copyright material: Mrs Evelyn O'Nolan; Mr Ciaran O'Nuallain; Granada Publishing Ltd; Hart-Davis MacGibbon; A. M. Heath & Co.

Introduction

THE PUBLICATION of *At Swim-Two-Birds* in 1939 immediately brought Flann O'Brien a number of loyal and interested friends; regrettably a very small number. Since the reissue of *At Swim* and the appearance in quick succession of *The Hard Life, The Dalkey Archive, The Third Policeman, The Best of Myles* and, recently, the translation of *An Béal Bocht,* the ranks of his admirers have increased to an army and now spread all over the world. O'Brien's books have been translated into French and German. Theses have been , and are being, written on him in France, Germany, Italy, Canada, America, Ireland and England. The importance of his books in the development of the modern novel and within the Anglo-Irish and native Irish or Gaelic traditions is now being fully realised.

A number of courageous reviewers have attempted to make sense of the delightfully complex world which O'Brien presented. A few critical articles have been written, and many personal reminiscences and anecdotes, but, to date, there has been no consideration of his work as a whole. My intention in this book is to attempt to fill this gap; to provide a general introduction to the work of Flann O'Brien — Myles na gCopaleen which I hope will interest both the student and the O'Brien devotee.

Since it is the first book on the subject, I have deliberately ordered it so as to provide as wide a discussion of O'Brien's work as possible. Much of that work is still unpublished and, since it is variable in quality, may remain so. Even some of the published work is difficult of access, since it appeared in relatively obscure journals and magazines or provincial news-papers and has not yet been collected in more available

editions. In the 1960s, for example, O'Brien wrote a substantial number of plays for television. These exist in
manuscript form in the library of the University of Southern
Illinois, but it is difficult to see how their publication could
ever be a commercial proposition. As a consequence anyone
who was not a close friend of O'Brien's, a frequent reader of
the *Irish Times,* a student of UCD in the 1930s, and an avid
television viewer, will be unaware of the great amount of
material that is available, much of which reinforces themes in
the novels or reveals the development of an attitude.

I have tried, then, to provide as complete a summary of the
unknown work as was possible, and to present both it and the
well-known material in a chronological manner in order to
give some idea of the development of O'Brien's interests and
skills as a novelist, journalist and playwright.

This arrangement has, of course, led to some difficulties.
O'Brien was often obsessive in some of his themes, and to treat
his work chronologically involves a certain amount of
repetition. He constantly returned to an attack on Joyce, for
example, yet I felt that to abstract this and treat it
thematically would, apart from offending against the
chronological arrangement of the rest of the book, give an
impression of a greater organisation and symmetry in
O'Brien's approach than it actually possessed. Furthermore,
O'Brien's stylistic achievements were sporadic, due primarily
to financial pressures which forced him to spend a good deal of
his time in hack journalism. It would have been better, in
some ways, to ignore the failures, but it is clear that some of
his most triumphant successes sprang directly from the
methods and concerns of this journalism and are often only a
hairsbreadth away from failure. This fact made it necessary to
deal with the frustrating years of provincial journalism and
unsuccessful articles, tedious as these often are.

Two quite different problems arose from my own
deficiencies. The more important of these is my ignorance of
the Irish language, both ancient and modern. O'Brien was a
writer who performed with equal fluency in both Irish and
English and who derived much of his unique vision of life from
the inspiration of early Irish literature. His book in Irish *An
Béal Bocht* is regarded as a classic of modern Irish writing, full

of subtle and complex linguistic jokes and allusions to contemporary events and leading personalities of the Gaelic revival movement. No translation can hope to convey the quality of that linguistic dexterity. From an appreciation of this aspect of O'Brien's work I and many of his readers are excluded. It is to be hoped that some Gaelic scholar will write (in English, please) a substantial account of the Gaelic element in O'Brien's work. In the meantime I have done what I could, using a number of authorities on the spirit and content of early Irish literature. I have used Patrick Power's translation of *An Béal Bocht* and could, of course, only comment on the more obvious elements in that book—the satirical presentation of the 'Gaeligore' and the attack on other Irish writers (whom I also had to read in translation). My hope is that what little I have done will, nevertheless, give some indication of this aspect of O'Brien's work and reveal the need for a more authoritative study.

The second problem derives from the first. O'Brien had a command of at least three languages (and probably more). The awareness of linguistic nuance that resulted from this command reveals itself in the style of all his novels and in the *Cruiskeen Lawn* column. I am aware of this but incapable of examining the characteristics of his style, I must leave this to someone more competent.

In this introduction to the work of Flann O'Brien I have attempted to give an analysis of dominant themes, attitudes and techniques in his writing. For the sake of the student who will, I hope, find this book of use, I have given a separate chapter to each novel and coherent body of writing, and presented my conclusions within that chapter. (It is my experience that students tend to read relevant chapters rather than complete books.)

I am, I hope, aware of all the deficiencies of this book. Even these, however, may prove useful, for I hope to raise such a number of unanswered questions that scholars will be compelled to reply, thereby initiating a debate that will result in a proper critical assessment of O'Brien's achievement and his place in modern literature.

Anne Clissmann

1

Biography: Brian, Flann, Myles

Born Paris 1691. Widely troubled. A connoisseur of
potheen and stirabout. Took part in 1898 insurrection.
Member of Seanad Éireann, 1925–1927. Minister for
Justice, May–August, 1931. Regius Professor of Potheen,
TCD. President of Ireland, 1945.[1]

WE FIND these intriguing details in one of the 'official
biographies' of Myles na gCopaleen. Myles is also Flann
O'Brien, John James Doe, George Knowall, Brother Barnabas,
the Great Count O'Blather, and many another, depending
on his mood and circumstances. The 'official biographies'
tell of Myles's long years in different countries and in-
carnations and recount in startling and overwhelming detail
the list of his many high offices, distinctions and deeds of
bravery.

Myles's readers had no difficulty in believing that such a
talented and long-lived man could have been President of
Ireland, an illegitimate son of Henry VIII, a count of the Holy
Roman Empire, and a famous detective. Flann O'Brien's
readers, however, usually wanted to know some particulars of
the 'real' man behind the pseudonym and O'Brien was very
obliging in revealing personal and heart-rending details of his
life to eager inquirers. One intrepid interviewer, who arrived
in Dublin in 1943 and sought out the great man with the
intention of obtaining a 'true-life' account for the American
magazine *Time,* was given an 'official' statement. This, the
first biography of 'Éire's columnist', gives the reader an
intimate picture of the great man's sad past and merrier daily
habits.

People who have sought O'Nolan since he became Éire's
favorite columnist have had a hard time finding him. A

conscientous, hard-working civil servant, adept at answer-
ing letters, his days are busy with many matters of state (e.g.,
settling claims for a recent orphanage fire). He passes as few
nights as possible with the metropolitan arty crowd; among
them he is a good drinker, poor conversationalist. He
prefers the talk at the tough bars and quayside pubs.

One of the few things O'Nolan takes seriously is chess. He
is equipped with a pocket chessboard, plays promiscuously
with chance acquaintances. He has informally beaten
World Champion Alekhine. He writes so easily that he
grows bored with it. *At Swim Two Birds,* O'Nolan's first
novel in English, is never concluded, just stops abruptly.

O'Nolan was a pale-faced, bucktoothed youngster of 23
when he scudded into Éire's Civil Service on a foam of
brilliant answers to such questions as 'How far is the earth
from the moon?' Born in Northern Ireland's County
Tyrone, he had lived until then without notable incident
save a visit to Germany in 1933.

There he went to study the language, managed to get
himself beaten up and bounced out of a beer hall for un-
complimentary references to Adolf Hitler: 'They got me all
wrong in that pub.' He also met and married 18-year-old
Clara Ungerland, blonde, violin-playing daughter of a
Cologne basket-weaver. She died a month later. O'Nolan
returned to Éire and never mentions her.[2]

This 'biography', though written by someone else, is so
much a work of fantasy, that it begins to resemble the 'official
autobiographies'. It indicates the length to which O'Nolan
and his friends would go when trying to protect, not O'Nolan's
identity, but his personality. O'Nolan was always full of
contempt for those he managed to fool, and he was later to
remark, even while elaborating the details of the *Time* story:

I am not the worst at inventing tall and impossible stories,
but what I produced on this occasion was a superb heap of
twaddle that would deceive nobody of 10 years of age. I
remember it contained an account of my marriage which
took place to a Cologne basket-maker's daughter on a
steamer going down the Rhine.   (*CL.* 13 Apr. 1960)

Indeed, O'Nolan need not have been so contemptuous; his

efforts to throw a screen of false information or pseudonymous personalities in front of himself undoubtedly make any attempt at biography very difficult. To a great extent he became something of a myth. Stories and anecdotes, most of them apocryphal, abound in Dublin, and it is always difficult to separate truth from fantasy or even to decide whether an account was written by the person who signed it or by O'Nolan himself. He hated the idea of biography and so went out of his way to resist the efforts of biographers to gain clear and unambiguous facts about his life. In his *Cruiskeen Lawn* column he wrote on 27 February 1957:

> *Auto*biography is not so bad — indeed it is probably advisable to get in first. But the type of biography that lifts the veil, hacks down the elaborate façades one has spent a lifetime in erecting — that is horrible.

That is why there are so many freely proffered autobiographies, so many pseudonyms. What we as readers are presented with is a multi-faceted life and personality so rich and varied that we could not possibly ask for more. Why should we? Is not the fantasy better than a thousand detailed realities? O'Nolan was a man who dramatised himself into a series of poses, each one sufficient for the moment; who laid a trail of false clues so that his essential privacy would not be violated. He was for most of his life a very public man and so he needed privacy as a defence against the onslaughts he had to face every day. It was almost as if, by putting Myles na gCopaleen forward, prepared to take on, and conquer, the world, Brian O'Nolan could retire to an impregnable and safe position. Whatever the reason for the adoption of pseudonyms and the self-dramatisation which is a notable feature of his work, the defensive stance became a part of his artistic practice. When he wrote, years later, of the essential prerequisites of the literary artist, he said that any writer needs

> a thorough education of the widest kind . . . an equable yet versatile temperament, and the compartmentation of . . . personality for the purpose of literary utterance.[3]

This 'compartmentation of personality' led to the versatility which is such a delight and yet remained a mode by which a vulnerable personality and deeply held beliefs could be protected from that mockery which O'Nolan was himself so well able to use. The feeling of a need for privacy and safety is summed up in a sentence used by the anonymous narrator of *The Third Policeman* as he comments on his conversation with Sergeant Pluck.

> I considered it desirable that he should know nothing about me but it was even better if he knew several things which were quite wrong.   (p. 57)

It is this impulse which makes O'Nolan express himself most characteristically in inversion, side-track and complication. His point of view, where it can be discerned, often emerges as the product of mutually opposed attitudes. He looks obliquely at life, concentrates on its unusual aspects and only reveals himself grudgingly and in hints.

Thus most of the biographical information which has been published about O'Nolan is incorrect in one way or another, but any attempt to rectify the errors can itself be correct only in outline.

Brian O'Nolan (or Brian Ó Nualláin, the Irish form of his name which he sometimes used) was born on 5 October 1911 at 15 The Bowling Green, Strabane, Co. Tyrone. He was the third of twelve children. The two older than himself were boys. Gearóid, three years older, went into business and Ciarán, one year his senior, is editor of the Irish weekly newspaper *Inniu*. Two of his sisters, Roisín and Maev, became nuns; three others married. Of his four younger brothers, one is a doctor, one an artist, one an academic, and one is in management. It is, then, a family of enormous and diversified talent.

Their father, Michael Victor O'Nolan, and their mother, Agnes Gormley, were born in Omagh, Co. Tyrone in 1875 and 1886 respectively, but they met in Strabane where the Gormleys had set up a business and where Michael O'Nolan was stationed as an officer in the customs and excise service. They married in 1906 and the first three children were born in Strabane.

As a customs and excise officer, Brian's father was subject to many changes of location, so, shortly after Brian's birth, the family moved to Dublin and were living in the suburb of

Inchicore at the time of the 1916 rising. Ciarán O'Nolan, then aged six, remembers, 'the rising, and also trips to the city before it took place'.[4] Brian, who was aged five at the time, may have remembered it too, and talk about the rising and the civil war may have enabled him to write some of the passages in *At Swim*.

At some time around 1917 Michael O'Nolan was promoted but was 'unattached', that is, he had no fixed location but could still be moved from place to place. In order to give his wife the comfort of being close to her relatives he took a house back in Strabane and the family remained there until 1920, when the father became 'established', with Tullamore, in the midlands of Ireland, as his district. The family had a house about two miles outside the town, and it may be the landscape around Tullamore which is described in *The Third Policeman*.

In 1923 Michael O'Nolan was promoted once more and the family returned to Dublin to 25 Herbert Place, a quiet road by the canal. (*The Hard Life* is set in the area around the canal.) It was when the family moved back to Dublin that the three eldest boys went to school for the first time. At home they spoke Irish among themselves. (Myles, in *Cruiskeen Lawn*, facetiously describes himself as having to learn English at the age of twenty-nine.) There was, apparently, no Irish on their mother's side of the family and they knew English as soon as Irish. They were, in effect, completely bilingual. They had obviously been well taught at home, for although they went to school late (Gearóid was fifteen, Ciarán thirteen and Brian twelve), they do not seem to have experienced any particular difficulty. Neither Brian nor Ciarán enjoyed the Christian Brothers' school in Synge Street. Synge Street school features in *The Hard Life* as a dreary, dirty place where corporal punishment was handed out with a little too much malicious glee. In *Cruiskeen Lawn* O'Nolan reiterates and emphasises his dislike of the place, but he could, occasionally, talk of it in more moderate terms.

> I read contemporary literature in five languages, thanks to the Christian Brothers and an odd hiding now and then.
>
> (3 Jan. 1957)

The boys were probably glad when, in 1927, they moved from

Herbert Place to Avoca Terrace in Blackrock and changed schools to Blackrock College. There is no mention of the college in any of O'Nolan's books, so we have no clue as to what he thought of it. However, he obviously liked the southern coastal area of Dublin because it occupies such a large place in *The Dalkey Archive*.

In 1925 Michael O'Nolan was appointed one of the three revenue commissioners in Dublin Castle and remained in that post until his death at the end of July 1937.

Brian left Blackrock College in 1929, matriculated at University College, Dublin, and entered the university in October. In the summer of 1930 he passed the first university examination in Arts with second-class honours in Irish, and in 1932 the BA examination in German, English and Irish — again, with a second-class honours. This was a very fine achievement in a university where very few students read the honours course; it was certainly very much better than that of James Joyce many years earlier. In 1933 he won a travelling scholarship to Germany and was probably abroad from December 1933 to June 1934. The scholarship was an eagerly sought-after prize and was intended to help students improve their linguistic ability. Brian went to the University of Cologne

and spent many months on the Rhineland and at Bonn, drifting gradually away from the strict pursuit of study.[5]

On his return to Ireland he began an MA thesis on Modern Irish poetry, and gained his degree in the autumn of 1935.

His years at university proved to be crucial in his development. His brother Ciarán says:

Whereas I, at the age of 11 or so, used to walk the two miles into Tullamore to buy a notebook in which to indite some rubbish purporting to be a 'novel', Brian never showed any interest then or for many years after in the writing game. It was only when he went to University that he began to write for the first time.[6]

UCD was to provide the first real stimulus for O'Nolan's creative imagination and was also to offer him a forum for his views. Yet his comments seem to reveal that he found little stimulation in his studies. Indeed, he seems to have despised UCD as an academic institution. It is difficult to take seriously a lot of what purports to be serious comment in *Cruiskeen Lawn,* but where an opinion reoccurs after an interval of years, it can be accorded some attention. Thus in 1958 we find Myles writing:

> I am myself a graduate of that place and certify that I found the level of 'learning' and tuition contemptible, and the standard set in examination papers just a joke.
>
> (28 Jul. 1958)

In 1966 he was to reiterate this.

> . . . what have I to show for five years of my life? . . . I paid no attention whatsoever to books or study, and regarded lectures as a joke — which, in fact, they were if you discern anything funny in mawkish, obtuse mumblings on subjects any intelligent person could master single-handed in a few months. The exams I found childish and in fact the whole university concept I found to be a sham. The only result my father got for his money was the certainty that his son had laid faultlessly the foundation of a system of heavy drinking and could be always relied upon to make a break of at least 25 even with a bad cue. I sincerely believe that if university education were universally available and availed of, the country would collapse in one generation. (2 Mar. 1966)

This, of course, is only partly true. What O'Nolan is presenting here is a portrait of himself similar to that of the student narrator of *At Swim,* who attends college very rarely, drinks heavily, watches billiards being played, and manages to get through his course without opening very many books. Brian O'Nolan certainly seems to have excelled at billiards and, according to himself, rarely attended lectures. This was, perhaps, due to his disappointment with the scholarship of Douglas Hyde, then Professor of Irish at UCD, afterwards first President of Ireland. O'Nolan liked Douglas Hyde as a man; he found him most kind and generous but said that 'he spoke Irish inaccurately and badly' and that 'his methods of lecturing were fantastic, often comic'. Nevertheless, he speaks of him with affection, and affection is not a quality which is abundant in O'Nolan's writing. In *Cruiskeen Lawn* he wrote:

> I was a sort of friend of his and purportedly a student under

his tutelage . . . After some experience of his lectures . . . I
decided to abstain from his tuition; a new billiards room
had been installed in the building. But one morning I found
myself accidentally in attendance and answered to my name
at roll-call. He blanched as if struck by lightning and
swivelled those extraordinary eyes. 'Ní féidir, ní féidir!'
[Impossible, impossible] he groaned. Apparently he had
assumed I was a myth.   (13 Aug. 1959)

Writing in a completely serious article about Hyde's 'heart
of gold', O'Nolan complained that his lectures were 'surprisingly elementary' and added:

Skipping lectures while contriving a prim presence at roll-
call became a great skill, particularly with poker and
billiards men.[7]

It seemed, indeed, that a large percentage of the students
found poker and billiards more absorbing than study;
however, this may have indicated merely that recreational
facilities in the college were astonishingly limited. When
O'Nolan first went to college, there were no sitting rooms, but
before he left a large 'students' room' had been

provided in the semi-ruinous remnant of the old Royal
University premises, which is still behind the UCD façade;
this room was destined to become the home of really
ferocious poker schools . . . Later a billiards table was
conceded, possibly in reality a missionary move to redeem
poker addicts.[8]

Life in college really centred round the main hall, where
groups of students lounged between lectures. The ladies of
college had a room to themselves, and the only place where the
sexes met in the college was a little tea-room. The students
were summoned to lectures by a large and noisy bell rung by
one of the hall porters; these gentlemen, called Ryan and
Redmond were 'made in the proportions of Mutt and Jeff'.[9]
They became important personages in the university
magazine, were often caricatured as de Valera and Arthur
Griffith, and were mercilessly satirised for their obsessive habit
of trying to trap students who were surreptitiously and illegally
smoking in the college.

The atmosphere, then, seems to have been restricted, the students still treated a little like children. Yet O'Nolan found stimulus for his writing there, and that stimulus came, not unnaturally, from friends and associates and from extra-curricular activities.

The students who were contemporaries of O'Nolan's were to become leading men in Irish society and letters. Among the more notable were Robin Dudley Edwards, Vivion de Valera, Cyril Cusack, Niall Sheridan, Donagh MacDonagh, Cearbhall O Dálaigh, Seán Ó Faoláin, Mervyn Wall and Charles Donnelly. With so many fine and lively minds transmitting ideas and opinions, it must have been a time of great excitement. Indeed, it would seem as if the college itself felt that it was going through a period of renewal after several years of mental somnolence. The year 1930 marked the university's anniversary, and during this same year the university became aware of itself as a distinct entity and wished to create literary and political organs to express that sense of identity. At the prompting of the oldest established society in college, the Literary and Historical Debating Society, a college magazine called *The National Student* was revived. The first issue of its new series appeared in March 1930 with the expressed intention of

> [furnishing] the College with a symbol of its essential unity, and [fostering] a keen *esprit de corps* among all College men and women.[10]

It went on to describe UCD as 'a College which has possibilities of greatness'.[11]

It was in this sort of atmosphere that O'Nolan began to write, not, it seems, for *The National Student* but for a successor and competitor, *Comhthrom Féinne,* the magazine of the newly awakened and expanding Students' Representative Council (SRC). By the time these magazines started, he had been in the college for some time. Niall Montgomery, a contemporary and lifelong friend of O'Nolan's, describes his first appearances in UCD. He descended on UCD, says Montgomery,

> like a shower of paratroopers, deploying a myriad of pseudonymous personalities in the interests of pure destruction.[12]

Niall Sheridan's memory of him was as

> a first-year Celtic Studies student, with a round, pale face,
> rabbit-like teeth and an alert and piercing gaze.[13]

He looked, Sheridan said, like a 'satanic cherub', and added
elsewhere that O'Nolan's

> air of demoniac innocence . . . was by no means mis-
> leading. Indeed, even in that astringent circle, he was
> known to be formidable in argument and deadly with the
> pen.[14]

These qualities did not, however, appear at once. They
were to emerge, fully developed, in the college magazine and
in the L & H Society, where O'Nolan held a notable and somewhat infamous position for many years. There is no record of
him until 1930, when in May of that year, in the first issue of
Comhthrom Féinne, we find mention of his performances at
the L & H. In the second issue of that magazine the stately and
goodly Brother Barnabas, O'Nolan's first pseudonymous
creation, made his debut.

From then on, Brother Barnabas appeared regularly and
O'Nolan was to become one of the leading college personalities
to be reported on, quoted, argued with and never forgotten.
A number of interesting comments about O'Nolan in the
college magazine give us an insight into several little-known
aspects of his character. It has been remarked how few women
there are in O'Nolan's novels and what little attempt there
is to present them as fully realised characters. An editorial
comment in *Comhthrom Féinne* seems to bear out O'Nolan's
dislike of women.

> Mr Ua Nualláin's opinion of college women, coming under
> the Amendment (Censorship of Publications) Act and in
> deference to already tender feelings of female members of
> the Pro-Fide Society, was very reluctantly blue-pencilled,
> but may be seen on application at our office.[15]

O'Nolan had, it seems, a considerable reputation as a 'hard'
man.

> We could tell you a thing of two about . . . Brian Ó
> Nualláin . . . but that our censor won't pass it.[16]

In spite of this, he was admired by certain young ladies and one, at least, was mocked for her *tendresse*.

The alluring and coy M-lly W-r,
As she swam in the Mull of Cantyre,
  Remarked to the fishes,
  'I've got all my wishes,
It's BRINE OH! NO LAND I desire!'[17]

O'Nolan in his writing in *Comhthrom Féinne* often mocked the members of a society called Pro-Fide. It was a Catholic social study group which debated social issues and sought for a solution to contemporary problems. Its members were much given to long walks on Sundays. O'Nolan's own name was, however, often associated with Pro-Fide by other writers. 'Doppelganger', the magazine's gossip columnist, names O'Nolan as director of Pro-Fide's newly-established 'information bureau', and later on someone else writes

BELIEVE IT OR NOT—

Mr B. Ua Nualláin goes for a three-mile walk on Sundays. **Pro-Fide** or **Bona-Fide?**[18]

O'Nolan must have read these comments on himself and he may have remembered them and worked them into his books. The Pro-Fide information bureau may have provided the germ of the idea for the various Myles na gCopaleen research bureaux, and the three-mile walk has an echo in the scene between the narrator, Brinsley and the uncle in *At Swim* when walking and piety are indirectly associated.

O'Nolan was often to attack the practices and personalities of the Church, but this did not prevent him from remaining a sincere and intelligent Catholic throughout his life. His membership of Pro-Fide, if he was a member, reveals a deeper and more concerned aspect of his personality than do any of his other university activities.

Another comment, unconnected with Pro-Fide, and quite frivolous, may have given O'Nolan the basis of the 'mollycule theory' which was to appear in *The Third Policeman* and *The Dalkey Archive*.

Mr Brian Ua Nualláin regrets the fact that he is becoming lantern jawed from riding his bicycle in the dark.[19]

Other comments reveal that O'Nolan's profession of indolence was accepted by his companions. Brother Barnabas, in his College Almanac for 1932, prophesied that O'Nolan, with others, would gain a first-class honours degree and a travelling studentship in the forthcoming exams. This news, so unexpected, would stun the recipients, who would have to be 'brought around with brandy afterwards'. Once created, the idea that O'Nolan did no work was readily accepted.

> BELIEVE IT OR NOT—!
> **Mr B. Ó Nualláin** is reading for his degree.[20]

On the other hand, the magazine also yields a letter written by O'Nolan protesting at the closure of the university library to allow a dance to be held. This complaint and the excellent examination results he achieved reveal that he must have been a very serious student indeed. One of his foremost personal characteristics (far from being indolence) was an intense energy which allowed him to plunge himself wholeheartedly into the many activities he undertook. As well as writing, studying, billiards, Pro-Fide and the SRC, he also acted in the UCD dramatic society, edited the magazine at one stage and, even more important, played a very prominent part in the L & H.

The L & H met every Saturday night to debate serious and not-so-serious topics. It was a rowdy and lively society much given to practical jokes of the type described in *At Swim*, though O'Nolan's position in it was by no means as detached and passive as his student narrator's. O'Nolan's position in the L & H was to some extent the result of the physical limitations of the college. The society met in 86 St Stephen's Green, 'a very dirty place and in bad repair'.[21] The largest lecture room was used but it had a seating capacity of only two hundred and the audience usually numbered about six hundred. The semi-circular auditorium was first filled to total capacity and then the hall outside was jammed with a swaying, shouting body of people who came to be known as the 'mob'. There was no question of coming early so as to get a place inside. Many people *chose* to remain in the vestibule. There were practical reasons for this. Ladies who attended the L & H and who had to leave at ten o'clock to return to their convent halls of residence had to fight their way out of the hall to the cheers and jeers of the assembled multitudes. Once in, it was practically impossible to get out. Outside there was more freedom. Students could retire for a game of cards on the steps or pay a quick visit to a local pub called 'The Winter Garden Palace', 'where it was possible to drink three or four strong pints at sevenpence each'.[22] The mob, in reality, controlled the proceedings. In theory, when the debate became too rowdy, the porter, Flynn, would control it. Flynn, however, was an incredible man 'whose eyes were nearly always closed, though not from an ocular complaint or mere sleep'.[23] In any case it would have been impossible for him to control behaviour where space was confined and lighting was by gas. O'Nolan gives us a memorable description of the scene.

> This most heterogeneous congregation, reeling about, shouting and singing in the hogarthian pallor of a single gas-jet (when somebody had not thought fit to extinguish the same) came to be known as the mob, and I had the honour to be acknowledged its president . . . A visitor would probably conclude that it was merely a gang of rowdies, dedicated to making a deafening uproar, the *obbligato* to some unfortunate member's attempts to make a speech within. It was certainly a disorderly gang but its disorders were not aimless and stupid, but often necessary and salutary. It could nearly be claimed that the mob was merely a severe judge of the speakers.[24]

O'Nolan, with his friend and 'special-effects manager', Jack Nevin, controlled the mob. What O'Nolan neglected to mention in his account was that the 'somebody' who from time to time extinguished the gas was Nevin, a mechanical wizard, who co-operated with O'Nolan to ensure the maximum effect during crucial stages of the proceedings. O'Nolan was always able to control the mob and he believed and argued, against much opposition, that any good speaker should be able to do so. He had little time for the other debating societies: they were too calm, there was no mob; indeed, he ceased to take any interest in the L & H when it began to meet in the big Physics Theatre in Earlsfort Terrace and the physical limitations which had called forth the mob were no longer there.

The standard of debate seems to have been high. O'Nolan admired J. C. Flood for 'his wit and his scorching tongue'[25] and Tim O'Hanrahan, who was 'a first-class debater on any subject under the sun'.[26] At the time of O'Nolan's admission to the college the auditor of the L & H was Robin Dudley Edwards. In 1931–32 Cearbhall Ó Dálaigh was elected. O'Nolan regretted Ó Dálaigh's obsessive interest in Fianna Fáil politics but approved of his attitude to the mob which was similar to his own. It is even possible that O'Nolan and Nevin supported Ó Dálaigh's candidature. A report in the magazine says that the 'Proletariat Party' met, with O'Nolan in the chair, and decided to support Ó Dálaigh. It was clear that O'Nolan himself would be in line for the auditorship of the society. He was the unofficial leader of the opposition, and there were many who greatly admired his debating powers and his ability to sway an audience. In 1932–33 he won the medal for impromptu debate. This was an important honour: the gold medal for oratory went, traditionally, to the auditor of the society, and O'Nolan's success was therefore an indication that he was, in fact, the best orator in the society. Years later, writing in *Cruiskeen Lawn*, he was to remark about the prize:

> Nothing surprising about that, for guff comes out of me as readily as a half-pint of Tullamore slips in.   (18 Dec. 1964)

One of the members of the L & H, R. N. Cooke, has left a most memorable account of O'Nolan's debates and of his candidature for the auditorship. It is worth quoting in full.

> O'Nolan was undoubtedly the best humorous speaker of my time. I feel certain that he never prepared a speech or made the most exiguous note for a speech in his life but I have seen him, I think in de Valera's year, hold the house alternately convulsed with laughter and almost shame-faced with pathos for a full fifteen minutes. In an impromptu debate he was given the subject, after he had stood up to speak: Sweet are the Uses of Advertisement. He said nothing for about half a minute while he felt in the outside pockets of his overcoat and then drew from the breast pocket a crumpled copy of the *Evening Herald*. Unrolling the paper slowly, he looked through it until he came upon the advertisement for Lux Soap Flakes and read the headline aloud:

'I wonder does he see that faded slip?'
From that on he dealt with the ludicrous aspects of the ad —
with occasional reference to the text, while the house shook
with laughter; but almost imperceptibly he changed the line
and analysed the danger of such advertising with a
thoughtful penetration of which few had believed him
capable. There was a dead silence when he finished and
then a real ovation. The meeting should have been ended
then, the rest was anticlimax. On another occasion he
finished a speech ridiculing the Blueshirt movement and in
particular the ladies' squad in the College with an
extempore parody of Colum's *Cradle Song* of which I can
recollect now only the final stanza, which he delivered half-
turned to the faithful without the door;

> O, men from the fields,
> Soft, Softly come through,
> Mavourneen is going
> From me and from you.
> O'Duffy pulls round her
> His mantle of Blue.

Poor stuff, if you will, and not an exact parody, but even
Bell, than whom no one was bluer, cheered him for it.

Unfortunately his fame as a funny man was such that he
was typed. The Society expected it from him and he seldom
disappointed it, but it meant that his real standing as a
first-class serious speaker was never acknowledged and it
gave the sun-bursters, of whom we had plenty, an
opportunity of running him down as a potential auditor of
which they availed to the full during our campaign.

Vivion de Valera on the other hand was in those days the
most serious-minded man in Ireland. It is only right to say
that he was probably the most fair-minded also. That
proved our and O'Nolan's undoing. At the last meeting of
the year, speaker after speaker poured out the most
nauseating tripe adulatory of the national aspirations which
Vivion was alleged, vicariously of course, to personify until
it seemed that a vote for O'Nolan was a nail in the coffin of
the Republic. O'Nolan was present. He spoke quietly and
with restraint in reply to the egregious nonsense of his
opponents, but some of his remarks were rather personal to

the President's vicar in College and the four of us drank our Saturday night coffee in the Savoy in solid gloom.[27]

O'Nolan was 'to retain his dislike of politics. Later in the year following his defeat he made another memorable speech, 'a magnificent satirical oration . . . in which he robed in ridicule the whole political set-up'.[28]

He seems, however, to have been bitter at his defeat, and this bitterness is manifest in his own account of the campaign.

The session 1932–33 was of some importance, for it was then I decided it was time for myself to become Auditor. My opponent was Vivion de Valera. The Fianna Fáil Party was by then firmly established, heaven on earth was at hand, and de Valera gained by this situation. I believed and said publicly that these politicians were unsuitable; so I lost the election.

As an Auditor, I would give de Valera, as in marking speeches, eight out of ten. The affairs of the L and H were cluttered with too many politicisms, objectionable not because politics should have no place in student deliberations, but simply because they bored. Perhaps I am biassed, for it was to be my later destiny to sit for many hours every day in Dáil Éireann, though not as an elected statesman, and the agonies entailed are still too fresh in my memory to be recalled without emotion.[29]

After 1934 O'Nolan began to drift away from the society, but he was to remember 'the magic those years held'[30] and one feels that his personality must have been then at its most confident and sparkling as he realised, and gloried in, his increasing powers to sway an audience to tears or laughter, to talk them, for a moment, out of their convictions and prejudices, to demonstrate the power and purpose of language, images, and style.

His departure from the L & H was not, however, a gradual withdrawing. It was to be attended by a controversy in which O'Nolan's attitude to the mob led to a spate of bitter invective directed against his personality and person. When the L & H was attacked as a 'barbarian' institution because its present auditor was unable to control the mob, O'Nolan defended it. His defence stirred up a real wasps' nest, though, on the face of it, his recommendations seem acceptable enough. Regarding public speaking as a practised art, requiring wit, personality and the capacity to be serious without being dull, he said:

> Do not address dock labourers on Canon Law, and if you must, speak to them in their own language. Silence them and compel their attention. Having compelled it, hold it. If you once flag, they will swamp you. But grip them at all costs, even at the expense of good speaking or 'parlour language'.[31]

It is clear that what O'Nolan learned in the mob and on the floor of the L & H, he was to apply later in his own persuasive, rhetorical columns, and his attitude to the generation of speakers which followed him contained a phrase which was to sum up one of his own most distinctive characteristics.

> It is a weak and spineless generation. The normal people are still standing in the unhealthy draught of the doorway. They will preserve the Society by their *destructive sanity* [my italics] and by refusing to accept spurious imitations until genuine speakers of substance and guts come along, as they inevitably must. They will continue to castigate pompous incompetents.[32]

The abuse which was showered on him as a result of this statement was deeply hurtful.

> For Mr O'Nualláin 'might-have been' has loomed largely in his College life — larger than his bantam strutting will admit.[33]

O'Nolan was also described as venomous, as a man in love with publicity, vain, lop-sided, and foolish.

In his answer to these attacks, O'Nolan signed himself thus for the first time. He was infuriated by the misspelling of the Irish form of his name, and he may have felt, as he did when adopting a pseudonym, that Brian O'Nolan was a different person to Brian Ó Nualláin, and it was the latter who was being attacked. The change of name at this juncture is perhaps significant in that it may re-emphasise the idea that a different name meant a different personality. Furthermore, one might argue that as O'Nolan was about to leave UCD he

was preparing a new personality to meet the new conditions he
was about to face. The article, as well as being a defence of his
position is also a conscious farewell to the college, and it is
likely that he would have preferred his farewell to be less
contentious. In a sad and restrained tone he wrote:

> And when Mr Fitzpatrick grows up, he will find that 'might-
> have-been' figures too largely in his own little life, as in
> everybody else's, to be safely employed as a weapon against
> others.
>
> In conclusion, let me say that, academically, I have been
> dead for two years. When a man matriculates, he is born.
> When he graduates and goes away, he dies. *De mortuis nil
> nisi bonum.*[34]

In June 1935 Niall Sheridan reported that O'Nolan had
begun work on a novel, and even though Brother Barnabas
was to make a belated appearance, in Irish, in the June and
July issues of *Comhthrom Féinne*, O'Nolan had effectively
finished his college life. The August issue of the magazine
describes him as a former student. The article sounds almost
like an obituary.

> Another newcomer to the Microphone was BRIAN UA
> NUALLÁIN, B.A., who gave fortnightly talks on books. Mr
> Ua Nualláin was called to the post of Junior Administrative
> Officer in the Civil Service at the beginning of this month.
> He is in the Department of Local Government. He was,
> under various pseudonyms, particularly that of Brother
> Barnabas, the most successful and popular contributor
> COMHTHROM FÉINNE has ever had. He is as able a writer
> in both Modern and Middle Irish as he is in English, and is
> a fine cartoonist. He was for three years the Leader of
> the Opposition in the L and H and was by far the most
> brilliant impromptu speaker that the Society produced
> within the past six or eight years.[35]

O'Nolan was to remain in the civil service until 1953, when
he retired after eighteen years of service. He worked himself
up through the Department of Local Government and was
private secretary to four successive ministers, eventually
becoming principal officer for town planning.

At the beginning of his term in the civil service he worked a five-and-a-half-day week and wrote *At Swim-Two-Birds* in his spare time. He was to remain a hard worker all his life and must have been very well organised to be able to carry out so many undertakings at once.

At Swim-Two-Birds was finished in 1938, and O'Nolan began to look for a literary agent and a publisher. In London A. M. Heath & Co liked the book, became his agents, and found Longmans to publish it. It was published in England in 1939, and the AE Memorial Fund gave O'Nolan a special prize of £30 for it.

In the January before the publication of *At Swim*, O'Nolan and Niall Sheridan began a controversy in the *Irish Times* with Seán Ó Faoláin and Frank O'Connor. They criticised what they called O'Connor's and Ó Faoláin's 'pretensions to high art'. A play of O'Connor's had been unfavourably reviewed in the *Irish Times*. Ó Faoláin defended the play, and O'Nolan and Sheridan the reviewer. An exchange of letters began, with O'Nolan using the pseudonym Flann O'Brien for the first time. O'Nolan enjoyed the controversy so much that he invented other names and wrote more letters to keep it going. The correspondence in the *Irish Times* continued for several weeks. William Burne of Longmans asked if he could see it. O'Nolan sent him cuttings and he replied: 'It is an amusing collection and bears out the Irishman's question, "Is this a private fight or may anyone join in?".'[36] But O'Nolan, clearly took the controversy seriously, for he refused to allow a copy of *At Swim* to be sent to Seán Ó Faoláin.

O'Nolan was, however, uneasy about using the pseudonym Flann O'Brien for *At Swim*. He did not want any of the rancour aroused by the feud to become associated with his first book. He proposed to use the name John Hackett instead, but this somewhat unfortunate choice was considered unsuitable by Longmans and the publication went ahead as planned.

It is interesting to note how seriously he took his desire for anonymity at this stage. He went to the length of writing to the author of 'College Notes' in the *Irish Press* to disavow his authorship of *At Swim*. Perhaps, now that he was in the civil service, he felt he needed anonymity even more, or perhaps the use of pseudonyms had become a habit with him. In a letter to Longmans he seems to refer to Flann O'Brien as his 'real' name.

Having finished the Ó Faoláin–O'Connor controversy, O'Nolan and Sheridan decided to initiate another. This one was also conducted in the 'Letters to the Editor' column of the *Irish Times*. It covered a vast range of almost totally unconnected subjects which were proposed and argued under a positive myriad of pseudonyms. The correspondence lasted for over a year and is a good example of the inventiveness of O'Nolan's and Sheridan's imagination. It is impossible to deduce who wrote the different letters. Niall Sheridan had demonstrated his comedic and parodic abilities in *Comhthrom Féinne,* and it is even possible that others joined in and that some of the letters which seem most comic are, in fact, quite serious contributions from authentic correspondents. Sheridan and O'Nolan began by taking names and addresses from Thom's Directory and then went on to invent others more appropriate to the subject in hand. Some of the letters were signed by

> An Irishman from Aberdeen
> A Glaswegian from London
> Earnest Christian
> Grandfather
> Lay Woman
> X-ray
> Commonsense
> Hilda Upshott

but the pseudonyms are far too numerous to be listed in full. The correspondence became very much like the argument between the Pooka and the Good Fairy in *At Swim*; the writers were like jugglers trying to see how many subjects could be kept going simultaneously. Letters were written in one name which contradicted those written in another, and it must have occasioned great glee when some unsuspecting outsider joined in and wrote seriously, signing themself 'Concerned' or 'Mother of Eight'. It was to prove an excellent training for *Cruiskeen Lawn* and was, indeed, to be the direct predecessor of it.

In the main, the subjects dealt with were nonsensical or fantastic, but this did not seem to matter to the readers of the *Irish Times*. The circulation of that newspaper increased spectacularly while the letters continued. It was a time of war, and it may be that nonsense and fantasy were badly needed as an escape-valve in a gloomy time. O'Nolan seems to have been of this opinion for, in *Cruiskeen Lawn* which was written all through the war, he rarely mentions the conflicts which were shattering the rest of the world. Only when the war was over did he castigate the Irish people for their complacency and inability to learn from the events of the past six years.

The increasing popularity of the *Irish Times* correspondence column led the editor, R. M. Smyllie, to wish to meet O'Nolan. He was very pleased at the growing circulation of the newspaper but was worried about the possibility of libel. Some of the people whose names had been taken from Thom's Directory and attached to miscellaneous letters were beginning to protest, but Smyllie did not want to lose O'Nolan's talents either. He knew Niall Sheridan, and Sheridan seems to have given the lion's share of credit for the correspondence to O'Nolan. Sheridan undertook to introduce them. They met in the Palace Bar, and in the course of the evening Smyllie asked O'Nolan to write a regular column for the *Irish Times*. This was the beginning of *Cruiskeen Lawn*. The first article appeared on 4 October 1940, but the famous pseudonym 'Myles na gCopaleen' was not used until the second article.

While the long newspaper correspondence had been progressing, O'Nolan had been writing *The Third Policeman*. It must have been started sometime early in 1939 or perhaps late in 1938. It was finished early in 1940. In 1939 William Saroyan had visited Ireland and had become acquainted with O'Nolan. Saroyan tried to persuade O'Nolan to renew the attempt to have *At Swim* published in the USA. Saroyan was confident enough of the successful outcome of his endeavours on O'Nolan's behalf to bet him $50. He lost the bet. Saroyan's agents in New York, Matson & Duggan, were not willing to promote *At Swim*, but they did find a publisher for a short story called *John Duffy's Brother*. When *The Third Policeman* was finished, O'Nolan told Saroyan about it and Saroyan tried once more to persuade Matson & Duggan to promote a book by O'Nolan but was again unsuccessful. Longmans in England had also refused it and O'Nolan must have been bitterly disappointed. He spread the story that the manuscript had been mislaid. Donagh MacDonagh, who had read and liked

the novel, was saddened by its supposed loss and wrote an article on it called 'The Great Lost Novel'. O'Nolan had put the manuscript away and refused to look at it again. His contemporaries in UCD had accused him of insensitivity, yet his reaction to the rejection of *The Third Policeman* shows a deeply wounded personality. The wound was to be so deep that even when *At Swim* was reissued and there was an eager audience for a second book, the manuscript of *The Third Policeman* was left where it was. O'Nolan had decided that it was not good enough and he rewrote what he still liked as *The Dalkey Archive*. *The Third Policeman* was not published until after the author's death.

The invitation to write a regular column for the *Irish Times* came at the right time to compensate, in a small way, for the disappointment of *The Third Policeman*. *Cruiskeen Lawn* was, in the beginning, quite a short column, but it grew in length and importance as the years passed. The first two articles were written in both Irish and English, but thereafter it was almost exclusively in Irish until the end of 1941, when English and Irish began to alternate day by day. This pattern continued throughout 1942. By March 1943 it was almost always written in English, and articles in Irish were a comparative rarity for the remaining twenty years of the column's life.

For the first year there were about three columns a week but then the number was increased to six. The *Time* reporter said that O'Nolan wrote all six columns on Saturday afternoon. It is hard to imagine how he found the time to write the numerous other pieces which appeared in these years. *An Béal Bocht* appeared in 1941, *Faustus Kelly*, *Thirst* and *The Insect Play* in 1943. As well as these more major works, there were numerous articles for *The Bell*, reviews, poems and short stories.

It can be argued that O'Nolan's best writing was done before 1945. By then he had two novels in English — some would say his best two — and *An Béal Bocht*. *An Béal Bocht* was a great success and was greeted as a masterpiece by Gaelic enthusiasts. The *Cruiskeen Lawn* column was at its best in the years up to 1945; imaginative, wildly funny, and not yet bitter or repetitive. *At Swim*, though not a great financial success, won many important and faithful admirers for O'Nolan.

O'Nolan was now at the height of his power, not yet subject to the long series of illnesses and accidents which were to bedevil all his later years. His job, though probably not absorbing enough for his vital and energetic mind, provided much of the material for *Cruiskeen Lawn* and left him enough time for 'spare-time literary activities'. The years after 1945, and even more after 1953, were quite different. These were years of disappointment, increasing bitterness, illness and frustration. It was hard to see in the irascible and contentious man of those years the brilliant wit, the dynamic personality who had swayed the rowdy L & H audiences, or the mind which seemed like a display of fireworks shooting sparks of ingenuity and insight all around him.

In 1941, however, this was all a long way off. Everyone, not excepting O'Nolan himself, was astonished at the sales of *An Béal Bocht*. It is surprising, considering its success, that O'Nolan did not write another full-length book in Irish. Instead, at Saroyan's suggestion , he turned to drama and wrote, in quick succession, *Faustus Kelly*, *Thirst* and *The Insect Play*. Even before *Faustus Kelly* was finished O'Nolan had been approached by the director of the Cork Opera House and by Hilton Edwards at the Gate Theatre. They both asked him for a play, but he had already decided to offer *Faustus Kelly* to the Abbey. Cahill & Co. offered to publish the play after it was performed. The edition was quite small. It soon went out of print and was not reissued until 1973. The play itself was a success with the audiences but was disliked by the critics. It was put on at the end of January 1943 and was still running at the end of March, but O'Nolan, writing in *Cruiskeen Lawn*, said that it had had a run of only two weeks and that the government ordered it to be closed. It is difficult to see how he got this idea; perhaps it came from the adverse critical notices, O'Nolan's dislike of politicians, and his growing obsession with censorship.

Before the production of *Faustus Kelly*, O'Nolan had adapted the Capek brothers' *Insect Play* and had sent it with a sketch called *Thirst* to Hilton Edwards. At the end of March Hilton Edwards staged *The Insect Play* at the Gate. The production began as *Faustus Kelly* was ending. It was not a success, and the rumour still exists in Dublin that, like *Faustus Kelly*, it was taken off because it satirised all the prominent government ministers. O'Nolan may have been confusing the two productions in his *Cruiskeen Lawn* account. *Thirst* was a mere sketch, but a successful one, and was produced in 1943 by the Dublin University Players. It was revived on stage and television on several occasions. *Faustus Kelly* was produced once on Radio Éireann but was never as popular as *Thirst*.

After 1943, O'Nolan's activity slowed down a little. Indeed, it could not be expected that it could continue at that pace for long. Most of his energy went into the writing of *Cruiskeen Lawn*, which was an excellent outlet for his fantastical imagination. The number of columns per week decreased after 1945. Early in 1946 there was nothing for a few days, and then about three a week. The pressure of O'Nolan's civil service job was greater at this time than it had been previously. With increasing responsibility he had to work longer hours and began to make trips to England and Europe to collect data on town planning. In July and August 1944 he had spent some time in New York, and he returned there in 1949. He was out of the country for varying amounts of time in 1947, 1948 and 1949. He had married in 1948, having met his wife Evelyn in the civil service where she also worked. The trip to the USA in 1949 may have had something to do with the fact that there was, finally, an American edition of *At Swim*. This was published by Pantheon in 1950.

O'Nolan's work was also hindered during this period by the first of the accidents which were to plague him for years. Some of the accidents were ludicrous, many others were serious. They were always frustrating since they stopped him writing. Nearly all of February 1947 was spent in a plaster cast. 1951 was a year of illness which kept him away from work and from the *Irish Times*. It may be this illness which is responsible for the absence of any mention of the American edition of *At Swim* in Cruiskeen Lawn. (Alternatively, O'Nolan's dislike of that book may have increased sufficiently for him to avoid talking about it.) Illnesses were to be very frequent after this, and even O'Nolan's prodigious energy could not battle against them. His literary output at this time is minimal. He was away from the *Irish Times* for all but a few weeks at the beginning and end of 1952, and the few columns which do appear are often

repeated from early issues. The absences from the *Irish Times*
were not always the result of illness: sometimes O'Nolan
resigned in a fit of anger and had to be coaxed back. Jack
White, who worked for the paper, remembers this time well.

> His work generally came in batches of three or four columns
> at a time typed by himself on foolscap paper, and usually
> accompanied by a scurrilous letter addressed to the Editor.
> He was particularly abusive if we had cut anything out of his
> column the previous week. He claimed to have an infallible
> ability to avoid libel; in fact, he was very successful in doing
> so.[37]

It was Jack White who was often 'sent out as an envoy to bring
him back again'[38] after one of his periodic rows with the
editor. O'Nolan's continued presence in the *Irish Times*
proved how successful White was in these embassies. In
passing, White reveals that O'Nolan used to refuse invitations
to speak at public meetings. Since everyone by now knew who
Myles was, White does not think that O'Nolan's motive in
refusing these invitations was due to an attempt to preserve
anonymity, but rather to the fact that he could no longer
speak in public with any success. This, more than anything
else, reveals how much he had changed from his university
days. In December 1952, when he returned to the column, the
number of articles was reduced even more. Sometimes there
was only one in a week. By June 1953 he was, however, back at
the regular six columns per week.

Early in 1953 O'Nolan resigned from the civil service after
eighteen years' service. The reasons for his resignation are not
clear, though there are many conflicting rumours. It is certain
that O'Nolan was exhausted by illness, frustrated because he
had little time to write and, as *Cruiskeen Lawn* makes clear,
he was becoming increasingly disillusioned and bitter about
the civil service. He may have found the work tedious; there
were difficulties with superiors and *Cruiskeen Lawn* had
offended many important people. Although there is no
proof that the tone of his column had any connection with his
departure, it might well have been embarrassing for the civil
service to have one of its prominent employees, whose identity
was an open secret, sniping at all the organs of Church and

State and mounting special attacks on the Abbey Theatre and Dublin Corporation. O'Nolan himself said he resigned because the atmosphere of party politics in his department made it impossible for him to do his job properly. This is certainly consistent with his known attitudes. That his departure was not friendly is well attested to by the fact that the *Cruiskeen Lawn* columns of the time all speak with contempt of government ministers and civil servants. Myles constantly points to the ignorance of the former and the inefficiency of the latter. In one column, writing about a man whom he admired, he said:

> He had the guts—in Ireland unique—to march out of the Civil Service because he found life intolerable there.
>
> (5 Jun. 1954)

O'Nolan had a pension from the civil service, but he probably found himself pressed for money, and this meant that he had to produce more for the *Irish Times* and, if possible, supplement his income by writing for other newspapers and journals. He hoped to be able to use his increased leisure to produce something worthwhile, but this was not to be the case. Most of the writing done at this time was pure hack journalism done in the interests of bread and butter and with little intrinsic literary merit. There are some trivial stories, another newspaper column, and an as yet unknown amount of advertising material for Guinness and the Irish Hospitals Sweepstakes.

The history of these years is painful. They show O'Nolan constantly on the search for alternative employment or literary commissions. He wrote to the editors of a number of provincial newspapers proposing a light, entertaining column that would be non-controversial, non-political and non-serious. When their editors accepted, he also wrote columns for newspapers in Skibbereen and Carlow. He also contributed formula-type stories to a pulp-detective magazine. *Cruiskeen Lawn* was kept up assiduously and faithfully, for O'Nolan refused to consider offers from editors in London and Manchester which would take him away from the *Irish Times*. He disliked this kind of writing even though he described himself as 'an accomplished literary handyman'. Much of his energy was going into these non-productive activities and he

began to look about for an acceptable form of non-literary
employment which would guarantee him a stable income and
still leave him free to write. He tried to find extra employment
in the *Irish Times* as a reader but with no success. Early in
1957 he wrote to Lord Moyne asking for a reference. He
wished to use it when applying to Trinity College for an
'Assistant Lectureship' in English. Later in the same year he
offered *The Boy from Ballytearim* to the newly created BBC
station in Belfast in the hope that he would become one of
their script-writers. He had an 'important project' in mind and
found that hack writing was 'difficult, distasteful' and
prevented him starting on the project. None of these ventures
met with any success, and relief, when it came was from a
quite unexpected and unsolicited quarter.

In May 1959, Timothy O'Keeffe of MacGibbon & Kee, the
publishers, wrote to O'Nolan to propose a new edition of *At
Swim*. Some twenty years after the book was written it was,
finally, to bring him fame. O'Keeffe told him:

> Along with a number of other people, I've been a great
> admirer of *At Swim-Two-Birds* and some time ago began
> making the preliminary moves to try to get the book re-
> issued here. I'm now glad to tell you that, provided the
> rights are available and that you wished to have the book in
> print again on this side of the Atlantic, that we would
> publish it.[39]

O'Nolan readily agreed to the reissue and sent O'Keeffe the
original Longmans contract. Longmans still held the rights,
which were however, due to expire in five months; it was clear
that they could not produce an edition in that time and they
were willing to surrender the rights to MacGibbon & Kee.
O'Nolan himself got busy in Dublin arranging for
announcements of the forthcoming edition and seeing where it
could be publicised. The MacGibbon & Kee issue was an
enormous success. Translation rights were sought and the
book was translated into German and French. It was widely,
and usually favourably, reviewed, issued in paperback, and its
extensive sales brought in badly needed money. Most
important of all, it gave O'Nolan's spirit a psychological boost.
In better spirits than he had been for many years, he began to
write *The Hard Life* and with its completion perhaps

accomplished that 'important project' he had been thinking about since 1957.

It was not only the success of *At Swim* that prompted him to write another book. The reissue had been timely but its effects were more long-term and there were still financial pressures. The long association with the *Irish Times,* not always easy, was undergoing serious difficulties. O'Nolan wrote to Brian Inglis and told him that the 'dirty *Irish Times*' continually suppressed his *Cruiskeen Lawn* material.[40] He now felt that even though *The Hard Life* was proving to be comparatively easy to write, it was incompatible with what he called '*Irish Times* slavery'.[41] He had decided to leave the newspaper if he could, but it was still his most certain source of money. The profits from another book would help to free him. On 16 August 1960 he wrote to Niall Montgomery:

> The *Irish Times* is continually suppressing my stuff, which means I'll get next to nothing from them in a few weeks. All this seems to mean that I had better get on with my dirty book.

The Hard Life was written very quickly, possibly in August and September 1960, but it was not completely finished and dispatched until January 1961. There was a good deal of other work to be done at the same time and O'Nolan was incapacitated by a cracked coccyx and an eye injury which necessitated an operation. In the USA Pantheon wanted to publish the book and sent a large advance. O'Nolan probably needed it badly by then, for he was fighting several legal battles. The Royal Hibernian Academy had exhibited what O'Nolan called a 'grossly offensive caricature' of him. He threatened to sue them unless they removed it from the exhibition. He was quarrelling with an insurance company and with the *Irish Times.* Another memorable battle was with the Electricity Supply Board, and in 1964 a real battle royal was joined with the Inland Revenue, who were trying to tax him on the royalties from his books. O'Nolan joined in these fights with a certain amount of gusto and a feeling of being more than a match for anyone. He wrote to his agents telling them of the tax claims against him and said that even though his father had been a revenue commissioner, the present set of 'bastards are quite afraid of me, for I have got quite a name here for damaging public vituperation in print'.[42] The vituperation was prepared in an article called 'A Writer's Writhings', but it is not clear if it was published anywhere.

Throughout 1960 O'Nolan was still looking for steady employment. In March he answered an advertisement for a job as an administrative assistant. In November a friend sent him a note telling him that interpreters were needed in the Dáil. He was at this stage supplementing his income by reading manuscripts for the Figgis publishing company. He seems to have disliked everything he read. In effect he was exhausted, and he made this clear on 31 May 1962 when he wrote on the original carbon manuscript of *The Hard Life*:

> I, who wrote *The Hard Life* guarantee that this is the original MS as typed (I always type) though the text as published was somewhat changed towards the end. I did the job, in addition to other jobs, in two months dead and found I was nearly dead myself.

The first copies of *The Hard Life* were sold out in the Dublin shops in forty-eight hours. The book had been eagerly awaited and was favourably reviewed. Graham Greene, to whom it had been dedicated, wrote to O'Nolan to tell him he was pleased with the dedication. He went on:

> *At-Swim-Two-Birds* has remained to my mind ever since it first appeared one of the best books of our century. But My God, what a long time it has been waiting for the next one.[43]

It had indeed been a long wait, but O'Nolan was determined to make up for lost time and was already planning his next book. *The Dalkey Archive* was conceived as a revised edition of some of the elements of the still unpublished *The Third Policeman*. It was, however, very different in spirit and outlook from the former book. It took a long time to write. This was due to the fact that O'Nolan was constantly ill in these years. In spite of this, he had recovered a lot of his good spirits and was able to do an enormous amount of work. *The Hard Life* was published in the USA in March 1962. At the same time O'Nolan was negotiating the paperback rights for it and *At Swim* and was soon dealing with translation rights as well. He resisted attempts to persuade him to allow an English

translation of *An Béal Bocht*, maintaining that its humour
was untranslatable. In May 1962 Tim O'Keeffe wrote to
O'Nolan reminding him that the following year, when
European translations of both books were scheduled to
appear, would be his continental *annus mirabilis*. O'Brien
continued to spread his talents in other directions, particularly
into the world of television. *Thirst* was produced by the BBC
at the end of 1960, and in November 1961 Granada Television
approached him with proposals concerning *Faustus Kelly* and
a possible dramatised version of *The Hard Life*. Hilton
Edwards, who was now head of drama in RTE, produced *The
Boy from Ballytearim* in 1962. There were other television
plays too. *The Time Freddie Retired* was produced early in
1962 and was followed by *Flight, The Man with Four Legs* and
The Dead Spit of Kelly; this last was an adaptation of the
short story *Two in One*.

Cruiskeen Lawn was still appearing but the number of
columns per week decreased steadily while the amount of
television writing grew. Eventually O'Nolan was asked to write
an entire television series. *The Ideas of O'Dea*, written specially
for Jimmy O'Dea, began in September 1963 and lasted for six
months. The series was weekly, each episode lasting fifteen
minutes. The original idea had been to unite two of Ireland's
greatest comics, but it did not succeed as expected. Both men
were ill. Jimmy O'Dea was ageing rapidly and O'Nolan knew
very little about the art of writing for television. His scripts
were not suitable. The speeches were too long, there was no
action, and O'Dea was by then not able to keep long speeches
in his head. The task of cutting the speeches, abstracting
suitable punch-lines, adding action and generally turning out
something suitable for a television screen fell to John
O'Donovan. He accepted it very unwillingly and requested
that his name be left out of the credits. He did not want
O'Nolan to discover who had been responsible for butchering
his script. O'Nolan's special brand of vituperation was
reserved for those who sinned in this way.

In the meantime work went ahead on *The Dalkey Archive*.
The plot was ready in outline by September, but O'Nolan
wished to have his facts correct before he started, and
'research' on the life and character of St Augustine of Hippo
took up a good deal of his time. He wrote to Professor Stanford

of Trinity College for essential information on St Augustine. This was a departure from his usual custom which was to consult an encyclopaedia. He had done this for *The Hard Life,* where the account of Guy Fawkes is only a slightly parodied version of that in *Encyclopaedia Britannica.* He must have felt that so distinguished a person as St Augustine deserved better treatment than Guy Fawkes, or perhaps the encyclopaedia did not tell him enough. He was much puzzled as to St Augustine's colour. Was he black or white? Such matters delayed the progress of the book, and O'Nolan felt that he needed an incentive to get him writing with consistent regularity. Accordingly he wrote to Tim O'Keeffe in January 1963 and told him that

> The electronic controls went askew and the vehicle burnt up on re-entering the atmosphere. A second launching was successful and it is now in orbit, but not yet attaining optimum velocity. I intend sending you a monthly progress report, as much for your information as a spur to my own industry.[44]

In February 1965 O'Nolan signed the contract for *The Ideas of O'Dea* but was unable to proceed with the series due to what he called 'infuriating and unprecedented interruptions and invasions'. A fall had disabled him so that he had to dictate letters. The letters reveal his frustration at his condition and his eagerness to press ahead with the book in spite of all obstacles.

By February he was able to report the completion of the first two chapters. Progress was slow in March, April and May. On 3 May Niall Montgomery wrote to Trinity College to recommend O'Nolan for a Junior Lectureship in English. Nothing came of it, or of a later application in May 1964 for the job of student records and calendar officer. These unsuccessful attempts illustrate that O'Nolan's position remained insecure and that he was still casting about for some form of permanent employment. When none materialised he went on with *The Dalkey Archive,* which was half finished by September. He had been ill again in June but by then was prepared to accept delay in a resigned and philosophical manner.

I think this enforced pause was no harm; I was going too
hard. What's a few weeks in a book that's to last several
centuries.[45]

He sent the manuscript 'as so far completed' to O'Keeffe in
September. In November illness struck again, and his
wife wrote at his dictation to Cecil Scott of Macmillan to
explain *The Dalkey Archive*. It was finally finished in
February 1964, almost two years later than O'Nolan had
expected. It was to remain his favourite book.

As always, he was planning the next book before the
previous one was published. By the autumn of 1964 *Slattery's
Sago Saga,* as it came to be called, was planned in outline.
There were other projects too. Hugh Leonard, who had
done an excellent adaptation of Joyce's *A Portrait,* wrote
to O'Nolan asking permission to adapt *The Dalkey Archive* for
the stage. O'Nolan was pleased with the idea, and the
dramatisation was to be a great success. It was finished by June
1964 and O'Nolan was so impressed with Leonard's dispatch
that he wrote to him saying: 'You undoubtedly have a thing I
used to have — a prodigious capacity for hard sustained
work.'[46]

The adaptation, entitled *The Saints Go Cycling In* was
presented at the Dublin Theatre Festival. It ran at the Gate
Theatre from the 27 September to the middle of November
and was an enormous success. O'Nolan himself almost missed
seeing the play; he was in hospital for most of its run. On 22
November he wrote to Cecil Scott and, in a casual enough
tone, described what he called his 'adventure'.

My adventure has been briefly as follows: a diversified pain
about the left side of the face, present and increasing for
about a year, made me seek medical advice about the end of
July. A 'specialist' diagnosed neuralgia, a quasi-fictional
disease meaning 'nerve pain'. Later, when I drew attention
to slight 'knottiness' in the neck region, my man said this
was a matter for a commoner sort of surgeon. I saw the
latter, who operated and immediately afterwards told me to
enter a certain hospital for 'ray treatment'. In my innocence
I thought this meant ultra-violet rays or some such harmless
cosmetic radiation. Too late I realised I was getting what is
called deep x-ray therapy, and under a reckless lout of a

doctor who exercised no supervision or control. Briefly, I was fried alive and, on a tide of vomit, had to enter another hospital to be decarbonised, or 'decoked'. I'm still under drug treatment and have to go back at the end of this month for blood transfusions. In other words — never a dull moment but total stasis of that literary project that has come to be called SSS — SLATTERY'S SAGO SAGA.

In between hospitals he had gone to the first night of *The Saints Go Cycling In* but was taken ill during the performance and had to leave the theatre. He had tickets for the play and intended going to see it before he went back to hospital for his 'decoking'. He did, finally, manage to see it and liked it very much, but the press photo taken of him at the theatre shows him to be very ill indeed.

Nevertheless, his capacity for hard work does not seem to have decreased as radically as he had implied in his letter to Hugh Leonard. He was working on *Slattery's Sago Saga* and on his second television series, *Th' Oul Lad of Kilsalaher*. This ran in weekly instalments of fifteen minutes each. It employed only two characters and consisted mainly of conversation. It ran for fourteen weeks, with the last programme being recorded on 14 December 1965.

When, in December, RTE decided not to continue the television series, O'Nolan was relieved, but he was already planning a third series. Inspired by *The Dalkey Archive,* it was to be called *The Detectional Fastidiosities of Sergeant Fottrell.* He discussed the idea with RTE's programme director, who was enthusiastic. Sergeant Fottrell had become a well-known character since his stage appearance.

Slattery's Sago Saga progressed slowly, but ideas for the new television series were beginning to emerge. O'Nolan had stopped writing for the *Irish Times* in 1962 but resumed his contributions in 1963. He was, however, having to rely on the *Irish Times* staff to take the material he sent them and 'knock it into shape' to keep the column going.

While in hospital, O'Nolan read what he termed the 'algebraic theosophy of Pierre Teilhard de Chardin', 'another bloody Jesuit'. He wrote an article for the *Manchester Guardian* called 'Can a Saint Hit Back?', laying the blame for his afflictions on St Augustine, who, he said, was repaying him for the cavalier treatment his reputation had received at

O'Nolan's hands. St Augustine was punishing O'Nolan as Orlick Trellis had punished Dermot Trellis, the author of his misfortunes. Years after *At Swim,* O'Nolan still believed that a character could object to being tortured and mishandled 'for the sake of a story-teller's book-web'. O'Nolan may have known that he had cancer; certainly his reading of Teilhard de Chardin demonstrates his continuing interest in Catholic theology, which may have become more important to him at this time. All the same, he had always seen laughter as a palliative of gloom, especially of that gloom occasioned by a knowledge of mortality, and so, with serious flippancy, he continued to make St Augustine a figure of fun. By this time in his life, O'Nolan had several times received the last rites of the Roman Catholic Church, so the dedication at the beginning of *The Dalkey Archive* may be more personal and sincere than has been assumed. Yet he gave no indication in his letters that he feared or suspected an imminent death, and his head was full of projects for the future.

It was about this time that Ian Sainsbury of the *Sheffield Telegraph* visited O'Nolan at his home in Dublin. O'Nolan was in very poor health. He called his complaint neuralgia and explained that he had to take a large quantity of drugs to relieve the pain. Sainsbury recalled the meeting in a letter to David Powell of Illinois and provided a description of O'Nolan, whom he obviously liked.

> I recall his manner as being like that of a benign schoolmaster. He asked me if I knew something or other (I can't remember what) and when I said I didn't know he gently persisted like someone eliciting an answer from a backward pupil. All with the utmost courtesy; he knew the answer, of course; it was part of some point he wanted to make.[47]

Nothing shows his industry better than his output at this time. Constantly ill, with almost persistent vomiting, he continued with his book, his newspaper column, and with a wide correspondence. He emerges as a man of great courage and endurance and, no matter how irascible he was in his middle life, all his friends must have felt a deep respect for him at this time. He may have continued to fill his mind with plans for new work so that he could stave off thoughts of the present and future, or he may genuinely not have realised the gravity of his illness, perhaps considering it merely as one more of the long series which had made his later progress through life such a painful affair. For whatever reason, then, he began negotiations with Shiel Associates to write a long popular history of Ireland called *Glorious Ireland, Then and Now.*

Cruiskeen Lawn continued. helped by his friends, one of whom had often substituted for him in the past, and by the reprinting of earlier pieces. In March, Gunnar Rugheimer, the programme director of RTE, wrote to O'Nolan reminding him of his Sergeant Fottrell idea. He told him: 'I [was] enthusiastic about this and still am and hope to see some sample scripts and a general plot outline from you fairly soon.'[48] O'Nolan replied on 15 March 1966 telling Rugheimer that his illness had delayed completion of the first script. He sounded hopeful of recovery: 'I am still very far from the land but one feature — vomiting several times every day — seems to have eased up.'[49]

In spite of all his own difficulties — or because of them — he had great plans for the Sergeant, a character who, unlike O'Nolan himself, would be able to overcome everything.

> When the Sergeant's personality and tongue form a countrywide treasure, the Sergeant may well take a hand in interfering with other people's programmes and ultimately could become the unofficial voice of TE. He would make his remarkable views known on Nelson, the Budget, Decimals . . . anything of current import; he transcends all his situations.[50]

O'Nolan wrote three pages on Sergeant Fottrell and then proved that, unlike his fictional counterpart, he himself could not transcend all his situations. He died suddenly on 1 April and might have taken comfort from such a comic augury.

Brian O'Nolan was probably a very difficult man to know. His closest friends describe him as irascible, loveable, shy, sensitive, wounding. His shyness was only overcome and his sensitivity revealed when he wrote, and there are a few remarkably emotional passages in the novels. Primarily he was a satirist and a mocker, a believer in balance who evoked it by skirting the edge of chaos. He constantly dramatised forth new personalities to protect his own, and what one recent writer has said about the 'Irishman' in general is, at least, true in O'Nolan's case: he is

> a chameleon, an expert at camouflage, who changes the colour of his personality according to his mood or the surrounding conditions. He is fluid, elusive, evasive . . . He will not . . . reveal his true feelings.[51]

Like many other Anglo-Irish writers, he regarded words as a consolation and 'a defence of the mind against being possessed by thought'. He was a fantasist, seeking to escape from a reality of which he was more than conscious. Once, replying to a correspondent who asked why he never talked about 'useful' things — things 'calculated to make life happy, contented, useful, satisfying' — he wrote:

> To sensible, thoughtful people, the thought of life, as life goes, must be something of a nightmare. It begins to look as if we humans were right until we developed consciousness, with its two children, Memory and Imagination. If man was not 'blessed' or cursed with Memory, he could not look back. And if he were not 'blessed' — or cursed with Imagination, he would think nothing about the future.
>
> (*CL*. 30 Jul. 1953)

He was to reiterate this later, adding that if a man

> has the courage to raise his eyes and look sanely at the awful human condition . . . he must realise finally that tiny periods of temporary release from intolerable suffering is the most that any individual has the right to expect.
>
> (*CL*. 2 Mar. 1966)

This was written in March 1966 shortly before his death, but it does sum up his vision of life. For himself, those tiny periods of temporary release were gained by transcending or avoiding normal consciousness, by blanking out the mind or filling it with new, fantastic, remarkable ideas.

> A blank paralysis comes over my mind after a prolonged severe bout of *(a)* concentrated brain exertion, usually of a literary nature and *(b)* ingestion of Irish Malt. Note this: there is really very little difference between *(a)* and *(b)*. But often on those occasions of blankness an idea which has nothing to do with anything preceding bobs up.[52]

For others, O'Nolan was determined to offer them release

through laughter. If life, as he said in 1943, is just 'comic maggot folly',[53] then the proper way to treat it is as a comedy. In a small notebook he wrote 'The meanest bloody thing in hell made this world,' and so made hell into a joke. He believed that satire could make the world better by pricking the bubbles of pomposity, hypocrisy and philistinism which were everywhere in evidence. He wanted people to see straight, but when they found the view intolerable he wanted them to be comforted with laughter and invention. He laughed because laughter was a defence against horror and because laughter with its side-track, its inversion, convolution and coincidence, was ultimately truthful. Laughter is, O'Nolan implies, an acceptance of chaos and a belief in the miraculous imposition of order. His vision has much in common with Beckett and Kafka, with Picasso and Charlie Chaplin. He deliberately concentrated on the erratic, the unfocused picture, the new combination of facts, the surprising perspective. His vision, which at times appears to be darkly insane, is a way to sanity and to balance; it is what O'Nolan himself called 'sane madness'. He argued that 'reason' was a dangerous faculty:

> The whole damn trouble lies in the incompatibility of the flesh and the spirit. Imbedded in the flesh (and by no means in the spirit) is this disastrous faculty of reason. It has ruined many a man the same reason.   (*CL.* 30 Jul. 1953)

Instead of reason he would substitute 'sane madness',[54] for if 'studied delusion' was the complement of sanity, could one not develop 'the potentialities of the human being's capacity for orderly hallucinations and delusion . . . in the interest of therapy and commerce'.   (*CL.* 5 Nov. 1953).

To create this 'studied delusion' and to remain, para-doxically in complete control of it, he turned to parody, exaggeration and fantasy, and set out to create a parallel world which allowed free range for man's limitless imagina-tion; a world in which everything, including disturbing and horrifying things, was possible. To save his own soul and to alleviate the 'sense of doom that is the heritage of the Irish Catholic'[55] he set out, like the ancient Gaelic poets, to detach himself from the distractions of the present to spin in the un-assailable privacy of his own mind a 'story-teller's book-web'.

2
Early Writing: Brother Barnabas and Other Celebrities

I T WOULD be difficult to overemphasise the importance of O'Nolan's six years at University College, Dublin. While he was there he began to write, to respond creatively and imaginatively to the *milieu* in which he found himself, to develop his characteristic style and outlook, and to lay the foundations on which he would build in later works.

The early writings are, of course, mixed in quality. Some can stand alongside his best writings, others are inept and tedious, the work of an obviously young man trying too hard to impress. In spite of their mixed quality, these early articles and stories make fascinating reading, since it is in them that O'Nolan first indulged his love of puns, his hatred of clichés, his delight in demonstrating his own brilliance, whether this manifested itself in the assembly of an enormous mass of pedantically correct, but quite incongruous, facts or in the mastery of numerous literary styles which were flaunted and parodied.

O'Nolan created two main fictional personalities at this time. Brother Barnabas became much better known than Count Blather, who only appeared in the five issues of the magazine *Blather*. The personalities and the pronouncements of these two characters laid the groundwork for aspects of *At Swim-Two-Birds* and *Cruiskeen Lawn*, neither of which can be fully appreciated without reference to the magazines *Comhthrom Féinne* and *Blather* in which they made their appearance.

A study of these magazines is a very rewarding venture for they reveal not merely how O'Nolan's art developed over this seminal period, but also how he was influenced by the writings of his contemporaries and the format of the magazines

themselves. Since most of this material is unfamiliar and not
easily accessible, the main intention in this chapter is to
present it rather than to comment on it. There is such an
obvious relationship between the early writing and the
Cruiskeen Lawn column that the technical devices and focus
of attention can be more appropriately discussed in Chapter 5.

Niall Sheridan, writing in the *Irish Times* on the day after
O'Nolan's death, gave this account of O'Nolan's emergence as
a writer.

> I was then editing the college magazine *Comhthrom
> Féinne*, and he proposed that he should contribute a sort of
> modern Decameron, to be written in Old Irish. He
> estimated that he would reach an audience of three (Osborn
> Bergin and two others) and explained that the latitude
> permitted to a writer increased in inverse ratio to the size of
> the audience.
>
> I was attracted by this conception of inverted censorship
> and we went ahead; but Bergin must have spread the
> gospel. Three instalments later I was called before the
> President, Dr Coffey, on the unusual charge of publishing
> bawdy and obscene stories in Old Irish.[1]

A search of the first few issues of *Comhthrom Féinne* did not
produce any article in Old or even Modern Irish which could
fit Niall Sheridan's description. There is, however, an article
in Vol. IV, No. 1 of the magazine, dated January 1933, which
is probably the one of which he was thinking. It is entitled

ECHTRÍ AGUS IMTHEACTAÍ NA NGRADUATÍ
1. SGÉL RÓ-DESS
Ag BRIAN UA NUALLÁIN

This story, said O'Nolan, was a very clean tale which he had
rendered unusually moral and wholesome. The figure '1' in
the title seems to imply that more stories were intended, and
the introduction gives thanks to all the Celtic scholars who
have aided him in its composition. There was no further story
in the magazine. It does seem to fit the description Niall
Sheridan gives, but if this was the story he was referring to in
the obituary, his recollection of events was a little indistinct.

By the time this tale was written Brother Barnabas, O'Nolan's pseudonymous persona at this time, had already been in existence for some time.

The first mention of Brother Barnabas was in the second issue of *Comhthrom Féinne*, in May 1931, when he appeared as author of an article on 'The L. and H. from the Earliest Times'. No attempt to establish the personality of the Brother was made in this article. The pseudonym as it first appeared was merely another pen-name, in no way different from 'Prospero' or 'The Janitor' who had appeared in the earlier magazine called *The National Student*. As the articles continued in the magazine, they came to have an introductory section which described the habits and revealed the personality of Brother Barnabas. He became a great comic character. His name was a byword in the college. He gradually attained the status of a living person and his activities were written about in the magazine's gossip column alongside those of the leading notabilities of the college.

> BELIEVE IT OR NOT —!
> **Mr Brian Ó Nualláin** was heard speaking to Brother Barnabas in a lonely corridor.
> 'Brian, I had to come back from Baden-Baden.'
> 'That's too bad then.'[2]

> **Brother Barnabas** has been seen at a Continental Spa other than Baden-Baden.[3]

Charles Donnelly, in a poem called 'The Dead' showed the poet numbering the tombstones of UCD's dead muses. The poet comes to the tomb of Brother Barnabas and the sight of it inspired this verse.

> Here Barnabas was thrown, whose Muse being lame,
> He mistook notoriety for fame;
> Loved of the ladies, as orator had he
> Every gift — save that of orat'ry;
> But, ah, although we smiled whene'er he 'spoke'
> We smiled not when he joked — that was no joke![4]

The creation of Brother Barnabas as a full and expansive character began with his second appearance. At first all that was known about him was that he was a scholar who was careful not to incur the wrath of the Censorship Board. He was also a humanist who ran an advice column for the ignorant and/or love-lorn. He was wise, sympathetic and unselfish. His knowledge was of a most catholic kind. In one advice column he answered queries about the history of the college, the titles of operas, the origin of the name 'Angela', the possible rhymes for 'kitty' as well as giving medical advice, suggesting prescriptions for various complaints, and recounting the various billiard scores achieved in college. Brother Barnabas was also a literary critic, though not indeed a very perceptive one, and although he was capable of giving very good advice to others, he was less able to follow it himself. He customarily had to go to Baden-Baden for the 'cure'. He was obviously a gentleman of expansive habits in the Friar Tuck tradition. He was paternal, pompous, simple, a supporter of social virtues and a man dedicated to the use of flowing and mellifluous English — an anachronism in his day, but a joy to the ear and a pleasure to pronounce.

> Brother Barnabas who has adjourned to Baden-Baden for the cure, sends his boys and girls of University College his Compliments and Greetings at the merry festival of Yuletide and hopes that they will apply themselves to their books with more ardour and industry in the course of the coming year than ever before, that they may become a credit to their College, a delight to their good parents, and a fragrant pink rose in the nostrils of their decent Professors; to Dr Coffey and the staff he renews his genial benediction and blessing, with the hope that he will be remembered with love, where e'er they gather in, when Dusk draws her mantle o'er the fields, in sober conclave to discuss the College, its students, or any other business that may arise, and likewise be remembered in their private prayers.[5]

Brother Barnabas was to grow more mellow and paternal with each succeeding issue. His depths of wisdom made him capable of understanding all the failings of mankind and he was always more than willing to reveal his secret remedies for all life's little ills and inadequacies as well as carefully to prognosticate future events. In 1932 he produced a College

Almanac. His character at this time positively glowed with
goodwill towards all his loyal followers.

> Brother Barnabas, who has left Baden-Baden and gone to
> Carlsbad for the waters, gives to each one of his lady readers
> a Saccharine Platonic kiss, a thousand times sweeter than its
> name, and to his gentlemen readers he bows courteously
> and cordially, but from a distance; to the Auditors and
> their assistant officers, the Staff of our Academic Life,
> Patient Dustmen of Life's Garbage-Waggon, Sweet
> Cigarettes to our Nicotine-craving Lungs, Corpse-washers
> in Life's Mortuary, Blessed beans of the gods, he extends his
> brotherly bonhomie, rich as treacle, a condiment that will
> sweeten the sourest Academic Pudding.[6]

With true generosity, Brother Barnabas sent a gift to the
college for the new year. It was a painting. It showed Brother
Barnabas

> walking through a snow-storm from Baden-Baden to
> Carlsbad, clad in white pyjamas, followed by a flock of
> white ponies. Overhead, as if leading the way, is a mystic
> white guillemot.[7]

The painting looked like this:

It was appropriate that Brother Barnabas should be
accompanied by 'a mystic white guillemot' for he had
gradually taken on some of the aspects of God and creator. He
predicted in his almanac that on 23 January 1932 'America
declares war on Japan; Brother Barnabas pares his corns.'
Like Joyce's artist, who was 'like God of creation, indifferent,
paring his fingernails', Brother Barnabas was far above the
general concerns of the world, though he was unfortunately
afflicted by the agony of corns.

A competition, conducted in the college by Brother

Barnabas himself, revealed his real position. One of the questions asked was 'Who is next year's Auditor of the L and H Society?'. The winner gave the following answer:

> That such a question be seriously asked in the Official Magazine of the SRC (even in a Competition) passes my understanding . . .
> Who, I ask, is the greatest figure in College?
> Who is our Chief Clown?
> Who is the one saving feature in an age of decadence and corruption?
> Who is *Comhthrom Féinne*?
> Who is he that thrills the hearts of our women students (and, some say, Professors)?
> Who is he, I say?
> He is Brother Barnabas.[8]

Just as Brother Barnabas had reached this height of power, influence and indeed, almost god-like omniscience, the classic, tragic fall came. Brother Barnabas was ignominiously thrashed in Baden-Baden by his rival Politicus. Politicus, an employee of the *Irish Independent* and a supporter of Trinity College, had long been attacking the inhabitants of UCD for their ignorance, naïvety and political ineptitude. Brother Barnabas was unfortunate enough to meet him on a train, and, not being aware of his identity, engaged him in discussion about UCD. Annoyed at something he said, the Brother, violent and impetuous at all times, challenged him to a fight.

> Details of the fight are rather meagre. It appears that a suburban hall was rented, an impromptu ring fixed up. Enormous crowds turned up, apparently taking it from the posters that the Church and State had finally decided to settle their long-standing differences in the old fashioned way. Photographers were excluded by special request of Brother Barnabas, who appeared, amid thunderous applause, clad in the College colours (by the special telegraphic courtesy of the Athletic Union); Politicus was clad becomingly in a singlet of Abbey Street puce and according to Brother Barnabas, 'Some people were understood to clap' when he appeared.[9]

Brother Barnabas was soundly defeated and slunk away leaving Politicus master of the field and centre of an admiring crowd. Nevertheless, the repercussions following on the defeat of such an important international figure were serious. 'The Free State National Loan lost eight points on the German Bourse.' President Hindenburg received 'a curt Note from the Free State Government' and 'repercussions [were] expected in the Far East'.[10] It was rumoured that, since UCD had been defeated in the figure of its champion, Earlsfort Terrace would be put up for auction and its students and professors sent to the Russian state farms 'where they will be put in charge of the "Aran Chief" potato-plots'.

In spite of his international reputation, then, and the fact that his services as an election agent had been 'requisited [*sic*] by Herr Adolf Hitler', Brother Barnabas was still socially naïve, and was never to become as suave and well-dressed as Politicus. He was friendly and open, quite without guile, impetuous and inclined to the use of improper language when seriously offended.

Brother Barnabas returned to UCD after his defeat and found another trial facing him. A competitor had arrived in UCD. The poet Mr Lionel Prune was a man of very different character to Brother Barnabas. He was

> tall and willowy, and groaned beneath a heavy burthen of jet-black hair long untouched by tonsorial shears. His eyes were vacuous but yearning and looked out on the world through a pair of plane lenses. These latter were held erect on his nose by the device known as *pince-nez* and from the edge of one of them a thick black ribbon descended flowingly to his right-hand lapel buttonhole. A slight trace of black moustache drooped cloyingly from his protruding upper lip. His neck was embellished by a flame-red tie. He wore a great nigger brown overcoat which stretched well below his knees. His right hand toyed with a walking stick and his left with a bulky dispatch case.[11]

Lionel Prune clearly epitomised the languid romantic poet and may be regarded, in particular, as a fairly accurate caricature of Yeats. The 'Special Representative' who wrote the article gave his readers examples of his poetic output, together with Mr Prune's 'deep' explanation of their meaning. Brother Barnabas was outraged. He proclaimed that 'LIONEL PRUNE MUST GO,' and revealed that he himself was a poet of far greater ability. Indignant that Mr Prune's puerile effusions had been printed on the verso of a page which bore his own immortal compositions, he felt that only the most scathing reprimand would soothe the feelings which were wounded by this threat to his position as literary leader of the college. He described Mr Prune as

> a superannuated plum. He is the shrivelled wreckage of a fruit, which though never other than sour and ill to look upon, is now bereft of the paltry juice which once gave it the claim to regard itself as young and green, and full of promise.[12]

He went on to call Lionel Prune 'a journeyman-dilletante, an upstart, a parvenu . . . a bowsy, a menace and an eye-sore, a thorn in the side of educated humanity', and in so doing demonstrated that the learned friar had a good store of invective at his command. To prove his point, Brother Barnabas showed, with examples, explanations and footnotes, what 'real poetry' was. Brother Barnabas emerged victorious from this struggle of literary giants and thereafter used the royal plural ('We have spoken, and it suffices for the times that are') in all his writings. Lionel Prune proved to be of too weak and nervous a disposition to sustain such an onslaught. He contracted a case of Eksaam fever and pined away watched over anxiously by his admiring followers. Brother Barnabas forgot about him and continued to make his knowledge and experience available to UCD students by devising, among other things, a special insurance scheme, with a prize for the person who suffered the oddest mode of death.

Brother Barnabas was by now such an indispensable institution that he was able to demand that his followers sign 'an Oath of Allegiance' to him. This was not really unreasonable since Brother Barnabas continued to make invaluable contributions to UCD in the form of special services guaranteed to make the participants taller, cleverer, richer and more confident. He also proved himself to be possessed of genius of a very high order when, after years of exhausting

study, he produced 'An Cóngar'. He had initially been
searching for the 'square root of a minus quantity', but
discovered instead a method of reducing the Irish language to
simple mathematical symbols. 'An Cóngar', he said, would
allow everyone to master Irish without any drudgery.

Eventually Brother Barnabas grew old and, afflicted by
illnesses, he was left only his memories. But what memories
they were! The old man now lived in retirement and flitted
about the countryside, absent-minded and simple,
remembering Vienna in 1912 when he thrashed Kaiser
Wilhelm or the time he shot the stag whose head hung in the
Reichstag Chamber. His life, in retrospection, became
infinitely extended in time and place, and, even if he was
suffering from 'convulsions, teething, whooping-cough,
mumps, rickets and a host of other infantile complaints', he
knew that he was the man who 'invented mixed dancing' and
'The two-egg omelet with three-egg lower'. He it was who
dissolved the Danish Reichstag in 1887, who first thought of
using starch on rashers, who stole the corsets of the Archduke
Nicholas, and who was, and remained, 'first in peace, first in
war and first in the hearts of his countrymen'.[13] Later Brother
Barnabas revealed the odd and unexpected fact that he was 'a
halfcaste Russian Jew . . . of good *kulak* stock', who had
had to leave the steppes and go to Spain with his violin. Even
there 'Russian disaffection' caught up with him and he turned
his face to 'that island of the west, to Ireland of the Welcomes'
and 'landed at Bannow Strand on the tenth of May'.[14] The
total absence of Communism made it possible for him to
remain in Ireland. He instantly joined the Gaelic League,
changed his name to An Bráthair Barnabas, and soon made
progress in the use of 'Gaelic obscurities'. He could not easily
accept the league's interdict on trousers or jazz, but he did
learn Irish dancing in order to obtain a job in the civil service.
Eventually he decided to go to UCD and while there met
Bernard Shaw, Yeats, AE Sherlock Holmes, Billy Bunter and
Mac Uí Hitler. He promised to tell the whole story sometime,
to reveal

> How Vernon-Smith ('The Bounder') was elected Auditor of
> the Commerce Society. How Fludd and Bernard Shaw lived
> for two days in Loreto Hall disguised as two little girls in

blue. How I discovered and hastily re-covered James Joyce. How I boxed a professor's ears. How I became President of University College. *It is a story of yesterday, but a grand story.*[15]

At last even Brother Barnabas had to die, but even in death he did not forget his faithful readers. He wrote, especially for them, a posthumous article. The article, 'Scenes in a Novel', gave an example of Brother Barnabas's methods of literary composition:

> Carruthers McDaid is a man I created one night when I had swallowed nine stouts and felt vaguely blasphemous. I gave him a good but worn-out mother and an industrious father, and cooly negativing fifty years of eugenics, made him a worthless scoundrel, a betrayer of women and a secret drinker. He had a sickly wheaten head, the watery blue eyes of the weakling. For if the truth must be told I had started to compose a novel and McDaid was the kernel or the fulcrum of it. Some writers have started with a good and noble hero and traced his weakening, his degradation and his eventual downfall; others have introduced a degenerate villain to be ennobled and uplifted to the tune of twenty-two chapters, usually at the hands of a woman . . . In my own case, McDaid, starting off as a rank waster and a rotter, was meant to sink slowly to absolutely the last extremities of human degradation. Nothing, absolutely nothing, was to be too low for him, the wheaten-headed hound.[16]

Sadly, Brother Barnabas had to recount that McDaid revolted against his creator. He refused to rob the poor-box in a church; when sent to a revivalist meeting to scoff, he had stayed to pray; and when his creator threatened him with literary extinction, he possessed himself of a paper-knife which figured in another part of the story. Brother Barnabas's life was in danger. He recorded, while waiting for a sudden death:

> The book is seething with conspiracy and there have been at least two whispered consultations between all the characters, including two who have not yet been officially created. Posterity taking a hand in the destiny of its ancestors, if you know what I mean. It is too bad. The only

objector, I understand, has been Captain Fowler, the drunken hedonist, who insists that there shall be no foul play until Chapter Twelve has been completed; and he has been over-ruled.

Candidly, reader, I fear my number's up.[17]

These were almost the Brother's last words. Having advised his readers to cherish them well, he passed out of existence. It was clear that he was now really dead, and even his ghost turned to pursuits other than writing for *Comhthrom Féinne*. A commentator in that magazine recorded his passing, and his subsequent spiritual treachery.

One dismal afternoon in early August, the wind whistled eerily along the muddy streets and ominous black clouds gathered over the Bank of Ireland as I made my way hastily up Dame Street. Suddenly the long-threatened shower burst, and the street became enveloped in one sheet of driving rain. . . I myself dodged into an adjacent doorway. The street was now quite deserted, save for a gaunt figure who stalked doggedly through the downpour. He passed swiftly by me, and as he passed, I caught sight of two copies of 'Comhthrom Féinne' sticking out of his coat pocket. I glanced keenly at his face, a haggard wasted face about which played a weird unearthly green light. I caught my breath; my heart pounded within me—it was the face of Bro. Barnabas, who had died in May!

Even as I stood horrified, he turned swiftly into a doorway. Drawn by I know not what awful magnetic force, I followed him, and was rewarded by seeing him enter the offices of 'Blather'. I waited outside in the rain. My journalistic curiosity was now thoroughly aroused and had overcome my superstitious dread. I was determined to interview him—if indeed it is possible to interview a ghost. But imagine the scoop—'Exclusive Interview with the Ghost of Br. Barnabas!'; 'How Bro. Barnabas picked the Lock of the Gates of Heaven with a Skeleton Key!' 'The Other World from the Inside!' etc., etc.

But though I waited until dusk fell he did not emerge. One by one the staff came down the stairs, and lastly the O'Blather himself. He locked the door, and passed me by with a knowing smile hovering about the delicately-modelled countenance. I felt sure that he had forestalled me, and I went home with a heavy heart.

A few days later, I was idly turning over the pages of the newly-issued 'Blather', when to my astonishment I caught sight of a passage which I could have sworn I had read before. I read it again; yes, those familiar words, which had filled, if not adorned, the pages of 'Comhthrom Féinne' not many moons before! How Bro. Barnabas thrashed the Kaiser; how the characters of his novel revolted against him. There it all was, staring shamelessly at me. Bro. B. had thinly disguised himself under an alias. That was all. So that was his little game: selling his soul for gold; dragging his lurid past from the decent obscurity of the files of 'Comhthrom Féinne' to satisfy the morbid desires of an idle world! My contempt for him in his self-abasement was not unmixed with a certain pity. He must have been badly off indeed in his eternal abode to descend to such depths.[18]

Brother Barnabas was no more. His place was taken, for a short time, by the O'Blather, but 'Scenes in a Novel' revealed clearly enough that his creator's thoughts had already turned to another direction. The plot of *At Swim* was being worked out. The main comic devices were already decided upon; the character of the villainous hero and his subsequent rebellion and attempt on the life of the author had been settled.

But if Brother Barnabas was dead, he had left behind him as his legacy a substantial body of writing, ideas, inventions and systems.

Brother Barnabas's first appearance in *Comhthrom Féinne* was as the author of an article on the history of the L & H 'from the Earliest Times'.[19] It was, of course, a satirical commentary on the proceedings of the 'oldest' society in college. Indeed, Brother Barnabas insisted its antiquity was unsuspected by even its most fervent admirers. To prove his point he quoted from the original minutes which stretched back 'far beyond the Paleolithic Age'. In his footnotes he regretted the fact that the granite blocks on which the minutes were carved had since been rendered illegible 'owing to the vandalism of Erse writers several centuries later, who covered the granite Minute-stones with crude "Ogham" notchings'. It was clear from the minutes that the members of the L & H had once had

tails, had told jokes which were not considered in good taste,
and had been as unruly in the past as they were in the present.
As the L & H began to emerge from the mists of prehistory
some of its auditors and members were named. They included
Mr F. McCool, B Agr Sc, Mr Yaf, B Naut Sc, 'who was suspected to be a Viking', Mr Oisin, D Litt Celt, who spoke 'in
metres too intricate to be recorded', Mr D. D. McMurrough,
BA (Legal and Political Science), and Mr Adam, BAO, 'the
Auditor who introduced women to the Society'. Later the
stones were replaced by 'fossilised goat-skin', and the new
series of members included, as guest speaker, Henry VIII, Deo
Grat. Rex, and Mr Guy Fawkes, who said 'he would endeavour
to make the Society go with a bang'.

Brother Barnabas next appeared in 'Humanists' Corner',
where he managed to poke gentle fun at many of his
companions in the college and to chide Cyril Cusack for
submitting for criticism a stanza of a poem which Brother
Barnabas felt was 'marred by sentimental sloppiness and crude
diction'. The stanza read:

> O what can ail thee, knight-at-arms,
>   Alone and palely loitering?
> The sedge has withered from the lake
>   And no birds sing.[20]

He followed this with 'Thumbnail Sketches of Our Latest
Alumni'. These included Robin Dudley Edwards, John Kent,
Domhnall O'Sullivan and Dionysius Jeremiah Cougheigh,
MB, who was

> Born Kerry, in the long nights after Samhain. Lived for five
> long winters on spuds that would be stark without their
> jackets and fish that might be stinking. Has got a schooling
> and a scholarship that the second man has not got then, and
> many's a long writing in the Dublin papers with his name
> forninst it.[21]

At Christmas he reviewed 'The Latest Books' and found most
interesting that by Ryan, the head porter of the college, who
had spent many years trying to find out why little 'wisps of blue
smoke' were emerging from the right-hand trouser pocket of
the 'many hundreds of male students' who were to be found

habitually lounging in the main hall.[22] In January 1932 he produced his 'College Almanac' with predictions for the coming year. It was primarily concerned with the billiards tournament in which many of the students won degrees from their professors. Brian Ó Nualláin won twenty-five B Comm degrees after the summer examinations had been postponed to facilitate the billiards players.[23]

Brother Barnabas now had to take his new position as savant seriously, and since *Comhthrom Féinne* was making an enormous profit, he proposed a free competition, the winner of which would receive £50 a week for life. The competition centred round questions as to the identity of Brother Barnabas, the relations between UCD's Pro-Fide Society and the *Irish Independent,* and the identity of the future auditor of the L & H Society.[24] The winner was 'Skate', who revealed clearly that Brother Barnabas was the greatest man in college.[25] Brother Barnabas then departed to Germany to face his defeat at the hands of Politicus which was reported 'by our Special Wire'. He was back in time to offer challenge to Lionel Prune and to offer his readers examples of his own poetic output. Having recited a poem called 'An Ceangal', Brother Barnabas remarked of it:

> In all due modesty, we consider this long poem a memorable achievement, whose Gargantuan eminence, however, cannot diminish or obscure the power and brilliance of some of our shorter, more delicate and more chaste specimens. Take, for instance, the mighty fragment 'The Cobbler's Son', written when we were twins, or, rather, when we were very, very young.

THE COBBLER'S SON

'The Cobbler's Son
Was a bookish fool
foul
full
of trix.

He went to church
And stole

a stole
Twere better had he plied
Atome
Atome, or like his pa
Soled soles
And not
Sold his soul
For a stole.'

Note the exquisite dominance of the 'o', the breath-taking transition from 'fool to full' by the celebrated U-STEP METHOD, the internal sense-metamorphosis, without in any way impairing the phonological beauty of the word. This is a poem that must be pondered upon. We earnestly recommend Prune to put it in his pipe and smoke it.[26]

Brother Barnabas's readers had known for some time that he had poetic potential, ever since his poem 'Accelerate' had appeared and had shown that Longfellow could be improved upon.

The shades of night were falling fast,
When through a Munster village passed
A road-hog bold, and for a trice,
You'd read behind, this strange device
'XLR-8'.

The adventures of the road-hog are recounted in grim detail and at the conclusion he meets a suitable fate.

The traveller, by the sergeant's hound,
Half-buried in the wreck was found,
Still grasping in his hand of ice
The wheel that steered that strange device
'XLR-8'.

There in the twilight cold and grey
Lifeless but beautiful he lay,
And from the sky, serene and far,
A voice fell, like a falling star

'Accelerate'.[27]

Having proved that he would brook no competitors of a literary nature, Brother Barnabas was free once again to turn to schemes of a philanthropic kind, and he introduced a 'Brilliant New Insurance Scheme'. The beneficiaries of this scheme were to be those members of UCD who suffered the most interesting death or mishap. Brother Barnabas promised an interview with the next-of-kin of the bereaved as a special bonus.

> The first reader to benefit under this novel scheme was Mr Bewley Box, a well-known graduate in the faculty of Science. It appears that Mr Box, being a penniless Communist, had set out on the day of May the first last to walk home from Dublin to Cork along the railway line and thus show his contempt for a capitalist company by refusing to use its system of transport. He walked all day and well into the following night. At approximately 5.49 a.m. on the morning of May the second, when some two hundred yards from Limerick Junction Station, apparently after he had been accepted by the North Signal Cabin, he was struck between the fifth and sixth vertebrae of the spinal column by a GSR train bearing several tons of the 'Irish Independent' and the 'Irish Times' (dep. Kingsbridge 3.55 a.m.). Mr Box, realising with admirable presence of mind that a mile-long cattle-train was due in two hours, endeavoured to drag himself from the metals with the aid of his one remaining limb; but before he had time to put his ingenious plan into operation, he was struck by the 'Irish Press' train (dep. Kingsbridge 4.0 a.m.) which came thundering through the night just then, and Mr Box was literally reduced to match-wood. The deceased was calm and collected to the last, the collection occupying four trained paper-spikes from Stephen's Green, who were rushed to the spot, some twelve hours. Funeral private.[28]

Brother Barnabas decided to inaugurate his 'Giant Free Insurance Scheme' by presenting readers of *Comhthrom Féinne* with free balloons, embellished with appropriate quotations from Chaucer and Eóghan Ruadh Ó Súilleabháin. In order to qualify for the free gifts, readers

when met by Brother Barnabas, must be carrying a copy of

'Comhthrom Féinne', conspicuously carried folded twice under the arm, a birth-certificate, copies of references from head of school or college or institution attended, a roll of Gaeltacht handwoven tweed, a copy of 'Ulysses' by James Joyce or Lord Tennyson, a complete set of snooker balls, a BA Hons. degree parchment, a tastefully arranged basket of home-grown tariff-free cut-flowers, a copy of an Oath of Allegiance to Brother Barnabas, four penny buns from the College restaurant, ten Irish-made coal-hammers, a copy of Morphi's 'Games of Chess', a set of new Dublin-made brow-knitters, a red flag, and a small green-coloured urn containing the ashes of the last issue of the 'National Student'.[29]

The Brother's next great venture was 'An Cóngar', the short cut to the mastery of the Irish language. An example shows how the word Séadna could be broken down in various Congars.

Shán Ó Cuív's Cóngar . . . . Shiana
Professor Bonnimann's (Berlin) . . . . S%En @
Our Congar . . . . x^2-y^2 [30]

The preface told his readers of the difficulties and toils undergone by Brother Barnabas and his devoted team of helpers and fellow researchers in their attempt to bring this breakthrough in learning to the Irish people.

The Epic of the CONGAR has yet to be written — the inspiring tale of all-night struggles with refractory tangents, thrilling combats to the death with intransitive logarithms and veritable faction-fights with swarms of subjunctive hypothenuses. Much trouble and a nett cash loss estimated at £3,500 per day were occasioned by a chance encounter with two Aorist Surds; these appear to have originated in the darker years of the Middle Ages, and to have made their way through the Primitive Indian Dialects, eventually arriving in Egypt about the year 1469. Gustav Krautz, a German traveller who died in 1674 records an encounter with them on the Aran Islands in his treatise *Ueber allen Gipfeln ist Ruh,* but no satisfactory confirmation of this curious statement has been forthcoming. Much credit is due to Brother Barnabas, who faced what may well be described as a menace to civilisation with coolness and courage; he placed his army of assistants at strategic points, imbued them with the requisite mixture of tact and firmness, and managed to obviate the very ugly scenes which would certainly have occurred with a less experienced man in charge of operations. Despite some efforts on the part of the Aorist Surds to retreat within the Great Wall, Brother Barnabas has the situation well in hand after 26 hours' stiff fighting.[31]

In the course of the investigations it was discovered that the search for 'An Congar' was raising questions about the very shape and nature of the universe. It is clear that if O'Nolan allowed free rein to his powers of fantastical speculation, he would eventually reach the inverted world of *The Third Policeman.*

> The old question regarding the rotundity or flatness of the earth, believed by many to have been definitely settled many years ago was resuscitated; and not for a hectic 54 hours was Galileo vindicated. On another occasion, starting from Belfast, gallant efforts were made to produce to infinity two parallel chalk lines drawn on the earth's surface. The attempt was eventually given up outside Sidi-bel-Abbes' owing to the coarse language of troopers of the French Foreign Legion, the callous conduct of four old Arabs, who trained their camels to dance on the line and obliterate it, the unwarranted and ignorant interference of the police throughout the world, and finally the persistent inclemency of the weather.[32]

The mental rigours of such a battle and the 'involved, advanced and abstract' nature of the subject reduced Brother Barnabas to a state of near insanity so that his next endeavour was, perforce, of a more relaxed and less demanding kind. He produced an account, in the appropriate style, of 'College Two Centuries Ago'. According to his tale, things had not changed very radically.

> A Fellow who with Especial Temerity was smoking in the Hall being apprehended by a Parcel of Porters was hanged

from a Tree for His Pains, it being a Just Dessert for the
Wretch and a warning to Other Lawless Fellows.[33]

This account was followed by material more personal to the
Brother himself. His own reminiscences, written under the
title 'Mein Kampf', recalled

> Vienna, 1912. Through the mind back to the glamorous
> days before the war. Live, laugh and love. Unter den
> Linden, the gay crowds promenading, the gipsy fiddlers,
> the moon, the cafes and Ach! the wein.[34]

Finally, there was his posthumous article and then Brother
Barnabas, his work, his writings and his expansive character
sank into oblivion and were replaced by Count O'Blather and
his idiot son Blazes.

The O'Blather was, initially, quite similar to Brother
Barnabas, since his first appearance was in an article entitled
'Scenes in a Novel' which was a compression of the articles
'Mein Kampf' and 'Scenes in a Novel' from *Comhthrom
Féinne*.

The O'Blather was, first and foremost, a 'great financial
genius'. It was he who determined the policy of the whole
magazine. *Blather* was, from the first, intended to be quite
different to *Comhthrom Féinne* and its different qualities were
determined by the personal quirks and opinions of its great
man. The first editorial read:

> BLATHER is here.
> As we advance to make our bow, you will look in vain for
> signs of servility or for any evidence of a slavish desire to
> please. We are an arrogant and a depraved body of men.
> We are as proud as bantams and as vain as peacocks.
> BLATHER **doesn't care.** A sardonic laugh escapes us as
> we bow, cruel and cynical hounds that we are. It is a terrible
> laugh, the laugh of lost men. Do you get the smell of
> porter?[35]

The paper was to be the only one in Ireland which was
'Exclusively Devoted to the Interests of Clay-Pigeon Shooting'.
It was purely comic. It contained no serious reports of

clubs or societies, no book reviews or drama criticism, though it had parodies in plenty. If *At Swim* was to be an anti-novel, *Blather* was, if such a thing is possible, an anti-magazine. An editorial described it as

> a publication of the Gutter, the King Rat of the Irish Press, the paper that will achieve entirely new levels in everything that is contemptible, despicable and unspeakable in contemporary journalism.[36]

In true Mylesian style, the editorial continued with the announcement that *Blather's* objects were

> the fostering of graft and corruption in public life, the furtherance of cant and hypocrisy, the encouragement of humbug and hysteria, the glorification of greed and 'gombeenism.[37]

Everything in the magazine was to be a parody, a satire or an exaggeration. It was excellently and wittily illustrated, probably by O'Nolan himself. It developed the use of favourite phrases and cartoons (in which Eamon de Valera was usually a main character). The editors who termed themselves 'we' conducted a running commentary on the subject of the magazine's merits and demerits.

> Our next issue is going to be the best yet. A man in a corner of the hall is understood to say that he doesn't think a whole lot of our first issue. He is perfectly right. It is pure twaddle; but he is guilty of a hasty judgment as our best stuff, acquired regardless of expense, has been held over owing to pressure of advertising.[38]

The material of the magazine consisted of sketches, short stories, puns, bad poetry, Irish lessons, improbable limericks and remarkable inventions. It contained advertisements that promised miraculous results, a 'letters to the editor' section, advice on how to make 'easy money', a 'monthly heart-to-heart', a competition, and various columns of a mock-serious kind. It was a remarkable and uninhibited vehicle for O'Nolan, who had by now developed many of his characteristic devices and points of view.

The O'Blather himself remained submerged in his

magazine. The readers knew of him only that he was the scion of a noble house which had connections in England, where it went under the name of O'Blether. The O'Blather was a great cricketer, a lover of rugby, a disappointed father (his son aspired to be a poet), a man whose anger and extensive contacts were to be feared, a man of wide talents ('publicist, playwright, poet, politician and press baron'),[39] an aged statesman commonly to be found in his boudoir. He was never as fully realised as Brother Barnabas. The character of the paper was his character, and his opinions were those we find expressed in the pages of his magazine. *Blather* was never unwilling to make its attitude felt on many and diverse subjects. A favourite target was the Irish language.

> At a time when some of our most bad-tempered judges are trying important cases in draughty, leaky and unsanitary court-houses throughout the provinces, the BLATHER attitude on the Irish language comes as a clarion call to the scattered ranks of the Geal [*sic*] throughout the world. BLATHER believes that *everybody* should be compelled to learn Irish, with the exception of Independent TDs and ex-Unionists who are eager to learn it voluntarily. BLATHER likes all the dialects almost equally well, strange as it may seem, but would like to see all the Particles in the language re-assembled, as it makes a mess of the page when they are littered about. The BLATHER attitude on Irregular Verbs is a peculiar and an intricate one, and will probably be explained in some future issue.
> But we promise nothing, mind.[40]

Blather never did explain its attitude on Irregular Verbs, but it did offer lessons in Irish as one of its essential services to the reading public. In the preamble to the lesson *Blather* mourned for those who wished to learn Irish but who had no opportunity to do so. Lest its readers suspected it of philanthropic motives, it hastened to add:

> Privately, of course, we regard all these people as illiterate rats, but outwardly we dare not shirk our responsibilities as Ireland's Senior Monthly.[41]

The lesson

GAEDHILG FOR ALL
ENGLISH DO CHACH

promised to make all those who were 'unilingual' become
'bilingual and bilateral, bi-heaven'.

IRISH	BEURLA
Gaedhilg blasta	Blasted Irish
Comhrádh Beirte	Comrade Bertie
Garda síothchána	Guarda Shove-on-a
Mo rogha	Guinness
Éamonn	Dev.
Cheap mé go raibh glas ar an doras.	Migawd, my wife![42]

In the preamble *Blather* had made its readers aware that the
sad plight of those who could not speak Irish 'is equalled only
by the thousands of men and women in Ireland to-day who
want to learn English'. Accordingly it turned to the teaching
of English, a knowledge of which was found to be essential for
those wishing to pass the clerical officers' exam. The low
standard of English spoken in this island was due, said
Professor Dr Otto Kindergarten, to the fact that 'the English
language was first invented by the Abbey Theatre'. When the
Civil Service Commission began to demand a reasonable
standard of Abbey English *Blather* undertook to educate the
'Great Ignorant Public'. Its first lesson provided an example of
Abbey English in the form of a dialogue between three men.

PHELIM: God bless all here. Have·ye heard the news,
the black, black news from the North?

SHAUN AND PEADAR (*together*): Nothing have we heard
for many days but the drip—drip—drip of the rain
as it drips, and the sighing of the wind as it sighs.

PHELIM: Indeed, troth, good cause has it to sigh.
For last night, at the grey coming of the twilight,
the redcoats seized a poor Croppy Boy as he watered
his stag in the glen. O woe, woe, woe!

PEADAR: Alas, alas, poor Yorick.

SHAUN: The pity of it. The pitiful pity of it is
heavy on my heart this day.[43]

With the Irish and English languages firmly set on the right

road, *Blather* turned to the continent, and to the provision of
'handy vocabularies' which provided useful phrases for those
who intended to holiday abroad.

> *Je me trouve mal, pourrai-je avoir un sceau.* This are
> French for 'I are suffering to endure stomach spasms, so
> kindly to produce me a bucket.' . . .
> *Le chauffeur est évanoui et Er hat das Bein gebrocken.*
> 'Honourable chauffeur are swooned and imbroken his
> leg.'[44]

In the quest for linguistic purity, the arts were not
neglected. One of *Blather's* most valuable services to its
readers was its offer to 'gut books' and extract the 'best bits'.
These it printed all together in a 'hash', thus obviating the need
for readers to spend money on books or read through reams of
rubbish before arriving at the 'good bits'. One of the benefits
offered to readers of *Blather,* then, was that they would be
kept up to date with the climactic moments of all the latest
detective, cowboy, romance, adventure and travel books and
so would be unable to dishonour *Blather* by an appearance of
ignorance or illiteracy.

> Solitaire sat thoughtfully on a bunk in one of the cells of
> the jail that had been built in the back part of the sheriff's
> office. He realised that he was in a very difficult position.
> He was a prisoner in a town where he was an utter stranger.
> *I was a white man* — the last product in the slow upward rise
> of mankind through the ages. I had to stop this thing if it
> cost me my life! . . .
> A feature of Moscow broadcasting is the regular relaying
> of ballets and operas from the Bolshoi Theatre, or Grand
> Opera House, Theatre Square . . .
> He was flat on his back, bound hand and foot, on the
> floor of the cabin of the launch.[45]

Blather obviously had so much to offer that it could not be
confined within the covers of a small magazine. It decided to
set up a radio station, the Blather Pirate Station, 2BL,
designed to 'give Athlone hell'. Its policy statement said:

Our broadcasts will be devoted to Communist propaganda,

the B LAT HER No Rates Campaign, and to the furtherance
of the O'Blather's League for Little People.[46]

The programme which was provided showed that Radio
2BL offered the same diet of news, gramophone records, Irish
and 'talks' on 'Roses' and 'Poultry-feeding in Mid-Winter' as
its competitor in Athlone. For lighter moments there was
poetry, but even the editors of *Blather* had to agree that
'There Is Really No Excuse for This Sort of Thing':

A Word to Our Daughters
Did you ever try oiling a vehicle,
Elizabeth, with trehicle?
Or do you smear syrup
On your styrup?
It's too expensive, don't do so,
You'll never save up for your troso.

In Darkest Ireland
Cockneys who hike with an Óige
Half believe they will meet with a tÓige[47]

Blather could, on occasions, even attempt a serious study.
One month, in the 'monthly heart-to-heart', it inquired 'Has
Hitler Gone Too Far?'. *Blather,* which had been circulating in
Germany under the title of the *Daily Express,* had been
banned. *Blather* was annoyed and resolute.

> The attempt to stifle legitimate comment and to browbeat
> the great national organs of other countries by the
> operation of bans and prohibitions is bound to fail.
> B LATHER receives the present ban unmoved. Arrangements
> are in hand by which the next issue of the paper will appear
> in Germany under the title of the 'Daily Mail'. Should a
> further decree be issued, B LATHER will have no hesitation
> in changing the title again to that of 'Our Boys'.[48]

The editors went on to campaign for greater politeness in
speech. They recommended the use of the word 'please' and,
in particular, objected to the gentry cursing the Lower Orders
who were, of course, debarred from replying.

Let us suppose you are going on a Yule-tide picnic. You

arise late. You cannot find your razor. You fly into a temper
and ring madly for your valet, Tomkins.
'Blast you, Tomkins,' you shout, 'Where is my blasted
razor, blast you?'
This is known as Tautology. The second 'blast you' is
redundant and unnecessary. It is saying over again what you
said before and is grossly offensive to the educated ear.
Tomkins is bound to notice it, and he will probably give you
a black look when your back is turned. Why not:
'My blasted razor, Tomkins. Where did you hide it, you
swine?'
That is immeasurably better.[49]

Finally, the O'Blather himself condescended to send a
message of hope and cheer to the Irish people on the eve of the
New Year. The O'Blather, writing from his boudoir and
realising that Kathleen Ni Houlihan was 'lying broken and
bleeding in the gutter of party politics' proposed the following
solution for her ills.

Let there be a big (if necessary an enormous) saw got, and
let there be two yokes or businesses erected, one in the
Atlantic and one in the Irish Sea, for working the big saw in
the manner of two men working a cross-cut. Let the country
be then sawed from its moorings from Antrim's coast to wild
Cape Clear. By the laws of physics (Boyle's Law, Principle
of Moments, etc.), the country will then float. Our
subjection to England will then be no longer dependent on
our geographical proximity to her. It is the first step in the
sundering of the chain.[50]

The O'Blather realised that Ireland might drift over to Wales
if there were no means of steering her in the right direction.
He thought that a large sail might be erected across the
midlands but remembered that the boys of Athlone would
probably ruin it by playing handball against it. He therefore
abandoned that idea and instead suggested that the Shannon
be diverted so that it entered the sea at Cobh, a place roughly
approximating to the stern of the island. A large rudder would
have to be erected at Cobh as well, and should be housed in
the government buildings, which would have to be transferred

there. This was logical, since whoever controlled the rudder controlled the destiny of the island. Once liberated from its geographical position, the island could roam at will. It could 'go abroad for the winter', choosing winter sports or tropical fruits as it wished. Foreign supplies would be much cheaper due to the absence of transport costs. Indeed, the whole island could act as a carrier between the 'New World and the Old, putting every shipping company in the world out of business'. O'Blather was very excited by his scheme. It had inestimable advantages.

> We can give the British hell as often as we feel like it by steaming past her coast and ruining the country with gigantic tidal waves. The possibilities are endless.[51]

Having put forward this ingenious scheme for the salvation of Ireland, and having invited comment on it, *Blather* bowed out of existence. Brother Barnabas, in response to editorial appeals, reappeared briefly in *Comhthrom Féinne,* where he wrote his final farewell in Irish. When O'Nolan left UCD all his energies were diverted into other channels, and these pseudonymous creations were forgotten until aspects of them appeared, reincarnated in the person of Myles na gCopaleen.

To discuss Brother Barnabas and the O'Blather is not, however, to exhaust the sum of O'Nolan's contribution to these magazines. An adequate assessment of his early adventures in writing necessitates a study of the three student magazines which appeared during his time in UCD.

In March 1930 the first issue of a revived magazine, *The National Student,* appeared. It was published regularly until June 1931, after which it disappeared for over a year and reappeared for only a few months in 1932 before vanishing completely. In May 1931 *Comhthrom Féinne* made its debut. Run by the SRC rather than by the L & H, it was intended to be a competitor to *The National Student.* It was published for many years but only retained the name *Comhthrom Féinne* until June 1935, when it adopted that of its now defunct predecessor and became *The National Student. Blather* ran for five issues only, from August 1934 to January 1935.

There is no direct evidence of O'Nolan's having contributed

to the early *National Student*. He had been in the college for
almost a year by the time it first appeared, yet there is no
signature or initial which indicates his presence in it. In
Comhthrom Féinne O'Nolan is easily identified as Brother
Barnabas. He also signed himself as Brian O'Nolan or Brian
Ua Nualláin and used the initials B.O'N. or B. Ua N. The
articles written over his name or his initials were generally of a
serious nature and included book reviews and drama criticism,
an article on Kevin Barry (in Irish), an account of UCD's rag
week, an article on the L & H Society, and a story of Finn
MacCool (also in Irish and not at all serious).

An editorial in April 1932 further extends the range of his
contributions, by remarking that

> We have seen some very good sketches over the name(s) of
> . . . Mr B. Ua Nualláin, who persisted in hiding his light
> under a bushel by using initials other than his own.[52]

Later on, another comment seems to indicate that there were
pseudonyms other than 'Brother Barnabas'.

> He was, under various pseudonyms, particularly that of
> Brother Barnabas, the most successful and popular
> contributor COMHTHROM FÉINNE has ever had.[53]

Even if it is argued that this was written after the appearance
of *Blather,* it does seem to indicate that the 'various
pseudonyms' referred to appeared solely in *Comhthrom
Féinne. Blather,* indeed, was the work of a group of graduates.
O'Nolan was undoubtedly its prime mover, but his brother
Ciarán contributed at least two articles, 'The West's Awake'
and 'The Mystery of the Yellow Limousine', and Niall
Sheridan probably had a hand in it too, as he did in the later
Irish Times controversy and in the making of *At Swim-Two-
Birds*.

The evidence therefore indicates that O'Nolan wrote more
for *Comhthrom Féinne* than is immediately apparent and that
he cannot certainly be said to be the author of all that appears
in *Blather*. In the light of this, an examination of the early
National Student for signs of his presence under another
pseudonym would seem justified; it should, one imagines, be
easy to ascribe to him articles which appear there and in

Comhthrom Féinne and which bear the marks of his characteristic turns of mind. In fact, it is very difficult to decide what O'Nolan did write beyond what can certainly be ascribed to him. The cause of the difficulty becomes evident on even a cursory reading of the two magazines.

Although *The National Student* was always a more serious production than *Comhthrom Féinne*, both magazines have in common a particular type of humour; and it was humour which bore an astonishing resemblance to many of O'Nolan's most characteristic pieces. The temptation, then, is to ascribe more to his pen than any man could possibly have produced. It is probably more accurate to conclude that this particular type of humour influenced O'Nolan to a very great extent so that he wrote largely in response to it and to satisfy the needs of a known audience.

Both magazines are filled with puns, parodies, satires, gossip columns, odd competitions and exaggerated advertisements. Comic devices which appear first in *The National Student* are to be found also in *Comhthrom Féinne* and in *Blather*. Catch phrases like 'the editor's decision is in all cases final and legally binding' and 'let us be your Fathers' are common to both the later magazines. Brother Barnabas wrote a parody of Longfellow's poem 'Excelsior', and in doing so was following an already long-established tradition of poetic parody which had begun with the first issue of *The National Student*. The chief exponent of this sort of parody was a student called Murray who wrote under the pseudonym 'Skate'. The predominance of parody and the extensive use of pseudonyms was fitting for productions which seemed unable to dwell seriously on anything for long. There are a few serious poems in both magazines, but the overall air is one of mockery and embarrassed self-consciousness which was well summed up in a poem by Cyril Cusack. It began as a love-poem and having described a romantic situation, went on to undercut its romanticism in the last line 'Oh, do not take me seriously, child!'. The contributors to the magazine sought to be witty, erudite and a little cynical. They were self-conscious primarily because the magazines were devoted to showing the world that the inhabitants of UCD were 'capable of greatness'. Their self-consciousness expressed itself in parody, satire, fantasy and exaggeration — those very modes which O'Nolan was to develop in his later work.

The magazines themselves were anonymous. It is rare that one can identify the owner of a pseudonym as one can with 'Skate'. Other pseudonyms used were Friar John, Prospero, Ianthe, Doppelganger, Silias, Alasper Yorick, Balliste, Pandora, Joyce Vea, Regis Poetae Nepos, Wheezer, Paterfamilias, Ukelele Marx (identifiable as Donagh MacDonagh), Samuel Hall, The Janitor, Gargantua, Biddy Mulligan, Lone Star Ranger, Tadpole, Tamam Should, Enol Rats, and Mr Grange Gorman. Most of these appeared only a few times and were chosen for their propriety to the subject of the article (e.g. Ianthe for a parody of Chaucer). Some were puns (e.g. Alasper Yorick), some were meant to give a clue as to the identity of the author; Regis Poetae Nepos offered a prize to the first person to identify him from his pseudonym. Many were merely ridiculous. Only a few, and among these Brother Barnabas was outstanding, allowed for the presentation of a persona, whose habits and characteristics could be developed from issue to issue.

O'Nolan's talent in the creation of comic characters might lead one to search among these few 'true' pseudonyms for his other contributions. One of these pseudonymous characters, Samuel Hall, was first presented as the eccentric genius who set up University College, Ballybrack, to cater for UCD dropouts and idiots. His activities were reported in much the same way as those of Brother Barnabas, and it was not long before he was found to be a dramatist of note. His first play, 'The Bog of Allen', was printed in *Comhthrom Féinne,* and its introduction contained many elements which were similar to those found in O'Nolan's writing.

> With almost hysterical pleasure we give below the first literary work of genius to come from the pen of Mr Samuel Hall, BA, QED, written at the request of a deputation from the Dramatic Society, Ballybrack, and now exhibited in advance to readers of Comhthrom Féinne for their diversion, edification and moral exaltation.
>
> When requested to undertake the work Mr Hall immediately agreed, and, letting his mind fester for the short space of five minutes, wrote the play in ten minutes,

and then absent-mindedly continued writing, using both hands and two pens. At the end of half-an-hour he had written, in addition to the play, five novels, a book of sermons on Temperance, an almanac and a pamphlet on Anti-vivasection [*sic*]. However, we are concerned here only with the play. It is a wholesome Irish play, racy of the soil and Samuel Hall, written in the real traditional style, and a masterpiece of characterisation and pregnant dialogue. Mr Hall apologised for his inability to introduce Blind Phelim fiddling at the cross-roads, and although this is a serious flaw—dammit all, what about it anyway? Mr Bernard Shaw, on being shown the play, made his usual witty remark—'It bears the Hallmark of genius.' He cryptically added 'The grave—it is waiting for me. I am old.' He evidently recognised that a new star had risen in the firmament, greater than his own. The play, Mr Hall tells me, is copyright in Yugo Slavia only.

All the rights are reserved, and are securely locked up in a drawer in Mr Hall's desk.[54]

The dramatis personae were Allen Bogg, a farmer; his wife, a woman; and a bog-trotter, a man. The scene was set in the Bog of Allen; the dialect was Anglo-Irish; the subject was the noble peasant living in the Celtic Twilight.

Several elements of this article (the address to the audience, the elements of clichés, bad puns, additional and ludicrous detail, the attack on the Abbey Theatre for the matter and language of its plays, the pseudo-critical comments, and the addition, for good measure, of a few non-sequitors) seem to mark this as possibly a production of O'Nolan's. Samuel Hall was, however, to appear again with another play. The second effort, entitled 'The West's Awake', contained a glorious accumulation of clichés derived mainly from cowboy romances. Peter, a Poor Idiot Boy, tells his grief-stricken mother, a widow:

I'm going away to a place where men are men, where everyone is bow-legged from riding horses, where people shoot straight and live crooked; where everyone has a marvellous physique and an iron constitution that even hard drinking can't destroy; where the moon is a shield of silver in the sky, and the sun a gold medal on the bosom of the heavens; where the wind ploughs waves in the prairy grass, where the buffulo [*sic*] and the an'elope play, where the leaves rustle in the breeze, and rustlers rustle beeves, and where it's Springtime in the Rockies far away.[55]

O'Nolan was to be described by Donagh MacDonagh in a later article in the magazine as someone who was characterised by his hatred of clichés. In the article 'Hash' in *Blather* (if it is O'Nolan's) and in the 'Circle N' episode of *At Swim* he demonstrated his ability to parody cowboy romances. It could easily be assumed that Samuel Hall was another of O'Nolan's pseudonyms were it not for the fact that the second Samuel Hall play, 'The West's Awake', was written over the signature Ciarán Ó Nualláin. It is possible that the articles dealing with University College, Ballybrack, and 'the Bog of Allen' were written by Brian and that Ciarán took over the character in time to write the second play. However, the very high standard which was maintained throughout the large number of contributions in all the issues of the magazine makes it very difficult to ascertain the authorship of any particular piece.

An article entitled 'College in 2000 AD (A Phantasy)', was submitted over the initials N.J.S. (Niall Sheridan). Its introduction, which gives a motley list of characters and things, is later imitated by Myles in *Cruiskeen Lawn*. A student called John J. M. Ryan wrote an article on the possible chaos which would ensue if the letter H were to be lost from the alphabet, and demonstrated in the process an imagination as fantastic and particular as O'Nolan's. Other writers showed an awareness of the dangers of clichés, and one, who signed himself 'Wheezer' (and whose style is quite different to any of O'Nolan's) included a sentence which shows that its author possessed the capacity, also shared by Myles, to draw a cliché out to its logically grotesque conclusion, to see what it really meant in physical terms.

I surged, I groaned, in very truth I was offended, but I didn't show it, no, sir, he is *so nice,* you know, and then a thought struck me—of course thoughts are always striking me, some day they will knock me out—.[56]

The magazines were full of parodies of Joyce. One of these

'The Day of the University Students' by 'Sezme', a parody of the style of *Finnegans Wake,* is very similar to one of the letters sent to the *Irish Times* in 1940. It is, however, possible that Niall Sheridan wrote both of these and that their presence points merely to the intense interest aroused by Joyce and his work which was to reveal itself in O'Nolan's writing as well as in Sheridan's.

It is very difficult, therefore, to identify those examples of writing which we're initiated by O'Nolan and those which he himself was responding to. In December 1933 an article appeared which will serve to highlight the whole problem. It was called 'Op.$^1/_8$' and was unsigned. It provided, in a mock serialisation rubric, a list of characters, a synopsis of the plot, and a parody of *Finnegans Wake:*

OP.$^1/_8$

SYNOPSIS

D. Mac D., cradlemaker, and fainting shadow in a world of mist opportunities, is the subject of a 'double exposure' by

MAC AN IOMAIRE, chief mourner to Heraclitus, gallantly assisted by

ELIZABETH CURRAN, cradlerocker, who agrees 70 per cent.

EXEGESIS by McGilkar, a Palgravedigger.

CROWD WORK BY: Joyce, Manet, Van Gogh, Yeats, Keating, Stein, Jolas, Dumas, Dickens, Lavery, Freud, and Dick Wittington Turner.

NOW READ ON:

Adagio Assisi the poor man's boredom. Peperit Monty et nascitur ridiculus mus Bach to our mousetraps. I am a fuguetive so are we all but he'll immortalise us. Sneer to-day and Don tomorrow till the last syllable of dischord in time.[57]

Could this be O'Nolan's work, and possibly one of the comic ideas from which he developed the plot of *At Swim?* Or is it the work of someone else, which O'Nolan read and enjoyed and which he was to remember later when he wrote his anti-novel with its own synopses, lists of characters, satirical approach to James Joyce, and parodic inclusion of many types of literature?

One cannot be sure which theory is correct. All that is certain
is that O'Nolan must have learnt a great deal from the fairly
coherent comic ethos of *The National Student* and
Comhthrom Féinne. The impulse to parody was to remain
with O'Nolan and it is not too much to say that this impulse
must have been prompted by the sustained and widespread
parody to be found in the college magazines.

The lay-out of the magazines, too, must have influenced
O'Nolan when he came later to write the *Cruiskeen Lawn*
column. Mr Grange Gorman, *Comhthrom Féinne's* 'special
correspondent', conducted a conversation with his editor
which is similar to many of those Myles was later to conduct
with the supposed editor of the *Irish Times.* The type-settings,
capitalisations, headlines, the mock 'letters to the editor' in
Comhthrom Féinne, the research bureaux and the exaggerated advertisements were all to reappear in *Blather* and
in *Cruiskeen Lawn.* Even a casual comment, printed in the
gossip column of *Comhthrom Féinne,* may be relevant for a
later work.

A student who is up before the President seems to have
position, but no magnitude.[58]

This sentence does not appear again in the magazine, but it
does reappear in *At Swim,* where it used to describe the Good
Fairy.

It is easy, then, to establish that O'Nolan worked in close
harmony with his contemporaries and friends, learning from
them and from the process of putting a magazine together,
responding to ideas and devices, and developing them in his
own articles. To prove that there was a community of interest
and outlook, with its members engaged in a reciprocal
relationship, does not, however, go far towards determining
what O'Nolan might have written and not signed or signed
with an unknown pseudonym. Nevertheless, in spite of the
general difficulties of ascription, outlined above, it is possible
to mark at least two unsigned articles which are almost
certainly his work. The first of these articles is entitled '"Let Us
Be Your Fathers". Hope for the Mind-Sufferers. Our Unique
New Service.' It announces the establishment of the
'Comhthrom Féinne Institute of Practical Psychology' which

undertakes to develop personality, to make people taller and more dynamic, to abolish their dandruff and make them relaxed and masterful. All that is necessary is that each worried man fill in the official form and send it to the institute. Each inquirer will then receive a copy of the institute's special booklet, *The Golden Road.* The form reads:

The Principal,
C.F. Institute of Practical Psychology,
University College, Dublin.

My Dear Sir,
I am a Professor/a Student and I am an Idiot Boy/a Boob/a Yes-man/a Spineless Waster/a Wreck/an Aumadhaun/a Flat Tyre. I cannot do any of the things you mention. I find that I cannot concentrate for one moment *on anything.* I have never passed an examination in my life but I have failed several. I find it hard to quit the bed in the morning. I often fail in that matitudinal struggle. Would you blame me? I feel that my only remaining hope is the Institute. You may make any use you wish of this letter. I enclose the requisite fee of six guineas, and I make this application only on the distinct understanding that should the Principal consider that my case is hopeless, he shall be in nowise compelled to accept my application or my money. I am interested in the following:

> Technocracy.
> Tautology.
> Totalisators.
> Trolley Trimming.
> Transvaal Transport.
> Journalism in the Home.
> Jansenism.
> Jamborees
>   and
> Accountancy.

And if I am, can you help me? I beg to remain,
> Dear Principal,
> Your Most Humble Servant
> ....

P.S. — I think your Institute supplies a long-felt want.[59]

This article is only one of the many satires on the advertising of quack remedies and panaceas, which can be found in both magazines. However, all the evidence points to O'Nolan as its author. The list of subjects taught is as heterogeneous as that offered by the 'brother' in his London University Institute in *The Hard Life*. The mixture of a list of nonsensical ambitions with a parody of personality-building courses can be found throughout *Cruiskeen Lawn,* where O'Nolan's normal method of satirical comment is to elaborate and exaggerate, to add as he does here, a cure for 'scurf', 'dandruff', 'falling hair and baldness', to a promise to teach people how to relax. The use of non-sequitors in the letter to the institute, even the idea for the institute itself, are devices in which O'Nolan always delighted. Finally, the article was printed in Vol. V, No. 2, of February 1933, the issue which O'Nolan himself edited.

The other article, which was included in the following issue, was entitled 'Are You Lonely in the Restaurant?' and is certainly a predecessor to the famous 'Buchhandlung' service of *Cruiskeen Lawn.*

> Professor Adolf Gleitzboschkinderschule of the Berliner Universität, the eminent psychologist, has repeatedly pointed out in the Paris editions of the *Leipziger Tageblatt* that the habit of eating alone is a pernicious one and one which leads to morbidity and undue contempt for one's own vices . . . . COMHTHROM FÉINNE, therefore, taking its duty of SERVING its public very much to heart, has much pleasure in announcing a NEW PROFESSION in an effort to cope with the present difficulty. COMHTHROM FÉINNE will provide EATERS, varying in quality and price to suit every client. YOU NEED NO LONGER EAT ALONE. Hire one of our skilled Conversationalists, pay and talk as you eat and avoid the farce of pretending that you are a THINKER to whom his own kind is sufficient for the day.[60]

As the condition of hire for the Eaters is outlined, it seems very clear that this article contained the germs not only of the Buchhandlung service but of the Myles na gCopaleen Escort Service as well. It did not, of course, develop as they did, but the idea of satirising pseudo-psychology and intellectual snobbery is there, as is also O'Nolan's often acute observation of character types. There are six types of Eaters, depending on the level of conversation offered.

CLASS B.

Are you a strong silent man? We can supply a great hulking lout who will GRUB with you, and munch, and chaw for an inclusive charge of about 2/6 per hour. These fine Eaters have been specially trained and must be provided with great lumps of beef, porter and whole loaves. Knives and forks are desirable but not essential. They will under no circumstances talk, but coarse animal grunts may be provided at a small extra cost. *Forte,* 2d. each, and *fortessimo* 4d. each.

CLASS E.

An exclusive and superior type of Eater belongs to this Class and must on no account be offered MASH or brown buns. They will discourse and converse on the subject of the drama, the theatre, the novel, the play, the tragedy, the comedy. Clients are warned not to make a *faux pas* in front of these Eaters, as they will not consent to stay with clients who betray an inferior intellectual level.[61]

As always, *Comhthrom Féinne* provided a coupon for those who wished to avail of its new service.

To the Editor, *Comhthrom Féinne.*
  A Chara,—I am a Professor/a Student, and I do be lonely in the Restaurant. Please send me a copy of your free booklet 'Golden Words' and arrange for the attendance of an EATER.
Class.............. on............... at.................o'clock.
         Signed..

I certify that this Client is ALRIGHT.
        Signed...............................
            Member of the Royal Irish Academy.

The similarities between this coupon and that provided by the 'CF Institute for Practical Psychology' are so evident that

one can assume, without going too far, that they are the work
of the same author.

There may be other articles in *Comhthrom Féinne* which
might be ascribed to O'Nolan. An early article, 'The
Be(r)ginnings of L & H', which purported to be a defence of
Brother Barnabas's first article, was a satirical account of
Celtic scholarship in the line of O'Nolan's later (signed) attack
on the triumvirate of Celtic scholarship, 'Binchy, Bergin and
Best'. The subject was always a favourite target for O'Nolan's
wit, and there are similarities in style. The cover of the issue
informs us that the article was written by 'Skate'. Nevertheless,
there is an obvious temptation to believe at least that O'Nolan
produced most of the articles for his own issue of *Comhthrom
Féinne*. The article 'Let Us Be Your Fathers' was followed by
'Ballade Cynicale' by Brother Barnabas and 'Thomas
Campbell'. There was then an unsigned inquisition on the
subject of 'What is the Most Popular Journal in Ireland?'.
Much of it is a parody of legal jargon. If it was written by
O'Nolan, it is the first example of the extensive attack he was
to wage on jargon of all kinds in the columns of *Cruiskeen
Lawn*. This article was followed by one dealing with the
establishment of University College, Ballybrack—the first
appearance of Samuel Hall. The article contains, in the form
of a sample examination paper, an attack on the pathetic level
of Irish required in oral examinations. Throughout the issue
the articles were broken up by boxes inset in the text. One of
these contained the message:

> If you are convinced that *Comhthrom Féinne* is no good
> and unworthy of your further support, TURN AT ONCE
> TO PAGE 20.

Page 20 contained the article 'Let Us Be Your Fathers'. On
page 38 appeared a 'Stop Press' account of a savage attack on
the editor of the magazine. No reason was given for the attack
which was perpetrated by two Donegal women. Readers were
assured that 'The Editor's condition is serious, but not
immediately critical.' It was known that 'Huge crowds visited
the scene of the occurence up to a late hour last night.' This
type of self-dramatisation, as well as the total lay-out of the
magazine, bear the stamp of O'Nolan's comic outlook.

O'Nolan may also have edited the following issue, in which

the 'Eaters' article appeared, but which does not carry the
name of its editor. Certainly his contributions to *Comhthrom
Féinne*, which had been steadily increasing in number, were
most numerous at this time. Shortly afterwards his interest
began to decline. Myles na gCopaleen, writing in 1960, barely
remembers the magazine. It was only by accident that,
searching through his papers, he found

> a silver-covered affair named the *National Student* and
> dated June, 1935. To my surprise I find myself mentioned
> in it *passim,* even accused of once having been editor of it,
> and bedamn but I appear again towards the end of it as the
> author of a discourse which was at once witty and serene.
> Much as I would like to reproduce it here, what would be
> the use? It is in Early Middle Irish, and of my kind not many
> now exist to understand a word of it.   (*CL*. 31 Mar. 1960)

In the course of writing for the magazine O'Nolan had
worked out many of his major interests. The Irish language,
and Celtic scholarship were to be major themes, though,
surprisingly, there was little actual writing in Irish. Pseudo-
science, jargon, Clichés, and advertising were already
favourite targets and the main devices of parody and satire
were used primarily to undercut intellectual pretensions,
humbug and hypocrisy. In the parody of Longfellow and in
the article introducing Brother Barnabas's Great Insurance
Scheme O'Nolan's tendency to allow his imagination to dwell
on the grotesque and horrible was revealed.

In all the articles he seems at his best where his imagination
is given full freedom to roam unfettered by the dictates of
time, place or subject. This is especially true of the O'Blather's
scheme for Ireland or the evocation of the Brother's great
memories. Wherever one finds a phrase like 'The possibilities
are endless' or the association in an article (in Irish) of Finn
MacCool and the 'Reds', it is clear that O'Nolan is using
pedantry, satire, parody, exaggeration — all his favourite
comic devices — in the service of fantasy. Where these devices
helped in the construction of a parallel imaginative world
without limitations or rules, O'Nolan seems to have been
happiest; it is certainly in such instances that his work is most
coherent and least open to the accusation of being
overstrained or using 'wit for the sake of wit'.

3
The Story-Teller's Book-Web:
At Swim-Two-Birds

At Swim-Two-Birds by 'Flann O'Brien' (the name by which
O'Nolan became known to thousands of readers and by which
he will be referred to throughout the rest of this study) was
published in 1939, having occupied its author some five years.
It was written during the latter part of his time at UCD (while
he was completing his MA thesis) and his early years in the
civil service. The book is first mentioned in *Comhthrom
Féinne* in June 1935. In an article entitled 'Literary
Antecedents' Niall Sheridan informed his readers that
ÓNualláin is now engaged on a novel so ingeniously
constructed that the plot is keeping him well in hand.'[1] Later
Sheridan was to realise that, as Brinsley, he 'shared with Finn
MacCool the honour of being one of the characters'[2] in the
book. O'Brien showed him the various sections as they were
written and when the book was completed gave him a free
hand to prune its excessive length.

None of O'Brien's other novels was to take such a time to
complete. In general, once he had the idea for its plot, each
book was written very quickly. The delay in completing *At
Swim* was due partly to the fact that it was started at a time
when O'Brien was engaged in many other activities. The basic
plot of *At Swim* was developed as early as 1934 when O'Brien
was still writing for *Comhthrom Feinne*. From that he went on
to write, illustrate and edit *Blather,* to complete his MA
thesis, and to pass the civil service exams and begin a new
career. In his job he worked a five-and-a-half-day week and
can have had little time to devote to the progress of the book.
It was, however, finished early in 1938, when O'Brien passed it
to Niall Sheridan for final comment. Sheridan claimed that it
was suffering from hypertrophy, particularly in the Finn

MacCool sections, and reduced it in length by approximately one-third.

O'Brien began to make the rounds of publishers and agents. On 31 January 1938 he wrote to C. H. Brooks at the office of A. M. Heath & Co., the literary agents, and told him about the book.

> It is called *At Swim-Two-Birds* and is a very queer affair, unbearably queer, perhaps. For all its defects, I feel it has the ingredients that make the work of writers from this beautiful little island so acceptable.[3]

O'Brien probably wrote this tongue-in-cheek, but however insincere it might have been, the letter had the desired effect. Brooks asked to see the book. He liked it, and A. M. Heath became, and remained, O'Brien's literary agent. Longmans in England were secured as publishers. At this time Graham Greene was with Longmans, and he was most enthusiastic about the book. O'Brien later showed his appreciation for this support when he dedicated *The Hard Life* to Graham Greene. Greene was not, however, the only person at Longmans who felt such enthusiasm. A. M. Heath reported to O'Brien that Longmans had written to them saying 'We are all rather excited over his MS. and would like to meet him.'[4]

The publication did not proceed without some difficulties, most of them of O'Brien's own making. He was discontented with the title, which he described as 'defective from the commercial viewpoint' and suitable only as the 'title for a slim book of poems'.[5] He suggested *Sweeny in the Trees* as an alternative. But by this time, the people at Longmans had grown accustomed to *At Swim-Two-Birds* and were reluctant to change it, though it is possible that O'Brien's suggestion might have been a better choice. Swim-Two-Birds (or Snámh-dá-én) is only one of the places visited by Sweeny in his flight through Erin, and the lay which he recited in that place was not included in O'Brien's translation. *Sweeny in the Trees* is a title derived from a line in the 'Conclusion of the book, ultimate': 'Sweeny in the trees hears the sad baying as he sits listening on the branch, a huddle between the earth and heaven.' (p. 314) The line is an important one for it highlights the importance of the Sweeny section in the book's overall plan. The change of title would have pointed even more strongly to the central importance of Sweeny in the structure and vision of *At Swim*. The title *At Swim-Two-Birds* leads the reader to expect some special significance from the section where Sweeny visits Snámh-dá-én but his expectations are baffled by the exclusion of the lay spoken there.

At one stage O'Brien decided to change his pseudonym from Flann O'Brien to John Hackett. He had first used 'Flann O'Brien' in the O'Connor-Ó Faoláin controversy and did not wish his book to be associated with that somewhat acrimonious dispute. He wrote to Longmans and told them that he did not want his 'real name' to be linked with anything that was not entirely orthodox.[6] But by that time it was (fortunately) too late to change it. 'John Hackett' would have been an unfortunate choice, whereas 'Flann O'Brien' carries with it the right sort of associations for this book. As O'Brien himself had pointed out to Longmans on 10 November 1938, it 'has the advantage that it contains an unusual name and one that is quite ordinary. "Flann" is an old Irish name now rarely heard.' The name 'Flann' means 'blood-red'[7] and was probably thought suitable for the angry opponent of O'Connor and Ó Faoláin, but it was also borne by the ninth-century scholar-poet Flann mac Lonán and by the seventeenth-century historical scholar Flann Mac Aodhagáin, while O'Brien was the family name of a number of kings of Ireland. The complete name therefore associates the author with the Gaelic royal families and with the early Irish literary and scholastic tradition.

The book, when it appeared on 13 March 1939, was called *At Swim-Two-Birds* and it was by 'Flann O'Brien'. Perhaps the date of publication was an inauspicious one, for the book was to prove a financial failure. Six months later only 244 copies had been sold. The outbreak of war may have made bookselling more difficult, or was O'Brien's own explanation correct?

> In the year 1939, a book curiously named A T S WIM T WO B IRDS appeared. Adolf Hitler took serious exception to it and in fact loathed it so much that he started World War II in order to torpedo it. In a grim irony that is not without

charm, the book survived the war while Hitler did not.

(*CL*. 4 Feb. 1965)

The book survived the war due to the fact that, although it
was not widely read, it was received with intense enjoyment by
a small but influential group of discriminating critics and
writers. It became, and remained until its reissue in 1960, a
coterie taste, a book which its small number of owners were
reluctant to let out of their hands — even to friends — because
they knew it would not be returned. It came to have a
reputation as a 'difficult', 'intellectual' book, its patterns of
parody and literary cross-reference only clear to the highly
educated.

Those enthusiasts who had greeted the book in 1939 did not
share this view. It was praised by Graham Greene and William
Saroyan, and Niall Sheridan's story of Joyce's reception of it is
well known. In a letter to MacGibbon & Kee he said:

In the spring of 1939 I brought a copy of the novel
(inscribed by the author) to Joyce in Paris. His eyesight was
then so bad that he could read very little. I was amazed to
find that he had already read, and greatly enjoyed, *At
Swim-Two-Birds.*

He took very little interest in contemporary writing, but
his verdict on Flann O'Brien's book was emphatic and brief:
'That's a real writer, with the true comic spirit. A really
funny book.' It was significant tribute, for he later went on
to speak of the pomposity and solemnity of many critics of
Ulysses. He felt they had missed the point, and he wished
that more of them realised that *Ulysses* was essentially a
funny book.

Joyce's interest in the book took a practical form. He went
to considerable trouble to have it noticed in French literary
circles and wrote to tell me of his efforts. He persuaded the
well-known critic Maurice Denhof to write an article for the
Mercure de France, but Denhof died suddenly and the
project came to nothing.

Although the war was now on and Joyce had moved to the
South, he kept on trying to interest various literary friends
of his in the book and was still writing from Vichy on the
matter only nine months before his death.

There's an interesting postscript to the story. Before moving to his last Paris residence (34 rue de Vignes) Joyce pruned his library drastically. After his death this reduced remnant of the library was sold by his Paris landlord. Paul Leon and some other friends managed to buy in about two-thirds of the books and among them was the copy of *At Swim* which I had delivered in 1939.

It is included in a catalogue of the salvaged books which was published by the Librarie la Hune (170 Blvd. Saint-Germaine) in 1949. The entry relating to *At Swim-Two-Birds* is followed by a notice in italics which reads 'Livre tres aimé de Joyce . . .'[8]

For one glorious week in April *At Swim* replaced *Gone With the Wind* as top of the best-seller list in Dublin. It was favourably reviewed in the Dublin newspapers and sold well until the middle of April, and again for a week in June, after which it disappeared and was not again available until 1960, more than twenty years later.

It was not published in America until 1951. The American branch of Longmans had decided in 1939 that 'it was a little too odd for the market',[9] and they rejected it. O'Brien wanted an American edition, so when William Saroyan offered to find a publisher, he accepted eagerly. Saroyan's efforts met with no success and it was not until 1951 that Pantheon decided to publish *At Swim*. There is some confusion about this publication. O'Brien made some visits to the USA in 1948 and 1949, but when he wrote to Tim O'Keeffe in 1959 he said that he had no knowledge of how the American publication had come about. O'Keeffe made enquiries and wrote to tell O'Brien that the book had been recommended to Pantheon by James Johnson Sweeney of the Guggenheim Museum. Seamus Kelly of the *Irish Times,* however, was under the impression that the publication was a result of the enthusiastic advocacy of Richard Watts, Jnr of the *New York Herald Tribune.* Richard Watts has himself confirmed this in a letter to the present writer. He said that when he was press attaché in Ireland in 1942 he had been introduced to O'Brien by Seamus Kelly. He was impressed by O'Brien's work and wrote a number of articles about him. He continued:

I finally persuaded an American publisher to bring out 'At Swim Two Birds' here. But the wonderful novel was ahead of its time here, and it sold virtually no copies. In fact, it drove the somewhat obscure publishing firm out of business.[10]

This letter adds to the confusion, as Richard Watts cannot here be referring to Pantheon. Were there two American editions of *At Swim*? The Pantheon edition of 3,000 copies appeared in March 1951. American reviewers were, simultaneously, both enthusiastic and puzzled. The book sold only moderately well and its popular acceptance had to wait a further ten years. There is no mention of an American edition in *Cruiskeen Lawn*.

By this time O'Brien's dislike of his book was quite well established. Indeed, his aversion to it may have begun as soon as it appeared in print. In the earliest letter to A. M. Heath, O'Brien had described it as 'queer', but he ordered two special copies to be sent, one to Donagh MacDonagh and the other to Denis Devlin in Rome. At the same time he sent a copy to Ethel Mannin with a covering note explaining that *At Swim* was

> a belly-laugh or high-class literary pretentious slush, depending on how you look at it. Some people say it is harder on the head than the worst whiskey, so do not hesitate to burn the book if you think that's the right thing to do.

Miss Mannin did not understand or like *At Swim*. She replied on 17 July 1939 saying that it was 'altogether too latter day James-Joycean.' She added: 'Perhaps I am over-simple. Leave it at that.' But O'Brien was never really allowed to leave it at that. The critics were often confused by *At Swim* but they were unanimous in noticing the influence of Joyce on it. The constant mention of Joyce in connection with his own work infuriated O'Brien. In 1961 he wrote to Tim O'Keeffe and told him: 'If I hear that word "Joyce" again, I will surely froth at the gob!'[11] By that time, ironically, *At Swim* was at last a success. Its reissue in England by MacGibbon & Kee had brought O'Brien the recognition he had long deserved, but at a time when he felt the object was

unworthy of the attention it was receiving. O'Brien decided to
do whatever he could 'in the promotional sphere' even while
protesting that he had, by then, no faith in the book. He
decided that 'at least 2,000 copies will be sold in this little
island alone' because the 'true worth' of the book was 'quite
irrelevant'.[12] In spite of the great popularity of *At Swim,* the
translations, reissues, and paperback editions, O'Brien's
opinion of it never changed. In 1965 he told Tim O'Keeffe:

> I am so sick of this *At Swim-Two-Birds* juvenile scrivenry
> that I just can't take it seriously on any level and absolutely
> loathe the mere mention.[13]

Later, in December of the same year, he added:

> If I get sufficiently drunk over Christmas I'm going to read
> that damned book for the first time. Those birds must have
> some unsuspected stuffing in them.[14]

By then it did not really matter what O'Brien thought of it.
Graham Greene remembered it vividly and his comments,
with those of Dylan Thomas and James Joyce, were included
on the jacket of the new edition. Review copies were sent out in
July 1960. Reviews were numerous and, on the whole,
favourable. On 17 August O'Brien wrote to Brian Inglis and
told him: 'The book is, of course, juvenile nonsense but I
understand that the sales are enormous and that it is "going
like a bomb".' It continued to sell well and to attract
increasing critical attention over the years. John Wain, in an
article in *Encounter,* described it as 'a gargantuan comic novel
which makes a simultaneous exploration on four or five levels
of Irish civilisation'.[15] Richard Harrity of the *New York
Herald Tribune* stated emphatically: 'This is a comic
masterpiece of modern Irish literature that is as dazzling as the
aurora borealis and twice as difficult to describe,'[16] and Vivian
Mercier writing in *Commonweal* asked 'How is an addict [of
O'Brien], lacking the powers of a Baudelaire or a De Quincey,
to convey to the as yet unensnared anything of the true nature
of his artificial paradise?'[17]

A number of critics, whilst expressing enthusiasm for the
book, speak also of the difficulty of categorising, or even

describing it. Their difficulty is quite understandable as a quick 'synopsis of the plot' will make clear.

The events of the book centre round the activities, thoughts, reading-matter and literary productions of an unnamed narrator who is a student at UCD. The story is related in the first person and the narrator's mind is the focal point for all its events and digressions. The reader learns of his daily life at university and at home, where he lives with an uncle. The narrator, whose attendance at his classes is desultory, is much engaged in 'spare-time literary activities'. These take the form of a novel he is writing about a man called Trellis, the owner of a public house, who, like his creator, rarely attends to his business and divides his time between writing a novel and sleeping. Trellis's novel is to be a warning to Ireland. He is much concerned about the decay of moral standards and plans an antidote in the form of a cautionary tale 'on sin and the wages attaching thereto'. Trellis knows that if his book is to be read at all, and his message pushed home, he must fill it with detailed descriptions of the very sins he is condemning. With his 'friend and colleague' William Tracy, a writer of cowboy romances, he has perfected a new scientific-literary device called 'aestho-autogamy', a method by which characters are created fully grown and matured, by a process involving neither conception nor fertilisation. Trellis uses this method to create the villain in his novel, a man called Furriskey, who is born at the age of twenty-six 'with a memory but without a personal experience to account for it'. Trellis does not normally have to create his characters, for it is usually possible for him to borrow or hire them from the work of other novelists, explain their duties to them in relation to his story and let them get on with it. For this 'great' book, however, he has to create two characters: Furriskey, an example of unparalleled depravity and Sheila Lamont, an ideal of beauty and goodness. Nowhere in former literature can he find two such extremes. Most of his other characters are borrowed: Finn MacCool from old Irish legend, Shorty Andrews and Slug Willard from the cowboy romances of William Tracy, Peggy the servant girl from stories of Dublin.

All these characters have wills of their own but are subject to

Trellis's wishes while he is awake. Although their personalities are developing in a manner which does not suit the roles devised for them by Trellis, he nevertheless obliges them to act according to his original plan; however, they quickly revert to their own inclinations as soon as he falls asleep. Furriskey, created to be a seducer and a rake, falls in love with Peggy. They marry, and while Trellis is awake are forced to 'simulate immoral actions, thoughts and words' (p.86). Luckily, Trellis spends most of his time asleep and then his tyrannical powers are suspended. Soon, in order to lead freer lives, the characters begin to drug him so that his creative powers will be suspended for longer and longer periods of time. The novel begins to get completely out of hand. Finn MacCool, who was hired to act as Peggy's father and guard her virtue, attempts to assault her himself. When Trellis creates Sheila Lamont, he does so in his own bedroom, and overwhelmed by her beauty, rapes her himself. A child, Orlick Trellis, is born as a result of the rape. Sheila dies of shame and the Pooka MacPhellimey and Good Fairy arrive to do battle for Orlick's soul. The Pooka wins (because the Good Fairy cheats at cards) and takes Orlick away with him to teach him evil. When Orlick returns to the Red Swan Hotel he is found to have inherited his father's literary gifts, and the other inhabitants persuade him to punish Trellis by writing a novel about him in which he will be forced to suffer unbelievable torments. These torments are imposed on him by the Pooka, who seems unable to distinguish him from mad King Sweeny, a character in one of Finn's stories who later makes his own appearance in the book. Trellis is saved from a gruesome death when, during a trial in which one of his accusers is a cow, his servant Teresa inadvertently burns the papers in which these rebellious characters were created, thus banishing them from existence or returning them to the literary world from which they were originally borrowed. Trellis is saved. In his own life the narrator passes his exams, is reconciled with his uncle, and the conclusion of the book bears only an oblique relationship to the rest of it.

We have, then, three books in all: the narrator's book about Trellis, Trellis's book about sin, and Orlick Trellis's book about his father. If we add Flann O'Brien's book about the narrator and his mind we have four narratives, one within the other. Within each narrative there are further extensions. O'Brien tells us not only about the narrator's mind, but gives extracts from the literature he and his friends read. Thus we have many extracts, of a varying nature, from *The Conspectus of Arts and Natural Sciences*, from a letter the student receives from a racing tipster, his recollection of the Christian Brothers' *Literary Reader* and from *The Athenian Oracle*, a book which his friend Michael Byrne has picked up at a shop on the quays. He remembers the wise sayings of the sons of Sirach, a quotation in which the verse of Milton and Keats is compressed together, dictionary definitions, odd scraps of poetry—in fact all the clutter and jumble of a mind which is varied and catholic in its background and tastes.

The narrator's book on Trellis is a hotch-potch of different styles. Trellis himself is described in a passage borrowed from *The Conspectus of Arts and Natural Sciences* describing an eighteenth-century gentleman called Dr Beatty. Trellis's house, the Red Swan Inn, is described in a parody of travel and legal jargon. His aims in writing his book on sin are expressed in a style that swiftly becomes a parody of crusading moralist literature.

Trellis's own book, having such diverse characters as Dublin cowboys, Finn MacCool, John Furriskey and the Pooka Fergus MacPhellimey, obviously requires a number of different styles. Here are included Dublin 'talk', a parody of the language of cowboy romances, folk stories and Finn tales.

Orlick Trellis writes his book in a parody of the style of Middle Irish romance mixed with folk-tale, occasionally shading off into the language of 1890s romanticism. In addition to this, the characters of Trellis's novel tell their own tales in their own manner. Shanahan tells the story of the attack on the Circle N ranch, a story of cattle-rustling in Ringsend, which includes among its characters cowboys and Indians, cattle rustlers and exporters, Dublin gurriers, the Dublin Metropolitan Police and Irish revolutionaries. He also tells of Jem Casey, 'Poet of the Pick and Bard of Booterstown', and recites Casey's famous poem 'The Workman's Friend'. Later he relates the story of Jumping Sergeant Craddock. Finn, drowsing in his corner of the room, recalls the feats of the Fianna and recites, in Middle Irish verse, the story of the madness of Sweeny.

It is often difficult to ascertain whose is the speaking voice in all of this. One narrative level often shades over into another. In the account of the multi-clause colloquy between the Pooka and the Good Fairy, is it Trellis or the narrator who is writing? Often it does not really matter. O'Brien's intention was to include as many different styles of speaking and writing as was possible within the scope of the book's 316 pages, and to juxtapose one style against another for comic and artistic effect. By the time the book ends it has presented some thirty-six different styles and forty-two extracts.

The complication of style, character and incidents is, consequently, enormous. The wealth of allusion, to English, Gaelic, classical and European literature, and the large number of cross-references from section to section increase the complication, while providing a kind of thematic and structural unity. Thus Trellis and the narrator share many characteristics in common — a great love of their beds, an impulse to write, an inclination towards alcohol. Trellis and the narrator's uncle have an equal number of shared characteristics. Both are moralists, and they are physically similar. Trellis and Sweeny are punished in the same manner, but in different sections of the book. It is, perhaps, significant that Trellis is so named, for his position in the book does indeed resemble a pattern of interlocking pieces.

There are, also, a number of stylistic parallels from section to section. What is first told in one manner will later be retold in a quite different style. Thus Orlick Trellis begins his novel about his father in the Sweeny manner, continues in the Pooka manner and tries for a time to write it in the narrator's periphrastic and artificial style. In his absence, Shanahan, Lamont and Furriskey continue the same subject-matter in the style of working-class Dubliners. Trellis himself is described first in the narrator's characteristic manner, then in eighteenth-century diction, and finally in a parody of the Finn style. This accumulation of styles gives the story an incredible sense of richness and variety which never becomes chaotic because it is all held within a surprisingly rigid framework.

The structure of the book is based on ten 'biographical

reminiscences'. As the narrator recalls memorable experiences in the immediate past, he also supplies excerpts from the part of his novel he was writing at the time, from the things he read or heard, or the loosely associated thoughts or memories which are provoked by some casual phrase or remark. His everyday experiences determine the structure of his novel. A quarrel with his uncle leads to the punishment of Trellis, the uncle's counterpart in the narrator's book. A pain in his tooth occasioned by the eating of a hard crust disturbs the flow of his imaginative life and recalls him to an awareness of his surroundings. His uncle's moralising or a chance meeting with a friend lead to a memory of cautionary literature read at school. All the digressions, extracts and complications are, therefore, aspects of the mental life of the narrator, and in their turn they condition his imaginative life. As Mary Ellman said in a recent review of Alain Robbe-Grillet's latest book *Project for a Revolution in New York*, 'In mentioning the plot, I do not mean to imply a logical sequence, which does not exist. I will merely say that the narrator survives from beginning to end.'[18]

In *At Swim* the plot is largely, though not completely, irrelevant. If this were not so, it would not have been possible for Niall Sheridan to reduce the book by one-third of its length without doing irreparable damage to its unity and development. The focus of the book is the mind of its putative author. Like Tristram Shandy's, his cluttered mind is the main unifying device of the book. All the digressions are interrelated in the prescience of the author, as the author himself demands that they should be. They are, however, also interrelated in that, though many of them seem quite arbitrary and coincidental, they bear a thematic relationship to each other. This relationship will become clear in the ensuing discussion of the book, though it does not account for all the extracts.

At Swim is thus an example of the 'stream of consciousness' novel, but it is made deliberately 'queer' in order to fit the prescriptions of the narrator's 'aesthetic' notions. The narrator's mind is the focal point of the book. It is a mind which readily and instinctively turns to parody and travesty and which constantly drifts between the 'real' world and the world of fantasy. Whenever the narrator wishes to escape an unpleasant event he retires into a world of his own making, 'the kingdom of my mind' (p.15). His perception of the world, his vision of reality is, then, composed of his awareness of the factual details of his own everyday existence, the constituent characteristics of his fantasy world, and his very 'literary' mind. He tends to translate events into literary clichés, to see things in terms of a previous literary style, and then, almost unconsciously, to parody that style and place it in immediate juxtaposition to another parodied style. For example, when he is invited by his friend Kelly to go for his first-ever pint, he immediately recalls the various warnings he has received in his years at school about the effects of alcohol. In particular he remembers the '*Literary Reader, the Higher Class, by the Irish Christian Brothers*', which begins its solemn warnings with a suitable quotation:

> And in the flowers that wreathe the sparkling bowl, fell adders hiss and poisonous serpents roll.			(p. 27)

Nevertheless, several of his acquaintances had assured him that the impairment of the mind which occurred under the influence of alcohol was a pleasant one. Determined to try for himself, he conducts a personal interrogation which illustrates his tendency to think himself into a suitable literary stereotype. If the Christian Brothers projected a stereotyped picture of the 'helpless imbecile, tortured at times by remorse and despair' (p. 28), he sees himself in quite the opposite role, the dionysiac reveller supping wine in bucolic happiness.

> Who are my future cronies, where our mad carousals? What neat repast shall feast us light and choice of Attic taste with wine whence we may rise to hear the lute well touched or artful voice warble immortal notes or Tuscan air? What mad pursuit? What pipes and timbrels? What wild ecstasy?			(p. 29)

The narrator's choice of language, his almost eidetic recall of various styles, prove that he often sees reality in terms of the way it is expressed. He is hyper-conscious of the way in which language and style condition perception. His parodic and fantastic turn of mind, his awareness of the relativity of reality, make him an unconscious satirist, intensely aware of the lunacies of many aspects of Irish life and literature , in particular of the inordinate claims of the Irish literary renaissance. *At Swim* was intended to be a book which would overturn and expose the conventions of literary creations. It is, as Vivian Mercier described it in *The Irish Comic Tradition,* 'an assault on the conventions of all fiction, but especially on those of the so-called "realistic" novel.'[19]

At Swim is, in fact, an anti-novel, in the sense in which that form is defined by M. H. Abrams:

> . . . a work which is deliberately constructed in a negative fashion, relying for its effects on omitting or annihilating traditional elements of the novel, and on playing against the expectations established in the reader by the novelistic methods and conventions of the past.[20]

This definition accounts for many of the formal elements of *At Swim,* but it is also much more than an anti-novel. It is a work of fantasy in which characters from Irish legend and folklore come alive and mingle freely (as they do in the works of James Stephens and Eimar O'Duffy) with the inhabitants of the ordinary world. It is a satirical exposé of the way in which language is misused, particularly in the cliché-ridden speech of racing tipsters, moralists, lawyers and writers of travelogues. It is a book which delights in the faithful representation of the Dubliner with his distinctive idioms, his great store of talk, his limitations, misconceptions and boundless confidence. It is a work of sustained parody, not just of the novel form, but of many other types of literature as well. It may be a work which would fit Northrop Frye's definition of 'Anatomy',[21] but it is certainly a book which has as its prime aim a discussion of the relative importance of reality and imagination, mimesis and myth. Both reality and imagination are presented and undercut in the course of the book. The examination of their relative merits, and their interrelationship is a part of the discussion of the relationship between literary forms and the different realities they embody and project which is implied by the parodic and digressive nature of *At Swim.* That parodic and digressive nature is, in turn, an aspect of the book as an anti-novel.

Finn MacCool presents us with an image of the book when he complains about the tyranny of writers.

> Small wonder, said Finn, that Finn is without honour in the breast of a sea-blue book, Finn that is twisted and trampled and tortured for the weaving of a story-teller's book-web.
>
> (p.24)

At Swim is a book-web. All the threads run into each other and are connected to each other in an intricate and diverse pattern. This pattern is connected in its parts by virtue of the spider who sits at the centre spinning a web which is ordered, bright, and capable of almost infinite growth. The interconnections and cross-references make it as difficult and as complex as an illustration in the Book of Kells. Like the animals who are coiled round and round themselves and who are eventually seen to be eating their own tails, the themes and structures of the book turn round and back on themselves, so that an unravelling of the threads is a hazardous and difficult venture.

As an anti-novel, *At Swim* seems to have undergone its structural development as a result of the rather heterogeneous sources from which O'Brien derived the ideas for the plot and framework. His interests were extremely far ranging and he garnered ideas from many directions. The article 'Scenes in a Novel' in *Comhthrom Féinne* demonstrates that he had in 1934 already developed the idea of a writer creating characters who then really come to life and turn on him. In Brother Barnabas's book, the characters already created can even plot with those who have not yet appeared. This *reductio ad absurdum* of the phrase 'to create character' was an obvious one for O'Brien to work on. Brother Barnabas had very quickly seemed to take on a life and a reality which was independent of his creator's control. This raised the whole question of the kind of reality possessed by characters in novels, some of whom have always seemed more familiar and fully alive than one's friends and acquaintances. Critics had often discussed the manner in which characters 'come alive' in a book. E. M. Forster, writing in *Aspects of the Novel,* declared that he would recognise Moll Flanders anywhere. This assertion implies that literary characters somehow have a life independent of the context of the work of art for which they are created. In one passage Forster seems to be providing the basis of the idea for *At Swim.* He says:

> The characters arrive when evoked but full of the spirit of mutiny. For they have these numerous parallels with people like ourselves, they try to live their own lives and are consequently often engaged in treason against the main scheme of the book. They 'run away', they 'get out of hand'; they are creations inside a creation, and often inharmonious towards it; if they are given complete freedom they kick the book to pieces, and if they are kept too sternly in check, they revenge themselves by dying, and destroy it by intestinal decay.[22]

Forster was, of course, using metaphorical language here. O'Brien, who may have read his book, or at least been familiar with the type of argument which it presented, created a plot in which what Forster said was treated as a literal statement. When Forster describes characters as 'getting out of hand', O'Brien makes them do precisely that in *At Swim.* Trellis's characters arrive when evoked but they are inharmonious towards his book. Furriskey, who is created to be a seducer to illustrate the 'main scheme' of Trellis's moral book, is really a quiet, prudish man who marries Peggy instead of seducing her. Furriskey and Peggy 'try to lead their own lives' in a little house, and to protect themselves from Trellis they commit treason against his book by joining with the other characters to write a book about him and so thwart his purpose. In like fashion Finn rebels against the book by his attempted seduction of Peggy. 'Fictional' life becomes indistinguishable from 'real' life and this process is given official sanction by the theory of aestho-autogamy propounded in the book. Trellis has invented it but it rebounds on him. If 'fictional' characters become 'real', 'real' characters can become 'fictional' by being made characters in someone else's book. Thus Trellis's existence is threatened when his own characters decide to sentence him to death. Readers of *At Swim* are expected to believe in the validity and efficacy of aestho-autogamy because they are told that it has been reported in the newspapers in overwhelming detail. Similarly, the birth of Furriskey at the age of twenty-six, after he has been 'created' by Trellis, is reported in the newspapers.

> *Extract from Press regarding Furriskey's birth:* We are in a position to announce that a happy event has taken place at the Red Swan Hotel, where the proprietor, Mr Dermot Trellis, has succeeded in encompassing the birth of a man called Furriskey. Stated to be doing 'very nicely', the new arrival is about five feet eight inches in height, well built, dark and clean-shaven. The eyes are blue and the teeth well formed and good, though stained somewhat by tobacco.
>
> (p.54)

There is no doubt whatever, then, that Furriskey and, later, Sheila Lamont are really there. Indeed, Sheila Lamont is so very real that she is raped and produces a son. The narrator comments on the 'queerness' which must pertain to a man who is the result of a union between a publican and the heroine of a novel. His situation (he, too, is fully grown when born) is similar to that postulated in the casuistical discussion between the Pooka and the Good Fairy on the possible results of a union between a human and an angel.

> Even if it were desirable, replied the Good Fairy, angelic or spiritual carnality is not easy and in any case the offspring would be severely handicapped by being half flesh and half spirit, a very baffling and neutralising assortment of fractions since the two elements are forever at variance.
>
> (p.149)

Aestho-autogamy and spiritual carnality have obvious practical results. In the first place, characters can be spared the long experience of growing up, or even created as old-age pensioners ready to provide their parents with a steady income from the pension. In the latter case, the corporal element in the offspring can be eliminated by careful breeding and the result might then be a 'houseful of adult and imperceptable angels' who need no clothes, shoes or food. The comic *reductio* here is complete. The idea of 'creation of character' carried to its logical conclusion is absurd and fantastic. It also raises the question of the kinds of difference between 'real' life and 'fictional' life. O'Brien continued to insist that there was *no* difference.[23] In *Cruiskeen Lawn* Sir Myles na gCopaleen enters his library and finds:

> Stretched on the floor in a most ugly attitude is a corpse. Sir Myles has already taken up the telephone and asked for a number. 'That you, Sergeant? Look here, those dreadful detective stories. Another corpse in the library this evening. Really you know, too much of a good thing. Fourth this week. No doubt trouble is shortage of libraries'.
>
> (13 Nov. 1942; *BM.* 156-7)

The possibilities, O'Brien might have said, were endless. Some of those possibilities he may have found already worked out in James Branch Cabell's fantasy novel *The Cream of the Jest.* O'Brien certainly knew of Cabell's work; once he even referred to him in *Cruiskeen Lawn* as 'James Joyce Cabell'. *The Cream of the Jest* deals with the life of Felix Kennaston, a novelist who moves, physically as well as mentally, between his drab real world and the magic world of Poictesme, where he is the clerk Horvendile, a character in his own novel. All the characters in Poictesme are his own creations but they too have reality. He falls in love with Ettarre, the beautiful heroine of his own story, but he tells her that she is only a figment of his own imagination. (Naturally, she refuses to believe him.)

> There was once in a land very far away from this land — in my country — a writer of romances. And once he constructed a romance which, after a hackneyed custom in my country, he pretended to translate from an old manuscript written by an ancient clerk — called Horvendile. It told of Horvendile's part in the love business between Sir Guiron des Rocques and La Beale Ettarre. I am that maker of romance. This room, this castle, all the broad rolling countryside without, is but a portion of my dream, and these places have no existence save in my fancies. And you, messire, and you also, madame, — and dead Maugis here, and all the others who seemed so real to me, are but the puppets I have fashioned and have shifted for a tale's sake, in that romance which now draws near to its ending . . . And it may be that I, too, am only a figment of some

greater dream, in just such case as yours, and that I, too,
cannot understand. It may be the very cream of the jest that
my country is no more real than Storisende. How could I
judge if I, too, were a puppet?[24]

It is, of course, the cream of the jest that Felix Kennaston, too,
is a puppet, the main character in a book by Richard Fentnor
Harrowby, who is himself a character in a book by James·
Branch Cabell.

There are many surprising parallels, both structural and
verbal, between *The Cream of the Jest* and *At Swim*.
Kennaston created Poictesme out of the need to escape from
his failed life, just as O'Brien's narrator retires into the privacy
of his mind and summons to him the 'God-big Finn'. whenever
he quarrels with his uncle. Kennaston apologises to Ettarre for
the anguish his plot has caused her to suffer. Trellis is put on
trial for his unfeeling and unprincipled treatment of his
characters. Kennaston's character Maugis d'Aigremont
resembles his creator, as Trellis resembles his student creator
in a shared predilection for bed. Kennaston decides that the
end of his book in which he makes Horvendile explain their
puppet-status to the other characters is too odd and instead
gives his book a conventional happy ending. O'Brien's
narrator, reconciled with his uncle at the end, relieves Trellis
of his punishments. He does not, however, decide on a
conventional ending. Indeed, he constantly draws attention to
the book's fictive devices. Kennaston, as author, constantly
borrows from other writers. Indeed, he remarks at one point:
'It is droll how we great geniuses instinctively plagiarise.'
O'Brien's narrator draws on as many kinds of literature as he
can fit into the scheme of his book and recommends that

> The entire corpus of existing literature should be regarded
> as a limbo from which discerning authors could draw their
> characters as required, creating only when they failed to
> find a suitable existing puppet.   (p.33)

Kennaston is a conscious stylist who is more than usually aware
of the structure and devices in his novel. He knows it is a
conscious artifact, its seeming realism the product of a
number of literary 'tricks', yet the characters of Poictesme do
attain a reality of their own and pursue him into other worlds

and other lives. Ettarre, especially, begins to have a life which is real at a mythic level and separate from his creation of her.

The Cream of the Jest and *At Swim,* then, are concerned with the relationship between an author and his characters, and with the relationship between the worlds of reality and imagination and the points where the two become indistinguishable. Reality, i.e. the twentieth-century world in which Felix Kennaston lives, is shown to be merely the result of a different set of literary devices. The deeper question in both books is about the nature of fictional reality—on a mythic as well as a realistic level.

Like Cabell, Aldous Huxley (whose novels the student narrator has in his room) put a novelist into his novel to see what would happen to the kind of reality that was presented therein. Huxley explains his aims in *Point Counter Point:*

> Put a novelist into a novel. He justifies aesthetic generalisations, which may be interesting—at least to me. He also justifies experiment. Specimens of his work may illustrate other possible or impossible ways of telling a story. And if you have him telling parts of the same story as you are, you can make a variation on the theme. But why draw the line at one novelist inside your novel? Why not a second inside his? And a third inside the novel of the second?[25]

O'Brien seems to have followed Huxley's directions. His novelist, the student narrator, makes a number of aesthetic generalisations, specimens of his work are given, and he explains difficulties experienced in telling part of his story. Inside his novel is another novelist, and inside *his* novel is a third novelist. The use of this particular structure ensures that attention is focused on the formal devices of the novel and the ironic perspectives created by its different modes of 'telling' rather than on the 'real life', the representation of which is often assumed to be a major objective of the novelist's art. The essence of *At Swim* lies in its attack on the idea that any one literary form can be said to portray reality. As a literary artifact it constantly draws attention to its own devices by introducing excerpts from other works, with memoranda-like insertions, formal headings and the provision of definitions. All these authorial intrusions are intended to emphasise the

point that this is not a coherent narrative but a deliberate
fabrication which constantly says 'Look how I did it.' The
narrator, as novelist, discusses with his friend Brinsley, and
with the reader, the difficulties he has had in writing certain
sections, in creating certain characters, and in describing the
birth of Orlick Trellis. He substitutes a synopsis of the plot for
some pages of typescript which he says he has lost. He is
careful, he tells us, to vary his 'telling', between 'direct' and
'indirect' modes of presentation. He explains his aesthetic to
Brinsley and reads extracts from his manuscript to illustrate
his point. He shows himself borrowing characters and
descriptions from previous authors, thus overturning all the
critical ideas about 'appropriateness' and 'artistic unity'. The
novel is *obviously* artificial. The processes of literature are
themselves the subject of the book.[26] The narrator's aesthetic
states that the novel should be 'a self-evident sham', and his
novel is just that. The cream of the jest is, of course, that this is
contained *within* a narrative about a particular character in a
particular time and place, and, as readers, we believe in his
existence. Furthermore, the first 'synopsis of the plot' is on
page 85. We are told that it is 'FOR THE BENEFIT OF NEW
READERS', but its place within the overall form of a novel
implies that the previous pages have been read in the usual
consecutive manner. This is the final comic irony of any anti-
novel.

   In creating his form of anti-novel O'Brien may have been
reacting against an article by Niall Sheridan in *The National
Student*. Sheridan argued that there had been a 'marked
improvement' in the techniques of novel-writing in the
twentieth century in that 'the advance has been towards a
better and more convincing realism'. He found a greater
'lifelikeness' in the lack of authorial intrusion and argued:

> We see less of the omniscient author. Reading Thackeray,
> for instance, it is almost impossible, (at least I have found it
> so) to escape the conviction that a story is being
> manufactured for us. The author is always there, disposing
> his material, dragging us hither and thither, butting in with
> often unwanted explanations. It would be mere stupidity to
> deny the richness of Thackeray's content; but in the
> arrangement of material *ars est celare artem*, and an

unquestionable advance has been made since Thackeray's time.[27]

O'Brien and his narrator, in adopting the pose of the omniscient, intrusive author are, surely, taking issue with Sheridan here.[28] If Sheridan sets out to prove that authorial intrusions and digressions are unacceptable in modern novels, O'Brien decides to make them acceptable by using Thackeray's methods and, indeed, regressing much further and accepting the novelistic topsy-turveydom of Laurence Sterne.

The apparent chaos of *Tristram Shandy*, where the only unifying device for all the digressions is the first-person narrator is an obvious model for *At Swim*. The narrator's desire for three separate openings for his book, his notes on constructive and argumentative difficulties, the fact that the novel begins with Chapter One and ends on page 316 without ever having reached Chapter Two, are, surely, influenced by Sterne's manner of writing.

What a work it is likely to turn out! Let us begin it.

CHAPTER II

It is with Love as with cuckoldom . . . but now I am talking of beginning a book, and have long had a thing upon my mind to be imparted to the reader, which, if not imparted now, can never be imparted to him as long as I live (whereas the *comparison* may be imparted to him any-hour in the day) — I'll just mention it, and begin in good earnest.
    The thing is this:-
That all of the several ways of beginning a book which are now in practice throughout the known world, I am confident my own way of doing it is the best. — I'm sure it is the most   religious, — for I begin with writing the first sentence, — and trusting to Almighty God for the second.[29]

Sterne begins with the first sentence and trusts to God for the second. O'Brien's narrator has a different, but equally idiosyncratic, method.

One beginning, and one ending for a book was a thing I did not agree with. A good book may have three openings entirely dissimilar and inter-related only in the prescience

of the author, or for that matter one hundred times as many
endings.   (p. 9)

The narrator is being consciously iconoclastic here, for one of
his own characters says that a story should have 'a beginning
and an end . . . a head and a tail' (p. 88). The narrator,
however, rejects this as being merely an illusion designed to
fool the reader, as is, indeed, the normal method of
delineating character.

> The novel was inferior to the play inasmuch as it lacked the
> outward accidents of illusion, frequently inducing the
> reader to be outwitted in a shabby fashion and caused to
> experience a real concern for the fortunes of illusory
> characters.
>   (p.33)

In his article, Niall Sheridan had discussed the
'psychoanalytic school of writers' (amongst whom he counted
Aldous Huxley) and their 'scientific' way of creating character.
O'Brien's narrator in part follows the modern trend by
providing a very scientific 'Memorandum of the respective
diacritical traits or qualities of Messrs Furriskey, Lamont and
Shanahan' (p.231). This, however, concentrates more on
external habits and appearance than on psychological
impulses. For the rest of the time O'Brien makes character
descriptions abrupt and noticeable. Thwarting the reader's
expectation that a description will be slipped in unnoticeably
in the text he produces instead a

> *Description of my uncle:* Red-faced, bead-eyed, ball-
> bellied. Fleshy about the shoulders with long swinging arms
> giving ape-like effect to gait. Large moustache. Holder of
> Guinness clerkship the third class.   (p.11)[30]

The narrator's characters are, then, delineated only in
external characteristics or by virtue of an overwhelming
obsession which dominates their lives. The uncle constantly
repeats the phrase 'Tell me this, do you ever open a book at
all?', while Trellis has an obsession which prevents him
reading any book unless it has a green cover. Sterne's
characters, with their various hobby-horses', may have been a
model here. Indeed, O'Brien may also have learnt the comic

efficacy of digressions (extracts) and the satiric use of pedantic erudition from Sterne. Early in the book Tristram Shandy announces his literary intentions:

> I should beg Mr Horace's pardon; — for in writing what I have set about, I shall confine myself neither to his rules nor to any man's rules, that ever lived.[31]

O'Brien in *At Swim* seems equally determined to side with the innovators and experimenters in an attempt to disparage experiment and grandiloquent claims for advances in story-telling techniques. However, some of the ideas behind *At Swim* may have been formed in response to another paragraph of Sheridan's essay:

> But I think it quite probable that the drabness of the photographic realists, and the errors of the psycho-analytic school are paving the way for a better type of imaginative novelist, who — by combining in their true proportions realism and idealism, subjectivity — will establish a closer and more satisfying relation between literature and life.[32]

Huxley and Sterne, Cabell and E. M. Forster had all, in different ways, directly or by implication raised the question of the relationship between literature and life. So had James Joyce. Trellis's characters accuse him of manipulating them for the sake of his story. They are puppets in his hands and he, as author, is God. Cabell referred to his characters as puppets and implied that everyone, including himself, was a puppet in the hands of, or a projection in the mind of, a greater author, God himself. Sheridan wrote about Thackeray, who explicitly referred to his characters as puppets. As intrusive author he, too, was God. Joyce agreed that the author was like 'the God of Creation', and added that he was not to be discerned in the work. He should remain outside his creation, 'indifferent, paring his fingernails'.[33] Sheridan, who was a great admirer of Joyce, was probably thinking of this idea of the novelist when he censured Thackeray. O'Brien clearly was rebelling against Sheridan's idea and, consequently, against Joyce's. Joyce had raised the question of the relationship between literature and life when he made his friends and acquaintances into characters in his novels. O'Brien turned the tables and eventually made Joyce himself a character in his novel *The Dalkey Archive*. *At Swim* as a whole can be seen, however, to be a sustained questioning of many of Joyce's assumptions. References to Joyce are pervasive in the book and the wish to parody or question Joyce's writing to a great extent determined the structure of the book.

The impulse to parody Joyce had begun as early as *Comhthrom Féinne*. The anonymous skit 'Op.$^1/_8$' connected a parody of Joyce with one of serialised novels and contained a 'synopsis of the plot' such as is found in *At Swim*. O'Brien could have found in 'Op.$^1/_8$', then, an already established association between Joyce and the form of the novel, and he was to extend this in *At Swim*.

The parody of Joyce is, perhaps, most obvious in the figure of the student narrator. Equally obviously the student is semi-autobiographical. It is, therefore, productive to look at those details of the narrator's life and character which are similar to O'Brien's so as to make it clear when the autobiographical elements end and the parody of Joyce begins.

The narrator is a student at UCD. He lives with his uncle, who constantly complains of his inattention and laziness. The student, on the whole, does not like his uncle very much, his descriptions of him are most unflattering and are usually provided at moments of irritation. The uncle's charges against him are, however, largely justified. He spends more time in bed and in idleness than in studying and his personal appearance suffers in consequence.

Whether in or out, I always kept the door of my bedroom locked. This made my movements a matter of some secrecy and enabled me to spend an inclement day in bed without disturbing my uncle's assumption that I had gone to the College to attend to my studies. A contemplative life has always been suitable to my disposition. I was accustomed to stretch myself for many hours upon my bed, thinking and smoking there. I rarely undressed and my inexpensive suit was not the better for the use I gave it, but I found that a brisk application with a coarse brush before going out would redeem it somewhat without quite dispelling the curious bedroom smell which clung to my person and which was frequently the subject of humorous or other comment on the part of my friends and acquaintances.   (p.11)

The narrator is forgetful and careless and resents his uncle's attempts to shake him out of his lassitude. The uncle is always ready with a homily, a proverb or a piece of 'Christian' advice for his nephew, who is much more interested in backing horses, drinking in Grogan's pub and pursuing women in company with his friend Kelly. Kelly is a countryman, a failed medical student and a man who

> was addicted to unclean expressions in ordinary conversation and spat continually always fouling the flowerbeds on his way through the Green with a mucous deposit dislodged with a low grunting from the interior of his windpipe. In some respects he was a coarse man but he was lacking in malice or ill-humour.   (p.26)

It was Kelly who first introduced the narrator to the joys of alcohol. He began with pints but soon changed 'to brown stout in bottle', and was prepared to accept the 'painful and blinding fits of vomiting which a plurality of bottles has often induced in me' (p.29). The after-effects of alcoholic indulgences are often so severe that the narrator is forced to stay in bed, hiding his ill-used suit under the mattress to disguise its sight and smell. On one occasion, pretending to have a chill, he lies in bed, exhausted and noisome, discussing art and literature with his friend Brinsley — a conversation which is quite at odds with the sordid state of his life and person.

> My dim room rang with the iron of fine words and the names of great Russian masters were articulated with fastidious intonation. Witticisms were canvassed, depending for their utility on a knowledge of the French language as spoken in the medieval times. Psycho-analysis was mentioned — with, however, a somewhat light touch.
>
> (p.32)

Brinsley, the narrator's closest friend, chief audience and major critic is described as

> Thin, dark-haired, hesitant; an intellectual Meath-man; given to close-knit epigrammatic talk; weak-chested, pale.
>
> (p.30)

He, too, is a student at the college, a poet and a billiards player.

The narrator obligingly provides a description of the college.

> *Description of College:* The College is outwardly a rectangular plain building with a fine porch where the midday sun pours down in summer from the Donnybrook direction, heating the steps for the comfort of the students. The hallway inside is composed of large black and white squares arranged in the orthodox chessboard pattern, and the surrounding walls, done in an unpretentious cream wash, bear three rough smudges caused by the heels, buttocks and shoulders of the students.   (p.45)

The student narrator describes the bell which announces the beginning of lectures, the hasty extinguishing of cigarettes, the bravado of some of the students. He spends much of his time in the old, ruined part of the college, in the 'Gentlemen's Smokeroom', which was usually occupied by 'card-players, hooligans and rough persons'. Here, he remains quite isolated from the general mass of the students, watching them in a cold and detached manner.

> I sat alone in a retired corner in the cold, closely wrapping the feeble citadel of my body with my grey coat. Through the two apertures of my eyes I gazed out in a hostile manner.   (p.46)

In cold weather even these infrequent visits to the college cease and the student spends all his time in his room concerned with his 'pulmonary well-being' (p.60). This results in his discovering, in February, that his person has become 'verminous', and the discovery shames him into a resolution to reform of his lifestyle. He draws up a timetable for a régime of 'physical regeneration which included bending exercises' (p.61), attends college every day and begins to walk about Dublin talking to friends and casual acquaintances. On these long walks he discusses poetry with Brinsley and pursues virgins with Kelly, with whom he also discusses 'dog-racing, betting and offences against chastity' (p.65). He attends meetings of the L & H Society and describes the gathering in vivid detail: the horse-play in the lobby, the extinguishing of the single gas jet, and the jokes played on various auditors. His stance during these 'diabolic' proceedings was to maintain

> a position where I was not personally identified, standing quietly without a word in the darkness.   (p.67)

Yet another friend is a Mr Kerrigan 'a slim young man of moustached features usually attired in inexpensive clothing' (p.70). With Kerrigan he visits the house of Michael Byrne 'a man of diverse intellectual attainments [whose] house was frequently the scene of scholarly and other disputations' (p.134).

At home, the narrator's relations with his uncle deteriorate as he is forced to listen to frequent lectures on the subject of his slothfulness. It is only when the uncle interests himself in the local musical society and in organising a céilí that he is left to his own devices. He then leads a life of 'dull but not uncomfortable character' which he itemises thus:

> *Nature of daily regime or curriculum:* Nine thirty a.m. rise, wash, shave and proceed to breakfast; this on the insistence of my uncle, who was accustomed to regard himself as the sun of his household, recalling all things to wakefulness on his own rising.
> 10.30. Return to bedroom.
> 12.00. Go, weather permitting, to College, there conducting light conversation on diverse topics with friends or with acquaintances of a casual character.
> 2.00 p.m. Go home for lunch.
> 3.00. Return to bedroom. Engage in spare-time literary activities or read.
> 6.00. Have tea in company with my uncle, attending in a perfunctory manner to the replies required by his talk.
> 7.00. Return to bedroom, and rest in darkness.
> 8.00. Continue resting or meet acquaintances in open thoroughfare or places of public resort.
> 11.00. Return to bedroom.   (p.212)

The narrator allots himself an average of 1.4 hours of study per day, but, despite this meagre allowance, passes his 'final examination with a creditable margin of honour' (p.301), thus exceeding the achievement of most of his companions. As a reward his uncle presents him with an antique watch, the gift of which effects a reconciliation between them and causes the narrator to see his uncle's character in a new light.

> *Description of my uncle:* Simple well-intentioned; pathetic in humility; responsible member of large commercial concern. (p.312)

It is clear, then, that a number of the events in the student narrator's life are paralleled by happenings in the life of his creator. They both attended UCD in the 1930s, though the narrator's dead-pan, peripatetic prose occasionally produces a deliberately archaic sentence like

> We went eventually to the moving pictures, the three of us, travelling to the centre of the city in the interior of a tramcar. (p.65)

In spite of his frequent use of this archaic descriptive style, the college which the narrator portrays is essentially the same place vividly described by O'Brien in his article on the L & H in James Meenan's book.

> I entered the big Main Hall at an odd hour on the second day of Michaelmas term 1929, looked about me and vividly remember the scene. The hall was quite empty. The plain white walls bore three dark parallel smudgy lines at elevations of about three, five and five-and-a-half feet from the tiled chessboard floor. Later I was to know this triptych had been achieved by the buttocks, shoulders, and hair-oil of lounging students. They had, in fact, nowhere else to lounge, though in good weather many went out and sat on the steps.[34]

In this article O'Brien went on to describe the smoking-room, the card-playing and billiards and the general chaos of L & H meetings in terms very similar to those found in *At Swim*. It is also clear that O'Brien's friends at college provided the models for the narrator's friends in *At Swim*. Brinsley is Niall Sheridan, his name in the novel being derived from that of Richard Brinsley Sheridan. When Niall Montgomery read the book he wrote in delight to O'Brien: 'You've got Sheridan so well it makes me nervous.' Niall Montgomery himself believes that he figures in the story as Kerrigan and complains that his clothing was never of 'inferior quality'. Kelly was a student called O'Rourke who came from Roscommon. He afterwards became a teacher. Donaghy, the poet which whom Brinsley and the student discuss 'the primacy of America and Ireland in contemporary letters' (p.62) was the writer Donagh MacDonagh and Michael Byrne was the painter Cecil Francis Salkeld who was, Niall Sheridan asserts, 'an expert on everything'.

Not only were these characters identified at once when the book was published, but some of the events of the story were recognised as having a basis in fact. On conferring night in 1934 O'Brien, O'Rourke and Sheridan drank in Grogan's pub on the corner of Stephen's Green and Leeson Street. Later on, near Lad Lane police station, they were accosted by one of the regular inhabitants of Stephen's Green, a man who usually wore a black coat with velvet reveres and a bowler hat. He made a practice of stopping students but this time he made a bad choice. In a state of extreme intoxication O'Rourke vomited all over him as he tried to interest them in the ideas of Émile Rosseau. The incident is reported in *At Swim* (p.53). The racing tipster's letter which the student reads to Brinsley was, in fact, given to O'Brien by Sheridan himself, who thought he would be amused by its stylistic extravagances. Brinsley's 'Lesbia' poem, which he recites to the student in Grogan's is a translation of a poem by Catullus and can be found under Sheridan's name in the *Oxford Book of Irish Verse*.

There are, however, as many differences as there are similarities between O'Brien's life and that of his student. In *At Swim* the narrator lives with his uncle; O'Brien lived with his parents during his time in UCD. The narrator does not play billiards and remains aloof from college life, particularly from the proceedings of the L & H; O'Brien was a leader and brilliant performer at the L & H and a keen billiards player. The narrator spends most of his day in bed, lying in an odour of stale stout with an unwashed, verminous body; O'Brien was a most active attender at college, a very hard worker, and not in the least verminous.

Why did O'Brien make these changes? Niall Sheridan thinks that the uncle may be a portrait of O'Brien's father, devised in that form because of O'Brien's wish to distance and protect his family affairs. This may be true, but it fails to account for the persistent emphasis on the squalor of the narrator's life, his cold and aloof bearing, his pose of hostility and general degeneracy.

The answer is, surely, that these aspects of the narrator's life are intended to be a mockery of the overstatements, conscious posturings and squalid habits of James Joyce's Stephen Dedalus. Joyce's presence in *At Swim* is pervasive both in style and content inasmuch as O'Brien mocks, albeit gently, aspects of *Dubliners, A Portrait of the Artist* and *Ulysses*. This mockery of Joyce is an important feature of the book; it is one of the strands which bind together many of its diverse elements, and it provides an important clue to O'Brien's own conception of the purpose and function of literature.

Like O'Brien's narrator, Stephen Dedalus was a student at what was to become UCD. He was lazy, inattentive, addicted to alcohol, verminous, given to pursuing women in the streets of Dublin. He takes long walks about the city, propounds an 'aesthetic' to his friend Lynch and is in rebellion against his family (particularly his father), his country and his church. He is aloof, self-consciously superior, pedantic and given to imagining himself as various literary stereotypes. He takes as his omen his namesake Daedalus, whose son Icarus flew too near the sun while escaping on waxen wings from the labryinth and fell to his death.

These aspects of Stephen are parodied in *At Swim*, primarily in the person and habits of the narrator (though O'Brien uses Orlick Trellis and Sweeny as other Stephen-figures in the book). We know immediately that he is at odds with his uncle[35] who is the 'holder of a Guinness clerkship the third class' (p.11). Simon Dedalus used to be 'something in Guinesses' so there is an association between the uncle, who irritates the student, and Simon, against whom Stephen rebelled. The uncle is a devout but naïve Catholic. At one point he tries to persuade Brinsley to join a religious order. He is, then, connected with the church which tried to claim Stephen but which he rejected. The uncle is a member of the

Gaelic League, a patriot, interested in the Irish language and Irish dancing. (He opposes the old-time waltz on the grounds that it might be regarded as 'foreign'.)[36] In this aspect he stands for the third force against which Stephen rebelled. In his quarrels with the uncle the narrator is, therefore, associated with Stephen.

The first lines of *At Swim*, self-consciously pedantic as they are, call Stephen's characteristic modes of expression to mind at once. Both characters conceive of themselves in terms of literary models, and the lives of both present a comic disparity between the squalor of their daily activities and the richness of their imaginations. Both characters are fascinated by language, both are lazy, drunken, dirty and aloof. Joyce tells us that Stephen 'chronicled with patience what he saw, detaching himself from it and tasting its mortifying flavour in secret'.[37] O'Brien's narrator describes his imaginative detachment: 'I closed my eyes, hurting slightly my right stye, and retired into the kingdom of my mind.' (p.15) this aloofness and detachment in the student is depicted as something silly and self-conscious.

> It was my custom to go into the main hall of the College and stand with my back to one of the steam-heating devices, my faded overcoat open and my cold hostile eyes flitting about the faces that passed before me. (p.61)

Stephen partially identifies himself with Lucifer, Prince of Light who became the Prince of Darkness; O'Brien's narrator has a habit of always sitting 'in the dark'. Stephen discusses the nature of faith with Cranly; O'Brien's narrator spends some of his time sitting in a pub with the Shader Ward, 'talking about God and one thing and another' (p.31). He is, indeed, as learned and intellectual as Stephen and has an equal tendency to blaspheme.

> We talked together in a polished manner, utilising with frequency words from the French language . . . The Holy Name was often taken, I do not recollect with what advertence. (p.62)

Stephen's long walks around Dublin and his encounters with prostitutes, his desire to sin with 'another of his kind'[38] are

---

paralleled by the perambulations of O'Brien's narrator with Kelly.

> Purporting to be an immoral character, I accompanied him on a long walk through the environs of Irishtown Sandymount and Sydney Parade, returning by Haddington Road and the banks of the canal.
> *Purpose of walk:* Discovery and embracing of virgins.
>
> (p.65)

Stephen's friends in *A Portrait* are paralleled by the narrator's friends in *At Swim*. Brinsley shares some of the characteristics of Cranly and Lynch. Stephen discusses his religious views with the former and his aesthetic theories with the latter. The student discusses his aesthetic theories with Brinsley, and Brinsley is also seen to be the more concerned with religion of the pair, since it is he who is approached on the subject of joining the Christian Brothers. The narrator, however, has no inclination towards the religious life, as his uncle recognises, neither does he show any evidence of religious doubt. Kelly corresponds to Lynch in his foul habits and to Davin in his rural origins. On one occasion in *A Portrait,* Stephen meets Temple who talks to him about Rousseau. O'Brien's narrator remembers a man in black who addressed him on the same subject.

In the parallels drawn between the two characters it is difficult to establish O'Brien's intentions. He may have been simply presenting a more obviously comic version of Stephen while being aware of the ironic undercutting which that character had received at Joyce's hands. Or O'Brien may, in fact, have been unaware that there was a real separation between Joyce himself and his creations. In later writings, when he speaks of Joyce as a 'heretic', O'Brien does seem to imply that Stephen's arguments are Joyce's. On balance it would seem that O'Brien's intention in presenting his narrator as a Stephen-figure was to mock Stephen and to imply that the events and circumstances which drove him to voluntary exile were no longer valid there. If this is so, then it might indicate a serious misunderstanding of Joyce's aims on O'Brien's part, or at least a failure to think out his own theories about artistic creation and apply them to Joyce.

In any case, it is quite clear that things have changed in Ireland. At least the brutality of the Prefect of Studies which Stephen experienced is a thing of the past. The uncle asks Brinsley if the masters are hard to please. When Brinsley replies that, on the contrary, they do not seem to care very much, the uncle comments that it was very different in his days for 'the old schoolmasters believed in the big stick' (p.36). Equally, Stephen's real experience with the prostitute is debunked by the 'purported immorality' of the narrator and Kelly.

> We walked many miles together on other nights on similar missions—following matrons, accosting strangers, representing to married ladies that we were their friends, and gratuitously molesting members of the public. One night we were followed in our turn by a member of the police force attired in civilian clothing. On the advice of Kelly we hid ourselves in the interior of a church until he had gone. I found that the walking was beneficial to my health.   (p.66)

The student's 'aesthetic' is a parody of Stephen's. Stephen saw drama as the most important of the literary arts because it was the most impersonal. 'The esthetic image in the dramatic form is life purified in and re-projected from the human imagination.'[39] O'Brien's narrator, too, places drama at the highest point of literary achievement, but for slightly different reasons.

> It was stated that while the novel and the play were both pleasing intellectual exercises, the novel was inferior to the play inasmuch as it lacked the outward accidents of illusion, frequently inducing the reader to be outwitted in a shabby fashion and caused to experience a real concern for the fortunes of illusory characters.   (p.33)

The narrator goes on to explain that 'the novel, in the hands of an unscrupulous writer, could be despotic'. It could, that is, impose the writer's vision of reality as the *only* reality. To counteract this he suggests that

> a satisfactory novel should be a self-evident sham to which the reader could regulate at will the degree of his credulity.
> (p.33)

Joyce's creator is an autocrat, a god, bending all the elements of his novel to his artistic will; O'Brien's narrator wants a democracy.

> It was undemocratic to compel characters to be uniformly good or bad or poor or rich. Each should be allowed a private life, self-determination and a decent standard of living.   (p.33)

In mockery of Joyce's levels of consciousness and the substratum of classical, biblical and historical reference on which his novels are based, the narrator prescribes that

> Characters' should be interchangeable as between one book and another. The entire corpus of existing literature should be regarded as a limbo from which discerning authors could draw their characters as required, creating only when they failed to find a suitable existing puppet. The modern novel should be largely a work of reference.   (p.33)

This prescription would, he predicted, preclude 'persons of inferior education from an understanding of contemporary literature' (p.33).

As Stephen explains his aesthetic to Lynch, an aesthetic which is based on ideas from Aristotle and Aquinas, Lynch listens inattentively and protests: 'Stop! I won't listen! I am sick. I was out last night on a yellow drunk with Horan and Goggins.'[40] Brinsley replies in similar vein at the end of the narrator's explanation. 'That is all my bum, said Brinsley.' (p.33)

The parallels between *At Swim* and *A Portrait* are by no means limited to the principal characters. In the Trellis section of the book the scope of the references is extended. If the student is O'Brien's Stephen Dedalus, Trellis is, in some aspects, his parallel for Leopold Bloom.

The references to *Ulysses* are introduced initially in the description of the Red Swan Hotel, where the mock legal language is a parody of the legalistic manner of the 'Ithaca' section of *Ulysses*.[41] Trellis's bed, 'a timber article of great age in which many of his forefathers had died and been born', draws the reader's mind to a memory of Shakespeare's second-best bed and thus to the sub-theme of Shakespeare and Stephen's theory about him in *Ulysses*. Joyce, who drank quite heavily, created an *alter ego* in Bloom who was relatively abstemious in that respect. Trellis is reportedly very like Dr Beatty, of whom it is reported 'that towards the close of his life he indulged to excess in the use of wine' (p.41); nevertheless, like Joyce who created an abstemious hero, Trellis as author forces his characters to refrain from the use of alcohol. Dr Beatty, on whose description in *The Conspectus of Arts and Natural Sciences* Trellis's character is modelled, has lost a beloved son. Bloom too had lost a son, but he finds in Stephen a spiritual son, rescues him and brings him to his house. There is a suggestion that Stephen might teach Italian to Bloom's wife Molly, though the idea that Stephen would be left alone with his wife worries the jealous Bloom. This is paralleled in *At Swim,* where Orlick Trellis is Trellis's literary-spiritual son, born according to the principles of aestho-autogamy. This process was developed by Tracy who managed to have his own wife delivered of a 'middle-aged Spaniard'. Although the Spaniard was Tracy's offspring, a sort of spiritual son, he refused to allow him to be close to his wife, in a kind of comic inversion of the Stephen-Bloom-Molly association.

In the 'Nighttown sequence of *Ulysses* Bloom undergoes a strange nightmare trial and punishment at the hands of Bella, the whorehouse madam. He is, metaphorically, turned into a pig. Trellis also suffers a nightmarish trial sequence when his characters put him on trial in a bar-room, where an orchestra plays and the drunken judges, jury and witnesses are all interchangeable. In the course of his punishment, Trellis is changed into a rat. His defence lawyers are two dumb Greek sailors, Timothy Danaos and Dona Ferentes, their names being a pun on Homer's lines which mean 'I fear the Greeks when they bring gifts.' This may be a parody of Joyce's classical substructure in *Ulysses*. To it could be added the Greek quotation which adorns the frontispiece of *At Swim* and the references to the world of the Odyssey contained in the extract of the argument of Falconer's poem 'The Shipwreck' which the student reads from *The Conspectus of the Arts and Natural Sciences:*

Ithaca, Ulysses and Penelope. Argos and Mycenae. Agamemnon. Macronisi. Lemnos. Vulcan. Delos. Apollo and Diana. Troy. Sestos. Leander and Hero. Delphos. Temple of Apollo. Parnassus. The muses.   (p. 306)

Trellis's character Finn MacCool is yet another story-teller, and he too has his connections with Joyce. The first 'Description of Finn' is given in an exaggerated manner which is itself a parody of the giantism of Joyce's description of the Citizen in the 'Cyclops' episode of *Ulysses*. Later Finn announces in phrases which unite him to some of the themes of Ulysses:

I am an Ulsterman, a Connachtman, a Greek said Finn . . .
I am my own father and my son,
I am every hero from the crack of time.

Finn's story is the tale of the madness of King Sweeny, who was cursed by St Ronan and caused to believe that he was a bird. The version of *Buile Shuibhne* as given by O'Brien in *At Swim* is very nearly a literal translation of the original Middle Irish romance. In certain places, however, he departs from the original and gives a variant version which is usually chosen because it draws a parallel between Sweeny and Stephen, or rather between Sweeny as bird-man and Stephen as Icarus falling to his death because his wings have melted. All the images of flight and falling in the Sweeny tale correspond with those implied by the Icarus-Daedalus theme in *A Portrait*. Stephen, in fleeing the 'nets' that are thrown to hold him down, is associated with Icarus fleeing the labyrinth. Sweeny too takes flight after a battle with the Church and has to strive to escape nets.

But being beseiged with nets and hog-harried by the caretaker of the church and his false wife . . .   (p.97)

Sweeny falls from his tree and is captured and the version in *At Swim* emphasises all the different ways he is imprisoned.

He fell with a crap from the middle of the yew to the ground and Linchehaun hastened to his thorn-packed flank with fetters and handcuffs and manacles and locks and black-iron chains.   (p.98)

The fourth story-teller in the book is Orlick Trellis, who is yet another Stephen figure, the artist of the 1890s, posing, concerned with art for art's sake. He is also a rebel in whom

the Pooka has sown the seeds of rebellion and 'non serviam'.
Orlick's literary style resembles the conversation of the student
and Brinsley. A few pages of his are found to contain portions
'of a high-class story in which the names of painters and
French wines are used with knowledge and authority' (p.236).
This reminds us of the student whose 'dim room rang with the
iron of fine words and the names of great Russian masters'
which 'were articulated with fastidious intonation' (p. 32).

As a story-teller, Orlick is very particular about his art,
which is, however, derivative. His story about Trellis is a
pastiche of Finn's story about Sweeny. He is, therefore, using
past literature as 'a work of reference'. When urged by
Shanahan, Lamont and Furriskey to get on with the violent
punishment of Trellis he rebukes them.

> You overlook my artistry, he said. You cannot drop a man
> unless you first lift him. (p. 240)

Trellis's fate is apparently to be similar to Sweeny's. He is to
be lifted, then dropped. Indeed, the style of the telling renders
Trellis almost indistinguishable from Sweeny. So Trellis
becomes, by identification, Stephen as well as Bloom. He too
has flown too near the sun in his aim for a 'great book'. As his
story proceeds, Orlick accuses Trellis of sins which are more
properly associated with Stephen.

> He corrupted schoolgirls away from their piety by telling
> impure stories and reciting impious poems in their hearing.
> (p.242)

> DRUNKENNESS, was addicted to. CHASTITY, lacked . . .
> DIRTINESS, all manner of spiritual, mental and physical,
> gloried in. (p. 245)

Orlick is dwelling on Trellis-Sweeny's battle with the
Church when his readers recall him to a proper sense of
values. 'You won't get very far by attacking the church, said
Furriskey'. (p.247) The hell to which Orlick sends Trellis is
remarkably like the hell which is so vividly evoked in the
retreat sermon in *A Portrait*. It has the same physical
qualities, noisome stenches and impenetrable darkness being
among its chief characteristics.

References to Joyce can thus be found in all the various levels
of *At Swim*. There are far more than have been mentioned

here. Niall Montgomery, writing to O'Brien before the publication of *At Swim,* told him: 'Your uncle is better than anything in *Dubliners',* and there may be a conscious reference to *Dubliners* during the tea-party at the Furriskey household when Lamont remarks: 'Paralysis is certainly a nice cup of tea'. (p.228)[42] Bloom's inadvertent tip about the horse Throwaway may find an echo in the casual mention of Grandchild by Brinsley, which reminds the student of the tipster's letter he had received. The juxtaposition between Brinsley reciting his 'Lesbia' poem and Kelly calling for 'three stouts' is stylistically similar to the scene in Barney Kiernan's pub, where the Citizen is described in mock-heroic manner and there is an abrupt transition to Dublin dialect. There are many other such stylistic similarities, but it would be tedious to enumerate them. It is certain that the parody of Joyce was conscious and widespread in *At Swim,* and the 'conclusion of the book, ultimate' provides the final comment, which draws many of the strands together.

> Was Hamlet mad? Was Trellis mad? It is extremely hard to say. Was he a victim of hard-to-explain hallucinations? Nobody knows. Even experts do not agree on these vital points. Professor Unternehmer, the eminent German neurologist, points to Claudius as a lunatic but allows Trellis an inverted sow neurosis wherein the farrow eat their dam. (pp.314-15)

The farrow are Trellis's characters who turn on him to destroy him. Joyce had said: 'Ireland is the old sow that eats her farrow.'[43] O'Brien presents a situation in *At Swim* where Joyce's remark is inverted, and in this inversion lies the reason for his mockery of Joyce. Trellis, Orlick, Sweeny and the student are all Joycean figures. Orlick's art is stylised and destructive and he is swept out of existence at the end of the book. Trellis's art is moral and committed to Ireland. He is forgiven and saved. Sweeny, through madness, is reconciled with the church he had attacked and dies honoured and befriended by St Moling. The student who translated his anger at his uncle into the treatment of his fictive counterpart, Trellis, is reconciled with his uncle at the end of the book. The uncle had, it is clear, represented the three forces which Stephen Dedalus rejected: church, country and family. Joyce's character rejected his Irish background, choosing exile rather than involvement. O'Brien's character consciously chose reconciliation and acceptance instead of exile and anger. O'Brien's parody of Joyce springs, then, from his mockery of Stephen's character and from his conviction that Joyce himself was wrong to accept exile, to reject his Irish heritage (here seen in terms of Gaelic literature)[44] and to accept a classical rather than an Irish model for the mythological basis of his book. O'Brien takes Finn MacCool rather than Ulysses for his hero and Finn himself tells us that he is 'every hero from the crack of time . . . an Ulsterman, a Connachtman, a Greek'.

In the reconciliation of hitherto opposed forces which occurs at the end of the Sweeny and 'biographical reminiscence' sections, and in the destruction by fire of Orlick who had been taught to declare 'non serviam' O'Brien was acknowledging his own allegiances.

To the generation writing after him it must have sometimes seemed that Joyce had said everything. Flann O'Brien was not prepared to accept this. His attack on Joyce may have been partly motivated by envy of the other man's great achievement but it was almost certainly inspired as well by the conviction that there were still other ways, equally valid ways, of looking at the world, other sources of myth, and other possible balances between reality and imagination than were to be found in the pages of Joyce's novels.

O'Brien himself held Joyce's greatest attributes to be his enormous humour and his ear for Dublin dialogue.[45] Like Joyce, O'Brien excelled in the presentation of the Dubliner; and some critics, such as Niall Montgomery, have even declared that he surpassed Joyce in his portrayal of particular characters. There are two types of Dubliner in *At Swim.* The uncle and his friends hover on the verges of the middle class, while Shanahan, Lamont and Furriskey represent the working class. The presentation of these two groups, together with that of the narrator's life, constitute the element of formal realism in *At Swim* and are those sections in which O'Brien's style and concerns seem closest to Joyce's.

At Swim-Two-Birds is abundant with a minutely described reality. We know the narrator intimately, and his uncle's habits are observed with a clinical detachment that is almost cruel.

> He speared a portion of cooked rasher against a crust on the prongs of his fork and poised the whole at the opening of his mouth in a token of continued interrogation . . . He put the point of his fork into the interior of his mouth and withdrew it again, chewing in a coarse manner. (pp.10–11)

This detachment and concentration on detail is evident throughout the book, and is particularly noticeable when something unpleasant is being described.

> Mr Corcoran, whom by chance I was observing, smiled preliminarily but when about to speak, his smile was transfixed on his features and his entire body assumed a stiff attitude. Suddenly he sneezed, spattering his clothing with a mucous discharge from his nostrils.   (p.133)

In some sections of the book, O'Brien devotes himself to catching the spirit of Dublin society with its peculiar attitudes and mannerisms. He shows the Dubliner as repressed, hypocritical, chauvinistic, slightly ridiculous in his pretensions and worried about entirely trivial questions. This is well illustrated at the quarrelsome committee meeting at which the uncle and his friends try to decide the details of a céilí they are planning to hold.

> Now I think it's a great mistake to be too strict, he said. We must make allowances. One old-time waltz is all I ask. It's as Irish as any of them, nothing foreign about the old-time waltz. We must make allowances. The Gaelic League . . .
> I don't agree, said another man.
> My uncle gave a sharp crack on the table.
> Order, Mr Corcoran, he said in reprimand, order if you please. Mr Connors has the floor. This is a Committee Meeting. I'm sick sore and tired saying this is a Committee Meeting. After all there is such a thing as Procedure, there is such a thing as Order, there is such a thing as doing things in the right way. Have you a Point of Order, Mr Corcoran?
> (p.189)

The uncle emerges as one of the most fully realised characters in the book. He is, with his stern admonitions, his anger, and his moments of kindness, quite unforgettable. He is created primarily in his speech which consists of a series of conventional statements and accepted wisdom.

> Oh indeed there is little respect for the penny catechism in Ireland today and well I know it. But it has stood to us, Mr Corcoran, and will please God to the day we die. It is certainly a grand thing to see the young lads making it their own for you won't get very far in the world without it. Mark that, my lad. It is worth a bag of your fine degrees and parchments. (p.131)

O'Brien usually allows the accuracy with which he has repeated the speech patterns of the various characters to reveal their particular preoccupations, but he does, occasionally, write a sentence which clearly reveals the artificial and stultified nature of most social responses. On one occasion, Mr Corcoran tells the uncle that his son has won a prize in Christian Doctrine. 'My uncle removed his smile in solicitous interrogation. Your boy Tom?' (p. 130) The same capacity is seen in the narrator's description of the behaviour of Kerrigan at college.

> He came forward quickly when he saw me and enunciated and answered an obscene connundrum. He then looked away and frowned, waiting intently for my laugh. I gave this without reluctance and asked where Mr Brinsley was. Kerrigan said that he had seen him going in the direction of the billiard-hall, he (Kerrigan) then walking away from me with a strange sidewise gait and saluting in a military fashion from the distance. (p.70)

The effect here, aided by the narrator's dead-pan manner, is of posed, unspontaneous action. The narrator habitually looks at people as if they were mechanical puppets or consciously posing for a stereotyped role. This is intended as a mockery of the realistic novelist who sets out to regard his characters as scientific objects to be observed in a detached manner. It is also an example of how a parody of formal realism can easily veer off into surrealism or fantasy. This tendency is evident in one of the descriptions of the uncle.

> My uncle, his back to me, also moved his head authoritatively, exercising a roll of fat which he was accustomed to wear at the back of his collar, so that it paled and reddened in the beat of the music.   (p.133)

O'Brien always seems to have found it difficult to keep within the bounds of realism. Often when he seems most realistic he is just about to depart into the wildest fantasy.

In the scene in the Furriskey household, O'Brien works primarily on the premise he outlined in *Cruiskeen Lawn*, where he said:

> I hold, however, that Ireland's king penguin is the Dublin man. I wish to attempt an analysis of this unique character and I shall endeavour from time to time to discover his more pronounced characteristics. These are embedded in the language he speaks, for he may be studied phrase by phrase.[46]

The language of Shanahan, Lamont and the Furriskeys show these Dublin characters to be masters of meaningless conversation which is indulged in purely for its own sake. They converse on a great variety of subjects which include the character of Emperor Nero, the best way to cure boils, preferred ways of dying and the peculiar benefits of the violin as compared to the human voice. No subject is beyond their scope, no knowledge too absolute for them to have a version of it. They swap old wives' tales and accounts of history which sound as if they could have come from *1066 and All That*. (Perhaps O'Brien would have used similar versions for the *Popular History of Ireland* he intended to write.)

These Dubliners are curiously embarrassed by their bodily functions and find a number of euphemistic ways of saying that they are going to the toilet. The more they avoid the issue, the more they giggle at the implications of their polite phrases. Mrs Furriskey, in particular, as suits her feminine role, is very 'refined' and dislikes any mention of basic or unpleasant facts at the tea-table. This, of course, allows great scope for Furriskey to shock her by being deliberately 'crude'.

Because when you were listening to my singing this morning, my good woman, said Furriskey stressing with his finger the caesura of his case, I was blowing my nose in the lavatory. That's a quare one for you.

Oh, that's a shame for you, said Mrs Furriskey contributing her averted giggle to an arpeggio of low sniggers. You shouldn't use language like that at table. Where are your manners, Mr Furriskey? (p.217)

The characters' stock phrases — and their speech is mainly composed of such — are often quite meaningless: 'The fiddle is the man' or 'I'll live if it kills me'. They relate strange events in hushed or melodramatic tones and have a tremendous appetite for horror. Suggesting that Trellis, as one of his tortures, be crushed under a steam-roller, Furriskey vividly evokes the scene and adds a refinement.

They drive away the roller and here is his black heart sitting there as large as life in the middle of the pulp of his banjaxed corpse. *They couldn't crush his heart!* (p.240)

O'Brien's Dublin is revealed as a city of useless talk, a place where anecdote parades as criticism, where the general is forever reduced to the particular, the familiar and, consequently, the trivial. Thus a discussion of the characteristics of the Irishman will conclude with the assertion that an Irishman, wherever he goes, will be known as a great jumper, because a Sergeant Craddock once jumped a mighty jump. In Dublin, says O'Brien, every man considers himself to be a savant, explaining things to his underprivileged fellows. Orlick Trellis, catching this attitude in quite different language, explains in a parody of their usual conversations, the great 'knowledge' possessed by Furriskey, Lamont and Shanahan.

Frequent use was made of words unheard of by illiterates and persons of inferior education, *exempli gratia* saburra or foul granular deposit in the pit of the stomach, tachylyte, a vitreous form of basalt, tapir, a hoofed mammal with the appearance of a swine, capon, castrated cock, triacontahedral, having thirty sides or surfaces and botargo, relish of mullet or tunny roe. (p.277)

Indeed, the assembled company have, in Orlick's account, discussed subjects of very wide application. They have illustrated a knowledge of chemistry, physics, history and innumerable (and quite pointless) statistics. A gasp of admiration accompanies Mr Furriskey's demonstration on 'How to read the gas-meter'. This whole section, some seven pages of solid pedantry, is a comic inversion of the conversation at the Furriskey household, where they had, in like manner, demonstrated a similar breadth of learning. Anthony Lamont, for example, shows himself to be possessed of extensive medical knowledge.

> I'll tell you what it is, explained Lamont, bad blood is the back of the whole thing. When the quality of the blood isn't first class, out march our friends the pimples. It's Nature's warning Mr Shanahan. You can steam your face till your snot melts but damn the good it will do your blackheads if you don't attend to your inside.   (p.225)

Paul Shanahan has his own expertise too. His *métier* is story-telling, and he possesses considerable skill in this line, as is seen in his exciting story of Jumping Sergeant Craddock.

> But wait till I tell you. The two of them lined up and a hell of a big crowd gathering there to watch. Here was my nice Bagenal as proud as a bloody turkey in his green pants, showing off the legs. Beside him stands another man, a man called Craddock, a member of the polis. His tunic is off him on the grass but the rest of his clothes is still on. He is standing as you find him with his blue pants and his big canal-barges on his two feet. I'm telling you it was something to look at. It was a sight to see.   (p.121)

Shanahan is not merely a story-teller; he is a connoisseur of poetry and a disciple of Jem Casey, the navvy poet, known popularly as 'the Bard of Booterstown'. Shanahan is able to recite, verbatim, an example of Casey's finest work, a poem called 'The Workman's Friend' which contains the immortal refrain 'A PINT OF PLAIN IS YOUR ONLY MAN'.

> When things go wrong and will not come right
> Though you do the best you can,
> When life looks black as the hour of night —

A PINT OF PLAIN IS YOUR ONLY MAN.

When money's tight and is hard to get
And your horse has also ran
When all you have is a heap of debt —
A PINT OF PLAIN IS YOUR ONLY MAN.   (p.108)

Shanahan, then, is a man who is sensitive to higher things, and Lamont has extensive medical knowledge. Nevertheless, both these men still need to rely on the greater and more universal wisdom of Furriskey. When Orlick Trellis, in his manuscript, describes Shanahan as 'the eminent philospher, wit and raconteur', Shanahan himself is not immediately receptive to this encomium.

> Wait a minute, he said. Just a minute, now. Not so fast. What's that you said, Sir? . . .
> Furriskey adjusted his neck so that his face was close to that of Shanahan.
> What's wrong with you man, he asked. What's the matter? Isn't it all right? Isn't it high praise? Do you know the meaning of that last word?
> It's from the French, of course, said Shanahan.
> Then I'll tell you what it means. It means you're all right. Do you understand me? *I've met this man. I know him. I think he's all right.* Do you see it now?   (p.268)

This Dublin, only slightly exaggerated for comic effect, is caught by O'Brien with remarkable accuracy. It adds, with the detail of the student narrator's life, to the impression of everyday reality which is strong in *At Swim*.

It is, however, quite clear that this everyday reality is represented in the novel so that it can be undercut. 'Realism' is undercut in three ways in *At Swim*. The first of these is the form of the book itself. The conventions of the anti-novel are, to some extent, based on the assumption that the novel's claim to represent reality is fraudulent. Secondly, realism is undercut when, as a result of the juxtaposition of many different literary styles, it is seen to be only one more style, the product of a series of accepted conventions as artificial as the dramatic soliloquy or the description of a character. Finally, realism is undercut by being contrasted with the products of 'pure' imagination.

Imaginative literature appears in *At Swim* in four different forms. These are exemplified in the presentation of Finn MacCool, in the story of Suibhne Geilt, in the journey of the Pooka and the Good Fairy to the Red Swan Inn, and in the presentation of the cowboys, the chief representatives of the 'American Dream'.

> Finn MacCool was a legendary hero of old Ireland. Though not mentally robust, he was a man of superb physique and development. Each of his thighs was as thick as a horse's belly, narrowing to a calf as thick as the belly of a foal. Three fifties of fosterlings could engage with handball against the wideness of his backside, which was large enough to halt the march of men through a mountain-pass.
>
> (p.10)

Finn in *At Swim* is primarily the comic giant of folklore. His presentation is a parody of the solemn and joyless or excessively romantic translations of the Ossianic tales which began to proliferate in the 1890s. Standish James O'Grady was the foremost exponent of the romantic school. In *Finn and His Companions* he wrote:

> St Patrick looked towards Tara and saw ten men coming towards him and now very near. The tallest of the tonsured Gaels and Britons who were with Patrick would not reach their shoulder-blades, and hardly to the waist of the man who walked before the others and seemed to be their captain. They wore shields and swords, and in their hands carried spears proportioned to their size and strength. Each man's mantle, blue, green, or scarlet, was folded round his shoulders and fastened on the breast by brooches the rings of which were like wheels of gold or silver. Their knees were bare, and their hair, escaped from the brazen helmets, fell in dense curling masses on their shoulders. Their port was majestic, and the meanest of them carried himself like a king.[47]

The translations of Kuno Meyer represent the other tradition. Part of his version of the 'Death of Finn', reads:

> And in that way he went forth, a famous tree of upholding battle, and a bush of shelter for brave warriors, and a stable

stake for hosts and multitudes, and a protecting door-valve for warriors and battle-soldiers of the western world; nor did he stop in his course until he reached the brink of the ford. Truly it was no wonder that the kingship of Erin and Scotland and the headship of the fian of the whole world would be in the hands of Finn Mac Cumaill at that time; for he was one of the five masters in every great art, and one of the three sons of comfort to Erin.[48]

Both these accounts accept the idea that Finn and the Fianna were men of great stature and noble bearing and that Finn himself was their leader by virtue of his greater stature, greater wisdom and enormous ability in battle. In this they partially disagree with Geoffrey Keating, the renowned seventeenth-century historian, who disputes the idea of Finn's great size with some vehemence.

> There were many among the Fenians . . . who were more remarkable for their personal prowess, their valour and their corporeal stature than Finn.

Finn, he says, was captain of the Fianna because 'his father and grandfather had held that position before him', and because

> He excelled his contemporaries in intellect and learning, in wisdom and in subtlety, and in experience and hardihood in battlefields. It was for these qualities that he was made king of the Fiann — not for his personal prowess or for the great size or strength of his body.[49]

O'Brien chooses to invert many aspects of these accounts of Finn and to accept instead the 'comic giant' Finn. From O'Grady he takes the idea of great size, while rendering it grotesque rather than noble and rejecting O'Grady's romantic picture. From Kuno Meyer he takes the style of the Finn versions, which he then parodies, while denying Finn intellect or wisdom. So, where Keating suggests that Finn was of normal size, but of great intellectual powers, O'Brien makes him gigantic and stupid. He treats the normally lofty descriptions of Finn in a jocular and undignified manner and style. In similar vein he provides a travesty of the Ossianic tales when he adds, in elaborate and fantastic detail, his own lists of

tests to those which had to be undergone by a prospective
member of the Fianna. When O'Brien begins this account he
could be translating, almost literally, from a fifteenth-century
manuscript source which is translated by Douglas Hyde in *A
Literary History of Ireland.*

> Of all these' . . . not a man was taken until he was a prime
> poet versed in the twelve books of poetry. No man was taken
> till in the ground a large hole had been made such as to
> reach the fold of his belt. and he put into it with his shield
> and forearm's length of a hazel stick. Then must nine
> warriors having nine spears, and a ten furrows' width
> between them and him, assail him, and in concert let fly at
> him. If he were then hurt past that guard of his, he was not
> received into the Fian-ship.[50]

O'Brien's version is, initially at least, quite similar to this,
allowing for his ever-present desire to burlesque literary forms
by exaggerating their conventions.

> Till a man has accomplished twelve books of poetry, the
> same is not taken for want of poetry but is forced away. No
> man is taken till a black hole is hollowed in the world to the
> depth of his two oxters and he put into it to gaze from it
> with lonely head and nothing to him but his shield and a
> stick of hazel. Then must nine warriors fly their spears at
> him, one with the other and together. If he be spear-holed
> past his shield, or spear-killed, he is not taken for want of
> shield-skill.   (pp.20-1)

Closely following this style, O'Brien goes on to produce his
own version of suitable tests, illustrating once again the
seemingly limitless extent of his imagination. His descriptions
become grotesque and fantastic and pass completely beyond
the bounds of probability when they stress the Fianna's
gigantic nature and magical powers.

> With the eyelids to him stitched to the fringe of his eye-
> bags, he must be run by Finn's people through the bogs and
> the marsh-swamps of Erin with two odorous prickle-backed
> hogs ham-tied and asleep in the seat of his hempen drawers.
> If he sink beneath a peat-swamp or lose a hog, he is not
> accepted by Finn's people . . . One hundred head of cattle

he must accommodate with wisdom about his person when walking all Erin, the half about his armpits and the half about his trews, his mouth never halting from the discoursing of sweet poetry. One thousand rams he must sequester about his trunks, with no offence to the men of Erin, or he is unknown to Finn.   (pp.21-2)

Yet if O'Brien's aim was to use parody and travesty to mock the conventions and translationss of Gaelic literature (and, in passing, Joyce's mockery of the Celtic 'hero'), his burlesque of those conventions is often surprisingly restrained. Douglas Hyde had pointed out that the whole Ossianic or Fenian cycle abounded with exaggerated verbosity and rhetoric. When he writes, Hyde says,

> the story-teller or prose-poet, passes everything through the prism of his imagination, and aided by an extraordinary exuberance of vocabulary and unbounded wealth of alliterative adjectives, wraps the commonest objects in a hurricane of—to use his own phrase—'misty-dripping' epithets.[51]

O'Brien's putative author becomes, for a time, a prose-poet of old Ireland. Like the traditional Gaelic poets, he composes his verses lying in darkness in his room, shut off from the distractions of the world about him. Under these conditions his mind can wander freely in time and space and pass easily through the boundaries of imagination and reality. Out of the mists comes the 'God-big Finn' who is, as the stories suggest, skilled in poetry and endowed with wisdom gained from the sucking of his thumb. Finn speaks, appropriately, in the heroic manner, but the student author, as the controlling mind, forces him to provide quite incongruous images for his parody of the Song of Amergin.

> I am the breast of a young queen, said Finn,
> I am a thatching against rains.
> I am a dark castle against bat-flutters.
> I am a Connachtman's ear.
> I am a harpstring.
> I am a gnat.   (p.19)

Finn's speech is full of compound words, formalised

apostrophes and replies, and alliterative patterns. Much of it is rendered comic by a process whereby the heroic is juxtaposed with the modern. Thus a Fenian warrior identifies himself with all his titles and then translates these into their modern counterparts.

The presentation of Finn is not, however, completely burlesque. It also emphasises certain qualities in Finn himself and in Ossianic literature which O'Brien thought important. This is clear in one of the earliest descriptions of Finn.

> After an interval Finn MacCool, a hero of old Ireland, came out before me from his shadow, Finn the wide-hammed, the heavy-eyed, Finn that could spend a Lammas morning with girdled girls at far-from-simple chess-play.
>
> (pp.15–16)

The narrator is fascinated by the colourful details of Finn's life. At one point he contrasts his own wasted and dull day with that of Finn. At another point where he talks of those things which are necessary for life he is echoing Finn's expression of horror at the thought of being deprived of mental and physical stimulation.

> There is no torture so narrow as to be bound and beset in a dark cavern without food or music, without the bestowing of gold on bards. To be chained by night in a dark pit without company of chessmen — evil destiny!   (p.17)

Finn's life is a multi-faceted one, a combination of sensuality (he likes 'comely, generous women') sensuousness, physical exertion (he spends one-third of a day in hunting or ball-play) and intellectual and aesthetic pursuits. He needs music, poetry and chess in order to survive and is acutely sensitive to the world of nature about him.

> When the seven companies of my warriors are gathered together on the one plain and the truant clean-cold loud-voiced wind goes through them, too sweet to me is that. Echo-blow of a goblet base against the tables of the palace, sweet to me is that. I like gull-cries and the twittering together of fine cranes. I like the surf-roar at Tralee, the songs of the three sons of Meadhra and the whistle of Mac Lughaidh.   (p.16)

Finn, in spite of being presented as a comic giant is, nevertheless, heroic in the sense that he is the many-rounded figure, the 'soldier-scholar-poet' of early Ireland, albeit in comic form. The narrator with whom he shares in common a love of poetry and of drink, an interest in women and in food, is quite different in that he is not an integrated person. The first lines of the book reveal a personality divided against itself, dominated by an active, free mind, but with a 'vacant' exterior. Even when the narrator is not deliberately withdrawing his powers of 'sensual perception' he seems little enough endowed with any. The workings of his mind fascinate him, but he is almost a stranger in the world of senses. Finn, on the other hand, is a 'mask' of feeling, responsiveness, physical courage and generosity; he is a mythical figure in that he represents possibilities rather than achievements. Finn is everything that the narrator is not. O'Brien's choice of Finn rather than Cuchulain was almost certainly due to Finn's reputation as a poet. O'Brien was far more interested in the characteristics and assumptions of Ossianic poetry than in the nobility of heroic saga.

No matter what danger threatened, Finn and his companions, did not cease from the reciting of melodious Irish. Their poems are all on nature, and they themselves, as the tests of entry to the Fianna prove, move through the woods and bogs of Ireland without disturbing even a leaf or a twig on the way. They are often able to perform great feats of magic and so prove that they are not bound by the limitations of the physical world.

Finn and the Fianna are, therefore, more than adequate as the mythological basis for *At Swim.* Ulysses has no more powers than Finn, who is almost omnipotent.

> Finn that is wind-quick, Finn that is a better man than God . . . Who has seen the like of Finn, or seen the living semblance of him standing in the world, Finn that could best God at ball-throw or wrestling or pig-trailing or at the honeyed discourse of sweet Irish with jewels and gold for bards, or at the listening of distant harpers in a black hole at evening? (pp.23–4)

Finally, it is noteworthy that the Ossianic stories of Finn and the Fianna are more often to be found in the repertoire of contemporary story-tellers than those of Cuchulain and the Red Branch. He is closer to the people and a character more capable of being twisted to suit the needs of the time, place and person.

Since Finn is ambiguously presented in that he is both hero and buffoon, it is to be expected that his telling of the tale of King Sweeny will be similarly ambiguous. Writing to Longmans in 1938, O'Brien explained that the Sweeny section of *At Swim* was his own translation of the medieval Irish romance, *Buile Shuibhne*. He had, he said, translated it independently of the version done by J. G. O'Keeffe for the Irish Texts Society edition of *The Adventures of Suibhne Geilt*. There are, certainly, many differences between the two versions. O'Brien's is a good deal shorter than O'Keeffe's as it excludes all the historical background detail dealing with the battle of Magh Rath. It also excludes many of the prose summaries of the lays and the poetic renderings of narrative sections already given in prose. Surprisingly, O'Brien's version also excludes the lay spoken by Sweeny at 'Swim-Two-Birds', though this can be said to be one of the most beautiful of all the lays in the tale.

The tale deals with the life of Sweeny, King of Dál Araidhe, who insulted and attacked St Ronan, threw his psalter into a lake and slew one of his acolytes. St Ronan cursed Sweeny, bidding that madness should overtake him so that he would think himself a bird and live in the trees, hungry, cold and isolated from human society. Madness did assail Sweeny during the battle of Magh Rath, and he fled from mankind and roosted in the trees, growing feathers on his body and gaining the ability to make enormous leaps through the length and breadth of Ireland. After many adventures and tortures Sweeny recovers his sanity and dies in the monastic settlement of St Moling. Both Sweeny and St Moling were renowned as great poets. The Book of Aicill, an early Irish law tract, makes this clear with reference to Sweeny.

Three were the triumphs (buadha) of that battle (i.e. the battle of Magh Rath): the defeat of Congal Claen in his falsehood by Domhnall in his truth, and Suibhne Geilt having become mad, and Cennfaeladh's brain of forgetfulness having been taken from his head. And Suibhne Geilt having become mad is not a reason why the battle is a triumph, but it is because of the stories and poems he left after him in Ireland.[52]

Like the Fenians who do not cease from the reciting of melodious Irish, Sweeny, too, translates his anguish into poetry and utters lays on the subject of his sufferings. His poetry primarily consists of hymns to the beauties of nature. Each lay speaks of the different qualities of particular places, or of the beauties of the trees of Ireland or its animals. In the composition of these poems, forced out of him by agony, he transmutes that agony, his madness and his sense of isolation into poetry which is life-affirming in its celebration of nature, of beauty, of normality and of man's relationship with God.

Of course, O'Brien parodies the conventions of this poetry by exaggerating the effect of the tense-structure and idiom of literal translation and by elaborating the tendency in Gaelic literature to make word-compounds and to use an excessive amount of alliteration and assonance. Nevertheless, the parody is usually quite gentle, as can be seen when his version is put beside O'Keeffe's.

O'Brien	*O'Keeffe*
The holy bell that thou hast outraged	That bell which thou has wounded
will banish thee to branches,	will send thee among branches,
it will put thee on a par with fowls—	so that thou shalt be one with the birds—
the saint-bell of saints with sainty-saints.	the bell of saints before saints.
Just as it went prestissimo	Even as in an instant went
the spear-shaft skyward	the spear-shaft on high,
you too, Sweeny, go madly mad-gone	mayest thou go, O Suibhne,
skyward. (p.92)	in madness, without respite.[53]

It is quite clear that words like 'fowls' and 'prestissimo' are incongruous here, even if there was not a line like 'the saint-bell of saints with sainty saints' to add to the parody. Nevertheless, when one compares other aspects of the tale, it seems clear that O'Brien has restrained his parodic impulse to give a real impression of its distinctive qualities. In the description of places, for example, there is a clear coincidence between O'Brien's version and O'Keeffe's.

O'Brien	O'Keeffe
All Fharannain, resort of saints	Cliff of Farannan, abode of
fulness of hazels, fine nuts	saints,
swift water without heat	with many fair hazels and nuts,
coursing its flank.	swift cold water
	rushing down its side.
Plenteous are its green ivies	Many green ivy-trees are there
its mast is coveted;	and mast such as is prized,
the fair heavy apple-trees	and fair, heavy-topped apple-
they stoop their arms.	trees
(pp.124–5)	bending their branches.[54]

The conceit in the last line of O'Brien's version, 'they stoop their arms', might even be regarded as superior to O'Keeffe's 'bending their branches'.

Buile Shuibhne is a romance. As such, it partakes of the characteristics of romance. While it could not be said to be chivalric in tone, its central figure is a king who undergoes a series of adventures which are, in essence, a journey from madness to sanity, from uncontrollable anger and resentment against the Church to reconciliation, peace and harmony with religion. The voice of the narrator is ever-present in the tale, which is, therefore, personal in tone. It contains many elements of the supernatural. Demons, headless and bodiless, chase Sweeny to confirm him in his madness. The tale is loosely structured and somewhat lacking in unity. O'Keeffe says of it that the story 'proceeds smoothly and naturally from stage to stage, but occasionally in the verse one is brought face to face with sudden and violent changes of subject'.[55]

The tale is often unrestrained in its evocations of nature and it presents a vision of an isolated, lonely figure cut off from the world and denied the benefits of society—those very things which Finn counted as essential.

Sad it is, Sweeny, said Linchehaun, that your last extremity should be this, without food or drink or raiment like a fowl, the same man that had cloth of silk and of satin and the foreign steed of the peerless bridle, also comely generous

women and boys and hounds and princely people of every
refinement; hosts and tenants and men-at-arms, and mugs
and goblets and embellished buffalo-horns for the
savouring of pleasant-tasted fine liquors. Sad it is, to see the
same man as a hapless air-fowl.   (pp.97-8)

Sweeny's madness teaches him, through deprivation and
isolation, the value of that order and restraint which he had
previously flouted.

O'Brien was drawn to this tale for a number of reasons. It is
thematically similar to the story of the narrator of *At Swim-
Two-Birds,* which also begins with anger and ends with
reconciliation. O'Brien's MA thesis on 'Nature in Modern Irish
Poetry' had shown him to be interested in nature poetry and
Buile Shuibhne is, in essence, a long nature-poem, containing
the famous and often-translated songs to the trees of Ireland.
The loose structure of the tale, the sudden digression, the
opportunity to include the world of the supernatural with that
of a vividly described actuality, may have offered a model for
At Swim as a whole. O'Keeffe, in his commentary, provides
another reason for its appeal.

> In a word, the *Buile Shuibhne,* like the Vision of
> MacConglinne . . . is a sustained literary *tour de force,*
> and, as such, furnishes an interesting example of the
> medieval attitude of mind towards literary creation.[56]

Literary creation, as seen in *Buile Shuibhne,* embodies an
attitude to man as a being who transmutes personal suffering
into a profound literary achievement and who transcends his
own loneliness and despair in a close and loving observation of
the world about him. In this, Sweeny is quite different to the
narrator of *At Swim,* who translates his discomfort into a
fictional torture of his uncle, and who seems incapable of
discovering the world around him, except possibly through the
medium of a literary model like Brinsley's 'Lesbia' poem.
Imagination in a medieval romance can have free rein. The
demons, and Sweeny's terrified flight from them, are vividly
presented but the emphasis on the supernatural does not
preclude an equally vivid representation of reality, for
Sweeny's sufferings are graphically and sympathetically
evoked:

In that glen it was hard for Sweeny to endure the pain of his bed there on the top of a tall ivy-grown hawthorn in the glen, every twist that he would turn sending showers of hawy thorns into his flesh, tearing and rending and piercing him and pricking his blood-red skin.   (p.94)

Reality does not serve to debunk imagination because, to Sweeny's poetic vision, poetry supercedes life, providing a consolation for the terrors of living and encompassing a greater reality than that of mere fact or sensory apprehension.

That Sweeny is accepted, in part, as the mouthpiece for the values of *At Swim* is illustrated in two ways. One is that both the title and the suggested alternative centre on him. The other is that the only really bitter satire in the book is directed towards Shanahan, Lamont and Furriskey as they react to the Sweeny tale.

As Finn tells his story, his listeners feel compelled to interrupt. They are incapable of listening to the end. They mock Finn by referring to him as 'Mr Storybook' and comment in an ignorantly condescending way on the story he is telling. Finn reminds them of the punishments due to those who interrupted a story, thus recalling the respected position of the poet in Irish society. Shanahan is impervious to Finn's droning voice since he wants to tell his friends about a modern poet who is, he says, 'a poet of the people'. Shanahan's stance is anti-intellectual, anti-art. His conception of poetry amounts to the fact that he thinks of it as doggerel to be learned by heart. Thus he makes extravagant claims for Jem Casey.

Just Jem Casey, a poor ignorant labouring man but head and shoulders above the whole bloody lot of them, not a man in the whole country to beat him when it comes to getting together a bloody pome — not a poet in the whole world that could hold a candle to Jem Casey, not a man of them fit to stand beside him.   (p.103)

Later, in an unconscious allusion to Sweeny, he goes on to call Casey 'as sweet a singer in his own way as you'll find in the bloody trees there of a spring day' (p.105).

They admit that Finn's 'stuff' was 'bloody nice' and

the real old stuff of the native land . . . that brought scholars to our shore when your men on the other side were

on the flat of their bellies before the calf of gold with a
sheepskin around their man.   (pp.105-6)

However, they still complain that such literature is not 'for the
man in the street' and, furthermore, that it becomes tedious if
listened to for too long. On the other hand, they say, Jem
Casey's 'pomes' never lose their freshness and have what can
only be called a quality of 'permanence' about them.

Since Casey's poem, hilarious though it is, is one which
recommends alcohol as the cure for all the ills of the world, the
contrast with Sweeny's life-transcending verses is clear. It is
rendered doubly clear by the fact that the refrain 'A PINT OF
PLAIN IS YOUR ONLY MAN' had previously been used by
Kelly, an ignorant man who thinks that Brinsley is talking
about alcohol when he is, in fact, reciting his 'Lesbia' poem to
the narrator. In both cases, while not understanding or
attending to the poem in question, the listeners are unconsciously infuenced by it.

The reactions of Shanahan and his companions are shown
to be typical of modern Ireland, which is escapist and whose
sensibilities are so atrophied that it can no longer respond to
the 'grand old stuff of the native land'. From a Gaelic scholar
of O'Brien's standing, it was a bitter complaint.

The third type of literature which O'Brien presents as an
alternative to formal realism is a contemporary form of myth.

The Red Swan Inn, though described in all its architectural
and historical reality, is, in fact, a house of imagination. The
cellar is full of leprachauns and one of the rooms is occupied
by cowboys. These cowboys, Shorty Andrews and Slug
Williard, are borrowed from the romances of William Tracy.
Cowboys are, of course, the folk-heroes of the American West,
the modern equivalent of Finn MacCool, creatures as large in
stature, in power, in good or evil as any of the folk-heroes of
earlier times. It is clear, in *At Swim,* that it is this type of
mythical image which is replacing the heroes of a former age.
The students go together to the 'moving pictures', and we are
told that the Antient Concert Rooms, in which the first
performances of the Irish Literary Theatre (afterwards to
become the Abbey) were held, has become a picture-house. It
was, of course, the Irish Literary Theatre which attempted to
revive Irish myth and legend in the awareness of the Irish

people. With its conversion into a cinema, the theatre in which Cuchulain might have spoken was given over to that main staple of twentieth-century popular culture — the cowboy film.

In *At Swim* it is Shanahan, that spokesman for 'popular' literature who tells the story of the cowboys' involvement in the adventures at the Circle N Ranch. Employed by Mr Tracy in a story of cow-punching in Ringsend, Shanahan, with Shorty Andrews and Slug Willard, 'the toughest pair of boyos you'd meet in a day's walk' (p.74), were busy with the normal activities of a ranch. They were 'rounding up steers, you know, and branding, and breaking in colts in the corral with lassoes on our saddle-horns and pistols at our hips' (p.74). At night all the cowboys gathered in their bunkhouse, drinking, singing, smoking and mixing with 'school-marms and saloon-girls'. Then one day they received a telegram instructing them to report to Tracy for further orders.

> Up we went on our horses, cantering up Mountjoy Square with our hats tilted back on our heads and the sun in our eyes and our gun-butts swinging at our holsters.   (p.75)

The telegram was a trap intended to lure the men away from the ranch while Red Kiersey's gang rustled their steers across the border into Irishtown.

> Red Kiersay, you understand, was working for another man by the name of Henderson that was writing another book about cattle-dealers and jobbing and shipping bullocks to Liverpool.   (p.75)

The three cowboys decide on revenge and set out by moonlight to regain their cattle and the negro skivvies who normally tended the bunkhouse and did the cooking in its well-equipped galley. When they arrive they advance determinedly towards Kiersay's hide-out.

> Down we got offa the buckboard to our hands and knees and up with us towards the doss-house on our bellies, our silver-mounted gun-butts jiggling at our hips, our eyes narrowed into slits and our jaws set and stern like be damned.   (p.78)

However, they are surprised by Red Kiersay himself, held at gunpoint and then told to go home. Having failed in their mission, they summon the police and a crowd of Indians who are stationed in Phoenix Park while working as characters in another of Tracy's books. Surrounding the ranch-house, the police, cowboys and Indians, after a pitched battle succeed in capturing all Kiersay's gang, except Kiersay himself, who is found to be saying his prayers in his tent. Next day all Kiersay's gang were tried and sentenced in the local court.

In some of its aspects the story is a parody of conventional cowboy adventure tales. It is wildly imaginative and manages to contain elements of many other types of adventure story as well. The cowboy jargon is mixed with the idiom of Dublin where the scene is set. The story moves easily between reality and fantasy. It contains realistic details suitable to Ringsend or Mountjoy Square as well as the flexibility of imaginative elements which is suitable for a romance.

As they sit at night in the bunkhouse the cowboys drink porter rather than whiskey and take their cigarettes off the 'chiffonier'. The company is entertained by a 'fiddler' who plays come-all-ye's and 'Ave Maria'. As they canter madly across the praries on a buckboard they overtake

> lorries and trams and [send] poor so-and-so's on bicycles scuttling down side-lanes with nothing showing but the white of their eyes.   (p. 77)

The police station to which they take their complaint is in Lad Lane. The case is taken in hand by the superintendent, 'a Clohessy from Tipp.', who lays on a whole detachment of the DMP and requests the fire-brigade to stand by. While the Indians are fetched from their wigwams in Phoenix Park, the superintendent and Shanahan 'get stuck into a dozen stout in the back-room'. A wholesale assault is then mounted on Kiersay's hide-out. The Indians gallop round and round it on their 'arab' ponies, while the police and cowboys hide behind the buckboard waiting for the gang to emerge from what has become a blazing inferno. Inexplicably the style of story-telling alters so that it refers to another kind of war. Kiersay and his men emerge 'prepared . . . to make a last stand for king and country'

(p. 80). They hold up a passing tram and take cover behind it. All the windows of the tram are broken, the world is full of snipers, the superintendent leads his 'brave bobbies' 'over the top', and the crowd of onlookers which has gathered calls on every man 'to do his duty'. The battle ends and Kiersay is found 'doing the Brian Boru in his bloody tent'. Shanahan laments the fact that he can do nothing to Kiersay, 'him there in front of me on his two knees praying'.

The battle in Ringsend conveys echoes of the battle of Clontarf, Shakespeare's *Hamlet,* the First World War, a street fight, cowboy and Indian sagas, the Irish Civil War — 'Shorty and myself behind a sack of potatoes picking off the snipers like to be damned' (p. 81) — and the *Táin Bó Cúalnge.* It is, however, more ˙ complicated than this, for the story is interrupted by several 'excerpts' which extend the possible range of meaning and allusion even more.

The first of these excerpts is from the press and reports Tracy's death. Like any obituary, it recalls his great achievements and personal qualities.

> A man of culture and old-world courtesy, his passing will be regretted by all without distinction of creed or class and in particular by the world of letters, which he adorned with distinction for many years. He was the first man in Europe to exhibit twenty-nine lions in a cage at the same time and the only writer to demonstrate that cow-punching could be economically carried out in Ringsend. His best-known works were *Red Flanagan's Last Throw, Flower o' the Prairie* and *Jake's Last Ride.*   (p.74)

Like all the excerpts in the book, this is both a parody (of obituaries) and is germane to the plot, for we are soon given an ironic reversal of many of the clichéd remarks which the extract contained. Tracy's 'old-world courtesy' is revealed in his single conversation with the cowboys.

> Get back to hell, says Tracy, I never sent any message. Get back to hell to your prairies, says he, you pack of lousers that can be taken in by any fly-be-night with a fine story.
> (p.75)

His 'economic' cow-punching is similarly deflated in a further passage which illustrates the satiric potential of this type of juxtaposition.

> On the land adjacent, grazing is available for 10,000 steers and 2,000 horses, thanks to the public spirit of Mr William Tracy, the indefatigable novelist, who had 8,912 dangerous houses demolished in the environs of Irishtown and Sandymount to make the enterprise possible.   (p.78)

Further oddities in the account allow for a more penetrating type of criticism. The 'little black maids skivvying there in the galley' are very casually mentioned in the beginning, so that the incongruity of having negro maids in such a setting is not immediately evident. As the story proceeds, this detail, apparently included only to complicate an already varied tale, becomes part of a criticism of the false assumptions of civilised society. The maids are referred to as 'nigger skivvies' and it is found that they have been stolen along with the cattle. Another relevant excerpt from the press makes the association between negro maids, galleys and cattle, a little clearer.

> An examination of the galley and servants' sleeping-quarters revealed no trace of the negro maids. They had been offered lucrative inducements to come from the United States and had at no time expressed themselves as being dissatisfied with their conditions of service.   (p.76)

Later the press account states that there was 'no intercourse of a social character between the men and the scullery maids'. The cowboys are regarded as socially superior to the negro maids. The existence of a 'galley' rather than a kitchen, in the bunkhouse, is beginning to have implications of slavery. Shanahan makes this attitude clear when he protests in pseudo-liberalism:

> I'm not what you call fussy when it comes to women but damn it all I draw the line when it comes to carrying off a bunch of black niggers — human beings, you must remember — and a couple of thousand steers, by God. (p.76)

A further excerpt from the press describes the Circle N Ranch with its mixture of Gothic, Elizabethan and Corinthian architecture. It goes on:

The old Dublin customs of utilising imported negroid labour for operating the fine electrically equipped cooking galley is still observed in this time-hallowed house. (pp.77-8)

O'Brien has used the disparity between realistic and imaginative detail, the total confusion of elements in the description of the house and the events of the tale, to make a number of social comments. Through the medium of fantasy and parody he points out that civilisation and 'custom' are at times close to barbarism and that the romance of lawlessness can only be seen when it is not placed in close proximity with an urban society which relies on the closeness of family ties and the presence of the police and fire-brigade to ensure its stability. The final excerpt from the press reduces the whole episode to a totally realistic level.

A number of men, stated to be labourers, were arraigned before Mr Lamphall in the District Court yesterday morning on charges of riotous assembly and malicious damage. Accused were described by Superintendent Clohessy as a gang of corner-boys whose horse-play in the streets was the curse of the Ringsend district. They were pests and public nuisances whose antics were not infrequently attended by damage to property. Complaints as to their conduct were frequently being received from residents in the area. On the occasion of the last escapade, two windows were broken in a tram-car the property of the Dublin United Tramway Company. Inspector Quin of the Company stated that the damage to the vehicle amounted to £2 11s.0d. Remarking that no civilised community could tolerate organised hooliganism of this kind, the justice sentenced the accused to seven days' hard labour without the option of a fine, and hoped that it would be a lesson to them and to other playboys of the boulevards.   (pp.82-3)

The gallops over the prairie are reduced to 'horse-play', the great battle to 'organised hooliganism', and the destruction wreaked in its course to two broken windows in a tram. It is not the whole story. There remains an importance which this realistic level has taken no account of. Shanahan's clichéd hyperbolic imagination has somehow managed to find a theme of almost universal human relevance. Not only has the juxtaposition of reality and imagination in the episode allowed scope for satire, it has also demonstrated an important human tendency. Shanahan has shown how a cattle-raid could gain epic proportion in the mind of the story-teller. He has demonstrated man's tendency to mythologise, to seek relevance in actions which are, in themselves, trivial until the mind of the story-teller has transfigured them. Once that transfiguration has taken place, no 'realistic' version is capable of accounting for all the associations and ramifications of the tale. O'Brien here both deflates and elevates the 'playboys of the boulevards' as Synge deflated and elevated Christy Mahon while showing how the transfiguring power of the imagination can close the gap between unheroic and disgusting reality and the aspirations to honour and significant action of each individual. The 'horse-play' is not, in essence, noble or heroic. The cowboys are like children when in their play they transform the streets into prairies and the lamp-posts into totem-poles. The cowboy in his own world stands for freedom, action and the moral powers of a deity. He has enthralled more imaginations than those of children, but it is children who, with their greater range of imaginative powers, have been less critical of their cult heroes. When the 'romance' of the cowboy's life is translated into, and contrasted with, the realities of Dublin's streets, it suffers in the comparison. Nevertheless, the mythic base, once touched on, cannot be easily dismissed.

No such comparison affects the final level of imaginative literature in *At Swim*. The Pooka and the Good Fairy are the inhabitants of the world of folk-tale; a world which is consistently a world of imagination. The reader is told that the setting is Ireland, but it is unlike any modern Ireland that we know. The Pooka and the Good Fairy journey through a forest, full of the creatures of fiction, a timeless place where Jem Casey can meet King Sweeny of Dál Araidhe. In all of these four types of fiction, the powers of the story-teller has created an imaginative, mythical landscape. Only in the Circle N episode does this landscape connect in any serious way with the 'real' world. The world of the Pooka and the Good Fairy corresponds to the Red Swan Inn, the archetypal house of imagination, that realm where all things are possible.

The Pooka, Fergus MacPhellimey, is 'a member of the devil class'.[57] The Good Fairy is a good fairy, a combination of Tinkerbell, a guardian angel and a scientific concept. The Good Fairy and the Pooka may also be compared with Ariel and Caliban, from whom their principal characteristics may be derived; this similarity becomes even more apparent when the two are placed in juxtaposition, as in the episode of the journey.

As a member of the devil class, the Pooka is endowed with magic powers. Like Finn MacCool, he uses his thumb to set those powers in motion. By making a magic pass in the air he wakens 'the beetles and the maggots and the other evil creeping things that were slumbering throughout the forest under the flat of great stones' (p.145). The Pooka has a tail, a club-foot and very sharp nails. He is often to be found uttering maledictions. He enjoys chess and plays it with skill. His wife is thin, black and smelly and possibly a very clever kangaroo, capable of disguising that fact by shaving the fur off her legs and so passing as a woman. In spite of his evil tendencies, the Pooka is courteous, well-dressed and clever.

The Good Fairy is quite different. He has no body, for he is like 'a point in Euclid, having position but no mass', yet he has a voice which is

> sweeter by far than the tinkle and clap of a waterfall and brighter than the first shaft of day.   (p.146)

He is far more educated than the Pooka, as he reveals in his questions to Jem Casey when they meet.

> Poetry is a thing I am very fond of, said the Good Fairy. I always make a point of following the works of Mr Eliot and Mr Lewis and Mr Devlin. A good pome is a tonic. Was your pome on the subject of flowers, Mr Casey? Wordsworth was a great man for flowers.   (p.170)

The episode of the journey through the forest is full of the elements of folk-story. It contains formalised exchanges, an awareness of the significance of names and magic numbers, and the motif where good and evil powers fight for control of the newly-born child. The Pooka expects to be in constant contact with the unseen because he deliberately refrains from mixing too much with the seen world. In this aim he is curiously similar to all the characters in the book who seek to escape to the unseen world through drunkenness or through sleep. The narrator and Trellis both sleep a good deal, and Michael Byrne, too, recommends sleep very highly.

> What is wrong with Cryan and most people, said Byrne, is that they do not spend sufficient time in bed. When a man sleeps he is steeped and lost in a limp toneless happiness; awake he is restive, tortured by his body and the illusion of existence.   (p.137)

In order to escape the illusion of existence, many of the characters turn to the reality of illusion or dream, or imagination. The Pooka is quite aware of the separation between reality and phantasy, as he explains to the Good Fairy:

> On account of the fact, he said gentlemanly, that I have at all times purposely refrained from an exhaustive exercise of my faculty of vision and my power of optical inspection (I refer now to things perfectly palpable and discernible — the coming of dawn across the mountains is one example and the curious conduct of owls and bats in strong moonlight is another), I had expected (foolishly, perhaps), that I should be able to see quite clearly things that are normally not visible at all as a compensation for my sparing inspection of the visible. It is for that reason that I am inclined to regard the phenomenon of a voice unsupported by a body (more especially at an hour that is acknowledged as inimical to phantasy) as a delusion.   (p.147)

As the Good Fairy tries to explain his particular mode of existence, which partakes half of the physical and half of the spiritual world, O'Brien seizes the opportunity to exploit comedy arising from man's inability to think in any but physical terms. This, strangely, is an inability shared by the Good Fairy himself. He tells the Pooka that he had no body and, consequently, no pockets. Nevertheless, he smokes cigarettes and is susceptible to bad smells, to being hurt, walked on, or even killed.

The conversation between the Pooka and the Good Fairy

becomes a 'multi-clause colloquy', each of the many subjects introduced being dealt with in turn within the scope of each successive paragraph. In conversation, the Pooka and the Good Fairy prove themselves to be casuistical verbal jugglers, capable of sustaining a conversation on the subject of the Good Fairy himself, the possible humanity of kangaroos, the subject of spiritual carnality, the relative importance and position of the good and bad numerals, the Pooka's name, the changing position of the Good Fairy, and how the Pooka manages to keep the number of his tails always even. The section is a comic *reductio*, a mockery of logic and of man's feeble attempt to discriminate and classify, as well as having important thematic connections with the rest of the book. In particular the problem of what happens if an angel should mate with a human is discussed at some length.

> Even if it were desirable, replied the Good Fairy, angelic or spiritual carnality is not easy and in any case the offspring would be severely handicapped by being half-flesh and half-spirit, a very baffling and neutralising assortment of fractions since the two elements are forever at variance.
>
> (p.149)

The arguments which follow, on the benefits of increasing spirit or body in further offspring, culminate with the suggestion that

> The spectacle of an unmarried mother with a houseful of adult and imperceptible angels is not really the extravagance that it would first appear to be. As an alternative to the commonplace family, the proposition is by no means unattractive because the saving in clothes and doctors' bills would be unconscionable and the science of shop-lifting could be practised with such earnestness as would be compatible with the attainment and maintenance of a life of comfort and culture.
>
> (p.150)

The argument bears a notable relationship with that proposal for aestho-autogamy, a process which is quite similar in that it joins physical presence with imaginative reality and could result in a houseful of old-age pensioners ready to draw their pensions and support their creator-parent. Both proposals join the physical with the immaterial, and in so doing they raise questions, not merely about the nature of the 'reality' of fictional characters, but about the conflicting nature of man himself. Man is, O'Brien says, half flesh and half spirit, and thus 'a baffling and neutralising assortment' forever at variance with himself and wandering in a puzzled fashion between the two worlds in which the different elements of his being are at home. This is not argued in the book; it is merely implied and then rendered comic by the implied association between the Good Fairy and the Holy Spirit which arises as the Good Fairy discusses, and dismisses as impractical, the possibility of union between an angel and a woman. The subject of mystical conception is further discussed in connection with aestho-autogamy. Sheila Lamont, the heroine of a fiction, was raped by her author and lived to produce a son. The narrator experienced difficulty in describing Orlick, an 'offspring of the quasi-illusory type'.

> It may be usefully mentioned here that I had carefully considered giving an outward indication of the son's semi-humanity by furnishing him with only the half of a body. Here I encountered further difficulties. If given the upper half only, it would be necessary to provide a sedan-chair or litter with at least two runners or scullion-boys to operate it. The obtrusion of two further characters would lead to complications, the extent of which could not be foreseen. On the other hand, to provide merely the lower half, *videlicet,* the legs and lumber region, would be to narrow unduly the validity of the son and confine his activities virtually to walking, running, kneeling and kicking football. For that reason I decided ultimately to make no outward distinction and thus avoided any charge that my work was somewhat far-fetched.   (p.207)[58]

This difficulty is not very far from the Good Fairy's agonised speculations or from the far more profound implied question on the nature of man.

> An act of quasi-angelic carnality on the part of such issue would probably result in further offspring consisting in composition of a half caro plus half the sum of a half and

half caro and spiritus, that is three-quarters caro and a
quarter spiritus.   (p.149)

O'Brien is at pains to explain that the idea of spiritual-
physical union and conception is a commonplace in the history
of man.

Aestho-autogamy with one unknown quantity on the male
side, Mr Trellis told me in conversation, has long been a
commonplace. For fully five centuries in all parts of the
world epileptic slavies have been pleading it in extenuation
of uncalled-for fecundity.   (p.55)

He even gives us an example of such a plea in one of the
obsessive questions in *The Athenian Oracle.*

Whether it be poffible for a woman fo carnally to know a
Man in her fleep fo as to conceive, for I am fure that this
and no other way was I got with Child.   (p.144)

The questioning about the interrelationship of *caro* and
spiritus, or imagination (mind-spirit) and reality (body-
world), has run throughout the whole book. The balance of
each element is different in the various sections of the book,
but the association is most evident in the Pooka section. The
Pooka's huge body thrusts itself through the mythical forest,
accompanied by a bodiless fairy who has only a voice. The
Pooka, large and clumsy as he is, nevertheless possesses an
active mind and a conscience, while the Good Fairy constantly
behaves as if he had a body. O'Brien thus points to the
difficulty of distinguishing and demarcating the two elements,
as he had earlier realised that perception was as conceptual as
it was sensory and that a character envisioned in the mind
often had as much reality as one seen in the street.

As the Pooka and the Good Fairy travel on their way to the
Red Swan Inn they meet the other characters of legend and
folk story who have appeared earlier in the book. First they
meet Shorty Andrews and Slug Willard who are searching for
a lost steer but who decide to join them on their journey to
Orlick's birth (that point at which all the speculation about
body-imagination will come to fruition). The world through
which they travel is abundant and overflowing with strange,
exotic plants.

The travellers then scattered apart for a bit about the wilderness of the undergrowth till they had filled their pockets with fruits and sorrels and studded acorns, the produce of the yamboo and the blooms of the yulan, blood-gutted berries and wrinkled cresses, branches of juice-slimed sloes, whortles and plums and varied mast, the speckled eggs from the nests of daws. (p.167)

Next they encounter Jem Casey, out of place, a working man in the middle of a forest, but temporarily united to the landscape around him by virtue of the language which unites him with King Sweeny, the nature poet, whose true environment this wilderness is. Finally they meet Sweeny himself, still making lays in the middle of a yew.

The journey possesses the conventional features of any symbolic journey. It is one which faces characters with situations which reveal their true qualities. Shorty Andrews is seen to be tough and violent. Jem Casey has a poet's understanding of another poet. The Good Fairy is transformed. He is seen to be aggresive, testy, snobbish and unchristian. It is the Pooka and Jem Casey who show the human response to the wounded Sweeny. The journey of the Pooka, the Good Fairy, Shorty and Slug, Jem Casey and Sweeny proceeds through a land overflowing with riches while they sing the songs of many cultures. Having arrived at the Red Swan, they play poker, a game in which the Pooka wins control over the soul of Orlick because the Good Fairy has cheated.

The journey of these characters is the central element of fantasy in *At Swim*. On this level the book is mythic. It is peopled with the creations of epic and folk-tale, sharing all the characteristics of the latter form; as K. H. Jackson puts it:

In this world any supernatural event may occur without incongruity because . . . that distinction between natural and supernatural which is the consequence of civilised thought has not yet been clearly drawn.[59]

At Swim, with its fairies and devils, ancient kings, the God-big Finn, cowboys and poets, sets out to create a world of imagination, where there is, as the theory of aestho-autogamy had postulated, no distinction between reality and imagination. As the characters meet together to play cards or walk through a world of wild nature to an inn that is at once in the centre of Dublin and at the heart of the wild wood, they transcend all the boundaries of time and place. Even when the style of folk-tale is transferred to what had hitherto been a realistic level of the book, that level takes on the characteristics of folklore. Trellis can thus be flying through the air at one moment, or uttering melodious and honeyed Irish as the Pooka torments him. At another moment, in a similar wild wood, he can meet Shanahan, Lamont and Furriskey trans-figured by the magic of Orlick's description of them. Again he can find himself on trial, one of his accusers being a talking cow. At this level, *At Swim* is close to the spirit of James Stephens's fantasy *The Crock of Gold,* and like all fantasy it asks fundamental questions about the nature of the universe and the human's perception of it and his own nature.

In the epilogue to their book *Celtic Heritage,* Alwyn and Brinley Rees write about myth in words that make it clear that O'Brien's vision is one that is directly derived from some of the characteristics of Celtic literature.

> In diverse ways myth and ritual loosen the grip of the temporal world upon the human spirit. Under the spell of the story-teller's art, the range of what is possible in this world is transcended: the world of magic becomes a present reality and the world of every-day is deprived of its uniqueness and universality. The story-teller like the juggler and the illusionist, by convincingly actualising the im-possible, renders the actual world less real. When the spell if over, the hearer 'comes back to earth', but the earth now is not quite so solid as it was before, the cadence of its time is less oppressive and its laws have only a relative validity . . . Not only is myth not bounded by the laws of nature, it transcends the limitations of common sense.[60]

It has been argued that Celtic literature as a whole is dominated by a particular cast of mind—one that expresses itself primarily in the terms and according to the implications of its oral literature. The Celtic imagination sees the com position and actual retelling of a tale or poem as a mythic almost religious, act. Celtic literature is concrete, lyric, non speculative and dominated by a mythopoeic point of view. There is little distinction in it between the natural and the supernatural: magic is seen as ever-present, mingling without contradiction with everyday reality. Past and present, the passage of time itself, were not necessarily distinguished.[61] If this can be accepted, it is clear that O'Brien's vision in *At Swim* (and at the starting point of *The Third Policeman*) is heavily influenced by this mode of perception.

It is intriguing to speculate that one of the elements of Irish myth may provide the overall model for the book. When the Good Fairy says 'Counterpoint is an odd number and it is a great art that can make a fifth excellence from four futilities', he directs our attention to the enormous number of references to significant numbers in *At Swim*. Three, five and nine seem to be particularly important. The book ends with a three, 'Goodbye, Goodbye, Goodbye', a trinity of farewell, but it is possible that five is, as the Good Fairy suggests, the more important number. There are four narrative levels in *At Swim*. Four, in Celtic numerology, is often the symbol for perfection. Yet Alwyn and Brinley Rees point out that there is a way in which each even number is not felt to be complete without the addition of a further unit. As the Pooka and Good Fairy argue that each number calls forth the next number, so too in Celtic numerology we find that four usually implies a hidden fifth. For example, if there are four directions in the world, the missing fifth is the centre of the world. We are told that 'Truth is an odd number,' so if the missing unit makes the original number an odd one, it must represent truth, unity and centrality. The additional numeral can also be the wild number which, while creating unity, also allows the possibility for an alien and free element to enter in. The fifth narrative level in *At Swim* is that of Finn, the Pooka and Shanahan. It is that level at which can be found the unifying symbols for the structure of the book: the idea of counterpoint, and that of the book-web. Finn, Sweeny, the Pooka and Shanahan seem to be largely independent of any of the narrators in the book. Their narratives work at a more primordial, mythic level. But if this level unifies many of the strands of the web by providing the alternative vision to realism, it also represents the 'wild' element. In characteristic manner, O'Brien uses this mythic aspect to undercut his own stress on the importance of the imagination. If myth is connected in *At Swim* with a trance-like or dream state which is withdrawn from the perception of the everyday world, it is clearly seen that there are dangers in that state.

The narrator is aware of these dangers. After Michael Byrne has finished his speech in praise of sleep, the narrator points out that Trellis is spending so much of his time asleep that he is losing control over the creatures his imagination had created, and he adds: 'There is a moral in that.' (p.139)

The moral of Trellis's punishment is that imagination is powerful and must not be uncontrolled. The Circle N story had demonstrated that imagination needed its own world in which to survive. The juxtaposition of a fantasy world of heroism and great acts with the world of law and social interdependence, had led to the degradation of the postulates of both worlds. In fact, all O'Brien's heroes in *At Swim* are fallen heroes.

Finn MacCool, who was 'a better man than God' was degraded to the position of playing father to a servant girl, living in a room of a Dublin pub, despised as 'Mr Storybook' by his uncomprehending companions. O'Brien's brother Ciarán had written a story called 'The Return of Finn' in *Comhthrom Féinne* in which Finn, returned to modern Ireland, was living in a cheap boarding-house in Rathmines, vainly trying to convince the inhabitants of his real identity, sitting like a 'human spider in the web of his fine thoughts', at length deciding to draw the old-age pension.[62] Finn's experiences are, then, a paradigm of the fate of the Celtic imagination in modern Ireland.

Sweeny falls from his tree into modern Ireland where he ends up playing poker in a room of a pub, his characteristic modes of expression a comic anachronism. The cowboys hunt for a steer in a forest or fight their battles in a built-up area. They are utterly degraded, for they are cowboys without horses, lost, and full of ignorant bravado. The Pooka, who was Puck, the goat god, is no longer the god of nature and of the irrational he had once been. His major characteristics are urbanity, conservatism and politeness. Unlike the Fianna who could run through Ireland without touching a twig, he crashes his way through the jungle, destroying everything in his path.

The heroes are fallen, unable to survive in the modern world. Writers are punished by rebellious characters who will no longer tolerate the liberated imagination but wish to impose the tyranny of fact and detail and require that all possible ends should be tied up.

The movement of the book is a dual one. On the one hand reality is undercut by juxtaposing it with imagination, but then, in its turn, imagination is degraded or punished, and is, because of the parodic and self-conscious nature of the book, seen as only one more artificial literary form.

Out of this dual movement and the basic juxtaposition of the worlds of reality and fantasy comes the resolution of the book. It is a resolution which asserts that the function of literature is a transfiguring and consolatory one which, nevertheless, looks at the most difficult questions about man's place in the universe, and that imaginative forms, if they can find a place in the modern world, are the most flexible forms to use. Even though the assumptions of imaginative literature are undercut, the emotional weight of the book is behind them. O'Brien, trained on the assumptions of the Gaelic poets, believed in the benefits of a complex and traditional technique where the conscious skill of the story-teller or poet was admired as much as the content of his stories or the apparent spontaneity or sincerity of his writing. For this reason, the awareness of the 'artificial' nature of all literary styles, including his preferred one, would not have worried O'Brien at all. The questions he would have put would have been about the flexibility, persuasiveness and appropriateness of any one style to the subject in hand. What angered him was the claim of proponents of one style, 'formal realism', that they alone were capable of representing the truth. O'Brien saw Joyce as one of the foremost practitioners of this style, and as a writer who could be faulted even on those occasions when he did turn to myth, for in doing so he rejected Gaelic models and chose Greek ones. For Daedalus flying triumphantly from his intricately wrought labryinth, or Icarus falling to his death, O'Brien substituted his own image, his own poetic counterpart, his own symbol of man's state.

Sweeny in the trees hears the sad baying as he sits listening on the branch, a huddle between the earth and heaven. (p. 316)

Sweeny is O'Brien's final unifying image. Sitting in the trees, 'a huddle between the earth and heaven', he represents man caught between reality and imagination, yet creating intricate and melodious evocations of the world about him to compensate for his loneliness, pain and the burden of consciousness.

4
Bicycles and Eternity:
The Third Policeman

The Third Policeman was begun sometime in 1939. It was finished, we know, by January 1940 when O'Nolan sent the manuscript to Patience Ross at A. M. Heath & Co. On 14 February O'Brien wrote to William Saroyan and told him:

> I've just finished another book. The only thing good about it is the plot and I've been wondering whether I could make a crazy . . . play out of it. When you get to the end of this book you realise that my hero or main character (he's a heel and a killer) has been dead throughout the book and that all the queer ghastly things which have been happening to him are happening in a sort of hell which he earned for the killing. Towards the end of the book (before you know he's dead) he manages to get back to his own house where he used to live with another man who helped in the original murder. Although he's been away three days, this other fellow is twenty years older and dies of fright when he sees the other lad standing in the door. Then the two of them walk back along the road to the hell place and start thro' all the same terrible adventures again, the first fellow being surprised and frightened at everything just as he was the first time and as if he'd never been through it before. It is made clear that this sort of thing goes on for ever — and there you are. It is supposed to be very funny but I don't know about that either . . . I think the idea of a man being dead all the time is pretty new. When you are writing about the world of the dead — and the damned — where none of the rules and laws (not even the law of gravity) holds good, there is any amount of scope for back-chat and funny cracks.[1]

The novel, when finished, was circulated in typescript

among O'Brien's friends in Dublin. According to Donagh MacDonagh,[2] it was lost in transit. What actually happened was that O'Brien sent it to Longmans, who had published *At Swim*. However, Longmans rejected the book. They wrote to A. M. Heath giving their reasons. Patience Ross, writing to O'Brien with the news, quoted them in her letter: 'We realise the author's ability but think that he should become less fantastic and in this new novel he is more so.'[3]

William Saroyan tried to have the book published in America using his own New York agents, Matson & Duggan. Harold Matson wrote to O'Brien and told him that he liked *Hell Goes Round and Round* (as it was then called) but was having little success in placing it. At one stage he lost the script and wrote to O'Brien asking for a replacement. This may have prompted the course of O'Brien's subsequent actions. *At Swim* had been a comparative failure, *The Third Policeman* had been rejected, and O'Brien was bitterly disappointed. He put the manuscript away out of sight and told everyone that it had been lost. Even after *At Swim* was reissued he did not attempt to retrieve it. He rewrote it as *The Dalkey Archive,* and the original manuscript was not published until after his death.

The Third Policeman must, however, be considered at this stage in my discussion of O'Brien's writing as it represents, in many ways, a continuation of some of the ideas expressed in *At Swim*.[4] O'Brien's own comment on it, 'It is supposed to be very funny but I don't know about that either,' expresses some of the strange quality of the book. It is, in parts, extremely amusing, but the overall impression is anything but funny. It could have allowed, as he said, scope for funny cracks but, in fact, there are comparatively few of these in a book which shows a fixity of purpose and clarity of theme which is surprising after the organised chaos of *At Swim*. It presents a vision which becomes steadily more horrifying. Its central concern is not, as in *At Swim,* with varying methods of presenting reality in fiction, but with reality viewed through the medium of scientific and philosophical concepts. This was a subject which had been preoccupying him for some time and would continue to do so long after *The Third Policeman* was put away.

O'Brien was well aware that the discoveries of modern scientists, particularly those of Einstein, had changed many ideas about the nature of the universe. In *Cruiskeen Lawn* he quotes a passage from A. N. Whitehead's *Science and the Modern World* in which the author describes his reactions to a proof of the validity of Einstein's theory.

> It was my good fortune to be present at the meeting of the Royal Society in London when the Astronomer Royal for England announced that the photographic plates of the famous eclipse, as measured by his colleagues in Greenwich Observatory, had verified the prediction of Einstein that rays of light are bent as they pass in the neighbourhood of the sun. The whole atmosphere of tense interest was exactly that of the Greek drama: we were the chorus commenting on the decree of destiny as disclosed in the development of a supreme incident. There was a dramatic quality in the very staging: the traditional ceremonial, and in the background the picture of Newton to remind us that the greatest of scientific generalisations was now, after more than two centuries, to receive its first modification.   (17 Dec. 1941)

Later on, O'Brien develops this idea further:

> 'There are less than a thousand people in the world who really understand the Einstein theory of relativity, and less than a 100 people who can discuss it intelligently.'
> This disturbing statement was made recently by Sir Arthur Eddington. It is nice news for those of us who have to fork out every year to maintain our grandiose university establishments. We have perhaps 30 or 40 well-paid savants whom we have always taken to know all about physics or mathematics or whatever kindred subject they profess. Now we are told that these people know nothing about Einstein's discoveries, and cannot make head or tail of his sums. What would we say if a similar situation obtained in relation to, say, plumbers? . . . whereas Einstein's discoveries entail the radical revision of conventional concepts of time, space and matter, and a person who undertakes to discourse on such subjects while ignorant of Einstein, must necessarily rely on premises shown to be inadmissable . . . It is now accepted everywhere without much show of reserve that the earth is a sphere, but these university professors I am talking about are still (in a relative sense) teaching their students that it is flat. That is a fair and perfect analogy, because there is

practically no limit to the mistakes you will make if the flatness of the earth is your fundamental *credo,* and you will fare no better if you choose to make pronouncements on the nature of the universe as if Einstein never existed.

(3 Aug. 1942)

Aware of the implications of these ideas, O'Brien saw in them a perfect situation for the exercise of his unique imagination, and presented, in the figure of the narrator, the ordinary man who is faced with scientific ideas which he can grasp only in an incoherent fashion and which seem to deny the validity of the world about him. When the 'Atomic Theory' has been explained to him by Sergeant Pluck, he remarks:

> The scene [around me] was real and incontrovertible and at variance with the talk of the Sergeant, but I knew that the Sergeant was talking the truth and if it was a question of taking my choice, it was possible that I would have to forego the reality of all the simple things my eyes were looking at.

(p.86)

He also presents de Selby, the savant,[5] whose 'wisdom' allows O'Brien full scope for the parody of pedantic learning and absurd philosophy he had used so often before. De Selby's philosophy is based on a number of inadmissible and comic premises such as that the earth, rather than being flat, is sausage-shaped.[6]

> The application of this conclusion to his theory that 'the earth is a sausage' is illuminating. He attributes the idea that the earth is spherical to the fact that human beings are continually moving in only one known direction (though convinced that they are free to move in any direction) and that this one direction is really around the circular circumference of an earth which is in fact sausage-shaped. It can scarcely be contested that if multi-directionality be admitted to be a fallacy, the sphericity of the earth is another fallacy that would inevitably follow from it. De Selby likens the position of a human on the earth to that of a man on a tight-wire who must continue walking along the wire or perish, being, however, free in all other respects. Movement in this restricted orbit results in the permanent

hallucination known conventionally as 'life' with its innumerable concomitant limitations, afflictions and anomalies. If a way can be found, says de Selby, of discovering the 'second direction', i.e. along the 'barrel' of the sausage, a world of entirely new sensation and experience will be open to humanity. New and unimaginable dimensions will supersede the present order, and the manifold 'unnecessaries' of 'one-directional' existence will disappear.   (pp.94-5)

Later in the book de Selby is reported as seeming to 'suggest that death is nearly always present when the new direction is discovered'. However, de Selby's premises and conclusions are inadmissable only in the normal world. They gain more validity while the narrator is undergoing his 'queer ghastly' adventures. We learn, at the end of the book, that these adventures and experiences have happened while he was dead and in hell, i.e. after he has found the 'second direction'. Some of this idea of the second direction, discoverable at death, was developed from the ideas of J. W. Dunne[7] in his books *An Experiment with Time* and *The Serial Universe,* both of which O'Brien quotes as a source.[8] Dunne puts forward the idea that death involves the continuation of the mind but on a different time scale which he calls 'time 2'. The mind, when it enters this different time scale, which is the 'fourth dimension' (a dimension which does not involve any kind of forward progression), wanders about in a daze and has to learn to control its focus of 'attention'. Otherwise its new world seems like the world of nightmare. Dunne says, in fact, that man, when he dreams, is entering this other dimension for a short time but in that brief moment lets his attention wander between 'time 1' (now) and 'time 2' (eternity). Just like a lost child he becomes confused and is 'glad to wake up and return to normal life, and he says that he had had a nightmare'.[9] The idea of death and nightmare as states with similar characteristics is important in *The Third Policeman.* The reader is unaware, until the end, that the main character is dead, so the world he finds himself in is presented as the real world, albeit a very strange corner of it. It seems, merely, as if his life has taken on a nightmarish quality.[10]

The plot is a development and variation of speculations like Dunne's, and its specific form is a result of parodying all speculation on the nature of life and death. It also continues and expands some ideas which were only suggested in *At Swim*. In that book the Pooka suspends the natural order so that Trellis can be punished by being tortured by 'phenomena which cannot be explained by any purely physical hypothesis'. The plot of *The Third Policeman* also deals with punishment. The unnamed narrator has killed old Philip Mathers and so is consigned to a hell of which the chief characteristic is that in it 'none of the rules and laws (not even the law of gravity) holds good'. He is sent to this kind of hell because he had committed a crime in order to gain money. The money was to be spent on producing a definitive edition of the works of de Selby. For de Selby, then, he commits his first and greatest crime. His punishment is fitting in that he is sent to a world where de Selby's mad ideas hold sway. De Selby had announced:

> Human existence being an hallucination containing in itself the secondary hallucinations of day and night (the latter an insanitary condition of the atmosphere due to accretions of black air) it ill becomes any man of sense to be concerned at the illusory approach of the supreme hallucination known as death.   (Epigraph)

In the narrator's world human existence does indeed become an hallucination: he is dead but is under the illusion that he is still living. Day and night and the passage of time also become illusory processes since the hero thinks he has been away from home for three days but, in fact, twenty years have elapsed.

For O'Brien's purpose, however, it is important that the reader should not know that this is a hell earned for the crime until the end, for this would make the story a fantasy rather than what seems to be, as it is read, a picture of dislocated reality. O'Brien goes to considerable lengths to make the reality seem convincing, though he does give many clues as to the true state of affairs, both at the moment of death and in the constant references to a negative state throughout the book. The choice of a first-person narrator serves to make the reader identify with the fear and bewilderment of the narrator as he goes through his strange experience. The narrator tells us in Chapter 1 of his childhood and of his life before the murder, but the detail is deliberately hazy ('I was born a long time ago') so that the dislocation of time and place which occur after he has tried to find the black cash-box do not seem quite as odd as they would have if he had not led such a strange life beforehand. His obsession with the ideas of de Selby make his transition to a universe where those ideas are acceptable seem a natural development. While he is in hell he constantly emphasises the normality of the natural surroundings, in spite of the strange phenomena which cast doubt on the very existence of those surroundings. However, the main factor which makes his experiences more normal is the presence in them of the policemen. O'Brien seems convinced that, no matter what magic powers are attributed to them, the sight and presence of huge policemen must imply security and order.[11] These consoling forces combine to add to the illusion that the hero has just walked a little way down the road to an odd corner of the parish and that if he can once reach home again, everything will be all right.

The first sentence points to death and to bicycles as central themes in the rest of the book.

> Not everybody knows how I killed old Philip Mathers, smashing his jaw in with my spade; but first it is better to speak of my friendship with John Divney because it was he who first knocked old Mathers down by giving him a great blow in the neck with a special bicycle-pump which he manufactured himself out of a hollow iron bar.   (p.7)

The references to death are continued in the discussion on de Selby's attitude to houses. De Selby defines a house as 'a large coffin', 'a warren' and 'a box'. His thoughts on the subject are our first introduction to his philosophy, and they reveal it as, essentially, nonsense. It is nonsense which has thematic significance, however, since all his reported thoughts throughout the book act as a sort of mocking chorus to the main action. Here the narrator's recollection of de Selby's ideas on houses were prompted by his approach to Mathers' house to recover the black box. Mathers' house is about to become his coffin, and later, with Policeman Fox, he will find it to be a warren of hidden corridors and rooms. Already, then, de Selby is beginning to be relevant.

At the moment of the narrator's death, which marks the beginning of the real substance of the book, there are several clues, in his own unaware account, as to his true state. He tells us that 'all my senses were bewildered all at once and could give me no explanation'. Neither can they give him any explanation for the strange occurrences of the rest of the book. His physical appearance closely resembles a state of death.

> My eyes remained open for a long time without a wink,
> glazed and almost sightless.   (p.23)

He feels that the earth may have stood still for a moment, that time may have been interfered with, daylight altered and the density and temperature of the air changed in some way. He experiences a strange interval which is difficult to describe in known words, except that 'Years or minutes could be swallowed up with equal ease in that indescribable and un-accountable interval.' He is describing a state of nothingness in which only his mind continues but in which all the laws and defining qualities of his world are changed. Known words could not convey it since they have reference to a different state of existence.

> The dusty floor was like nothingness beneath me, and my
> whole body dissolved away, leaving me existing only in the
> stupid spellbound gaze.   (p.24)

At this point he is confronted by the figure of the man he had murdered. When he hears Mathers' cough, 'soft and natural yet more disturbing than sound that could ever come upon the human ear', he has crossed over into the other world and his comments on his reactions to the cough are a confirmation of his new state.

> That I did not die of fright was due, I think, to two things,
> the fact that my senses were already disarranged and able to
> interpret to me only gradually what they had perceived, and
> also the fact that the utterance of the cough seemed to bring
> with it some more awful alteration in everything, just as if it
> had held the universe standing still for an instant,
> suspending the planets in their courses, halting the sun and
> holding in mid-air any falling thing the earth was pulling
> towards it.   (p.23)

At this moment he knows, in a confused way, that the laws of the universe have been overturned. He thinks, however, that this state of affairs is to be only temporary. In fact, it is to continue throughout the book and he is tormented and bewildered by expecting events and explanations to conform to the pattern he has known.

At this moment of entry into hell he notices many things which are to become motifs in the book. He sees the horror of Mathers' eyes and terrifies himself with speculations about them.

> Looking at them I got the feeling that they were not genuine eyes at all but mechanical dummies animated by electricity or the like, with a tiny pinhole in the centre of the 'pupil' through which the real eye gazed out secretively and with great coldness. Such a conception, possibly with no foundations at all in fact, disturbed me agonisingly and gave rise in my mind to interminable speculations as to the colour and quality of the real eye and as to whether, indeed, it was real at all or merely another dummy with its pinhole on the same plane as the first one so that the real eye, possibly behind thousands of these absurd disguises, gazed out through a barrel of serried peep-holes.   (pp.24-5)

His speculations, which he admits may have no foundation in fact, are, nevertheless, frightening. The image of the eye hiding behind many peepholes leads to speculations about what is real and unreal, and the image is very similar to that of all the boxes, one within the other, which create a horrified response in the narrator later in the book.[12] He is now in a situation where his reason can give him no assistance, where he knows Mathers is dead and yet sees him sitting alive before him. This pattern is to continue throughout the book. Reason is overthrown and a coherent type of unreason takes its place. The narrator has to accept with his senses what his reason tells him is impossible. He does not know whether he is in the middle of a nightmare but decides in any case that

> the best thing to do was to believe what my eyes were looking at rather than to place my trust in a memory. (p.26)

Even this proves to be only a temporary solution for, from this point on, the book develops with a consistent pattern of horrifying experience followed by the reassertion of sanity through evocation of ordinary scenes or actions. When he is speaking to Mathers the normal sound of his voice helps to calm him down, and he is further calmed by the journey to the police barracks which he begins next day. He is totally unaware that he is dead and emphasises this fact by his constant references to his fear of death. Joe (his soul, who is remarkably like the Good Fairy) tells him that he will be dead if his soul leaves him, and the threat to his life from the policemen and Martin Finnucane go a long way towards convincing the reader that he is certainly alive. It is clear that he has had a terrible experience and that this has worked some change in his state. He has discovered the existence of his soul, he has forgotten his name, and his personality seems to be divided into two sections, each working independently of the other. He describes himself as

> thinking my own thoughts with the front of my brain, and at the same time taking pleasure with the back part in the great and widespread finery of the morning.   (p.38)

This great and widespread beauty of the morning is the most reassuring fact of all. The narrator expresses a belief in the permanence and validity of the world about him. That, at least, is something which can be comprehended and relied on.

> The day was brand new and the ditch was feathery. I lay back unstintingly, stunned with the sun. I felt a million little influences in my nostril, hay-smells, grass-smells, odours from distant flowers, the reassuring unmistakability of the abiding earth beneath my head.   (p.42)

There are some discordant elements in this near paradise. There is something strange about the scene: it is almost too perfect, too well arranged.[13] The road is only a few miles from where he has lived but it is completely unfamiliar. The night before, when he left home, it had been winter; now it is high summer.[14] Yet he ignores these doubts and is reassured by the normality, the order and the beauty of the scene. It is only in the world of ideas, explanations and concepts that any confusion arises because these explanations with their seemingly convincing logic are at odds with the natural world. The hell undergone by the hero is to have a mind which clings to a faith in the natural universe and the experiential laws it seems to embody, but which also believes in the truth of

concepts which are totally opposed to that belief. For the
moment none of these doubts assail him and his feeling of
exhilaration and well-being continues (with only a brief set-
back in the meeting with Martin Finnucane and his gloomy
account of life) until he reaches the barracks.

During his journey he muses in a condescending way on de
Selby's theory that 'a journey is an hallucination'.[15] This
theory, says the hero

> seems to discount the testimony of human experience and is
> at variance with everything I have learnt myself on many a
> country walk.   (p.50)

Indeed, most of the theories which he is to encounter in this
world will discount the testimony of human experience, but
his meeting with Mathers or even with the chaotic logic of
Martin Finnucane has not yet convinced him that this is to be
a general rule. Here, his mockery of de Selby, whose work is to
gradually gain the status of a vision of this very universe, is a
mark of too much confidence in his own reason.

> Human existence de Selby has defined as 'a succession of
> static experiences each infinitely brief', a conception which
> he is said to have arrived at from examining some old
> cinematograph films which belonged probably to his
> nephew. From this premise he discounts the reality or truth
> of any progression or serialism in life, denies that time can
> pass as such in the accepted sense and attributes to
> hallucinations the commonly experienced sensation of
> progression as, for instance, in journeying from one place to
> another, or even 'living'.   (p.50)

The narrator's comments on this illustrate quite clearly that he
has not yet grasped any of the contradictory realities of this
world. He has not yet comprehended that the defining
limits of normal reality like time, motion and gravity are
meaningless here, that whereas de Selby's assertion that
motion is an illusion was nonsensical before, now it has
become truth. The narrator is not walking down a road which
leads from Mathers' house to a police barracks, even though
he thinks he is. His journey is, therefore, an illusion and to
insist that it is not is to engage the mind in the terror of
uncertainty. Yet the narrator says:

> It is a curious enigma that so great a mind would question the most obvious realities and object to things scientifically demonstrated (such as the sequence of day and night) while believing absolutely in his own fantastic explanations of the same phenomena. (p.52)

The point is, of course, that 'the most obvious realities' are open to question here, and are found to be false, while the most 'fantastic explanations' like that of the 'Atomic Theory' can be scientifically demonstrated and will have to be believed.

The narrator's confidence that his mind is superior to de Selby's and that he can be reassured by the 'abiding earth' is abruptly shattered when he arrives at the police barracks.

> As I came round the bend of the road an extraordinary spectacle was presented to me. About a hundred yards away on the left-hand side was a house which astonished me. It looked as if it were painted like an advertisement on a board on the roadside and indeed very poorly painted. It looked completely false and unconvincing. It did not seem to have any depth or breadth and looked as if it would not deceive a child. That was not in itself sufficient to surprise me because I had seen pictures and notices by the roadside before. What bewildered me was the sure knowledge deeply-rooted in my mind, that this was the house I was looking for and that there were people inside it. I had no doubt at all that it was the barracks of the policeman. I had never seen with my eyes ever in my life before anything so appalling and my gaze faltered about the thing uncomprehendingly as if at least one of the customary dimensions was missing, leaving no meaning in the remainder. (pp.52-3)

His horror arises from the apparent lack of perspective in the building, from the fact that the totality of his expectations have been disrupted. It arises too from the fact that this time he cannot believe his eyes which tell him that the building is two-dimensional; instead he has to believe his mind which tells him that there are people in it. His former confidence is wiped away and he is full of fear. He can find the barracks with his 'simple senses' but must pretend to himself that he understands what he sees.

When he enters the barracks and meets Sergeant Pluck his sense of disquiet is not immediately removed since, although the Sergeant seems, in his various parts, to be normal enough, the totality of those parts gives an air of unnaturalness. No matter how familiar the policemen become, they are still frightening and somewhat inhuman. At first the Sergeant seems merely eccentric, obsessed with the subjects of teeth and bicycles, but as the story progresses he comes to stand more and more for the processes of illogic. His seemingly nonsensical speech and misuse of language are nevertheless a valid expression of the laws of his universe. He moves through it ponderously but with security, able to accept without question its contradictory nature. His obsession with bicycles is at first amusing but his inability to think in any other terms eventually drives the narrator to distraction. However, he feels superior to the Sergeant and recovers confidence when he thinks that he can fool him. He speaks mockingly of the Sergeant's indication that time in this world does not follow the normal rules: 'This is not today, this is yesterday'. (p.60) He must accept, however, that his own willingness to believe what his eyes see is not a universal habit, for the Sergeant is quite willing to believe that what he sees in front of him is not there at all. If the narrator has no name, he does not exist, even if he can be touched and seen. This is the reversal of the empirical method.

The narrator's education in the invalidity of empiricism is continued in his interview with Policeman MacCruiskeen, whose defining characteristic is his use of convoluted and complicated language. De Selby's ideas once again provide an introduction to this scene. De Selby's investigations into the nature of time and eternity by a system of mirrors provide a parallel to the revelations in MacCruiskeen's room, and bear a very close resemblance to some kinds of speculation which currently pass as philosophical thought. As the idea is presented here, it is a travesty of logic, but it is not at all clear where logic ends and nonsense begins.

If a man stands before a mirror and sees in it his reflection what he sees is not a true reproduction of himself but a

picture of himself when he was a younger man. De Selby's
explanation of this phenomenon is quite simple. Light, as
he points out truly enough, has an ascertained and finite
rate of travel. Hence before the reflection of any object in a
mirror can be said to be accomplished, it is necessary that
rays of light should first strike the object and subsequently
impinge on the glass, to be thrown back again to the
object—to the eyes of a man, for instance. There is
therefore an appreciable and calculable interval of time
between the throwing by a man of a glance at his own face
and the registration of the reflected image in his eye.

So far, one may say, so good. Whether this idea is right or
wrong, the amount of time involved is so negligible that few
reasonable people would argue the point. But de Selby, ever
loath to leave well enough alone, insists on reflecting the
first reflection in a further mirror and professing to detect
minute changes in this second image. Ultimately he constructed the familiar arrangement of parallel mirrors,[16]
each reflecting diminishing images of an interposed object
indefinitely.[17] The interposed object in this case was de
Selby's own face and this he claims to have studied
backwards through an infinity of reflections by means of 'a
powerful glass'. What he states to have seen through his
glass is astonishing. He claims to have noticed a growing
youthfulness in the reflections of his face according as they
receded, the most distant of them—too tiny to be visible to
the naked eye—being the face of a beardless boy of twelve,
and, to use his own words, 'a countenance of singular
beauty and nobility'. He did not succed in pursuing the
matter back to the cradle 'owing to the curvature of the
earth and the limitations of the telescope'.   (pp.64-5)

De Selby takes a fact about the speed of light and, leaving out
of consideration other important aspects, carries it to a
conclusion which is completely illogical but which has all the
trappings of logic and as much detail as is necessary to confuse
the issue completely. The humour of the account lies in this
parody of the method and, of course, in the end result of the
whole elaborate experiment. O'Brien here is illustrating the
type of Irish humour which depends for its effect on a close
connection between the sublime and the ridiculous and on

the results of 'thinking too closely' about an imperfectly understood law. The narrator is aware that de Selby's conclusions are invalid and scornfully dismisses them. Yet he is immediately forced to face a situation in which premises are tested and conclusions reached in a manner as in admissible as de Selby's. The conclusions arrived at in this way, though nonsensical to a rational mind, are true and can be proved so by reference to the senses. MacCruiskeen's spear stings the narrator and makes him bleed, even though he cannot see its point. His attempt to visualise or understand the invisibility of the point leads to complete bewilderment.

> Now the proper sharp part is so thin that nobody could see it no matter what light is on it or what eye is looking. About an inch from the end it is so sharp that sometimes—late at night or on a soft bad day especially— you cannot think of it or try to make it the subject of a little idea because you will hurt your box with the excruciation of it.   (p.68)

The point of the spear is like many forces in physics. It must be there because it has effect, so even if it can never be seen or measured, its presence must be inferred in order to explain those effects. O'Brien is once again mocking the inability of the human mind, tied to the need to visualise, to embody or fully understand its own rationalisations. The narrator can no more understand the invisibility of the spear than the cowboys in *At Swim* can understand how the Good Fairy can be 'like a point in Euclid, having position but no mass'. Where the mind cannot translate mental concepts into physical images, it becomes bewildered. Sometimes the narrator is bewildered because he cannot believe his eyes; here he is bewildered because he cannot believe his mind. He can see the effect of the spear but cannot understand or conceive the spear itself since this is an understanding that excludes the senses. The situation is confused by the fact that although MacCruiskeen has made the spear and knows what it can do, he sometimes has his own doubts about its existence.

> It is so thin that maybe it does not exist at all and you could spend half an hour trying to think about it and you could put no thought around it in the end. The beginning part of the inch is thicker than the last part and is nearly there for a

fact but I don't think it is if it is my private opinion that you
are anxious to enlist.   (pp.68–9)

The narrator tries desperately to understand this, but it is
beyond his comprehension. He is faced with what is, in his
terms, the impossible and the unknowable, a quasi-object
which *almost* exists and which is an inch long and thicker at
one part of the non-existent or nearly existent point than it is
at another.

This conversation takes place in the middle of guessing
games and the continuing obsession with bicycles which
MacCruiskeen shares with the Sergeant. It remains comic
until MacCruiskeen shows his chests to the narrator. As each
one is revealed within the other but precisely similar in every
detail, the narrator becomes more and more frightened and
incoherent. All pretence of even trying to understand, or of
attempting to reconcile what his eyes see and his brain
comprehends, vanishes.

> 'Those chests', I said, 'are so like one another that I do not
> believe they are there at all because that is a simpler thing
> to believe than the contrary. Nevertheless the two of them
> are the most wonderful two things I have ever seen.'   (p.72)

At this stage he is beginning to talk like the policeman, but the
torture continues in that he must persevere in trying to make
sense out of the world, must realise that he is unable to do it,
must talk nonsense and yet be aware that it is nonsense.

> It was so faultless and delightful that it reminded me
> forcibly, strange and foolish as it may seem, of something I
> did not understand and had never even heard of.   (p.72)

The chests, like the original view of the barracks, become
'invested with some crazy perspective'. Eventually they become
so small that they disappear altogether and, like the spear,
their presence must become almost a matter of faith. At this
point the narrator panics.

> At this point I became afraid. What he was doing was no
> longer wonderful but terrible. I shut my eyes and prayed
> that he would stop while still doing things that were at least
> possible for a man to do.   (p.73)

But MacCruiskeen does not stop. He goes on producing chests that are completely invisible. The supreme incongruity of this scene is a hallmark of O'Brien's comic method; the effect is attained by his presentation of its most horrifying elements combined with the most trivial and ordinary concerns. Thus MacCruiskeen, the demonic manufacturer of these impossible chests, worries that he will need 'spectacles with gold ear-claws' to enable him to read the fine print on official forms. As always, it is the superfluous additional detail which both adds the final touch of horror and relieves the scene during its blacker moments by returning the narrator, and the reader, to the world of normal, mundane concern. The narrator whistles 'The Corncrake Plays the Bagpipes' to reassure himself, as he did with Mathers, with normal human noises and then goes off with the Sergeant in pursuit of a lost bicycle.

The dislocation of reality which has taken place is forgotten once again in a pleasant walk and in trivial conversation about the merits, demerits and analogues of the three-speed gear. After the terrifying experience with MacCruiskeen, the Sergeant's obsession with bicycles seems like a pleasant oddity until he mysteriously finds the lost bicycle with a technique that seems to owe nothing to forensic science. The narrator asks him to explain how he did this because, as he admits,

> I find it is a great strain for me to believe what I see, and I am becoming afraid occasionally to look at some things in case they would have to be believed.   (p.82)

In answer to this, the Sergeant confuses him still further by explaining to him the rules and implications of the 'Atomic Theory'. According to the Sergeant, if you take the idea that all things are composed of atoms to its logical conclusion you have to recognise that bicycles are becoming people and people bicycles.[18] Nothing else will explain why men lean against the wall on one elbow and why crumbs are found at the wheels of bicycles. Apart from the inherent hilarity of the extension of this idea to the sexual morals of the parish, it illustrates a further step in the narrator's education in unreason. By now he has lost faith in the logical approach to such an extent that he feels that any confusing statement must be a wise one.

'Your talk', I said, 'is surely the handiwork of wisdom because not a word of it do I understand.'   (p.84)

The Sergeant, himself, is a little puzzled by the theory, since atomics can only be solved by algebra, a study in which you can prove things that you do not really believe. Joe, the hero's soul, provides the obvious comment at this stage.

'Apparently there is no limit,' Joe remarked. 'Anything can be said in this place and it will be true and will have to be believed.'   (p.86)

The series of shocks which the narrator receives are only possible in a world without limits, where *everything* is possible. He knows at this stage that the thing from which he derives his sense of order, the 'real and incontrovertible scene' around him, must be discarded if the chaotic physical laws advanced by the Sergeant and verified by MacCruiskeen's artifacts and Gilhaney's strange behaviour are to be accepted as truth. As a character who has always felt that the speculations of de Selby were important and that the world must be explicable in conceptual terms, he must accept logic and believe in the scientific method, no matter how chaotic seem to be the conclusions it produces and how much these are at variance with the other reality he recognises with the other, separate, part of his brain — the reality of the external world. Having come to the realisation that he may have to 'forego the reality of all the simple things' his eyes were looking at, he returns to the barracks. Once there, he receives a 'severe shock' which sets him thinking of de Selby, who regards all the saliencies of existence, bereavement, death, old age and sin as 'unnecessary'. This conclusion is the direct result of de Selby's theory that the earth is 'sausage-shaped'. The narrator is not sure whether this idea is a joke but recognises that de Selby argued it seriously enough. This comment, perhaps, expresses much of O'Brien's feeling about intellectualism (much attacked in *Cruiskeen Lawn).* The narrator remarks about de Selby:

The humanising urbanity of his work has always seemed to me to be enhanced rather than vitiated by the chance obtrusion here and there of his minor failings, all the more pathetic because he regarded some of them as pinnacles of

his intellectual prowess rather than indications of his frailty
as a human being.   (p.92)

One could assume from O'Brien's attack on intellectualised
abstraction in *Cruiskeen Lawn* that he, like the narrator,
thought that what men often vaunted as the height of
intellectual prowess was, in fact, an indication of the frailty of
the human mind.[19] De Selby sets up elaborate experiments to
prove that things are quite other than they seem. Some
philosophers actually do this, and their effort is regarded as
noble. O'Brien, however, mocks this idea by showing how de
Selby's experiments are ludicrous because he has not
understood the very laws he is examining. De Selby by a
process of reasoning and assumption decides that man can
move in only one direction and then tries to find the other
direction. His search is made ridiculous by being recounted in
detail.

> He seems to have thought at one time that gravitation was
> the 'jailer' of humanity, keeping it on the one-directional
> line of oblivion, and that ultimate freedom lay in some
> upward direction. He examined aviation as a remedy
> without success and subsequently spent some weeks design-
> ing certain 'barometric pumps' which were 'worked with
> mercury and wires' to clear vast areas of the earth of the
> influence of gravitation.   (p.95)

Like all de Selby's ideas, these are not very far from actuality.
In fact, all the scientific explanations in the book are both
comic and acceptable because they are only an exaggeration
of the ordinary man's visualisation. Here there is a parody of
the tendency to think of gravity as a 'thing' which can be
removed by a machine worked by wires and mercury. The
other ideas, of flight representing freedom and of heaven lying
in an upward direction, are perfectly normal and only acquire
comic overtones when combined with the ideas about gravity.
O'Brien generally achieves comic effects by a combination of
ideas which, by themselves, are not comic but which, in
totality, become incongruous and surprising.

However, the ideas of de Selby, while being parodied in
themselves, are an integral part of the plot, and the narrator's
mention of a 'second direction', a concept formed under the

stimulus of de Selby's ideas, is an introduction to the idea of his forthcoming death and his desire to escape in any available direction from the confines of a world whose illogic, which before merely upset him, now threatens his life. Mathers has been found dead in a ditch and the narrator is arrested for the murder. A weird kind of justice is at work here but it is not one that the narrator appreciates. Previously he had thought that the Sergeant was foolish. Not the same Sergeant proves that his pieces of wisdom, which had hitherto seemed nonsensical, have a very practical relevance and are a very efficacious guide to action. The Sergeant intends to hang the narrator for the murder, not because he thinks he did it, but to save himself from the fury of the Inspector. He will be very pleased if the narrator will regard the whole incident as a joke. The narrator, on the contrary, is paralysed with fear but eventually protests, vigorously, nonsensically, and to no avail.

> 'I will resist,' I shouted, 'and will resist to the death and fight for my existence even if I lose my life in the attempt.'
>
> (p. 98)

The terrifying thing about the Sergeant's responses is that, compared to the sense of life held by the narrator, they are totally unemotional, and he expects standards of moral behaviour from the narrator while having none himself. While the narrator protests that this is 'unfair, unjust, fiendish', the Sergeant worries about how his bicycle will have to be taken out of the cell, and simply says, with great truth: 'It is the way we work in this part of the country.' Justice and fairness can only exist where there is a conception of order and balance. Unable to call on justice and order, which he had violated but nevertheless relied upon, the narrator is in the same emotional position as the child who feels that the whole world is against him because he cannot understand its rules. It is fitting punishment that he feels life most strongly when it is about to be taken away from him by a process about as fair as the way in which he murdered Mathers. He attempts to win his way out of the situation by the use of superior intelligence, by trapping the Sergeant in his own logic. He points out that if he does not exist because he has no name, then he cannot be hanged. The Sergeant, however, is not to be defeated and argues with equal weight that even though everything the narrator does is a lie, and nothing that happens to him is true, for that very reason he can be hanged; since his hanging will be a lie, he will not, in fact, have been hanged at all. He will merely be a piece of 'negative nullity neutralised'. All this is sophistry to the narrator, who has finally come up against the one surety in the universe, the one thing he can believe in passionately even if the Sergeant does not — the truth of his own being and consciousness.

> I felt so sad and so entirely disappointed that tears came into my eyes and a lump of incommunicable poignancy swelled tragically in my throat. I began to feel intensely every fragment of my equal humanity. The life that was bubbling at the end of my fingers was real and nearly painful in intensity and so was the beauty of my warm face and the loose humanity of my limbs and the racy health of my rich red blood. To leave it all without good reason and to smash the little empire into small fragments was a thing too pitiful even to refuse to think about.   (p.102)

The first layer of irony here lies in the emotional quality of the thought of smashing the little empire into fragments, as opposed to the previous unemotional callousness of 'Not everybody knows how I killed old Philip Mathers, smashing his jaw in with my spade.'[20] The second layer will not be evident until the final revelation that even as he evokes life in such vigorous detail, he is, in fact, dead.

Soon after his arrest, and following an interval for discussion on the 'readings' on a mysterious machine and an anecdote relating to the hanging of a bicycle for murder — a ludicrous parallel to his own forthcoming fate — the narrator is left alone with MacCruiskeen for another of what he later calls 'unthinkable conversations'. MacCruiskeen plays a music box which is completely inaudible to everyone except himself. However, the silence which is a result of this music takes on the quality of sound.

> The silence in the room was so unusually quiet that the beginning of it seemed rather loud when the utter stillness of the end of it had been encountered.   (p.105)

MacCruiskeen then takes out his patent mangle and uses it to produce light and then to turn that light into sound for

'diversion and also for scientific truth'. He uses this phenomenon, which greatly frightens the narrator, to explain
the general principles of the universe. Everything that exists,
he claims, has as a common prime constituent an essence
called omnium.

> 'Some people', he said, 'call it energy but the right name is
> omnium because there is far more than energy in the inside
> of it, whatever it is. Omnium is the essential inherent
> interior essence which is hidden inside the root of the kernel
> of everything and it is always the same.'   (p.110)

Later he says that 'Some people call it God.' (p. 111) He
then goes on to explain how everything is made of omnium
in different forms so that light and sound, all essentially
consisting of omnium, can be changed into each other. The
narrator at last feels that he understands something. He now
thinks he knows what the basic essence of the universe is, what
it is actually made of. With a grasp of this fundamental fact he
can concentrate more on the immediate problems which face
him — his continued survival, and his desire to find the black
box and know what valuables are inside it. These problems
and his experiences during the day find expression in his
sensations as he falls asleep and his ensuing dream.

> Lying quietly and dead-eyed, I reflected on how new the
> night was, how distinctive and unaccustomed its
> individuality. Robbing me of the reassurance of my
> eyesight, it was disintegrating my bodily personality into a
> flux of colour, smell, recollection, desire — all the strange
> uncounted essences of terrestrial and spiritual existence. I
> was deprived of definition, position and magnitude and my
> significance was considerably diminished.   (p.116)

This description is very similar to his sensations in Mathers'
house, and is, above that, a very accurate record of what
happened to him afterwards. Just as his 'life after death' is a
nightmare, so his dream after falling asleep in a way that
closely resembled that death, is also a nightmare. In the
nightmare he fears death and is obsessed both with his attempt
to understand the nature of the world and with the relationship between his knowledge of the world and what it
actually is.

> Was I in turn merely a link in a vast sequence of
> imponderable beings, the world I knew merely the interior
> of the being whose inner voice I myself was? Who or what
> was the core and what monster in what world was the final
> uncontained colossus? God? Nothing?   (p.118)

It is noticeable that in this attempt to comprehend his place
in the world, he has used an image like that of the boxes within
the boxes and the eyes within the eyes, which both times in the
past have meant horrified speculation.[21] Now, however, his
questioning as to whether Joe could have a body which is
within a body which is within . . . (and so on *ad infinitum*)
makes Joe so angry that he announces that he is leaving. Once
again the narrator must face fear which he tries to dispel by
reason. He is also afraid, though, that he ties himself in knots
in his speculation as he tries to explain his paradoxical
awareness.

> Puzzled and frightened I tried to understand the
> complexities not only of my intermediate dependence and
> my catenal unintegrity but also my dangerous adjunctive-
> ness and my embarrassing unisolation. If one assumes—
>   (p.119)

He has no time, however, to follow through any assumption
because Joe interrupts to 'explain things' and his pronouncements are a culmination of all the references to
negation and 'nullity' which have run like a *leitmotiv* through
the book.

> When I leave you I take with me all that made you what you
> are—I take all your significance and importance and all the
> accumulations of human instinct and appetite and wisdom
> and dignity. You will be left with nothing behind you and
> nothing to give the waiting ones.   (pp.119–20)

The narrator knows then that he is dead and listens, in his
coffin, to the lid being hammered down. This is only a dream,
but it is exactly similar to his real state. He is dead but still
conscious. Joe has announced the importance of the soul as a
positive definitive element of personality. The narrator is, in
reality, without a soul and so is (as is suggested in passing and
proven by his lack of name) a negative quality.
Normality returns with the daylight, and the narrator is

introduced to the idea that eternity is just down the road and can be reached by a lift. On the way to eternity, the narrator is once again calmed by the order and pattern of the world of nature. His contemplation of these scenes, the 'unexplainable enjoyments of the world' (p.125) relieves his senses from 'the agony of dealing with the existence of the Sergeant'. Joe is very sceptical about eternity, a subject on which he claims to be an authority, but the narrator has had enough of his presuppositions shattered and no longer doubts that anything may be possible. He is, at first, disappointed by eternity. which seems to consist only of long passages with lots of wires and pipes, but he learns after a while that in eternity time does not pass, the cigarette never burns to the end, the beard does not grow, the hands of the clock do not move, the day, when they get back to it, is at the same moment as when they left. Eternity has no size and in it all directions are the same direction, and no matter which way you travel you will arrive back at the same point. In eternity, omnium can be manufactured into anything at all, no matter how valuable. It is used to make two things which bewilder the narrator, a glass which magnifies to invisibility, and some box-like objects which have no determinate shape or colour. They seem, therefore, to embody the essence of this strange place.

> They had another quality that made me watch them wild-eyed, dry-throated and with no breathing. I can make no attempt to describe this quality. It took me hours of thought long afterwards to realise why these articles were astonishing. *They lacked an essential property of all known objects.* I cannot call it shape of configuration since shapelessness is not what I refer to at all. I can only say that these objects, not one of which resembled the other, were of no known dimensions. They were not square or rectangular or circular or simply irregularly shaped nor could it be said that their endless variety was due to dimensional dissimilarities. Simply their appearance, if even that word is not inadmissible, was not understood by the eye and was in any event indescribable. That is enough to say.   (p.135)

Throughout the book O'Brien has shown an awareness of the problem of translating the · untranslatable into semasiological terms. Language is bound to express a particular set of physical laws and the problem of the scientist is to find new terms, and sometimes even new grammatical forms, in which to express new concepts. Here the objects the narrator sees partake of no qualities inherent in the world and so can only be described in terms of what they are not.

The other objects that the narrator is impressed by are a part of his punishment. The unreason of the world is designed to punish him for committing a crime for the sake of de Selby, the attempt to hang him is to punish him for the actual murder, and the quantity of gold and jewels which he acquires in eternity and is allowed to carry as far as the lift is to punish him for his greed in wanting Mathers' money. The physical laws of eternity make it impossible for him to take these things with him. His bitter disappointment is placed in a comic light when it is juxtaposed with the policeman's discussion about creams, jelly babies, sugar barley, carnival assorted and dolly mixtures: the narrator has just had to leave a fortune behind him, and MacCruiskeen kindly offers him a sweet to console him. In a state of great distress he returns to the barracks and sleeps.

The overwhelming problem now is his forthcoming execution, which is planned for the immediate future. Even in the moments before the hanging, the Sergeant, who has become something evil and a complete opposite to nature, has a story to tell of a man who went into the clouds in a balloon and failed to return. The narrator, however, is more concerned with thoughts about his own possible rescue by the 'hoppy men'[22] and with speculations about what kind of life he will have after death. Predictably he sees the afterlife in the natural terms which are the only things he emotionally trusts. He becomes, at times, almost a parable of man divided against himself, unaware of the real impulses of his nature, trusting his intellect at the expense of his senses and, in so doing, creating a crisis of personality and of identification.

Down into the earth where dead men go would I go soon and maybe come out of it again in some healthy way, free and innocent of all human perplexity. I would perhaps be the chill of an April wind, an essential part of some indomitable river or be personally concerned in the ageless perfection of some rank mountain bearing down upon the mind by occupying forever a position in the blue easy distance. Or perhaps a smaller thing like movement in the grass or an unbearable breathless yellow day, some hidden creature going about its business—I might well be responsible for that or for some important part of it. Or even those unaccountable distinctions that make an evening recognisable from its own morning, the smells and sounds and sights of the perfected and matured essences of the day, these might not be innocent of my meddling and abiding presence. (p.159)

At the very moment of death he is rescued by a crisis in eternity to which the policemen must attend. He escapes from the barracks on a curiously human bicycle and finally reaches Mathers' house once again. Here he faces the final trial—the meeting with Policeman Fox, the Third Policeman. Policeman Fox is in a room in Mathers' house which was not there before and which, indeed, does not seem to be there at all when the narrator tries to find it. The light which streams from this room is mysterious and alarming, but, impelled by curiosity about the black box and greed for its contents, the narrator continues to search for the source of the light even though he feels that he is 'standing within three yards of something unspeakably inhuman and diabolical which was using its trick of light to lure me on to something still more horrible'. His attempts to find the light are moments of tension interspersed with moments of comfort when he returns to the bicycle and feels its reassuring normality. Eventually the tension culminates in his meeting with the policeman who is characterised by

his overbearing policemanship, his massive rearing of wide strengthy flesh, his domination and his unimpeachable reality. (p.180)

The impression of the policeman's 'unimpeacheable reality' is quickly shattered when his face is revealed, for it proves to be the face of old Mathers, somewhat changed but still recognisable: 'The eyes had been charged with unnatural life and glistened like beads in the lamplight.' (p.183)

Policeman Fox presents the greatest shock of all to the narrator for he questions his one surety, his belief in his own self. He asks how the narrator is still alive. The narrator replies that he escaped and Fox asks: 'Are you sure?' He is, therefore, questioning the reality of the narrator, asking if he is really alive. It is significant that Joe has been completely silent since their conversation on the scaffold. The hero is shattered, and the shock makes him physically weak and ill.

> Was I sure? Suddenly I felt horribly ill as if the spinning of the world in the firmament had come against my stomach for the first time, turning it all to bitter curd . . .
> I felt my brains struggling on bravely, tottering, so to speak, to its knees but unwilling to fall completely. I knew that I would be dead if I lost consciousness for one second. I knew that I could never awaken again or hope to understand afresh the terrible way in which I was if I lost the chain of the bitter day I had had. I knew that he was not Fox but Mathers. I knew Mathers was dead. I knew that I would have to talk to him and pretend that everything was natural and try perhaps to escape for the last time with my life to the bicycle. I would have given everything I had in the world and every cashbox in it to get at that moment one look at the strong face of John Divney.   (p.183)

The shock of having his own existence questioned is enough to make him toy with the idea of relinquishing the black box. For the moment, however, he does try to pretend that everything is normal by asking mundane questions about the police barracks. Perhaps this is an exemplification of the typical reaction of man when faced with such crises of identity. At last he asks about the black box, unable to forget it, no matter what his protestations to the contrary. He has, finally, achieved the aim of the visit to the police barracks. In answer Fox asks him about his impressions of eternity and the narrator finds this question reassuring for it seems to confirm the reality of his experiences.

> I reflected that this talk of the strange underground region with the doors and wires confirmed that it did exist, that I actually had been there and that my memory of it was not the memory of a dream — unless I was still in the grip of the same nightmare.   (p.187)

The reassurance of another consciousness sharing the same knowledge and experience is, then, only partial, for that other consciousness may be merely a part of the original hallucination.

At this point there is a complete reversal in the narrator's fortunes, and he is pushed to the height of exhilaration and joy by the possession of the black box, which is found to contain not money but four ounces of omnium. Fox comes to represent, at this stage, perhaps God, perhaps the devil, but certainly the moving principle of this world and the chief agent in the punishment of the narrator. The narrator himself is now carried away by visions of his god-like power to change, 'destroy, alter and improve the universe at will', to make, see or do anything with 'no limit to my powers save that of my own imagination'. He will have the same powers as Fox had when it was he who possessed the omnium.

> If I could believe him he had been sitting in this room presiding at four ounces of this inutterable substance, calmly making ribbons of the natural order, inventing intricate and unheard of machinery to delude the other policemen, interfering drastically with time to make them think they had been leading their magical lives for years, bewildering, horrifying and enchanting the whole countryside. I was stupefied and appalled by the modest claim he had made so cheerfully, I could not quite believe it, yet it was the only way the terrible recollections which filled my brain could be explained.   (p.188)

It seems to the narrator that everything has been explained. His mind likes such an all-inclusive pattern as that suggested by the policeman and his use of omnium. It also offers him complete and terrible power over the policemen and his erstwhile associate in crime, John Divney. It compensates for the disappointment of eternity. With these advantages before him, he does not examine the explanation too carefully. He mocks the policeman for his 'oafish underground invention'. Fox no longer seems to be a threat; he is merely lumpish and unintelligent, reducing the great power of the omnium to a way of getting his eggs boiled just right. The narrator has forgotten that he has Mathers' face, and that Mathers is twice dead. He believes that he is free and about to be master of the world: 'enormous, important, full of power. I felt happy and fulfilled.' (p.195)

Just as he is at the peak of happiness, comes revelation.

> There was nothing altogether unnatural in what I saw but I
> encountered another of those chilling shocks which I
> thought I had left behind me forever.   (p.195)

He discovers Divney, looking twenty years older, married, and
terrified by the apparition at his door. As he collapses in
fright, the narrator tries to help but Divney's wife does not
seem to be aware of his presence. It emerges, from Divney's
garbled speech, that the narrator has been dead for sixteen
years, blown up by a bomb placed in Mathers' house by Divney
himself. For a third time the experience of Mathers' house is
recreated.

> My mind became quite empty, light, and felt as if it were
> very white in colour. I stood exactly where I was for a long
> time without moving or thinking.   (p.197)

This indicates that the narrator is beginning to move again
into the same state of being as that experienced at the moment
of death. The stiffness of his walk as he leaves the house is a
reference to his state. The landscape through which he moves
is dead, stunted, wild and angry. His mind in response to this
is void and negative, though his eyes, like dead eyes, are still
open. This state of non-awareness, similar to the 'indescribable, unaccountable interval' which had ensued in
Mathers' house, is gradually replaced as he becomes conscious
of his surroundings. Rounding a bend he sees before him a
building which surprises and frightens him because it seems to
lack an essential dimension. It is the police barracks. The
period of non-consciousness over, he, joined by Divney,
advances towards the barracks to experience the same terror
all over again.

> Joe had been explaining things in the meantime. He said it
> was again the beginning of the unfinished, the re-discovery
> of the familiar, the re-experience of the already suffered,
> the fresh-forgetting of the unremembered. Hell goes round
> and round. In shape it is circular and by nature, it is
> interminable, repetitive, and very nearly unbearable.
> (Note by O'Brien, p.200)[23]

The importance of the *Third Policeman* lies in its presentation of a vision of hell which implies man's reliance on order, pattern and harmony. O'Brien believes that these things are inherent in man's world even if the sophistries of philosophy seek to convince him that they are not. The emotional stress of the book lies always in the evocation of nature and in the belief that it is this kind of perception which defines what is best in man.

This vision of horror and this perception of tranquillity in nature is subsumed within an overriding comic apprehension which can allow for the terror of bewilderment and negation at the same time as it presents simple guessing games and strange stories. The embellishment of a sinister and night-marish story with pleasant and amusing detail proves how near is the vision of comedy to chaos and unreason. That O'Brien conceived of comedy—and art—in these terms is evident from two pieces in *Cruiskeen Lawn* which were written at about the same time as *The Third Policeman*. The first is a parody of the pretentious jargon of art critics, yet some sentences are close enough to the spirit of *The Third Policeman* to allow us to accept it as, at least, semi-serious.

> I admit, of course, that you occasionally come across a painting from which you start back almost frightened by the queer, but authentic, incomprehensibility of it. Here, you say, is something that devolves, not from *Krondt, Liebz* or the *Munich Group* but from that myopic, almost intuitive, awareness of naturalistic cosmic function. Here is something, you add, that Yeats himself might have acknowledged without remorse. Then you walk around with the queer picture in your brain all day, vainly asking yourself whether you are really mad.   (31 May 1941)

Queer but authentic incomprehensibility that makes you wonder if you are mad seems an adequate description of the ethos of *The Third Policeman*. The second piece was written a year later and deals with the nature of comedy. The reference to the book seems to be a joke though the extract seems, on the surface, to be straight-faced.

> Some weeks ago I suggested that the stuff should be printed without warning under different headings 'Births,

Marriages and Deaths, To-day's Radio Programmes, and so on. I began to brood on this and soon came to the conclusion that the supreme if somewhat esoteric expression of comicality was *not to appear at all.* Just abstraction, blankness, nullity for one day. Can you not try to realise the superbness of that gesture, the . . . um . . . incomprehensible felicity of the nothingness of it all. I mean, get hold of Schaspman's 'Anatomy of Laughter' and turn to page 95 and you will find a footnote there that will enlighten you considerably.   (5 Aug. 1942)

Can we postulate, therefore, that the comic essence of *The Third Policeman* lies in its being the comedy of negation, nullity and abstraction? The comic *reductio* tends to lead to the world of the absurd, and this was a world in which O'Brien was unable to live for very long. The new world which he had created out of fragments of philosophy, ideas of the Celtic otherworld and the topsy-turveydom of Sterne, proved to be unbearable, and when he put *The Third Policeman* aside and rewrote it as *The Dalkey Archive* O'Brien moved from the horrors of illogical abstraction and turned to the promise of accepted mysteries.

5
'Our Gaelic Satirist':
Cruiskeen Lawn

I sat in a comfortable lounge in Dunleary
Puffing tobacco smoke, talking with learned
Companions about statistics, Mervyn Wall
Beside me at a small table and near the wall,
His back to us, the bold Sir Myles na Gopaleen,
He turned to order another round and leaning
Across the counter, remarked: 'We'll go on a skyte'.

Then, we were belting up into the sky,
Fast in his stationary monoplane,
Anxiously looking down at the map-rolling plain
Of Leinster. Myles, being a cracked pilot,
Had jerked the joystick, avoided eleven pylons:
Soon he was running the light machine along
A road between stubble-fields. Light was longer.
Why were we all in a motor car: the miles
Chasing us on with hill and thicket? Myles
Turned at the wheel, our Gaelic satirist,
To glance at the tiny dial on his wrong wrist,
Luminous as a miniature city.[1]

So the late Austin Clarke, himself primarily a satirist, saw
Flann O'Brien in his persona of Myles na gCopaleen, and the
terms in which Myles is described show Clarke's sensitive
apprehension of some of the salient characteristics of the
Cruiskeen Lawn column. The poem from which these lines are
taken is 'More Extracts from a Diary of Dreams', and the
events described in it share the suddenness and illogic of a
dream. The men are at one moment sitting in Dunleary, then
they are abruptly transferred to an aeroplane; finally, with an
equally abrupt transition, the aeroplane becomes a motor-car.
The guide to the dream-world is Myles na gCopaleen, the

'cracked pilot' who seems to be able to inhabit the sky at one
moment and to return to earth in the next. His very nature is
contradictory: he is 'cracked' but learned, a man who is in
control of illogic, yet a man who discusses statistics. His
aeroplane as it belts 'up into the sky' is 'stationary'. His watch
is on the 'wrong wrist', his view is universal yet minute. From
his height above the land he can see for miles, yet, even when
back on earth, the 'tiny dial' on his wrist is luminous as a
'miniature city'.

The *Cruiskeen Lawn* column is often fantastic, inverted and
convoluted. It is pedantically learned, yet despises learning.
Its interests range from the most universal to the most
parochial. Like Austin Clarke's poem, it is full of outrageous
puns and verbal games. Its chief characteristics are a sense of
mad and eccentric contradiction, an evocation of the variety,
richness and unexpectedness of the world, a discerning, often
wicked, awareness of the hypocrisies and idiocies of public life
and personal characteristics, a tendency towards fantasy, and
a love of all the intricacies of language. Myles had ample scope
to develop these, and other, characteristics in a column which
continued, with only a few interruptions, for more than
twenty-five years.

The first appearance of the column on 4 October 1940, was
quite inconspicuous. Placed on page four of the *Irish Times,*
beside the much larger *Irishman's Diary,* it was headed
'Cruiscín Lán' and signed 'An Broc'. It contined, predictably, a comment on the Irish language. Its next
appearance, six days later, was in both Irish and English, and
was signed 'Myles na gCopaleen'. This issue, too, contained
comment on the Irish language and those who sought for its
revival as the common speech of the Irish people.

The first article was written in response to a leader-writer
who had asserted that Irish could not deal with the facts of the
modern world because it did not have the vocabulary of
modern warfare or politics. He wrote, as Myles reported him:

Parents who confine the family meal-time discussions to
conversations in Irish must find it very difficult to explain
such words as air-raid warden, incendiary bomb, non-
aggression pact, decontamination and Molotoff bread-
basket. Has Gaelic ingenuity, for that matter, stretched so

far as to provide a really expressive and indigenous
equivalent for the well-known 'Axis'?   (4 Oct. 1940)

Myles replied to this by providing an imaginary and comic
meal-time conversation in Irish using all the terms for which
the correspondent had said there could be no Gaelic
equivalent. He went on to complain about the 'ghoul'-like
mentality of those people who accompanied their breakfast
with conversations on such dreadful subjects, and he asserted
the flexibility and inventiveness of Gaelic by proving that not
only could it provide verbal equivalents, but equivalents which
were more than mere translations, in that they were puns or
ambiguous and allusive terms.

From this first article, Myles was to pursue a continuous
policy of attack on those who doubted the flexibility of Gaelic
when they themselves were not competent in the language. It
might have been expected that this defence of the language
would have won him powerful friends among the Gaelic
Leaguers. In fact, quite the opposite happened. Members of
the Gaelic League, especially those whose command of the
language was not great and who saw the revival of Irish in a
purely nationalistic light, objected to the playfulness with
which Myles discussed what were to them serious, almost holy,
subjects. The Irish language was a noble tongue; it was not a
medium for comedy.

As a result of this feeling, reactions to the column were soon
to appear and were to take a rather odd form. The 'Letters to
the Editor' section of the *Irish Times* soon carried a large
correspondence on the subject of *Cruiskeen Lawn*. There were
some letters of praise, but more of condemnation. Opinions
veered between those who felt that the *Irish Times,* that
stronghold of the 'West Briton', was at last beginning to cater
for Gaelic, Catholic, nationalist opinion, and those who felt
that Myles was attacking both the Irish language and Irish
speakers and was, thus, yet another example of West-Briton
contempt. On 10 October 1940, in his second article, Myles
had written:

The Irish language will probably become invaluable as an
instrument of self-expression in these changing times, when

most of us are sure of nothing. The Irish speaker, being the most equivocal of God's creatures, expresses his ambiguous existence by two separate and dissimilar verbs 'to be'-'is' and 'tá'. If he says 'is fear mé', he means that he is the external masculine, fundamentally and utterly a man; but if he says 'tá mé 'mo fhear', he means that he is just man-like with trousers and looking as if he needed a shave as distinct from boy-of-twelve-like with pimples on his jaw and a sling in his pants pocket. (Apart from which verb is used, the speaker is not infrequently merely a gawm). The *tá* sense is, therefore, an inferior temporal excrescence on the skin of the timeless and imponderable *is* (pronounced like the middle 'is' in 'hiss'). 'Is' is really a god-word unusable in its strict sense by mortals. Possibly Irish speakers are not mortals.

Responses to this were immediate. One correspondent who signed himself 'West-Briton Nationalist' pointed out that while he was a member of the Ascendancy who was faithful to 'King, Country and Empire', he had always been tolerant of the opinion of others. For that reason he asked:

> But what are your inspiring motives in the little 'skits' you have started in the *Irish Times*. I understand the idea of poking fun at what is ridiculous, unless it be too pitiable to ridicule. I understand the nausea that untutored puppies with a knowledge of Irish sometimes induce in those who come in contact with them. I understand also that people that are not sure of themselves are very thin-skinned. But I do not understand what worthy motive can inspire your 'skits' on the Gaelic language and its students as such. It sounds very much like fouling one's own nest.
>
> I have heard many adverse comments on Irish. But you are spewing on it.[2]

Other correspondents complained that *Cruiskeen Lawn* was not 'sensible', and was written by an 'embittered' man. Myles was accused of 'pettiness' and of trying 'to sabotage the propagation of the language and things Irish'. 'West-Briton Nationalist' wrote again to say that he did not think that the Gaelic movement was sufficiently 'strong to stand satire', and, giving a definition of the proper function of the satirist, he criticised Myles's attitude.

> Satire has a searing but healing fire. Light humorous articles, ironical, quietly rubbing up the ridiculosities of the movement and its disciples are one thing. For humour to do good to a movement it wishes well to, the humorist must love that which he satirises . . . To my reading, there is no love of the Irish language discernible in the articles, especially in the initial article, of 'Cruiskeen'.[3]

In an article years later Ben Kiely was to comment that

> The more rigid, old-fashioned Gaelic revivalists were driven up the walls by his mockery — in Gaelic and in a rare mixture of Gaelic and English — of their idiosyncrasies. Yet the very style of his mockery was one good proof that a revival had taken place.[4]

Even at that time there were people who recognised the truth of this. O'Brien's personal papers contain a note signed 'Constant Reader', which laments the fact that Myles has written some columns only in English. This sums up one of the responses to *Cruiskeen Lawn.*

> You are the best advertisement in Ireland for learning Irish and the Gaelic League ought to subsidise you heavily.[5]

Other correspondents pointed out that Myles was demonstrating the 'elasticity and adaptability' of Irish, inviting it to advance by relating it to the world, and putting life into it. Myles was compared to Stephen Leacock by a writer who said:

> This type of article really fills a long-felt want. Years ago I discontinued reading the fulsome, fatuous 'sixth-standard-essay' type of article which passes for Gaelic journalism in the other metropolitan newspapers. Now I find myself looking forward to Myles' next appearance in your columns.[6]

A correspondent who praised Myles's 'mature humour and graceful diction' was reproved by Oscar Love on 18 October. Oscar Love had played a prominent part in the controversy fomented by O'Brien and Sheridan which was the immediate predecessor of the column. He was one of the most prolific letter-writers and it is likely that both he and 'West-Briton Nationalist' were pseudonyms used by O'Brien to continue the correspondence about the column and to draw attention to it. Oscar Love pointed out that Myles's aim was not to produce 'graceful diction' but to use nonsense to define what was, in itself, nonsensical.

> The Irish have not discovered that nonsense is a new sense. This sense is unknown to dictators. If present-day dictators possessed a sense of nonsense the world might be rocked with laughter instead of shocked with bombs.[7]

Another correspondent agreed. He wrote that he had become tired of the melancholy twilight aspect of Gaelic writing and pleaded: 'Let us laugh, even if at ourselves, sometimes.' This theme was continued in the letter which arrived to reprimand 'West-Briton Nationalist' for his misreading of the intentions of the column.

> A 'West-Briton-Nationalist', in my humble opinion, misses the whole point of Myles's articles. They are not 'skits' on the language or on its students, but a rebellion in satire against the awful 'tripe' which is dished out day after day in news sheets all over the country in 'the Irish'. These hypocritical, guinea-making effusions—turned out like sausages from a sausage-machine—are mere sops to the extreme, impractical Gaelic-here-there-and-everywhere minority. These are the articles which really cause mental spewing in rational Gaelic-speaking circles.[8]

By the time the correspondence petered out the point of the column had been well explained. The attitude to bad Irish and to nonsense, laughter and 'sane madness' were typically Mylesian, no matter who had signed the letters pointing this out. Myles himself, with his supreme knowledge of the ambiguities and nuances of Irish, had a better claim than most others to castigate those enthusiasts who succeeded only in bastardising his 'mellifluous and noble' tongue. The double attack on opponents and supporters of Irish was to remain a permanent feature of the column which, despite its initial hostile reception, became enormously popular and eagerly sought after, particularly in Dublin.

At first quite short, the articles grew in length until they came to be about seven hundred words each. The whole article might be on a single topic or, more usually, on three or four topics which could be totally unrelated. Until the end of September 1941 they were written mainly in Irish, and appeared approximately three times a week. Thereafter they were written alternately in Irish and English and appeared daily. (There was no *Irish Times* on Sundays.) By the end of 1943 Irish was appearing only once or twice a week, and articles in Irish virtually ceased early in 1944, when Myles began to write almost exclusively in English. For the remaining twenty-two years of the column's life an article in Irish was a very rare exception, though Irish as a *subject* was never abandoned. It is possible that writing in Irish was abandoned because it could command only a very small readership. It is possible, however, that as O'Brien's pseudonymous creation grew in stature Myles wished to have a broader scope for his imagination. He certainly realised that the proper mastery of Irish would remain a rare achievement. On 24 February 1955 he wrote:

> It is far too difficult, its vocabulary, syntax and general grammar structure too linguistically alien to the mother-tongue of most Irishmen, which is English.

In any case, people who worked with Myles on the *Irish Times* found it increasingly difficult to persuade him to write anything in Irish.

Essentially, then, *Cruiskeen Lawn* began as an instrument intended to scourge the inept but arrogant Irish speaker. It soon had many more purposes than this. Through the pseudonymous character of Myles na gCopaleen, O'Brien was able to extend the range of his interests to cover every aspect of Irish life, and many of a more international nature. *Cruiskeen Lawn* covered most of O'Brien's life as a writer. It is important in a number of ways. As a substantial body of ephemeral, satirical writing it is almost unique in Irish literature. It emphasised and reflected themes and concerns which afterwards appeared as central aspects of his novels. Often the genesis of a novel can be traced to a *Cruiskeen Lawn* article written many years previously. The column is, in fact, a sort of notebook for the novels. Finally, it provides an invaluable insight into the events of O'Brien's own life, and it contains, often under the guise of mockery, a number of serious comments which enshrine his vision of life.

Cruiskeen Lawn is not an ordered and consistent piece of writing. It is a collection of some thousands of articles, written over twenty-five years in varying moods and under quite different circumstances. It presents an impressive number of different comic and satiric devices and an enormous number of different subjects. Throughout this long period Myles had always to retain the interest of his readers, to present an ever varied and surprising column. It could never be allowed to fall into any predictable pattern. *Cruiskeen Lawn* is, therefore, a jumbled, paradoxical, inconsistent, pedantic, funny, bitter, sad, and sometimes humourless series of writings. The format of the daily column meant that each thought and each episode had to be compressed within a small space, while the certainty of continuance from day to day, meant that jokes, ideas and subjects could be developed over a long period.

This very format, the enormous range and variety of the individual articles, creates difficulties in approaching *Cruiskeen Lawn.* The fact that the column extended over so many years explains not only the great change in attitude from year to year, but also the noticeable variation in quality from article to article. The constant need to turn out daily articles must have taxed Myles's abilities to the utmost. Often a joke fails or is repeated, the subject-matter becomes turgid and unrewarding, or a successful device is used too frequently. A second difficulty stems from the fact that the columns rely heavily on contemporary events for source material. *Cruiskeen Lawn,* even at the height of its popularity, was an intimate affair, aimed primarily at Dublin audiences, and even then sometimes only fully appreciated by those 'in the know'. Many of the columns, predictably, deal with Myles's own world, that of the civil service and its inter-departmental battles. References in these columns would often have been clear only to a small number of people, even in Dublin, a city where the biggest secrets are the most widely discussed topics. The long series of articles on Andy Clarkin's clock is a good example of this characteristic. At first the joke centred on the inability of the clock to keep time, but as the discussion continued it became clear that more was involved than Myles's eye for the unusual or ludicrous. Andy Clarkin was then Lord Mayor of Dublin, and the constant assaults on his inaccurate clock were a way of attacking him and Dublin Corporation which Myles always detested. These personal and contemporary references are now largely unintelligible to us. Even casual references to war news or post-war planning will soon need footnotes to elucidate the point of the joke.

The solution to some of these difficulties was found in the creation of the Myles persona. Myles na gCopaleen became the mind, the memory and personality which would bind together all this amorphous mass of material, from the most precise and pedantic to the most universal and transcendent. The development of Brother Barnabas had shown that O'Brien's imagination was, to some extent, dramatic. In the creation of an aesthetically distanced and expansive superman, Myles found a medium through which he could impose a minimum of order and continuity while allowing a completely free reign to his increasingly confident imagination. A major aim in the selection of a new pseudonym was that it should reflect different aspects of O'Brien's personality to those seen in the novels. The creation of the Myles persona was a matter of some importance to O'Brien and he put a good deal of thought into deciding its basic characteristics.

In a semi-autobiographical and semi-serious article in *New Ireland* magazine, O'Brien explained the importance of a pseudonym.

In twenty-five years I have written ten books (that is, substantial *opera*) under four quite irreconcilable pen-names and on subjects absolutely unrelated. Five of those books could be described as works of imagination, one of world social comment, two on scientific subjects, one of literary exploration and conjecture, one in Irish and one a play (which was produced by the Abbey Theatre). On top of that I have produced an enormous mass of miscellaneous material consisting of short stories, scripts for radio and

TV, contributions to newspapers and magazines, and even book reviews.

This is work and can be very rewarding financially, often surprisingly and unpredictably so. But is it insufferably hard work? Not necessarily.

Apart from a thorough education of the widest kind, a contender in this field must have an equable yet versatile temperament, and the compartmentation of his personality for the purpose of literary utterance ensures that the fundamental individual will not be credited with a certain way of thinking, fixed attitudes, irreversible technique of expression. No author should write under his own name nor under one permanent pen-name; a male writer should include in his impostures a female pen-name, and possibly vice versa.[9]

The first issue of *Cruiskeèn Lawn* appeared without a specific signature. The title, translatable as 'the full jug' (Dinneen), was sufficient indication that O'Brien intended to cover a multiplicity of subjects in a variety of forms: the chief characteristic of the column, clearly, would be 'fullness' and—since the title 'Cruiscín Lán' is taken from a folk-song which praises the joys of alcohol—a sense of intoxicated variety.

The pseudonym he chose for *Cruiskeen Lawn* and used for *An Béal Bocht* and some of the short stories, was Myles na gCopaleen ('Myles of the Ponies')) and was adopted from Gerald Griffin's novel *The Collegians*. Dion Boucicault had also used the name for his version of *The Collegians* called *The Colleen Bawn*. In the latter work and, to some extent, in the former, Myles is part hero, part romancer, part clown, part law-breaker. If he has little sense of responsibility towards the law of the land, he is faithful and self-sacrificing in personal relationships. He is a great comic figure, a good story-teller who can make a simple incident into a strange and vivid story. Griffin had emphasised his heroic rather than his comic status and described him in language which O'Brien almost certainly had in mind when he created his own character.

The door opened, and the uncommissioned master of horse made his appearance. His appearance was at once strikingly

majestic and prepossessing, and the natural ease and
dignity with which he entered the room might almost have
become a peer of the realm coming to solicit the *interest* of
the family for an electioneering candidate. A broad and
sunny forehead, light and wavy hair, a blue cheerful eye, a
nose that in Persia might have won him a throne, healthful
cheeks, and a mouth that was full of character, and a well
knit and almost gigantic person, constituted his external
claims to attention, of which his lofty and confident, though
most unassuming carriage, showed him to be in some
degree conscious.[10]

This character must have appealed to O'Brien both in its
comic aspect, its power as story-teller, and in its role as
'shaughraun' wandering through the world with an irreverent
and satiric eye. There could, of course, be little connection,
other than in these basic features, between the character of the
novel and of the column. The novel and the play presented a
coherent character with a particular mode of speech, a
constant attitude and more or less predictable behaviour. The
newspaper column, by its very nature, demanded versatility
and a wide range of interests and modes of expression. Indeed,
the point of using a pseudonym was to guard against certain
'ways of thinking, fixed attitudes, irreversible techniques of
expression'. Like Brother Barnabas before him, Myles in
Cruiskeen Lawn developed into a many-headed hydra, an
indefinable character who changed his personality with each
thing he satirised. He was a multiplicity of characters — at once
a Dublin 'gutty', a famous journalist, an art critic, banker,
archaelogist, inhabitant of Santry, aesthete, civil servant,
social commentator, and anything else he wanted to be
according to the dictates of his mood or as a likely subject for
satire or parody presented itself.

The development of the character of Myles became one of
the chief aims and comic aspects of the column. Myles was, of
course, a man of extensive experience in all walks of life. A
scholar and diplomat, he was, nevertheless, at home with the
ordinary people of Ireland. Never a modest man, he was fond
of telling his readers of his many brave exploits. From time to
time he accounted for his pre-eminence in the world of art,

sport, business, the professions, politics and international intrigue by providing his readers with an 'official' biography. Each of his biographies (they were mostly autobiographies!) is different from its predecessor, though *in toto* they provide an unparalleled illustration of the great man's talents and importance. His readers neither expected, nor received, a coherent narrative. Myles, like his predecessor Brother Barnabas, transcended time, space and continuity — all the human limitations. Even death could hold no sway over him. He died and revived frequently, and he enjoyed lying in state watching the millions mourn over his demise until death became tedious and he decided to live again. Myles was the greatest of all O'Brien's creations. He was omnipotent, omniscient and omnipresent, a 'greater man than God', a perfect example of the ability of myth to defy commonsense. Born in many different times and places, dying and being resurrected, changing from youth to age and back to youth again with astonishing rapidity, Myles inhabited a world where everything was possible. Hardly a year passed without some account of his exploits, the new honours that were daily piled on him, the superhuman achievement of which he alone was capable.

There was one series of 'official biographies' which ran from 15 to 21 December 1960 and continued, after an interval, from 17 to 24 January 1961. This, entitled 'The True Biography of Myles na gCopaleen', was written in the third person. This series by no means exhausted the subject which had been dealt with, on and off, almost continuously throughout the history of the column, occurring most often in the first ten years.

He was born in Paris, in Montevideo, in London's Paddington station. His origins were both lowly and noble. He lived in Europe for 'seven or eight centuries' playing his part in all the great events of history, befriending the greatest men of each age, his achievements rivalled only by 'Leonard O'Davinci'. There was no activity to which he was a stranger. He was particularly active in politics. He helped Clemenceau to restore order in France, fought for small nationalities during the Great War, was invited to 'take care of the Irish Sea' by the prime minister, and rose to be head of state himself. He was forced to recall the Minister of the Phillippines and investigate the political régime in Portugal. From all sides came pressure to be President of Ireland. He was well fitted for the role since he was the man who had advised Truman not to annexe Russia.

As a musician he had studied under Scarlatti, and, in 1931, had entertained Kreisler with violin solos. He had a voice like that of his friend John McCormack. As scientist and philosopher he was known to have been tutor to Einstein and a number of other prominent European philosophers. Even Kierkegaard referred to him as 'the communicator of truth'. He thought he had written (but could not properly recall) in 1844 a work on etiquette under the name of the Earl of Chesterfield. His acquaintance with the world of letters did not end with that. He was known to have been a drinking companion of Joyce's father and to have referred to Horace as 'uncle'.

A man of great personal courage and physical prowess, it was he who taught the famous air-aces how to fly, and set a transatlantic speed record in his plane *Cruiskeen*. He could turn his hand to anything and so was not surprised when UCD offered him its vacant chair of architecture. He was, however, offended that he should be thought likely to accept such a lowly office after all his great achievements. In 1946 he complained that his honorary doctorates were being delayed, but he was nevertheless generous enough with his time to spend a period as Provost of Trinity College.

In his spare time he was District Justice of Ballybrophy and, as such, never had a judgment questioned or reversed. A great patriot, after he was executed by the British for treason, he returned to Dublin to take leave of those too infirm to attend the funeral in England and then announced that he was not dead at all.

Like all great men, he had to suffer for his pre-eminence. He was so busy, he said, that he must be the most bored man in the world. He was in demand everywhere. On one occasion he wrote that he had just returned from Paris after acting as 'honorary valet and adviser to His Grace the Duke of Edinburgh'. He had a place at all the great peace conferences, and even though his own country was slow to honour him,

titles and distinctions flowed in from all over the rest of the
civilised world. The English offered him a title which he
accepted. In fact, an English minister went so far as to
condemn the Irish government for its cowardice and stupidity
in ignoring and alienating Myles who was 'undoubtedly the
best man in Ireland'. Myles was never burdened by false
modesty and had a clear awareness of his own importance; he
even demanded to be told was he *not* the greatest Irishman of
all time. As such he once called upon the Irish nation to
abdicate from its position in the world. He had aggressively
demanded to know whether there was anyone who would say
that he was unfit to be President of Ireland. Horrified at not
being elected President of WAAMA when he had actually
indicated his willingness to stand, he set up his own rival
organisation. He was the head of a great house, of a banking
corporation and of the Research Bureau, his own brain-child,
established because of his desire to serve the Irish people.

In his own honours list for 1951 he made himself 'Duke of
the World', and why shouldn't he? A man whose real status
was indicated by the more sinister title 'His Satanic Highness'
was surely entitled to give himself any earthly title he desired.
In gentler moods he was the 'the Sage of Santry', inhabiting
Santry Hall, the defender of the rights of the Little Man, the
benevolent, paternalistic, wise old aristocrat.

He ascended and descended the social scale with a rapidity
which would have been intolerable in a mere human. He
could be 'Titular Head of the Wholly Human Empire' and 'the
Man in the Hat'. Other titles pointed to his formidable talents.
He was 'the Gaelic Demosthenes', 'the Wordsworth of Ireland',
'the Irish Disraeli' and 'Ireland's Own Hatchetman'.

However, like all men, and even gods, he was not without
fault. He had sometimes been found to be in violation of the
laws which, on other occasions, he administered. He tried to
get married without his parents consent. He attempted to
smuggle Irish whiskey out of the country. He was fined more
than two million pounds for cashing bad cheques on the
continent and was arrested with 'a woman of the gipsy class' on
a charge of larceny. He was alleged to have stolen four bicycle
tyres and a tram.

Myles, an eternal shape-changer, was more than human

and yet remained recognisably human in single and separate
parts of his existence. Through his transformations, O'Brien
was able to approach every aspect of Irish society and
comment upon it. The autobiographical columns were never
devoted solely to building up Myles's character. The new event
in which he was an actor, or the new aspect of character
revealed, usually provided a way in to a criticism of Irish
politics, or habits, social classes or personalities.

It is probable that certain features of *Cruiskeen Lawn* were
modelled on the *By the Way* column in the *Daily Express*. The
column was written by J. B. Morton under the pseudonym
'Beachcomber' and had been in existence since 1924.
Contemporary readers of *Cruiskeen Lawn* recognised the
affinity. In September 1941 an *Irish Times* correspondent, E.
V. Briscoe, wrote that, as a contender for 'the title of best
European humorous columnist', Myles was Beachcomber's
nearest rival. Beachcomber had developed several devices
which Myles probably adopted. He had a whole series of
incredible characters with rather Dickensian titles. One of
these was Dr Strabismus (Whom God Preserve) of Utrecht, a
mad scientist. Another was Prodnose, whose main function it
was to interrupt Beachcomber and inform him that he was
being tedious, or to correct his facts. Beachcomber was a great
parodist, especially of sentimental or 'romantic' material. He
disliked 'artiness' and had a marvellous time at the expense of
academic, critical, and legal jargon.

Another possible influence was 'Father Prout' (Francis
Sylvester Mahony), who wrote in *Fraser's Magazine* in the
nineteenth century. Father Prout was an authority, pedantic
but completely assured, on *everything*, and, like Myles,
wandered through history claiming acquaintance with
its great figures. According to Myles, Father Prout was one of
the consortium which had 'really' written Joyce's books, and,
indeed, he was enough of a pseudo-scholar, parodist and
linguist to be considered eligible by Myles.

Ten years after its inception, and with characteristic eccentricity, Myles wrote (on the wrong date) 'CRUISKEEN LAWN
IS 10 YEARS OLD TODAY', and summed up its achievements.

As a long-term feat of denunciation and abuse, I do not

think it has ever been equalled; certainly it has never been surpassed.   (23 Oct. 1950)

He was quite correct. In the limited space of a few pages, it is quite impossible to give an adequate idea of the range of subjects, attitudes, devices and flights of fancy which Myles presented in the columns of *Cruiskeen Lawn.* It is possible, though unavoidably misleading, to clarify the issue a little by separating aspects of the column and discussing it under two headings: as what might be called 'pure fun', and as satire.

Under the heading 'pure fun' come those articles with little satiric content. In a letter to Gerald Gross on 16 January 1962, Myles talked about the English attitude to humour. He said that the English were

> very hard to amuse—they look for overtones, undertones, subtones, grunts and 'philosophy'; they assume something very serious is afoot. It's disquieting for a writer who is only, for the moment, clowning.

Myles was often 'only clowning', particularly during the early war years when he felt that 'nonsense' was needed to uplift the depression brought on by a solid diet of war news, and when the Irish were still learning the important and difficult lesson of how to laugh at themselves.

Most of the column is, however, satiric in intention. Myles in *Cruiskeen Lawn* is primarily a satirist and his satire embraces an enormous scope. The column, as a whole, was completely unpredictable and often bizarre and intentionally disturbing; it could sometimes even be deeply wounding to those at the receiving end of Myles's very sharp barbs.

In the realm of 'pure fun' or 'nonsense' came the findings and inventions of the Research Bureau, the antics of the 'brother', the Keats and Chapman stories and the catalogue of bores.

The Myles na gCopaleen Central Research Bureau made its first appearance in 1941. It is a direct successor to the various Institutes of Practical Psychology and similar establishments in *Comhthrom Féinne* and *Blather* which formulated devices, miraculous schemes and ingenious inventions as panaceas for all possible (and some impossible) ills. Myles, as mad scientist, was a composite of Beachcomber's Dr Strabismus, and O'Nolan's friend Jack Nevin, the mechanical wizard who had probably been the first to fill him with a love of miraculous mechanical machines. Myles was, quite obviously, fascinated by scientific and pseudo-scientific devices and usually accompanied his descriptions of the Research Bureau's intricate and quite useless gadgets with a detailed drawing. Myles had, in fact, a vivid visual imagination and some of the best columns were those which illustrated the outdated marvels of the old Corkaguiney, Dingle and Muskerry Railroad and its amazing machines and modes of propulsion, or showed a coach-and-four actually being driven through an act of parliament which is suspended across the road. On a number of occasions Myles commented on the separation between visual and verbal awareness which he saw as detrimental to the former.

> At dinner some nights ago I said with great bitterness Do have some Carrageen mBás. No one laughed at this shiny sarah (or brilliant sally). I decided immediately that this oral mechanism is a very poor affair. It cannot communicate an essentially visual joke.   (22 Feb. 1943)

A few days before he had written about illiteracy:

> Think of the illiterate's acute observation of the real world as distinct from the pale print-interpreted thing that means life for most of us!   (12 Feb. 1943; *BM*.238)

The illustrations and the precise descriptions were intended to convey, in so far as it was possible, a visual dimension to the column. A good many of Myles's readers were taken in by some of the more likely-looking devices and wrote to him wishing to purchase the Research Bureau's newly patented tea-saving teapot or some such item. This delighted Myles. He spent a good deal of time designing a snow-gauge, trying to run street-lamps on sewer-gas, or finding a way of helping keep candles alight in railway tunnels. In addition, he invented intoxicating ice-cream and midnight oil, and found a way to generate 'jam from second-hand electricity'. The more fantastic and impractical the gadget, the more it was enjoyed, and the Research Bureau was always more concerned with a demonstration of sheer mental dexterity than with the kind of analysis of the processes of scientific thought which is to be found in *The Third Policeman*. Most of the gadgets, of course, had a strictly *practical* application.

> Before the leaves of autumn fall, the Research Bureau, spurred on by the exhortations of Sir Myles na gCopaleen (the da) will have provided new patent emergency trousers for the plain people of Ireland. These garments, conventional enough in appearance, will be fitted with long eel-like pockets reaching down to the ankles. The pockets will be the exact diameter of a bottle of stout and not by any coincidence, for they are designed to deal with the nuisance of those brown-paper Saturday-night parcels. It will be possible to stow four stouts in each leg. At first, walking in the 'loaded' position will necessarily be rather slow and straight-legged but practice will tell in the long-run, which should be undertaken only after short runs have been mastered. (10 Sep. 1943; *BM*.126)

One of the most popular features of the column was the series of Keats and Chapman stories. These stories, which always concluded with an excruciatingly bad pun, were rendered more comic by the association of quite incongruous antics with the translator of Homer and the romantic poet. In the stories, Keats and Chapman operate in a classic comic mode. Chapman is usually the actor, Keats the commentator. It is normally Keats who delivers the punch-line, while Chapman, playing the role of audience, responds to the awful pun with groans, howls and, often, physical collapse. The long build-up of the story to the final deflation in the punch-line is another example of a classic comic device. Many of the puns depend on the scholarship of the readers; the humour derives partly from the unexpectedness yet inevitability of the resolution, the skill employed in the telling of the pre-story, and the sense of conspiracy between the reader's powers of recognition and Myles's inventiveness and sense for incongruous associations of ideas.

Once Chapman, in his tireless quest for a way to get rich quick, entered into a contract with a London firm for the supply of ten tons of swansdown. At the time he had no idea where he could get this substance, but on the advice of Keats went to live with the latter in a hut on a certain river estuary where the rather odd local inhabitants cultivated tame swans for the purposes of their somewhat coarsely-grained eggs. Chapman erected several notices in the locality inviting swan-owners to attend at his hut for the purpose of having their fowls combed and offering 'a substantial price' per ounce for the down so obtained. Soon the hut was surrounded by gaggles of unsavoury-looking natives, each accompanied by four or five disreputable swans on dog-leads. The uproar was enormous and vastly annoyed Keats, who was in bed with toothache. Chapman went out and addressed the multitude and then fell to bargaining with individual owners. After an hour in the pouring rain he came in to Keats, having apparently failed to do business. He was in a vile temper.

'Those appalling louts!' he exploded. 'Why should I go out and humiliate myself before them, beg to be allowed to comb their filthy swans, get soaked to the skin bargaining with them?'

'It'll get you down sooner or later,' Keats mumbled.

(4 Mar. 1944; *BM*. 192-3)

The characters of Keats and Chapman, like the character of Myles himself, became infinitely expandable in these stories. They shared a great variety of adventures, tried many different occupations, lived in different countries; in short, they had a rich and varied existence. Keats and Chapman stories became, and remain, a rage in Dublin with everyone trying to best Myles in making up ingenious plots and worse puns.

The 'brother' was another minor character who came to be a kind of Everyman figure. His adventures and opinions were expounded on at great length by a 'Dublin' character who trapped listeners at a bus-stop. His most customary audience was a gentleman of refined expression and sceptical nature whose speech and obvious disbelief are in pointed contrast to

the story-teller's Dublin idiom and credulous attitude.
According to him, the brother can do anything. There are
those who doubt the existence of the brother, and they are not
to be blamed, for he is such a fabulous creature that it is
difficult to see how he could be human. The brother was a
sworn enemy of the Dublin Corporation whom he had
continually on the run, a man of extensive learning, medical,
historical and linguistic. He was a politician, an inspired
engineer and doctor. Tyrannical as he was on matters of
health, hygiene, and moral behaviour, the other inhabitants
of the 'digs' went in terror of him, and when he spoke his word
was law. Even his dog shared his cleverness and was so
outstanding as to be considered a suitable applicant for the
Guards. The brother always knew someone who was 'in the
know', and he himself was often called upon to hold the
national fort in times of emergency.

> Half the crowd above in the digs are off to Arklow for a
> week Tursda. On their holliers, you know.
> *I see. Is your relative travelling also?*
> The brother? Not at all man. Yerrah not at all. Shure the
> brother can't leave town.
> *Is that a fact? Why not?*
> The brother has to stop in town for the duration of the
> emergency. The Government does be callin the brother in
> for consultations. Of course that's between you and me and
> Jack Mum. The brother gave a promise to a certain party
> not to leave town during the emergency. He has to stand by.
> Because if something happened that could only be fixed up
> be the brother, how could your men be chasin after him on
> the telephone down to Strand Street, Skerries, where he
> goes every year to the married sister's?
> *Admittedly it would be awkward.*
> Sure you couldn't have that, man. You can't run a
> country that way.
> *I agree.*
> You couldn't have that at all. And do you know what I'm
> going to tell you, if ould Ireland isn't kept out of this
> business that's goin on, it won't be the brother's fault. And
> all the time he'll keep the Guards right, too. The ould

weather-eye never leaves them boyos, no matter what
consultation he's called in on. They needn't think they can
take it easy because he's busy. He has the eye at the present
time on a certain boyo in plain clothes.

I see.

I was thinking of takin a week myself in August. Down as
far as Bettystown with Charlie. Would you say that'd be all
right?

*I think the nation would be reasonably safe, especially
since your relative has undertaken to remain in the capital.*

Begob, I think you're right, I think I'll chance it. Here's
me bus. Cheers.   (29 Jun. 1942; *BM*.51-2)

The 'brother' is a direct descendant of Messrs Shanahan,
Lamont and Furriskey, and he reappears in *The Hard Life*,
re-embodied in Manus, the supreme con-man, innovator and
'chancer', who begins his career at an early age by teaching
people, through a correspondence course, how to walk over
the Liffey on a tight-rope.

Throughout *Cruiskeen Lawn* Myles illustrates some of the
qualities which determined the peculiarities of the novels. He
demonstrates an ability to create detailed comic fantasy. This
ability stems from a constant tendency to postulate a situation,
work it out to its conclusion, taking in all the possibilities on
the way, and in the process, convincingly demonstrate the
illogic of logic. The relentless reasoning is skilfully exploited to
create the 'brother's' fantastic conclusions and the long lead-
ups which gives the Keats and Chapman puns their dreadful
impact.

I've a quare bit of news for you. The brother's nose is out
of order.

What?

A fact. Some class of a leak somewhere.

I do not understand.

Well do you see it's like this. Listen till I tell you. Here's
the way he's fixed. He starts sucking the wind in by the
mouth. That's OK, there's no damper there. But now he
comes along and shuts the mouth. That leaves him the nose
to work with or he's a dead man. Fair enough. He starts

sucking in through the mose: AND THEN DO YOU KNOW WHAT?

What?

THE—WIND GOES ASTRAY SOMEWHERE. Wherever it goes it doesn't go down below. Do you understand me? There's some class of a leak above in the head somewhere. There's what they call a valve there. The brother's valve is banjaxed.

I see.

The air does leak up into the head, all up around the brother's brains.   (26 Jun. 1942; *BM*.49)

Myles was always able to see the real meaning, in pictorial and often physically grotesque terms, of a particular word or phrase. He had demonstrated this in *Comhthrom Féinne* in the macabre detail in which he invented a story around the phrase 'the train made matchwood of him'. Thus, in another article, Myles describes a visit to his editor's office, where the editor sits talking to a reader about the state of the nation. Myles describes what he sees.

But wait . . .what . . .*what is this?* It is too terrible but no, I must, I'm paid for it . . .there, cowering before him [the editor] on the other chair is a skeleton, faultlessly (not faultfully) attired in a bowler hat and spats, his bones scarcely dry. And that's not all. What on earth is that roseate jelly that trembles on the floor near the window, that appears to be making a colossal effort—Oh, stop! stop!—to *move,* yes to crawl across the floor? What is that strange brown fur? That sparkling rapid-congealing pink liquid? I looked at the man behind the roll-top (not roll-bottom) desk and he must have seen the agonised query in my eyes. He interrupted his discourse long enough to say:

Just one of our readers, old man—I'm making his flesh creep.   (3 Mar. 1943)

The fantastic, visual quality of Myles's imagination was most often present in conjunction with the Research Bureau, Keats and Chapman and the 'scientific' explanations of the 'brother'. It is usually allied to a habit of vivid description and the ability to 'catch' characters for ever by evoking their most frequently used phrases, or by classing them among the set of universal comic stereotypes. Thus the 'brother', although a chameleon-type character, is also a composite-character, a summing-up in one person of all those separate types who are classed as 'bores' by Myles.

Myles's bores are usually 'pub' characters, comic stereotypes, one-dimensional in their particular obsessions. Myles catches the characteristic turn of speech, the habitual pose, the clichéd response with a cruel and immensely precise eye and ear, and is helped in this by the fact that his 'bores', like his Dubliner (there is often little difference), can be analysed phrase by phrase. He presents us with 'The Man Who Buys Wholesale', 'The Man Who Is His Own Lawyer', 'The Man Who Never Gives Pennies To Beggars', 'The Man Who Doesn't Look His Age', 'The Man Who Has Read It In Manuscript', 'The Man Who Does His Own Carpentry And Talks About It', and — greatest of them all — 'The Man Who Spoke Irish At A Time When It Was Neither Profitable Nor Popular'. Myles himself says:

> The sort of bore I have been attempting to define in recent notes is a bore and outright bore; boring other people is his sole occupation, enjoyment, recreation. No thought of gain would he permit to sully his 'art', indeed, many of them are prepared to lose money — to *stand* drinks — if they see a good opportunity of pursuing their nefarious vocation.
>
> (13 Dec. 1945; BM.294)

Of course, this type of analysis is more serious than the verbal gymnastics of the Keats and Chapman puns. It gives, at times, a sense of the intolerable misery and 'thereness' of the everyday world, of the desperate obsessions of mankind trying to convince itself that it has purpose, of the neurotic need for an audience for one's trivia. Myles, who often sensed that for Everyman the world was intolerable, might have been more sympathetic. But sympathy was not his purpose in *Cruiskeen Lawn*. His primary aim was satire. He wished to castigate, not to tolerate, the follies of the world. He was to be the observer, watching all that went on about him, always detached, selecting special weapons for each attack. He would be mocking or deflating if that were effective, wounding and denunciatory if it were not. In 1956 he wrote in the column:

> I sometimes flatter myself that I am a most valuable person
> (or public institution) because I ventilate certain disquiets
> and resentments widely held, but mostly by people who
> have no means of public expression.   (18 Jan. 1956)

The parenthetical idea was not wholly fanciful. In a special
sense Myles did become a 'public institution' supplying something that was felt to be necessary in Irish life. When he
was absent from the *Irish Times,* people wrote to him to ask
him to return. Every society probably needs its sardonic jester
to castigate its follies, sting it into a sense of moral awareness,
and give it a broader perspective than its own parochial
interests. Since Myles's death, only Donal Foley, writing *Man
Bites Dog,*[11] has corresponded in any way to the mixture of
fantasy, nonsense, irony and inversion which Myles used to
attack the idiocies of bureaucrats, the pretensions of idealists,
the lunacy and danger of certain social attitudes. He hated
complacency and humbug and refused to let them be
sanctioned by the name of 'tradition'. He was a satirist in the
classic sense of attacking the hypocrisy of men and manners.
Little of his satire, unlike Austin Clarke's was directed at
particular social evils. His war was waged against recurring
characteristics in man and his institutions. There have been
many occasions since his death when Ireland would have been
the better for his presence.

Only a very brief idea can be given of the range of Myles's
satire, but it is important to remember that each subject called
for the use of specific comic devices and that Myles's
deployment of an incredible range of such devices can only be
regarded as brilliant.

Myles turned his attention to the full range of Ireland's
social spectrum, beginning with a presentation of the typical
Anglo-Irish family.

> The baronetcy, of course, is one of the oldest in the
> country. Sir Myles is reckoned to be the 57th of that ilk. Lady
> na gCopaleen is one of the Shaughrauns of Limerick, a very
> distinguished country family. Round after round of
> spontaneous applause has been won by her seat and hands
> at countless point-to-points. A lover of Scotch, she is

reputed to be one of Europe's foremost bottle-women.

Miss Sleeveen na gCopaleen came out only last season. She is very popular with the younger set and is one of the most interesting personalities one meets at hunt balls. After a week in the saddle, she finds her relaxation in poetry, play writing, novel writing, dancing and film work. She is very popular with the younger ballet set and tells me that her hunting experience helps her considerably in this sphere. She is not in the least self-conscious when off a horse. At the moment she tells me that she is organising a Comforts Fund for the troops. 'I do definitely think that life is rather wizard, actually,' she remarked to me the other day.

(2 Jan. 1942; BM. 154-5)

Here Myles is using caricature, and a conglomeration of the characteristics popularly attributed to the Anglo-Irish Ascendancy. The social commentator's laudatory manner is undercut by the rather odd syntax which is used when discussing Lady na gCopaleen's 'hands' and 'seat' and by the names and antecedents of the family. The article, to the frequent reader of *Cruiskeen Lawn*, would have gained extra effect from its place in the large number of articles dealing with Sir Myles na gCopaleen's family and from its association with the long series of jokes about horses in Irish life (why shouldn't they be made ministers?) and about ballet. (Myles devised patent exploding ballet pumps to help the profession rise higher.)

Having demolished the Ascendancy, Myles turned his attention to the peasantry. By this term, however, he did not mean people living on the land. He meant anyone he disliked. The word 'peasant' came to have distinctly perjorative associations. Myles tended to reserve his most violent antipathy for members of local government or semi-state bodies. In 1946 he described what *he* meant by a peasant. A peasant, he said, was a man of middle size who was not a farmer, though he had kept hens in his youth, but was now a university graduate who knew Greek and Latin and could quote (a little) from Homer and Virgil. He had a thorough knowledge of Gaelic language and literature but could neither speak nor write it; nevertheless he was always hoping to meet another peasant whom he could dominate and impress. He had visited Rome,

Berlin, Paris and Madrid once for one week each, and he
visited his home once every five years. This home was described by Myles in cruel and apposite detail and it is clear that
his peasant is a civil servant or a politician.

As a politician himself, Myles's mission was to 'tell the truth
in this damn country'. He saved most of his wrath for de
Valera, whose speeches he parodied. By considering de Valera
to be a stereotype of the politician, he was able to extend his
satire to cover the whole political establishment. He thought
de Valera was wordy, arrogant and ignorant, dishonest and
self-seeking. Most of the attacks on politicians, some of them
violent and bitter, came in the late 1940s and early 1950s, a
time when Myles also waged a campaign against CIE, the
ESB, and the Censorship Board. Politics and censorship had
been obsessive themes since his earliest writings and they
joined his other favourite enemies, lawyers, doctors, bankers,
journalists and academics, as the major subjects of his satire
throughout the column. The professions were, in fact, attacked
so often that it was possible to set up the Myles na gCopaleen
Central Banking Corporation, the Royal Irish Academy of the
Post-War World, the Myles na gCopaleen Institute of
Archaelogy and the Cruiskeen Court of Voluntary Juris-
diction, and under these headings to provide satiric accounts
of fantastic or ludicrous practices which exposed the
normal mode of behaviour of such institutions. Myles often
found it sufficient to abstract a report of court or local council
proceedings from the national or provincial press, and
comment on it at his leisure.

> The Town Clerk (Mr A. J. Powell) informed Cobh
> Council that three plots in the Council's field at Newton,
> under the Allotments Scheme, had disappeared during the
> week. — *Irish Press*, 17.3.'41. I have often heard of land
> hunger. Can it be that ravenous rustics took away the plots
> and ate them?
>   In the old Brehon code the theft of land was regarded as a
> very serious matter. In gravity it ranked next to the theft of
> other people's wind, the filching of private shadows, and the
> sequestration without authority of communal sunlight. A
> miscreant found in possession of a missing farm was

required to put it back where he found it. This done, he was
instantly executed with the old-fashioned *tuagh* and
interred in the bosom of his quondam plunder.

Not a little of the credit for our present scenery is due to
foresight of those old law-givers. They discouraged sternly
the larceny of mountains and gave no quarter to that
despicable mediaeval nuisance, the lake-thief. Moreover —

But no matter.   (29 Mar. 1943)

Mostly, Myles attacked bureaucrats and professionals
through their use of jargon, illustrating in the process his own
command of parodic language.

In the first case the plaintiffs sought a plenary injunction
for trespass, a declaration of fief in agro and other relief.
The defence was a traverse of the field as well as the
pleadings and alternatively it was contended that the
plaintiffs were estopped by graunde playsaunce. (*BM*.137)

The middle classes, upper and lower, were formed by Myles
into a sort of composite character known as 'The Plain People
of Ireland', who usually interrupted Myles in the middle of one
of his flights of fancy, bringing him back to reality with a
bang. The Plain People of Ireland were only semi-educated,
cranky, and very positive about their misconceptions. The
Plain People are, in fact, very much like the uncle in *At Swim*.
They constantly crave variety and demand 'jokes'. They dislike
the serious and sublime. They are, without a doubt, the voice
of confident mediocrity, the spawning-ground for bores,
politicians and civil servants. Their speech is totally cliché-
ridden.

Contemplate Little Britain Street bloch by bloch, Joe,
and drop me a postcard telling me in your own words about
the remote faded poignancy of elegant proportions, minute
delicacy of architectural detail balanced against the charming squalid native persons who sort of provide a contra-
puntal device in the aesthetic apprehension of the whole.
The Plain People of Ireland: How about those jokes.
Myself: Well wait till I see. Would you say that the cousin
of the French Pretender is the Duc de Guise?
The Plain People of Ireland: Whaa?

Myself: And I wonder would he be anything to the Wild Geese?

The Plain People of Ireland: Dear knows some people are very smart, these County Council scholarships to the universities above in Dublin do more harm than good, young gossoons walking around with their Sunday suits on them on week-days when they're home at Easter, ashamed to be seen out with their fathers and O no thanks, I'm not going to give *any* hand with the sowing, I have to attend to me studies, I've an exam in two months. And that reminds me, I want five pounds for books. Sure it's all madness. You say you'd like a joke or two for a bit of crack and the finger of scorn is pointed at you. It's madness, the country's in a right state. Madness. There's no other word for it. Madness.

(25 Mar. 1942; BM.93)

What passes for thinking, among the Plain People is a stereotyped, expected response produced in some 'time-honoured' pattern of words. Eventually, in order to reveal this in its full horror, Myles set out to produce a 'Catechism of Cliché',

A unique compendium of all that is nauseating in contemporary writing. Compiled without regard to expense or the feelings of the public. A harrowing survey of sub-literature and all that is pseudo, mal-dicted and calloused in the underworld of print.   (27 Mar. 1942; *BM*.202)

Myles was deeply concerned with the increasing misuse of language and the use of modes of expression which harm definition and destroy discrimination. He constantly attempted to make his readers aware of linguistic forms and the importance of correct speech.

An irascible and anonymous (indeed, incognitable) correspondent has communicated with me on questions of grammar and such like. He claims to be a native speaker, and finds that his use of words and syntactical accretions is in conflict with standard *opera*, lexicographical and grammatical . . . He asks me what he is to do.

I can only advise him to do as I do. Ignore all rules of grammar that do not suit your book, to the devil with all obsolete impudence that requires you to think before you write. Give words the gender that seems appropriate in the light of your God-given reason, and do not hesitate to import into the linguistic texture of your matter the same incredibly low standard that you reach in its intellectual content.   (19 Apr. 1941)

Myles constantly emphasised clichés, and played linguistic games in order to make his readers aware of both the subtlety and the increasing deadness of English speech. He makes much use of parenthesis and italics:

(All musical Dublin) (is agog) (with expectation) of the new symphony by Milesius Chapaline which will form the main item in next Thursday's concert at the Antient Concert Rooms.   (22 Jul. 1942; *BM*.208)

Incidentally (a word that adds absolutely nothing to what I'm saying) I was coming home late Saturday and fell to wondering why Ireland which has no high-speed industrial week, should also dedicate this night to organistic pot-astrophies. My whimsical mood of wonder was prompted by the sight of two 'men' in a tram. I call them 'men' rather then men because they were in inverted commas.
                                                        (1 Mar. 1943)

The Catechism of Cliché began in 1942 with the explanation

A CLICHÉ is a phrase that has become fossilised, its component words deprived of their intrinsic light and meaning by incessant usage. Thus it appears that clichés reflect somewhat the frequency of the incidence of the same situations in life. If this be so, a sociological commentary could be compiled from these items of mortified language.
                                                        (27 Aug. 1943; *BM*.227)

The clichés which Myles presented covered every aspect of life, and almost every set phrase. Some were devoted to only one subject, others covered a whole range.

DEAD ENGLISH

Life can be bitter. Did you ever notice how easily the
amateur can eclipse the industrious professional like myself
in the (sphere) (of cliché)? I take this wonderful thing
from the current issue of the Journal of the Irish Medical
Association.

'The returns show that the outbreak was by no means
confined to the Dublin area as rumour had suggested and
prove, if proof were needed, that Dame Rumour continues
to justify her reputation as a lying jade.'

Now let me follow up with a few poor efforts of my own.
When things are few, what also are they?

Far between.

What are stocks of fuel doing when they are low?

Running.

How low are they running?

Dangerously.

What does one do with a suggestion?

One throws it out.

For what does one throw a suggestion out?

For what it may be worth.   (14 Oct. 1942; *BM*. 222-3)

The form of the catechism had demanded that the reader
had to supply the cliché for the elaborate form Myles had
proposed in its place. Myles's aim in this was to make people
think about the real meaning of the words they used, and
hence about the real meanings of words used by others. On the
whole he was pleased with the response. Discussing the
catechism in an important article only a few weeks before his
death, Myles explained his attitude very clearly. Referring to
the Catechism of Cliché as 'the most cautionary (material) I
have ever written', he said:

Once upon a time in that slow, inevitable, forbidding,
dim and crepuscular archive known as Cruiskeen Lawn
there appeared an exegetic survey of the English Language
in its extremity of logo-daedalate poliomylitis, anaemic
prostration and the paralysis of incoherence. It is a
syndrome usually epitomised in the word cliché, a French

printing term which in English has come to denote language without anterior meaning or import, words for words' sake, speech destitute of communication, babble in which no mind is involved. The method I used was the catechetical and it was sinisterly efficient in bringing out the empty horror of this most modern of human abberations — a portrait of man in the nadir of his dessicated surcease.

Many intelligent editors, radio and print managers as well as countless headmasters, had the series preserved and reproduced and, as occasion demanded, summarily served a copy on delinquent subordinates. A result has been that today many people write English who otherwise would be manipulating a clueless code. A residual curiosity is that when a man is capable of expressing himself, he finds he had something to say, while, when linguistically mum, the astonishing side-result is that he is incapable of thinking: that it to say, meaningful words are often the actual stuff of thought. The verbal expression of thought is often thought itself in the process of formation. Perhaps this cerebral mystery is best exemplified in the case of poetry, where language is the real pith and magic as it disguises and embroiders thought.   (7 Mar. 1966)

Myles had early developed a loathing of cliché and this was to remain all his life. Even his bores are most boring in their stereotyped linguistic responses.

> Christmas come and gone, eh? Let's associate for a moment a few banalities and bores associated with the season.
>
> Easily first is the person, usually a woman, who says: 'Christmas? Do you know I wish it was over.'
>
> Next possibly is the person who says:
>
> 'Christmas? Do you know, I do always think it is a sad time.'
>
> Next:
>
> Well well. Another Christmas! The way time flies is something shocking.   (27 Dec. 1944; *BM*. 286)

There was a clear association in Myles's mind between the

degeneration of language and the ease with which people responded to fraudulent rhetoric, whether it be in advertising, politics or in stirring calls to arms. He saw language as a tool which could be manipulated in the interests of power if people were unaware of what was being done. For this reason he wrote on 14 April 1945:

Is it not time that you Irish woke up to the unsuspected fragility of the human intellect?

His letter to the man who was careless of syntax had clearly revealed the association between intellect and grammar. The fragility of the intellect, he thought, expressed itself in many ways but primarily in the attitudes of the Irish towards themselves and their assumptions about Ireland. Myles himself had no time for the romantic ideals; these, of all things, were prime examples of mental sloppiness. One of the reasons for his prolonged attack on the Abbey Theatre was its propagation of an image of Ireland which Myles found intolerable. Myles's perception of Ireland often seemed oddly distanced. He would refer to his own countrymen, possibly in a satire on Ascendancy attitudes as 'You Irish'.

When, I wonder — *when* will I get to the bottom of you Irish?   (10 Jan. 1945)

In general, rejecting both the conventional stage Irishman of popular knowledge and the Celtic stereotype which had replaced it and which personified the Irish as 'simple, unspoiled, God-fearing' people, he castigated the Irish for stupidity, ignorance, complacency, rudeness, brutality and hypocrisy. He referred over and over again to 'we awful Irish louts', and was to develop this point in *An Béal Bocht*, which exploded the myth of the Gaelic-speaking peasant and his idyllic life. Ireland, he implied, was not fairyland; it was often more like hell.

These comments only began to appear as the war was drawing to a close. While it was continuing, Myles saw his role as a transcending and consolatory one. After the war he was free to deride the optimism of post-war planners, and the blindness of a people who had learnt nothing about human nature from the events of the past six years. His favourite

device here was the presentation of an innocent and naïve
'But their feeling for matière is so profound and . . .
peace and prosperity, until brought face to face with a
conflicting and surprising fact. From surprise he goes on to
develop the fantastic possibilities of the situation.

No doubt you saw at the Planning Exhibition the big
map of Ireland laid out on the floor, you stopped and saw
the bulbs go on showing where everything would be in the
future. You were very interested in it all and left, reflecting
that at no far distant day Ireland would take its place
among the nations of the earth . . .
In certain of their moments, the planners surprise me. At
one point they turned on a little forest, one at every important point in the country. Do you know what these lights
stood for?·*Great new sanatoria!* Do they . . . do they mean
to tell me that we are going to have . . . *disease* . . . in the
new planned Ireland? Have they a dastardly scheme under
which *pain* will still be possible? Are we — great heaven! — to
be permitted to . . . to . . . *to die* in the new Ireland? If the
answer to these questions is yes, then I say all this planning
is a ramp. I solemnly warn Pat to look out for himself.
Hospitals are being planned for him, clinics, health centres,
stream-lined dispensaries. I can see the new Ireland all
right, in mime-hind's eye. The decaying population tucked
carefully in white sterilised beds, numb from drugs, rousing
themselves only to make their wills in Irish. Outside, not a stir
anywhere to be discerned — save for the commotion of
funerals hurtling along the vast arterial roads to the vast
arterial cemeteries — planned by architects, need I
say — where tombs and tomb-stones are prefabricated in
plastics. It is my considered view that Paud keeping step
with world hysteria in the belief that he is being 'modern' is
a woeful spectacle, is nowise funny. He has got himself a lot
of graphs and diagrams and is beginning to babble about
'built-in furniture'. Give him just a little rope and he will
demolish any descent houses he may have and go and live in
insanitary 'prefabricated' shells, the better and the sooner to
qualify for the new glass-brick sanatorium.

(10 May 1944; *BM*. 382-3)

555

Sometimes Myles was simply violently angry. Speaking of the 'morbid sub-human pretences adopted by the Keltured idiocated Dubliners', he discussed the campaign to preserve Georgian Dublin and all it had represented, and dismissed it.

> But what are the facts about this Georgian ramp? I'll tell you (they'll get me for this but my public comes first) I'll tell you the inside guts of it. Dublin is a slum. Dublin is a slum, do you hear me. At its best (in Fitzwilliam Square) a well-preserved flat-riddled professional slum. At its worst (in Bride Street, the Liberties, Summerhill, Mountjoy Square) a sprawling dung-hill on stilts, giving off a constant odourless vapour of rancid, unwashable profit-rents.
>
> (25 Mar. 1942; *BM*. 92)

The point of much of this was far more serious than anything Myles had attempted before. He was, essentially trying to force another kind of awareness on his audience. Playing the role of iconoclast, he wished now to destroy the precarious security brought about by the end of the war and to examine the sources of violence. In typical fashion he examined violence in all its aspects, from the excesses of war to a casual quarrel on a sportsfield. War was, in fact, one of the few subjects which Myles dealt with directly.

> War is to be understood only in terms of man; man only in terms of war. There is no third war. There is only one war and to think that it will cease within the bournes of humanity's tenure of the soil is to think as one thought in the nursery . . .   (25 Sep. 1944)

Myles was referring here not to war as a temporary outburst of international strife, but to the greater, and permanent, struggle between good and evil, which manifests itself in the very nature of man himself. As he had written 'the meanest thing in hell made this world', so too did he write about the difference between war and peace.

> When the world is at peace, horror camps are not photographed.   (23 Jun. 1945)

This sounds like Manichaeism, and perhaps it is, but it is a part of Myles's concern with the basic facts of human existence. It is clear that he felt that one of the basic facts was language and man's attitude to it. At times he almost seems to have thought that someone or something was setting out to sabotage meaning and coherence. Evil was quite often the result of perverted language or intellect — in effect, the same thing.

Myles makes it clear in *The Third Policeman* and *The Dalkey Archive* that he hated scientists and philosophers who invented their own language (and thus their own universe) which other men did not understand and so distorted. The result was chaos, and chaos became Myles's great fear. But he manifested that fear in satiric form. Myles laughed at chaos to distance it, and made men aware of it to alert them to its dangers. He believed that the 'fragile' human intellect needed the protection of order and discipline to keep it and its unlimited fabrications within bounds. The freedom of the imagination, in which he gloried, carried with it its own dangers. Language created everything. Perverted linguistic contrivances and usages led the way to evil, when mental sloppiness and conventionalised statements replaced wisdom. Since language defined and created reality, it must be made an incisive moral and humanitarian instrument and serve to protect man from gloom and obfuscation, inspire him with hope, and remind him of what lay outside process and expediency. It could not, as he saw it doing, continue to create valueless, chaotic, relativistic worlds in which a simple man was lost and credulous because he had been taught to believe in the achievements of an essentially weak and foundless intellect.

Because, men were not capable of distinguishing between 'true' and 'false' statements, where all statements were propagandist and clichéd, they were unable to see the full implications of the horrors of Hiroshima and Nagasaki, to which Myles reacted with disgust. He warned his readers:

Scientists and governments are very worried about the possibility that people may not die, or may not expire in sufficiently gigantic numbers, and, *in order to make sure* they have devoted much thought and treasure to research on this subject. The most efficient device yet evolved appears to be this 'atomic bomb'. I do not find that the quest for it is an adult performance.   (20 Aug. 1945)

As early as *At Swim* Myles had been aware of the dangers of transferring childish fantasies of violence and 'heroism' into the adult world. So he was terrified by the development of the bomb and argued that man could not be trusted to control it.

> Everyone wants to be a bombmaster . . . Everybody wants to mind it just really for everyone else's own good.
>
> (11 Oct. 1945)

The subject was to continue to be important in the column. He adopted a mock-stoic, sometimes defeatist role, calling on strontium as the cure for all ills, negator of the need for all effort.

If Myles disliked the confusions of scientists and philosophers, he found those of artists even more appalling. A major source of concern to him was the fact that artists said so little about the problems of the world; indeed, they even added to the confusion by creating the jargon of criticism and pseudo-aestheticism, a jargon which Myles parodied in article after article.

> Search any old lukewarm bath and you will find one of these aesthetical technicians enjóying himself. He is having a lukewarm bath, it is rather good, it is something real, something that has its roots in the soil, a tangible, valid, unique, complete, integrating, vertical experience, a diatonic spatio-temporal cognition in terms of realistic harmonic spacing, differential intervals and vector (emmanuel) analysis, of those passional orphic inferences which must be proto-morphously lodged in writing with the Manager on or before the latest closing date.
>
> (15 Apr. 1944; *BM*.249)

He was irritated by the pretensions and pretences of artists, and often supplied a passage which reveals this very clearly.

> It is, I think, natural for a person of my stamp (as poor Rowan Hamilton used to say) to embrace all human perfections and accomplishments (but excluding such as may be evil) within the mastery of my superb intellect gracing

not myself but all humanity with an artistic pre-eminence
that is withal saturated with an exquisite humility.

'But . . . don't you ever run short of ideas? How can
you *always* write so . . . interestingly . . . so . . . so
authoritatively about such a variety of things. Seldom, I
mean, have . . . so many things been written for so many
people . . . by so few a man.'

My reply is simple and, as always, truthful. 'Madam,
writing is the least of my occupations. Many other things,
many many other things contribute to the sum of my cares.
Vast things, things imponderable and ineluctable, terrible
things, things which no other mortal were fit to hear
of—things I must think upon only when utterly alone.
Writing is surely a small thing, indeed. Difficulties,
Mmmmm. One is not conscious of them. There are, of
course, five things and five things only that can be written
about and though for me they have lost all interest as
problems, I continue to write out of the depth of my feeling
for dark groping humanity.'   (22 Jan.1944; *BM*.377)

Not just the artists, but their followers and admirers,
annoyed Myles. He disliked, in particular, wealthy men who
have not the intellect nor the sensitivity to read but who wish,
nevertheless, to make a showing in the world of culture. For
these, as one of his services to mankind, Myles invented the
'book-handling service'. This undertook to mark books, insert
old theatre programmes, underline paragraphs, and in
general give a man's shelves of books a well-used look. The
wealthy would never again 'be put to the trouble of pretending
to read at all'. For the really culturally ambitious, comments
could be written in the margins of books like 'I remember poor
Joyce saying the very same thing to me' and 'Quite, but
Boussuet in his Discourse sur l'histoire Universelle has already
established the same point and given much more forceful
explanations'. The 'Traitement Superbe' version of the service
provide for the inclusion of messages purportedly from the
author to the owner, such as:

Dear A.B.,—Your invaluable suggestions and assistance,

not to mention your kindness, in entirely re-writing chapter 3, entitles you, surely, to this first copy of 'Tess'. From your old friend T. Hardy.   (10 Nov. 1941; *BM*. p.21)

The Myles na gCopaleen Escort Service was provided for those who had no books but who still wanted to be thought educated. Ventriloquists could be hired by the ignorant to accompany them to parties and the theatre, there to make brilliant remarks about art, music, ballet and literature which would seem to be the pronouncements of the hirer. Like the much earlier 'Eaters' service in *Comhthrom Féinne,* the skill and the cost of book-handling and Escorts varied with the amount of cultural snobbery they produced. One would have to pay very highly for the following conversation, which is 'one of the most expensive on the menu'. The misunderstanding, contained in it is, says Myles, designed to make 'the thing appear extraordinarily genuine'.

'Well, well, Godfrey, how awfully wizard being at the theatre with you!'
'Yes, it *is* fun.'
'What have you been doing with yourself?'
'Been trying to catch up with my reading, actually.'
'Ow, good show, keep in touch and all that.'
'Yes, I've been studying a lot of books on Bali. You know?'
'Ballet is terribly bewitching, isn't it? D'you like Petipa?'
'I'm not terribly sure that I do, but they seem to have developed a complete art of their own, you know. Their sense of décor and their general feeling for the plastic is quite marvellous.'
'Yes, old Dérain did some frightfully good work for them; for the Spectre, I think it was, actually. Sort of grisaille, you know.'
'But their feeling for matière is so profound and . . . almost brooding. One thinks of Courbet.'
'Yes, or Ingres.'
'Or Delacroix, don't you think?'
'Definitely. Have you read Karsavina?'
'Of course.'

'Of course, how stupid of me. I saw her, you know.'
'Ow, I hadn't realised that she herself was a Balinese.'
'Balinese? What *are* you driving at?'
'But —'
'But —'.   (8 Dec. 1941; *BM*.25-6)

If this represented culture, it, and its adherents, were irrelevant and worthless. Myles had his own ideas about the nature of art and literature. 'True literature is for pleasure, catharsis and instruction.' (21 Feb. 1949). The purpose of art, he said, was communication. In 1950, quoting J. Donald Adams of the *New York Times* who had said that Eliot and Joyce express confusion by employing confusion, Myles had commented sarcastically that it was not true that 'communication' was the first principle of art. Chief among writers, Joyce fell into the category of those who, like scientists and philosophers, destroyed language and substituted their own. *Cruiskeen Lawn* contains almost eighty comments on Joyce. They occur at all stages of the column's existence. Some of them occupy only a few lines; others constitute complete articles. Taken all in all, they reveal more ambivalence than coherence on Myles's part, but they shed light on Myles's continuing obsession with Joyce and indicate some of the reasons for it. The articles range from attacks on those who put an apostrophe in *Finnegans Wake* or comments on the difficulty of translating *Ulysses* into Irish, to a mock biography of Joyce (6 Dec. 1965), and imaginative reconstructions of various meetings with him. Among these articles can be found the genesis of the treatment of Joyce in *The Dalkey Archive* (23 Dec. 1961).

Myles attacks both Joyce's work and his personality, but primarily it is Joyce's attitude to language of which he disapproves. 'Twenty years ago . . . poor Jimmy Joyce abolished the King's English.' (27 Nov. 1942; *BM*. 103) This idea was repeated often in the column. In 1944 he wrote:

I hear there's not two consecutive words of English in that book 'Flanagan's Awake' matteradamn what anybody says. Could we . . . make that the national language?
                                                    (18 Mar. 1944)

In 1958, Myles wrote that the *Irish Times* was guilty of misplacing the word 'only' in sentences. He continued:

> It is not proper that they should presume to align themselves with Klee, Picasso, Joyce, Alban Berg and other demolitionists of the accepted modes of communication.
>
> (3 Mar. 1958)

A few months later he repeated this charge.

> His [Joyce's] attempted disintegration, dissipation and demolition of language was his other major attainment, if you can call it that'.   (7 Jul. 1958)

In Myles's mind the demolition of language was always accompanied by a state of confusion, and Joyce's works were no exception.

> Joyce is not living—though that indeed were a minor accomplishment on the part of one who reduced the entire literary world to a state of chronic and hopeless exegesis.
>
> (12 Sep. 1949)

In fact, Myles accuses Joyce of obfuscation, of not communicating clearly. He complained that *Finnegans Wake* was 'unreadable' and invented an interview with Joyce where Joyce criticised a 2,000-page-long 'fragment' of Myles's as 'incomprehensible', while still admitting that 'the inspiration was profound' (15 Sep. 1950). Deriding Americans for their interest in Joyce, Myles stated that 'nobody but a Dublin Paddy could get more than 10% of its [*Ulysses*] meanings', and went on to talk of 'the magic of misunderstanding' that surrounded Joyce's work (10 Feb. 1953). He complained that Joyce was illiterate, that his use of foreign languages was always incorrect, and that he was too fond of the literary *tour de force*. He wondered if Joyce was to be taken seriously at all, if *Finnegans Wake* was anything more than the 'ultimate fantasy in cod'. (16 Jun. 1954)

In 1957 he summed all this up and, returning to an earlier point, emphasised that art is communication. Hence his surprise that other writers, who also say that art is communication, still praise Joyce.

> because he was incommunicate, incoherent, or simply did
> not know what he was talking about.   (10 Apr. 1957)

Joyce's 'original simple and pure aim' was, Myles suggested,·
'not to be understood, certainly not to be misunderstood, but
to be un-understood' (10 Apr. 1957).

In a long, semi-serious article, in which Myles deals with
Joyce's language, he shows how intimately he connected the
idea of the destruction of language, with the destruction of the
universe.

> What would you think of a man who entered a restaurant,
> sat down, suddenly whipped up the table-cloth and blew his
> nose in it? You would not like it — not if you owned the
> restaurant. That is what Joyce did with our beloved tongue
> that Shakespeare and Milton spoke.
>
>   I suppose all experiment entails destruction, and every
> one of us may yet pay with our lives for certain nuclear
> experiments being now conducted by the Americans and
> the Russians.   (7. Jul. 1958)

Joyce's character and attitudes were equally disliked.
Referring to Joyce as 'James Aquinas Joyce' (21 Mar. 1944),
Myles tells of how he refused to verify a point about a place in
Dublin for Joyce, 'telling him that I lived in Santry and did not
run on messages for spoiled Jesuits' (6 Jun. 1957). Talking
about Jack Yeats, Myles said in his praise:

> Unlike Joyce, he was not an abominable prig and expressed
> himself freely instead of taking refuge in Joyce's peculiar
> form of 'silence'.   (11 Apr. 1957)

He objected to Joyce's attitude to Ireland. Always referring
to him as 'Poor Joyce' or 'poor Jimmy Joyce' and sometimes
playing the role of the man, a friend of Simon's, who had
known 'Jimmy' in his youth while he still showed some
promise, he would make comments like:

> The only decent man [in Dublin] was poor Mr Joyce, who
> left Dublin the better to libel it.   (17 Mar. 1943)

Other criticisms were more forthright. He also referred to
Joyce as

> a complete prig, a snob, and a person possessed of
> endownment unique in the archives of conceit. (6 Jun. 1957)

He spoke of Joyce's 'arid and cold view of life' (5 Apr. 1944),
called *Finnegans Wake* 'a wallet of literary underwear' (6 Jun.
1957), and announced that Joyce's publisher had better guard
against charges of obscenity (5 Apr. 1944). Myles sometimes
dropped the mocking, bantering tone and exploded into real
venom, as when he wrote that Joyce's 'pedantry, aridity and
tourdeforcity [were] something well within the compass of any
literate senior schoolboy'(6 Jun. 1957).

Nevertheless, Myles was forced to praise Joyce for his 'true
felicity' in 'writing comic stuff ' and for his 'almost supernatural skill in conveying Dublin dialogue' (6 Jun. 1957).
Joyce and Yeats, he said, were the only two Irish literary figures
of the last century who were men of genius (1 Sep. 1944).
In a somewhat ambiguous comment, Myles said that

> Joyce was a great master of the banal in literature. By
> 'banal' I mean the fusion of uproarious comic stuff and
> deep tragedy.   (20 Jul. 1955)

Some months later he asserted that *Ulysses* was not difficult or
obscure, but that its

> mental ingestion in full calls for intelligence, maturity, and
> some knowledge of life as well as letters.   (9 Feb. 1956)

Myles did not expect the members of the Censorship Board
('Smut Board') to be able to understand *Ulysses*. Later he was
to recommend both *Ulysses* and *Finnegans Wake* as
'invaluable reference works to chaos, Christian doctrine,
myth, history and hagiology' (19 Dec. 1957). He was continually to castigate the insensitivity of Joyce's critics and to
demand why Joyce had never received the Nobel Prize.

It is possible that Myles's comments on Joyce might not have
been so embittered if the Joyce critical industry had not been
so thriving. Certainly he was unrestrained in his criticism of
scholars and exegetists, and it is helpful to remember that his
comments on *At Swim* were equally violent. At best, it can be

said that Myles's comments on Joyce throw light on his own
conceptions, and that some of them are comic in themselves.
At worst, Myles's obsession with debunking Joyce was an
indication of his own insecurity and was quite senseless.

Joyce was not, of course, the only writer mentioned in·the
column. Myles's attitudes to other writers, past and present,
were more often scathing than praising, but a number of them
are particularly interesting in that they express his own
opinions. He disliked Dickens for his 'ridiculous' langauge, yet
Dickens, C. S. Lewis, William Saroyan and Shakespeare — an
odd combination — are respected for their ability to separate
themselves from their works. Myles praised them because they
make it impossible for the reader to discover, from their
works, what kind of persons they were (5 Mar. 1957). De
Quincey received unstinted praise; he was, said Myles,

> an excellent writer having, above all other symptoms of
> mastery in literature — discursiveness: and irony, un-
> obtrusive, as it always should be.   (4 Oct. 1954)

He was also capable of 'devilishly funny gravity'. He
commented favourably on some of Mark Twain's works and,
in a letter to his agents, pointed to the 'eerie resemblance
between certain departments of his thinking and my own. As
we say here, he is very derogatory.'[12]

Among Irish writers, he most particularly disliked Synge,
Frank O'Connor and Seán Ó Faoláin. The story of his battle
with O'Connor and Ó Faoláin was a long one, but apart from
his wish to debunk what he considered to be their pretensions,
he disliked their writing. It was unrealistic. They wrote, he
said,

> stories about wee Annie going to her first confession, stuff
> about country funerals, old men in chimney nooks after 50
> years in America; will-making, match-making — just one
> long blush for many an innocent man like me, who never
> harmed them.   (4 Oct. 1954)

If possible, he disliked Synge even more than this.
'Cornerboy of the Western World is my name for that fellow.'
(12 Nov. 1955) He claimed that Synge was a 'moneyed
dilettante coming straight from Paris to study the peasants of

Aran'. From Aran he came back to Dublin 'to pour forth a
deluge of home-made jargon all over the Abbey Stage'. He
referred to Synge as 'an ignorant and affected interloper in a
uniquely decent, stable and civilised community' (4 Oct.
1954).

Myles's dislike of Synge was part and parcel of his dislike of
the Abbey Theatre. He had begun to subject the Abbey to
derogatory attack in the pages of *Blather,* where he revealed
'Abbey English' as a very distinct and nauseating form of sub-
language. Apart from that, the Abbey propagated its own
particular brand of 'stage-Irishmen' whose character and
language Myles was to parody in article after article with as
much gusto as he parodied the works of Thomas O'Crohan in
Cruiskeen Lawn and in *An Béal Bocht.*

> A vanatee, agraw, would ye put out me supper like a colleen
> dhas, a bowl of stirabout med with injun meal and a noggin
> of buttermilk; surely?   (4 Oct. 1954)

He described the Abbey as an association of halfwits,
eccentrics and long-suffering martyrs, and to make their lot
easier was eternally suggesting improvements to the theatre.
Realising that people often had to leave before the end of the
play and that, indeed, the actors often got bored with their
parts he suggested that the play should be written out and
demonstrated on huge scrolls at the back of the theatre. It
would then be possible for the audience, by turning round, to
read what was to come next and depart happily. Commenting
on the type-casting that went on, particularly in the plays of
Synge and O'Casey, he suggested that it might be better never
to replace the original actor in a part, as the appearance of a
new Joxer or Juno caused so much distress to actors and
audience alike. There would naturally be difficulties as old
actors died, but it should be possible to continue the play
without them. Eventually Myles suggested a formula for
potential Abbey playwrights to save them the trouble of
devising new plots.

> What must you have to father a 'successful Abbey play'?
> Easily answered: a priest (and if he is a canon, also a
> curate); a will; a comic housekeeper; a civic guard; a

testamentary, agrarian, or matrimonial mix-up for 'plot'; a young idealist who writes poetry and despises everybody; copious mention of fairies; a rough-looking fellow who is on the run; and a learned cranky old grandfather who is working at a secret invention.   (22 Sep. 1955)

The themes and actors of the Abbey had become clichés, stereotypes; the theatre was a purveyor of untruth.

In the world of art, apart from literature, there is often a comment or an article which explains some of Myles's comic views. We know that he admired Charlie Chaplin, Groucho Marx and, even more important, Walt Disney. His comments on Walt Disney are, more than anything else, an adequate description of his own methods and outlook.

Now take a gander (or a donaldduck) at Disney. This man (milord) would mind mickeymice. He was the best man in the world for clever honest fun, for sneering at bores, buffs and bowsies, the best man for drawing, invention, imagination and vituperation.   (8 May 1942; *BM*.230)

Myles, too, was a great man for sneering at 'bores, buffs and bowsies'. Invention and imagination are prime qualities of his column, and many a Dubliner was most anxious to escape his vituperation.

But, the topics covered in *Cruiskeen Lawn* were by no means limited to art, literature and language. Myles dealt also with European politics, the American administration, the vagaries of fashion, the ascent of Everest, the possibility of life in space, and the conflict between capitalism and communism, neither of which he approved. Tourists, doctors, women and ballet dancers were his subjects, as were horses, hospitals, strikes and bicycle thefts. He had something to say on bargains, advertising, the church and prison, existentialism, trees and baby-minding. A list of the subjects dealt with in *Cruiskeen Lawn* takes on the same air of ludicrous incongruity as the syllabus for the London University Academy in *The Hard Life*.

As the column progressed, articles were repeated and the original freshness and wild variety went. It became increasingly bitter and began to lack the sublety of irony. In part this was due to a flagging of Myles's powers of invention and the decreasing hold of the Myles persona on the attention of the readers. Most of Myles's great adventures came in the first ten years of the column; after that, except for brief resurgences, the rapport which had existed between Myles and his readers began to decline. Increasingly he failed to explain his absences in terms of achievement; instead, as O'Brien's own life became more and more difficult, he began to take the place of his character. An absence was no longer due to attendance at a peace conference; it was the result of a spell in hospital, and Myles, less and less detached from O'Brien, grumbled about nurses and doctors and his quarrels with the ESB. This all lacked the distance, the expansiveness and the variety of the original Myles persona. What the readers wanted was the omnipotent, the superman—what they got in the last years was too normal, too human, too close to be acceptable. As an ordinary human, subject to time, to change and to death, O'Brien could no longer be the omniscient watcher, judge, and ultimate authority through whose eyes so many readers had felt and judged and discriminated and become aware.

As a final example of Myles's transcendence and in an ironic reversal of the mood of the last years, the *Irish Times* on the day after O'Brien's death was still printing the latest articles as if the passing of the man who had written them was quite irrelevant to their continuance.

6
Gaeilgeoirí, Politicians and the Devil: *An Béal Bocht* and Other Writings 1940–60

In the years between 1940 and 1960 O'Brien produced a substantial amount of writing. He did some excellent translations from poems in Irish, and wrote several short stories, a number of newspaper articles, plays, other newspaper columns, and a book in Irish, *An Béal Bocht*.

Some of this material is of a high standard, equal to that of his most interesting writing; much of it is, however, mixed and even inferior in quality due to the pressures of financial need or to a desire to experiment in unfamiliar forms. Looked at as a whole, it presents an amorphous mass in which can be seen some of O'Brien's most characteristic habits of style and some of the ideas which underlay all of his work. But his manner of presenting his work was undergoing a marked change. In the course of these years O'Brien was becoming less fantastic in outlook, less concerned to communicate his ideas through a distorted mirror which yet revealed all clearly. He was now more angry and came to be more concerned with society and social evils and to speak of them directly and without all the stylistic resources available to the satirist.

This tendency is most obvious in the other newpaper column, *A Weekly Look Around* written by 'John James Doe' for the *Southern Star*, Skibbereen, from 1955 to 1956. O'Brien chose the pseudonym to accord with his promise to the editor not to present anything controversial, or anything connected with politics or serious crime, but to be 'light' and 'enter-taining'. It was in many ways an unfortunate choice of pseudonym and he was to be much happier in the column written in the early 1960s for the *Nationalist and Leinster Times*, Carlow, where he became 'George Knowall'. Indeed the latter pseudonym would have been much more

appropriate for the earlier column, in the first article of which
O'Brien had said:

> Here, every week, I hope to give the reader the benefit of
> my thoughts, my wide reading, my wisdom and — where
> called for — my advice. Not at all, do not thank me. It is a
> pleasure to help.
>
> My field of study will be the whole world, but on the
> understanding that Ireland is the centre of it. If, from week
> to week, you hear of something interesting or important or
> funny which has escaped my notice, I hope you will write
> and let me know about it.
>
> I shall try to distinguish clearly between what I invent and
> what I merely record or quote. Sometimes it is not easy for
> even the most conscientious scribe to be sure. We can all be
> mistaken, occasionally.   (*WLA*. 15 Jan. 1955)

This sounds more like the bragging self-importance of Myles
na gCopaleen than the retiring timidity of a Doe, and it might
seem to imply that the column would contain *Cruiskeen
Lawn's* sense of fun and satire, loosely intermingled with wild
fantasy. O'Brien did not , however, ever bother to create a
character for John James Doe, except on one occasion where
John James's friends comment on the state of his hat. Nor was
there much invention in the column, which was mainly made
up of incidents reprinted from other provincial newspapers or
from old copies of the *Irish Times*. Occasionally there was a
pun or a joke or an amusing misprint, the implications of
which would be dealt upon in loving and amused fantastic
detail, but these elements were rare and were often an
indication that the column had been reprinted from *Cruiskeen
Lawn*. It was often possible to find sections of the column
which were reprinted from issue to issue. O'Brien seemed to
forget that he had already included them. An anecdote about
how two chimpanzees arriving in Israel were able to defeat
rationing by being classed as 'diplomats' was repeated within a
few days of its first appearance. It seems as if O'Brien was
uninterested in the column for he was often careless in matters
like this. Apart from the verbatim reports of district court
proceedings, or the lengthy deliberations of local urban and
rural district councils, or the odd incidents and peculiar

headlines culled from other papers, the column was a reverse image of *Cruiskeen Lawn* in that it shared its major concerns and themes but reported them 'straight'.

An enormous percentage of the fifty-six columns was devoted to reports of violence, comments on violence, on war and on the dangers of space exploration, of intellectual pretension and artiness. O'Brien dealt occasionally with contemporary writing and drama—he disliked O'Casey's late plays, finding them 'boring' (12 Mar. 1955)—and often raised the question, as he had done in *Cruiskeen Lawn*, of the relation between language and reality. crystallising his awareness in one important passage.

> It has occurred to me many a time that momentous concepts and events would be quite forgotten if the name they went by got, by some chance, quite lost. The name can sometimes transcend the thing. This is a commonplace in the sphere of theology. The inverse is equally true—give something false and base a nice name and it is cheered and respected.
>
> The real enemy of true belief is the infinity of human credulity.   (*WLA*. 13 Mar. 1955)

This kind of awareness is not frequent in the column; it may be transferred from *Cruiskeen Lawn,* but. it is strikingly associated with the concern with war and violence, which is a major theme of the *Weekly Look Around* and which is in turn associated with scientific concepts. Science, scientific gadgets, scientific concepts and discoveries are everywhere discussed, from Leonardo's description of air to the launching of America's first satellite.

Another of the column's most constant topics is popular recreation: gambling, steeplechasing, rugby, hurling, the Spring Show and local dances. At least four of the articles which O'Brien wrote in this period are concerned with the same thing: 'The Trade in Dublin', 'Going to the Dogs', 'The Dance Halls' and 'Drink and Time in Dublin', deal with dog-racing, dancing and drinking, those great stalwarts of Irish entertainment. Indeed, O'Brien seemed generally concerned with what one could term 'popular culture' and often discussed it in the column and in other articles. At the centre of popular culture is the newspaper and the radio broadcast, and O'Brien reached a stage where he castigated individuals for their rejection of popular newspapers and for their contempt for the pursuits of the ordinary man. This was a logical development, of course. Contempt for the 'aesthete' would naturally find an outlet in praise of the unsophisticated response. In a way O'Brien's respect and contempt for art, literature, music and, indeed, learning, was the shaping tension that underlay his work, and manifested itself in the discussion between Finn and Shanahan in *At Swim* and in the censure of publicans in 'The Trade in Dublin'. This article was written specially for the first appearance of *The Bell*. Its general tone was one of contempt. It deplored the changes taking place in the décor of Dublin pubs and regretted the replacement of the old 'snugs' by the tubular monstrosities of the publican's new dream environment — an environment from which the pint-drinker was completely excluded. A social revolution had taken place, based on the model of American films; sham gentility had taken over, and pubs were now classified into 'lounge' and 'public' bar. Dances in Ireland, as O'Brien reveals in 'The Dance Halls', are another occasion on which social snobbery can be asserted. The dress dance with its evening-suited males and beautifully attired women, is very different to the threepenny 'come-as-you-are' in which everyone squeezes into a jammed hall and is afterwards condemned by the parish priest. O'Brien was here on the side of the ordinary man and makes this clear in an article on 'Baudelaire and Kavanagh' in which he finds a similarity between the two writers in their rejection of popular journalism and their contempt for the 'herd'. O'Brien finds this attitude 'silly and invalid' and makes an appeal for tolerance of the 'herd', that vast mass of ordinary humanity who wanted to read about greyhound-racing rather than poetry. O'Brien recognised that 'Denouncing the herd and its habits is . . . a legitimate and valuable exercise,' but he warns, in a sentence which is peculiarly appropriate to his own practice as a satirist:

> But do not denounce in bitterness in the hope of sneering them into being more elevated and less vulgar, more like yourself, for that connotes a desire to standardise society.[1]

The 'herd', he says, must remain varied and vital, a mass of idiosyncrasy and wild humour, for the herd, in so far as it must be given a literary significance, is the property of the artist: 'it is from the herd he milks his wares'. O'Brien regards what other people call 'the lower orders' as 'the main heart of humanity' and he announces his intention to oppose anyone or any movement that tries to impose uniformity of thought on it. In his own work he made a conscious effort to capture the idiom, the dialect, the characteristic mode of expression of 'the main heart of humanity'. In a note for *The Boy from Ballytearim* he wrote: 'An attempt is made to achieve comedy by the exploitation of the regional accent, after the manner of O'Casey and the Dublin accent.'[2] Many of the stories and the plays written in this period are no more than an excuse for extended dialogue or for a developed anecdote, usually about a drinking bout.

Of all the Irish activities, drinking is dwelt on more than any other in this period. 'The Trade in Dublin' gives a history of the city's most renowned drinking-houses and the peculiarities of their clientèle. O'Brien also comments on the odd effects of some of the licensing laws, and he is able to make a story, *Donabate,* and a play, *Thirst,* from the points he made in the article about after-hours drinking and 'bona fide' travellers.

The article 'The Trade in Dublin' is memorable for its descriptions of the old-style pub, its awareness of the psychology of the Irish drinker and the importance to him of the 'curate'—part mine of information on politics, women, the GAA and the horses; part confessor and adviser, extending to each of his customers a welcome and a warmth that they found lacking in their homes. Drinking was usually an all-male preserve, and a definite social stigma attached to it. Thus even a moderate drinker sneaking into the privacy of a snug would feel degenerate and sinful. Respectability was maintained by drinking while the wife was away, or in a hotel where it would be assumed one had gone for a meal. These aspects of the phenomenon provided the basis for the article 'Drink and Time in Dublin' and the first part of *A Bash in the Tunnel.* 'Drink and Time in Dublin' is no more than an account, intended to be humourous, of a monstrous drinking session. It is quite unimportant except in so far as it reflects a general interest of O'Brien's and in that it is written in the kind of

format used for the 'brother' articles in *Cruiskeen Lawn*. The
narrator and drinker is a Dubliner; his interlocutor is a man of
the middle class whose English is of the 'superior variety'. It is
the way in which the drinker describes his experiences that is
important in this article-cum-story. *A Bash in the Tunnel* was
the editorial essay in a Joyce issue of *Envoy*, but the first part of
it is concerned with another account of a drinking debauch.
However, O'Brien uses the peculiarity of this drinker, who
goes on his binges sitting locked inside the toilet of an
unhitched railway carriage, as an image of the artist in
Ireland.

> Sitting fully dressed, innerly locked in the toilet of a locked
> coach where he has no right to be, resentfully drinking
> somebody else's whiskey, being whisked hither and thither
> by anonymous shunters, keeping fastidiously the while on
> the outer face of his door the simple word ENGAGED.
>
> (*SP.* 206)[3]

O'Brien had already said that the writer was on the same
economic level as the labourer who was excluded from the
heaven of the lounge bar. It is clear then, that he associated
drink and creativity. The publican in *Thirst* is a master of
language in his own way. The artist, like the drinker, is a
degenerate. The glow of creativity is like the glow gained from
alcohol which transforms the world; a win at the dogs transforms the world in the same way. Yet this sense of well-
being is, like everything associated with enjoyment in Ireland,
accompanied by a sense of sin. Even the simple pleasure of
dancing is seen as a 'dark rite', carried out under the juris-
diction of Satan himself. As Dan says of his son in *The Boy
from Ballytearim*, written some fifteen years later,

> And where is that fellow this night? In some dirty dance hall
> across, full of fallen women . . . and *sheep-shucks* with
> next to nothing on them.

The column and the articles, then, faithfully reflect
O'Brien's main interests in this period. The stories and the
plays are a further development of these interests. Mr Kelly,
the protagonist of *Faustus Kelly,* is a publican, chairman of
the urban council, and closely associated with the devil. *An
Béal Bocht* continues the examination of the 'Gaeligore' which

had started in *Cruiskeen Lawn*. *Two in One* in many ways continues the violence of *The Third Policeman*. Yet it must be said that, in spite of this thematic continuity, many of the articles are confused and badly written, memorable only for the odd piece of vivid description, the occasional good image. The short stories are little more than extended anecdotes, ineptly handled and quite trivial. The plays, on which O'Brien spent a great deal of time, prove him to have been no dramatist.

The most substantial single piece of writing undertaken during this period was *An Béal Bocht*, O'Brien's only major work in Irish, written in 1941. The version referred to here is the translation by Patrick Power published in 1973.

Myles wrote extensively about *An Béal Bocht* in *Cruiskeen Lawn*. He began to write the book to satisfy a desire to attack those who had objected to his column, and to satirise modern Irish writing in general and the writings of Tomás Ó Criomhthain and Séamas O Grianna in particular. The first aim is evident in a speech made by one of the Gaeligores at the feis in Corkadoragha, when he uses a phrase reminiscent of that used by 'West-Briton Nationalist' in his attack on Myles's first article. The context of the article is also recalled by this speech.

If we're truly Gaelic, we must constantly discuss the question of the Gaelic revival and the question of Gaelicism. There is no use in having Gaelic if we converse in it on non-Gaelic topics. He who speaks Gaelic but fails to discuss the language question is not truly Gaelic in his heart; such conduct is of no benefit to Gaelicism because it only jeers at Gaelic and reviles the Gaels. (p.54)

Myles himself, in letters and in retrospective articles in *Cruiskeen Lawn*, told his friends and his readers of his second aim. He intended the book to be a satire, of the 'Gaeligore', of the translators of Irish, and of the conventional image of the Irish peasant. He wrote in *Cruiskeen Lawn* that *An Béal Bocht* was 'a ferocious and highly technical assault on the Gaels' (25 Oct. 1950), and reiterated this in a letter to Timothy O'Keeffe, when he described the book as

an enormous jeer at the Gaelic morons here with their
bicycle clips and handball medals, but in language and
style . . . an ironical copy of a really fine autobiographical
book.[4]

The autobiography referred to here was *An tOileánach
(The Islandman)* by Tomás Ó Criomhthain. First published in
Irish in 1929, it had been translated five years later by Robin
Flower, who had visited the author on the Blasket Islands and
learned his Irish there. It is almost certain that Myles did not
approve of the manner of its translation. All through 1941
Cruiskeen Lawn contained article after article parodying the
style of *The Islandman*. Myles's method was simply to print
what purported to be a passage from the book making no
comment on it other than that implied in the heading
'Literally from the Irish'. It was, probably, the literalness of
the translation which annoyed him. In a long article on
Standish Hayes O'Grady, the Gaelic scholar whom he
evidently admired, O'Brien had praised O'Grady for his
'profound learning' and for that 'humour and imagination
which enabled him to deal with early texts in a lively creative
way that lifted his work far out of the repellent rut traversed by
most philologists'.[5]

What O'Brien objected to in translators of early Irish, Myles
objected to in translators of modern Irish. The end product of
'literal' translations which were unenlivened by 'humour and
imagination' was a colourless, unnecessarily complex and,
accidentally, comic prose. O'Brien praised O'Grady for doing
as he himself had tried to do; for creating a 'curious and
charming English . . . in an effort to render to the student the
last glint of colour in any Irish word'.[6] Without the 'glint of
colour', the translation of any Irish work would only
exacerbate the dislike of Irish, making it seem an impossible
language, overloaded with peculiar tenses, alliteration,
compound words, 'peasant' phrases, and completely noun-
centred. To reveal the full horror of such translations O'Brien
parodied 'literal' translations ruthlessly. One passage in Robin
Flower's edition read:

A while after this my brother Pats came over from America
to me. I was amazed at his coming over this second time, for
his two sons were grown up by this; and I fancied they were

on the pig's back since they were on the other side. When I
saw my brother after his return, anybody would have
conjectured from his ways that it was in the woods he had
spent his time in America. He was hardly clothed; he had
an ill appearance; there wasn't a red farthing in his pocket;
and two of his brothers in America paid for his passage
across with their own money.[7]

Myles's 'literal' translation of this passage renders it in
exaggerated fashion.

> A time after that my brother Paddy moved towards me
> from being over there in Ameriky. There was great surprise
> on me he is coming from being over there the second time,
> because the two sons who were at him were strong hefty ones
> at that time; and my opinion was that they were on the pig's
> back to be over there at all. On my seeing my brother on his
> arrival, there was no get-up on him — as would appear to
> any person who threw an opinion with him — save that it was
> in the woods he had spent his years yonder. There was no
> cloth on him, there was no shape on his person itself, there
> was not a dun-coloured penny in his pocket, and it was two
> sisters to him yonder who had sent him across at their own
> expense.   (*CL.* 8 Sep. 1941; *BM*.276)

In 1957 Myles wrote in *Cruiskeen Lawn* that when he read
The Islandman: 'Its impact was explosive. In one week I wrote
a parody of it.' However, some seven years earlier, he had said
that the book had taken him 'a mere month or so'. (*CL.* 25
Oct. 1950). He went on to relate how Browne & Nolan had
asked if they could publish it, but had eventually decided
otherwise because their reader had sent in a negative
recommendation. Myles was able to repeat it verbatim.

> I can safely assert that in an experience of sixty years this
> is quite the craziest piece of Irish I have ever met.
> What most surprises me is the self-assurance of its
> author — a man who demonstrates twenty times on every
> page that he is the veriest tyro in the Irish language. For
> want of knowledge he cannot begin, or continue or finish a
> sentence properly. Constructions such as he writes have

never before been seen in Irish, and one earnestly hopes that nothing of the kind will ever be repeated.

The late Stephen McKenna at one time proposed to write a book:

HOW TO WRITE IRISH

BY

ONE WHO CAN'T

and here, I am convinced, we have an author who could take up his project with every hope of success.

Chapter II of the typescript is devoted, almost entirely, to a description of a sickly and stinking pig whose odoriferousness was such as to cause a horse to turn back, and to drive a certain family into exile! The author may reply that the whole thing is an extravaganza, but if every word of his text were a *genuine* pearl, jem, or jewel, the inferiority of the Irish would damn the production.

At first I put a pencil mark against every solecism of his, but the marks became so numerous that I was obliged to give up the idea and to erase those I had made.

My advice to you is — to spend none of the firm's money on this work. (*CL.* 25 Oct. 1950)

Myles assured his readers that the report was 'absolute gospel. Even the word "jem" is exact.' Whether the report was authentic or not, the book was, in fact, published in November 1941 by the National Press. Myles reported, gleefully, that it had sold 12,000 copies, and that this exceeded what any other English or Irish writer could hope for.

At the time of publication, he had written in much the same vein:

I am rather pleased at the reception given to my book, 'An Béal Bocht'. It is gratifying to know that an important work of literature receives in this country the recognition that is its due. Scholars, students, men-about-town, clerics, TDs ladies of fashion, and even the better-class corner-boys have vied with one another in grabbing the copies as they pour from the giant presses. How long will the strictly limited edition of 50,000 copies last? A week? A month? Who can tell? Suffice it to say that you cannot order your copy too soon. Paper difficulties make it doubtful whether another edition of 50,000 will be possible, in our own generation at any rate.   (*CL*. 12 Dec. 1941)

Myles was, of course, exaggerating the success of the book, but it was a very great success. It was well received by the critics and hailed as 'a classic of writing in Irish'. Many people consider it to be Myles's best book. Jack Carney, a friend of Sean O'Casey, suggested that O'Brien might send a copy to O'Casey. O'Casey liked it and wrote to O'Brien praising it and telling him: 'There is, I think, the swish of Swift's scorn in it, bred well into the genial laughter of Mark Twain.'[8] O'Brien's reply reveals how very important was his knowledge of the Irish language in creating his attitude to literary composition.

It is by no means all you say but it is an honest attempt to get under the skin of a certain type of 'Gael', which I find the most nauseating phenomenon in Europe. I mean the baby-brained dawnburst brigade who are ignorant of every-thing, including the Irish language itself. I'm sure they were plentiful enough in your own day. I cannot see any real prospect of reviving Irish at the present rate of going and way of working. I agree absolutely with you when you say it is essential, particularly for any sort of a literary worker. It supplies that unknown quantity in us that enables us to transform the English lanugage and this seems to hold of people who know little or no Irish, like Joyce. It seems to be an inbred thing.[9]

O'Brien was master of three languages and had a good acquaintance with several others. It was, almost certainly, his intense awareness of the nuances of different languages that created his sensitivity to the colour and weight of words and phrases and to the awareness of the untranslatability of certain idioms and concepts. This led, in turn, to the realisation of the connection between language and concepts, language and reality. In this, while not being in advance of his time, he was certainly in tune with the findings of philosophers, psycho- and socio-linguists and modern novelists. This awareness was never developed into a systematic pattern but underlies and is implied by many seemingly casual phrases like 'Here is a story that simply won't do in Irish.' Intensely aware of language as a cognitive structure, he responded by playing word games, by inventing phonetic Irish, writing English in Gothic script, or producing hybrid languages like his marvellous Irish-sounding English or the cross between German and Latin which occur frequently in the pages of *Cruiskeen Lawn.* On many occasions he wrote articles about the range and characteristics of a particular language. Most often, in defiance of its detractors, and with an ironical tone, he asserted the flexibility and impressive descriptive power of Irish.

> There is scarcely a single word in Irish (barring, possibly Sasanach) that is simple and explicit. Apart from words with endless shades of cognate meaning, there are many with so complete a spectrum of graduated ambiguity that each of them can be made to express two directly contrary meanings, as well as a plethora of intermediate concepts that have no bearing on either. And all this strictly within the linguistic field. Superimpose on all that the miasma of ironic usage, poetic licence, oxymoron, plamás, Celtic evasion, Irish bullery and Paddy Whackery, and it is a safe bet that you will find yourself very far from home.
>
> (*CL.* 11 Jan. 1941)

In the translation of *An Béal Bocht* there are a number of passages which are stylistically similar to *The Third Policeman.* The description of the Rosses is a good example of such a passage.

> In every direction, the variegated colours of the firmament pleased the eye. A soft sweet breeze followed at our heels and helped us while we walked. High up in the skies there was a yellow lamp known as the sun, shedding heat and light down upon us. Far away there were tall blue stacks of mountains standing east and west and watching us. A nimble stream accompanied the main road; it was hidden in the bottom of the ditch but we knew of its presence because of the soft murmuring it bestowed on our ears. At both sides was a brown-black bog, speckled with rocks.
>
> (pp.65-6)

It is possible that the very distinctive style of *The Third Policeman,* which seems the least 'Irish' of the books, is the direct result of the presence of Gaelic linguistic structures underlying and transforming the English in which it is written.

An Béal Bocht itself is so linguistically complex that Myles himself said that its humour was untranslatable.[10] What he seems to have done was to take an original Irish text, parody its translation and then translate literally back into Irish that parodied translation. In the process all the linguistic habits attributable to Irish and used freely in literary Anglo-Irish dialect are exaggerated to a hitherto unknown extent. Any translator who has to render in comprehensible English a parodied translation of a parodied translation has a very difficult job. It is impossible for any but a true expert in the subtleties of Irish to comment on that translation, to say if it does, in fact, catch the complexity of the original. It *is* possible, reading Patrick Power's translation, to realise to what an extent Myles was satirising the accepted, romantic 'Abbey' image of the 'peasant', the pretensions of the Gaeligore and the works of Ó Criomhthain and other Gaelic writers.

Myles's book was subtitled *A Bad Story about the Hard Life.* Its English successor, *The Hard Life,* was subtitled *An Exegesis of Squalor,* but this description would be more than apt for *An Béal Bocht* written twenty years previously. The 'putting on a poor mouth' which means, according to the lexicographer Dinneen (whom Myles professed to despise), simply 'grumbling' or pretending to extreme poverty and misery in order to stave off the appeals of friends or the demands of creditors. It is a most suitable title for a book which deals, in overwhelming detail, with poverty and misery.

The events of the book are related by Bonaparte O'Coonassa, an inhabitant of Corkadoragha. Corkadoragha is a Gaeltacht area, where all the riches possessed by the inhabitants are the words of sweet Irish in their mouths. The peasants who inhabit this place are not the serene, noble peasants of popular conception; they are poor, hungry, badly clothed and miserably housed. They are thieves and 'chancers' and are generally without initiative or practical intelligence. But, most important of all, they have no knowledge whatever of the facts of life—a characteristic which makes them truly 'Gaelic'. To this extent, Corkadoragha is like any of the other Gaeltacht areas mentioned in the book; in fact, it is a composite of them all, being miraculously placed in a position whence can be surveyed the whole of the west, and parts of the north and south coasts of Ireland.

However, concerning the house where I was born, there was a fine view from it. It had two windows with a door between them. Looking out from the right-hand window, there below was the bare hungry countryside of the Rosses and Gweedore; Bloody Foreland yonder and Tory Island far away out, swimming like a great ship where the sky dips into the sea. Looking out of the door, you could see the West of County Galway with a good portion of the rocks of Connemara, Aranmore in the ocean out from you, with the small bright houses of Kilronan, clear and visible, if your eyesight were good and the Summer had come. From the window on the left you could see the Great Blasket, bare and forbidding as a horrible other-worldly eel, lying languidly on the wave-tops; over yonder was Dingle with its houses close together. (p.21)

The view was certainly the best thing about the house. In all other ways it was like all the houses of the true Gaels, built, traditionally, in the worst position in the valley, undivided and, in true stage-Irishman fashion, housing the animals and the humans in an odoriferous cohabitation. In particular, it held pigs. Tomás O Criomhthain in *The Islandman* had described his house thus:

We lived in a cramped little house, roofed with rushes from the hill. Often the hens would nest in the thatch and lay a dozen eggs there. We had a post bed in the corner, and two beds at the bottom of the house. There used to be two cows in the house, the hens and their eggs, an ass and the rest of us.[11]

Myles, not to be outdone, crams his house with, in good times, 'two cows, a cart-horse, a race-horse, sheep, pigs and other lesser animals' (p.18). At the time of writing, times were bad, so the house was less inhabited.

Our house was undivided, wisps of rushes above us on the roof and rushes also as bedding in the end of the house. At sundown rushes were spread over the whole floor and the household lay to rest on them. Yonder a bed with pigs upon it; here a bed with people; a bed there with an aged slim cow stretched out asleep on her flank and a gale of breath issuing from her capable of raising a tempest in the centre

of the house; hens and chickens asleep in the shelter of her
belly; another bed near the fire with me on it.   (p. 18)

In particular there is one pig, originally a pet, which grows
too big to get out of the door, swells in size and in ferocious
odoriferousness until it drives people, horses, sheep and even
neighbours well away from its vicinity. Eventually the pig,
mercifully, dies from its own smell just as the woman of the
house almost expires from its stench. The idea of stench,
poverty, discomfort, and the 'hard life' which has 'always been
the destiny of the true Gaels' is prevalent and repeated
throughout the book.

Corkadoragha, unlike its neighbouring areas, never sees the
sun. Indeed, when on one memorable day, a chink of sunlight,
the first ever to shine there, does make its way through the
thick clouds, the narrator's grandfather, the 'Old-Grey-
Fellow', believes that the end of the world is at hand. Every
night brings with it a complete downpour and sometimes this
persists into the day, making the fields indistinguishable from
the sea and forcing the people to eat fish instead of the
potatoes which they otherwise devour incessantly. Almost the
sole task of Bonaparte's mother is boiling great pots of
potatoes for the pigs or to 'stave off the day of famine'. Indeed,
there is so little difference between people and animals that a
grandmother's cry in the night can sound like a sheep
bleating, and piglets dressed in grey-wool trousers pass for
children in the gloom of the house. Indeed, if the noise of the
pigs convinces a government inspector that they are children
speaking English and entitled to two pounds a head for their
expertise, another pig grunting in the middle of a huddle of
old men leads a travelling scholar to the conclusion that it is
one of the men speaking Irish. The scholar, of course,
'understood that good Gaelic is difficult but that the best
Gaelic of all is well-nigh unintelligible' (p.44), so he tape-
recorded the grunting of the pig as it lay hidden. Then the
scholar

journeyed to Berlin, a city of Germany in Europe and
narrated all that the machine had heard in the presence of
the most learned ones of the Continent. These learned ones
said that they never heard any fragment of Gaelic which was
so good, so poetic and so obscure as it and that they were

sure there was no fear for Gaelic while the like was audible in Ireland. They bestowed fondly a fine academic degree on the gentleman and, something more interesting still, they appointed a small committee of their own members to make a detailed study of the language of the machine to determine whether any sense might be made of it. (pp.44-5)

The Gaels were not always the subject of such interest. Any schoolchild who could not speak English on his first day at school had his head broken by the irate schoolteacher. As Bonaparte's mother explains after he has undergone a similar experience,

Don't you understand that it's Gaels that live on this side of the country and that they can't escape from fate? It was always said and written that every Gaelic youngster is hit on his first school day because he doesn't understand English and the foreign form of his name and that no one has any respect for him because he's Gaelic to the marrow. There's no other business going on in school that day but punishment and revenge and the same fooling about *Jams O'Donnell.* Alas! I don't think that there'll ever be any good settlement for the Gaels but only hardship for them always.

(pp. 31-4)

At the end of the book Bonaparte is sentenced to life imprisonment in an English-speaking court for a murder he did not commit. He was unable to defend himself because he did not understand the proceedings.

However, life was not always so bad. The district soon began to be full of the 'Gaeligore', whose first appearance was greeted with horror and amazement. The Gaeligore had his particular preconceptions. He was annoyed if a word was in common usage which did not appear in the books of An tAthair Peadar Ó Laoghaire, the ultimate arbiter of Gaelic purity. He also believed that linguistic purity 'grew in proportion to one's lack of worldly goods'. A particular favourite of the Gaeligores was Sitric O'Sanassa who 'possessed the very best poverty, hunger and distress also'.

The gentlemen from Dublin who came in motors to inspect the paupers praised him for his Gaelic poverty and stated that they never saw anyone who appeared so truly Gaelic.

One of the gentlemen broke a little bottle of water which Sitric had, because, said he, it spoiled the effect.   (p.88)

Eventually, however, even Sitric failed to draw the regular stream of Gaeligores to the area. They began to decline in numbers and the Old-Grey-Fellow set out to discover why. The answer was found in the terrible environment of Corkadoragha.

1. The tempest of the countryside was too tempestuous.
2. The putridity of the countryside was too putrid.
3. The poverty of the countryside was too poor.
4. The Gaelicism of the countryside was too Gaelic.
5. The tradition of the countryside was too traditional.

(p.50)

To induce the visitors to come back to the area, the Old-Grey-Fellow decided to hold a feis to raise money for a Gaelic college.

The description of the feis brought Myles's rather savage humour to a climax, as he described the dress (kilts), the pet-names, the speeches and the complete insensitivity of the Gaeligores. They talk and talk; they offer prizes for marathon performances in speaking, singing, and dancing, quite oblivious of the poverty, hunger and exhaustion of the peasants. The satire is made more black by being deliberately underplayed by the apparent innocence and fatalistic accept-ance of the narrator. About the building of the platform, erected at night by a team of men, he says:

None of these fellows ever had good health again after the downpour and storm of that night while one of those who did not survive was buried before that platform was dismantled on which he had laid down his life for the cause of the Gaelic language.   (p.51)

The narrator never condemns; he simply wonders and believes all that he is told. The contrast between his descriptions of events and the statements he makes in praise of the Gaeligores create the ironic perspectives of the tale. He has been told that the men who wear kilts are truly Gaelic and, believing this, he goes on to comment:

There were men present wearing a simple unornamented

dress — these, I thought, had little Gaelic; others had such nobility, style and elegance in their feminine attire that it was evident that their Gaelic was fluent. (p.51)

It is in the pathetic willingness of the peasants to live up to the image of Gaelic Ireland created for them by well-fed, well-clothed gentlemen from Dublin that the ridiculous pretensions of the Gaeligores are most exposed. As the peasants listen to interminable speeches, or participate in a competition to determine 'who was most in earnest about Gaelic', or perform the long dance, which was the most Gaelic of all Gaelic dances, they are engaged in activities which require a stamina and health they they do not possess. So, in the endless events of the feis, the participants are stricken with madness or overcome by death, but, as Bonaparte says,

Even though death snatched many fine people from us, the events of the feis went on sturdily and steadily, we were ashamed to be considered not strongly in favour of Gaelic while the President's eye was upon us. (p.59)

Myles goes on to extend his satire from the Gaeligore himself to the whole of Gaelic writing. Even while not under the eye of the Gaeligore, the inhabitants of Corkadoragha are forced to arrange their lives according to the prescriptions of the 'good Gaelic books'. These prescriptions act as the force of tradition. The Old-Grey-Fellow is upset that Bonaparte is being brought up in a clean house: he is not 'rising up according to old Gaelic tradition' as a 'child among the ashes' (p.16), sitting in the ashes of the fire, the droppings of hens and the muck of the floor. Later, the Old-Grey-Fellow describes the conditions that are to be expected in the Rosses, using for his authority, not personal experience, but the descriptions in the Gaelic books. Then, as in *At Swim,* what is described in literature becomes true in reality and all things are found to be as the books describe them:

Did you ever read *Séadna* said the Old-Fellow sincerely,
We continued conversing lightly and courteously together for a long while, discussing the affairs of the day and talking of the hard times. I gathered quite an amount of information about the Rosses from the other two during the

conversation and also about the bad circumstances of the people there; all were barefoot and without means. Some were always in difficulty, others carousing in Scotland. In each cabin there was (i) one man at least, called the 'Gambler', a rakish individual, who spent much of his life carousing in Scotland, playing cards and billiards, smoking tobacco and drinking spirits in taverns; (ii) a worn, old man who spent the time in the chimney-corner bed and who arose at the time of night-visiting to shove his two hooves into the ashes, clear his throat, redden his pipe and tell stories about the bad times; (iii) a comely lassie called Nuala, or Babby or Mabel or Rosie for whom men came at the dead of every night with a five-noggin bottle and one of them seeking to espouse her. One knows not why but that is how it was. He who thinks that I speak untruly, let him read the good books, or the *guid buiks.*'   (p.65)

The 'guid buiks' in this instance were the stories of 'Máire' (Séamas Ó Grianna), which are here carefully and comically anatomised and schematised. There are many other references to 'Máire' in *An Béal Bocht*, all of them derisory. One of 'Máire's' clichés was the phrase 'a child among the ashes'. Another was the habit of describing children as if they wore nothing other than a pair of 'grey-wool breeches'. Thus, Myles describes Bonaparte as going to school in 'grey-wool breeches, but otherwise unclothed above and below' (p.29).

However, the main point of satiric reference in the book is to *The Islandman,* and here the parallels are numerous. Myles makes the similarity obvious from the outset when he bases the format of his chapter headings on that of *The Islandman.*

CHAPTER 1
MY CHILDHOOD

My people — The old woman next door — The turf basket — The palm oil — My breeches — The porpoises — The wheat ship — Myself and the conger-eel.[12]

Myles subdivides his chapters in the same way.

CHAPTER 1

Why I Speak — My Birth — My Mother and the Old-Grey-

Fellow — Our House — The Glen Where I Was Born — The
Hardships of the Gaels in Former Times.   (p.11)

Both writers are impelled to set down their history from the
same motive. They realise that all the people they know are
dying, that their very way of life is dying, and they wish to
testify to the future, for, as Bonaparte says, repeating a phrase
from Ó Criomhthain, 'our likes will never be here again'. The
parallels between the two books continue with the writers'
description of their respective mothers and of the houses they
lived in; the brevity with which Ó Criomhthain describes his
marriage and his life with his wife is matched by Myles's
chapter, the shortest in the book, on O'Coonassa's marriage,
the disorder of his wedding night, his life with his wife, the
birth of his child and the subsequent abrupt demise of wife
and child.

Myles also creates comic effect in the way he overturns
aspects of Ó Criomhthain's book. Thus, while the Islandman
is brave and skilful as a fisherman and hunter and industrious
as a father, Bonaparte O'Coonassa is lazy and timid, disliking
the imagined discomforts of hunting. The episode where Sitric
O'Sanassa sets off on a seal-hunt and remains with the seals is
also intended as an inverse account of the many descriptions of
seal-hunting is *The Islandman*.

Most of the comedy in the book, when it is not directly
satirical, comes from the effect of repetition. So, when all has
been explained to Bonaparte about the way of life of the
Rosses, he sees it for himself and describes it in exactly the
same terms as those in which he heard it. He goes wooing in
the traditional manner, and the shanachee tells his story in the
customary style, as outlined immediately beforehand. As
expected, all the women are down by the sea waiting for the
boats to come safely to land. The same incident will be
described three times over, gaining impetus from the previous
entirely similar and utterly dead-pan retellings.

In the course of the book Bonaparte has two adventures. He
meets the Sea-cat and he goes on a journey to find Maeldoon
O'Poenassa. Maeldoon had, many years before when the land
was flooded in a particularly heavy downpour, sailed away
taking with him the valuables of all those who had perished in
the flood. Bonaparte sets out to recover these valuables from

the corpse of Maeldoon and keep them for himself 'against the time of famine'. After much hardship and unwonted physical exertion he finds Maeldoon still alive in a cave which is running with fountains of whiskey. Legend is proved true. Maeldoon is, in fact, a very old shanachee, who repeats, in Middle Irish, the story of the Captain which Bonaparte had already heard from the shanachee in the Rosses. Myles is able to extend his satire of the conservatism of modern Gaelic writing to old Irish legend as well. What he is presenting is a mock version of the voyage of Maeldune, the poetic saga which had inspired both Yeats and Tennyson. Maeldune is now presented as a thief and a drunkard, but the story he tells is old and the shanachee in the Rosses who tells the same story as if it were the tale of a man he knew personally is unaware of its even greater antiquity. Myles is mocking the idea of the 'permanence' of the essential facts of life in the Gaeltacht, by insisting that *nothing* changes from year to year except, possibly, that conditions get worse. While proving the unchanging nature of peasant life, Myles also manages to introduce a comment on the kind of source and inspiration used by Synge for *Riders to the Sea*. As the Old-Grey-Fellow and Bonaparte arrive in the Rosses they find all the houses deserted. The Old-Grey-Fellow explains:

> 'Tis clear, wee little son, said the Old-Fellow, that you haven't read the good books. 'Tis now the evening and according to literary fate, there's a storm down on the sea-shore, the fishermen are in difficulties on the water, the people are gathered on the strand, the women are crying and one poor mother is screaming: Who'll save my Mickey? That's the way the Gaels always had it with the coming of night in the Rosses. (p.67)

When Bonaparte meets the Sea-cat and escapes a terrible fate he finds, when drawing the monster he had seen for the benefit of his grandfather, that it closely resembles a map of Ireland turned sideways. This provides an element of visual comedy for the book. Other comic aspects are the truly marvellous names of the characters and the stylised way in which starving peasants address each other. Bonaparte gives his name in the proper fashion as:

Bonaparte son of Michaelangelo, son of Peter, son of Owen, son of Thomas's Sarah, granddaughter of John's Mary, granddaughter of James, son of Dermot . . .   (p.30)

Bonaparte calls his son Leonardo, and thus continues the mockery of the idea of the innate nobility of the peasant and the basis of classical learning he had gained from the hedge-school teacher. The splendid names of the peasants and their ancient lineage contrast ironically with the squalor of their lives and environment.

As well as satire and irony, Myles uses nonsense and fantasy in *An Béal Bocht.* The people of Corkadoragha seem to be completely unaware of the facts of life. The arrival of a child is always a great surprise, the method a total mystery. Small babies are, in any case, indistinguishable at first glance from piglets. So the arrival of Bonaparte's son surprises him, though hardly as much as his birth surprised his father and the neighbours, and

The people and that my mother was not expecting me either and it is a fact that the whisper went around that I was not born of my mother at all but of another woman.

(p.13)

The child whose coming was so unlooked for was, not surprisingly, a strange creature. At the age of ten months he had an odd conversation with the Old-Grey-Fellow. Replying to the Old-Grey-Fellow's comment on the heat of the fire, he said:

There's an awful lot of heat in that fire truly . . . but look, sir, you called me son for the first time. It may be that your're my father and that I'm your child, God bless and save us and far from us be the evil thing!   (p.15)

This linguistic fluency is not, unfortunately, accompanied by a corresponding physical development and the child grows up fairly normally, though later he is hard put to it to know why he is not married. He is, however, clever enough to note that 'men married women and women married men always' (p.79).

The character of the Old-Grey-Fellow is one of the triumphs

of the book. He is the aged repository of ancient wisdom, reading the weather and foretelling the ever-expected doom of the true Gael. Simple and innocent, yet shrewd, cunning and eternally resourceful, he is a conglomerate of all the 'peasant' vices and virtues, and, in some of his aspects, very like Myles na gCopaleen.

> According to what I had heard, he was the best man in the Rosses during his youth. There was no one in the countryside comparable to him where jumping, ransacking, fishing, love-making, drinking, thieving, fighting, hamstringing cattle, running, swearing, gambling, nightwalking, hunting, dancing, boasting and stick-fighting were concerned.
>
> He alone killed Martyn in Gweedore in 1889 when the aforesaid person attempted to take Father MacFadden a prisoner to Derry; he alone assassinated Lord Leitrim near Cratlough in 1875; he alone first inscribed his name in Gaelic on any cart and was prosecuted on that historic occasion; he alone founded the Land League, the Fenians and the Gaelic League. Yes! he had had a busy broad life and it had been of great benefit to Ireland. Were it not that he was born when he was and led the life he had, conversational subjects would be scarce among us in this country   (pp.63-4)

A number of these elements are not finally drawn together and subjected to the black satire which provides the book's predominating framework. There are some inconsistencies, some loose ends, but an overall unity is achieved by the overwhelming sense of atmosphere, an atmosphere which is created by the constant repetition of the key-words, 'downpour', 'potatoes', 'hardship', 'misery', 'the destiny of the true Gael'.

An Béal Bocht is, probably, a book whose existence was inevitable. It is close to many of the mainsprings of Myles's creative impulse. It represents a logical continuation of many of the battles he had begun in *Comhthrom Féinne* and carried forward into *Cruiskeen Lawn*. Stylistically, it is an intermediary between the worlds of those very dissimilar books, *At Swim* and *The Third Policeman*. The prose often

recalls *At Swim* in the use of specifically Gaelic phrases such as
those in the episode where Bonaparte faces the Sea-cat.

> The bitter lean fear, the small smooth cowardly fear, came
> suddenly upon me. Within me arose a storm of blood, a
> well of sweat and excessive fuss of mind.   (pp. 75-6)

However, if phrases recall *At Swim* the similarity to *The
Third Policeman* is even more marked. There is a noticeable
resemblance between the language of the passage in which
Bonaparte finds Maeldoon, and that in which the narrator of
The Third Policeman sees Philip Mathers whom he thinks he
has killed.

> However what almost took the sight from my eyes was an
> old person, half-sitting, half-lying by the flames and away
> from me, a species of chair beneath him and his appearance
> suggested that he was dead. A few unrecognisable rags were
> wrapped around him, the skin of his hand and face was like
> wrinkled brown leather and he had an appearance totally
> unnatural about him. His two eyes were closed, his black-
> toothed mouth was open and his head inclined feebly to one
> side. A fit of trembling seized me, stemming from both cold
> and fear. I had finally met Maeldoon O'Poenassa!   (p.107)

By these stylistic devices *An Béal Bocht* unites the world of
Gaelic literature with the black comedy of satire and
disassociation and looks forward to the squalor of *The Hard
Life*.

After *An Béal Bocht,* the most important work of this
period was the play *Faustus Kelly*. In his letter to Seán O'Casey
O'Brien had said that he was to begin a play. The desire to
experiment with drama may have developed as a result of
Niall Montgomery's enthusiastic reception of *At Swim*. 'The
court scene at the end makes me say, Why Not Make It Into A
Play?'[13] William Saroyan who had borrowed the rejected title
Sweeny in the Trees for a very successful play of his own was
also encouraging him to attempt a play. When O'Brien wrote
to Saroyan about *The Third Policeman* he told him that he
was considering 'making a crazy . . . play out of it',[14] and this
scheme seems to have stayed in his mind, though he did not do
anything about it. He began writing *Faustus Kelly* with a

desire to attack two old enemies, the local government man and the Irish politician. Before the play was finished, the news of its composition was rumoured and O'Brien received two requests to see the script. One was from Michael Walsh of the Cork Opera House, the other from Hilton Edwards. In his reply to Michael Walsh O'Brien said that he had just written a play which 'seems good in a commercial sense' and that he intended offering it to the Abbey. He went on to tell Walsh that he had another play in mind, 'a comic business with a very serious idea at the back of it'.[15] He said much the same thing to Hilton Edwards.

> As regards a play, I wrote one somewhat hastily recently and sent the rough draft to a party connected with the Abbey with a request for an opinion as to whether it would be acceptable if finished off properly and submitted. I have not yet had a reply. It is an 'Abbey Play', called Faustus Kelly and deals with a man who sells his soul to the devil in order to become a TD. The faust theme being parallel throughout in what is meant to be an uproarious play.[16]

If one remembers what Myles had said in *Cruiskeen Lawn* about 'Abbey Plays' and looks at the description of it as 'good in a commercial sense', the ambiguity of 'what is meant to be an uproarious play' and the obvious speed with which the play was written, it is easy to conclude that O'Brien's whole mind was not in the writing of *Faustus Kelly*. Indeed, as he had done in the letter to Michael Walsh, he immediately went on to talk of another projected play.

> I have in mind another play . . . mostly funny but ultimately involving the audience in horrible concepts of time and life and death that would put plays like *Berkely Square* into the halfpenny place. I think my idea is quite new and if the play can be written out (which I doubt) nobody else but yourself could produce it.[17]

If O'Brien was thinking of an adaptation of *The Third Policeman*, it is clear that he never did get it written out. Instead, when the Abbey accepted *Faustus Kelly*, he busied himself with the task of revising it and preparing it for the stage. It was necessary for him to break up some long speeches and exclude some of the repetition of the early draft.

Furthermore, both the prologue, showing the signing over of Kelly's soul, and the final appearance of the Devil had to be worked out for dramatic effect. Cahill & Co. had offered to publish the play after it was produced, and in October 1942 they sent the printer's proofs to O'Brien. The play itself was ready for performance in January 1943.

From the outset it had been planned as a satire of political corruption. At the end it is seen that even the Devil himself cannot bear the loquaciousness, incompetence and corruption of Irish politics. He tells the audience:

> Not for any favour . . . in heaven or earth or hell . . . would I take that Kelly and the others with me to where I live, to be in their company for ever . . .and ever . . .and ever. Here's the contract, his signed bond. (*He shows the document and tears it up savagely.*) I WANT NOTHING MORE OF IRISH PUBLIC LIFE! (p.124; *SP.*196-7)

Myles had always disliked politicians, particularly those of the Fianna Fáil party, and he was intending to settle his score with them for good. However, even after he had written the play he was to return to the subject on many occasions. In an article entitled 'The Fausticity of Kelly' written in the 1960s, O'Brien sketched the history of his acquaintance with the Faust legend and went on to talk of the genesis of the play.

> Many years afterwards I entered the civil service (from which I was later to escape, thank God) and for some seven years my duties as a private secretary necessitated almost daily attendance at Leinster House. Garrulity is a feeble word to describe what I encountered in Dáil Éireann and my innocence at the beginning may be judged from the fact that I marvelled a certain poorly-dressed deputy could speak French so rapidly that I could not grasp his meaning. Some weeks went by before I realised he was speaking English of the Cork intonation.
> The play *Faustus Kelly* arose somehow from that Leinster House gab . . . Many people told me afterwards in strict confidence that it was a very bad play. Maybe. I personally find Shakespeare's *King Lear* unendurable.[18]

This was written long after O'Brien's resignation from the civil service, but his bitterness had increased rather than decreased in the passage of years. At the time of the play's composition, O'Brien was still a member of the civil service and was therefore worried that he might have gone too far. He wrote to the Abbey about the play:

> There are certain political implications in it which, as a
> state employee, I'm not too sure about.[19]

It was possibly this feeling which led to his mistaken conviction that the play was closed down due to government pressure after only two weeks. (*CL.* 5 Jul. 1957) As his bitterness at the government grew his idea of the merits of the play increased as well.

> But I confess, as in conscience I must, that [*Faustus Kelly*] is a masterpiece, saturated with a Voltaire quality, and penetrating human stupidity with a sort of ghoulish gusto . . .
> Why did we all, including myself, think it so bad? In that now distant year, I thought I had gone too far, that the play (though straight farce) had hurt too many people, and that that sort of thing doesn't pay in this country. I also thought it exaggerated some notorious national failings.
> Re-reading it in this different age, I am convinced I was right, but that the work takes on a new importance by reason of life and facts catching up on it. It had an unsuspected oracular and prophetic content.
>
> (*CL.* 3 Apr. 1954)

But *Faustus Kelly* was not to be O'Brien's last word on the Irish politician. The bitterness which O'Brien felt at his 'explosive and extravagant language' (*CL.* 5 Jul. 1957) was to emerge in *Cruiskeen Lawn* in the 1950s, and to form the basis of O'Brien's last novel, the uncompleted *Slattery's Sago Saga*, which was at one stage envisioned as an attack on de Valera.

The play opened to a full house on 25 January 1943. F. J. McCormick played Kelly, and Cyril Cusack, O'Brien's contemporary at UCD, played the Town Clerk. Other parts were played by such famous Abbey actors as Eileen Crowe and Ria Mooney, Fred Johnston, Liam Redmond, Michael J. Dolan, Brian O'Higgins, Denis O'Dea and Gerard Healy. In general, audiences liked it, though the critics found it impossible to classify and thought that only the very excellent

acting had compensated for weak structure and characterisation. *Dublin Opinion* magnanimously decided that
though the play was defective, it showed its author to have
'potential'.

Undoubtedly most of these critics were right. If the play
failed it was not because the government disliked it or because
the satire was too savage; it was because it was tedious and
badly structured. The speeches, though shortened, were still
very lengthy; there was a minimum of action and very little
development or suspense; Act I seems interminable and there
was much unnecessary repetition.

The play tells the story of Mr Kelly, publican and chairman
of the urban district council, who sells his soul to the Devil in
return for help in becoming a TD and in gaining the woman
he loves but who will not marry him because she thinks she has
a late vocation and because she suspects him of being a secret
drinker.

Act I is set in the council room of the urban council.
O'Brien's aim was to satirise the tedious pusillanimity of the
councillors and their interminable trivial conversations. This
he does in this act by a faithful representation of the council
meeting in the course of which the Devil, 'Mr Strange', is
appointed as rates collector in order to give him a reason to
remain in the area and to give him access to the electoral
register.

Act II opens with the election campaign well under way.
Mrs Crockett, Kelly's reluctant mistress, is treasurer of the
election campaign fund, and the election meetings therefore
take place in her house. Mr Strange has been raising money,
persuading some voters and bribing others. Kelly looks like a
clear winner until Captain Shaw, Mrs Crockett's brother,
arrives from England, prepared to defend her reputation.
After a melodramatic scene he decides to run against Kelly.

Act III takes place on election night. The votes are being
counted; Kelly is sure to win, but then disaster strikes. Mrs
Crockett, instead of being ensnared, rejects Kelly for his bad
influence on her brother who arrives, quite drunk, to concede
victory to Kelly. Mr Reilly, a member of the council who
bitterly opposed Mr Strange's appointment, arrives to tell him
that the department has not 'sanctioned' him; bureaucracy
has won, and Mr Strange's life is as good as over. Mr Strange

retreats, defeated, as a guard is on his way to question Kelly. A petition has been launched against his election because two ballot-boxes have been found to be full of ashes. Kelly leaves to fight his corner and the Devil reappears to reject him and to return, a tired man, to hell.

The Faust theme is, therefore, reversed. Kelly sells his soul, is given many chances to repent, but persists in his self-delusion. Even the love and honesty of a good woman cannot save him. However, he is not carried to damnation. The 'department', all unwittingly (and aided by the unquestioned adherence of the Irish people to any sort of authority), defeats the Devil, and even he cannot tolerate the verbosity of Kelly.

The audience know from the beginning that Kelly has sold his soul, and that Mr Strange is the Devil. This provides great scope for dramatic irony. Kelly's honour is forfeit, and we know anyway from Act I that the local council is a hot-bed of nepotism and political jobbery. But Kelly is carried away by the force of his own rhetoric and ends up believing that he is a man of principle who will expose corruption, a dedicated public servant who 'IS NOT FOR SALE!'. He believes himself to be upright, fearless in exposing the jealousies and self-interest of others. Everything that he says is undercut by the audience's knowledge of his true position, by the Town Clerk's surprise at his passionate denunciation of malpractice and by Mrs Crockett's honest outburst.

> I'm finished with you all—for ever. FOR EVER, do you hear me? You talk about Christian charity . . . and decency . . . and reforming all the nasty things one sees today in this country. What are you, the whole lot of you, but vulgar despicable hypocrites, a gang of drunken louts, worrying all day and all night about your delicate hides! I'm sick of you . . . absolutely sick . . .   (p. 104; *SP*. 185)

But Kelly is quite impervious to the falsity of his position. Drunk with his own oratory, he overlooks reality, believing himself to be the last Christian left, surrounded by jealous time-servers, but trying to serve God and country to the best of his ability. The defection of the Devil and the contempt of Mrs Crockett eventually fall on deaf ears. No blow is enough to teach him humility. His final speech illustrates the extent to which his speeches have gained a hold over his mind, which is now unutterably self-deluded.

> Ashes? . . . A Petition? . . . A Petition? (*He strides about feverishly.*) A Petition? (*He becomes defiant.*) To the devil with their petition! TO THE DEVIL WITH THEIR PETITION! Simply because I chose to make a few Christian principles the basis of my scheme of life, they hate me — they *loathe* me — they seek to fling me aside . . . TO RUN ME OUT OF PUBLIC LIFE! But they will not succeed — do you hear me? — THEY WILL NOT SUCCEED. I owe a debt to this old land that bore me. That debt I will repay. THAT DEBT I WILL REPAY. And no contemptible conspiracy, no insidious intrigue, no treachery or trickery shall stand between me and my rightful place in the free parliament of the sovereign Irish people. IN . . . THAT . . . NATIONAL . . . ASSEMBLY I will lift a *fearless and unfettered voice* to lash and castigate the knaves and worse than knaves who have sold out the old land on the altar of mammon, I will assail without mercy the gombeen men, the time-servers, the place-hunters . . . the fools and flunkeys and godless money-changers — I'll outwit them and destroy them, DESTROY THEM FINALLY. (p. 121; *SP.* 195-6)

Kelly has here cast himself in an almost messianic role. But he will be a destructive messiah. Even as he talks of Christian values and 'mammon', his attitude is a reversal of the Christian and he is, closest to Satan. He is truly damned, though not in hell; and at this level the play works well, for the hypocrisy and venality of men is seen to be more evil than the Devil, who is a bit of a juggler, not very competent, and even a little likeable.

For much of the time, however, the irony is rather crude. Kelly's behaviour is paralleled by that of Reilly, who is, he says, furious at the thought of any jobbery or nepotism, although his own niece is employed by the council. His language, however, is repetitive; he is simply the angry bull-headed man who always shouts, hoping to howl down all opposition. The Devil's position is used as a source of comedy in throwaway sentences like that in which Mr Strange is praised for his endeavours on Kelly's behalf.

> Shure he worked like a steam-injun and he got hundreds of
> pounds from nowhere, wherever the devil he collected it.
>
> (p.94; *SP.* 179)

This element of the play is only amusing in the first instance;
after that it becomes tedious and predictable.

One of the problems of the play is that of classification.
O'Brien himself described it as 'pure farce', but it is not quite
that or, rather, it is only sometimes that. The basic situation is
fantastic, but, for the most part, the speeches and settings are
so realistic that they give the impression of having been
collected with a tape-recorder. This is particularly the case in
Act I which captures the atmosphere of the council meeting so
well. The bureauocratic jargon, the clichés which are the
characters' sole mode of conversation, the disinterest of those
present — these are all presented with such accuracy that it is
painful to watch. Act II, however, is largely melodrama.
Captain Shaw appears and, using words like 'cad', 'rotter',
'bounder' to describe Kelly, seems the conventional stage-
Englishman, complete with stereotyped phrases and attitudes.
He has come to save his sister's reputation and in the process
impugns it. He postures as the stern brother, she as a maiden
of outraged honour, and Kelly as the innocent victim of
slander as he asks in a superb line:

> What poisonous tongue or pen has been sowing discord and
> slander and calumny?   (p.70; *SP.* 164)

Act III becomes, to some extent, farce, with the Devil
disappearing into, and reappearing from, a cupboard in Mrs
Crockett's sitting-room. These different dramatic elements are
usually accompanied by that realism in dialogue and idiom
which became an obsession with O'Brien but which means that
the elements of the play are not subsumed under some
coherent dramatic pattern.

The greatest vitality in the play comes from the language.
Characters are seen only in terms of characteristic turns of
phrase or obsessive concerns, and this sometimes results in a
vivid image or a striking idiom. It is in Kelly himself, however,
that the play's real power lies. If most of his speeches are
examples of political posturing or an assumed pity for 'poor
sinful humanity', one speech at least is unforgettable for its

amazing accumulation of clichés and misconceptions about
the whole scope of Anglo-Irish relations.

Kelly, having expressed to Captain Shaw (whom he thinks is
English!) his liking and admiration for the English people and
for 'the mighty nation that lives and has its being at the other
side of the Irish Sea', turns his attention to the British
government and demands, in a superbly excessive, baroque,
often wildly imaginative flight of rhetorical fancy:

> With what pitiless and inexorable terminology will I lash
> and lash again those debased minions who have presumed
> to tamper with our historic race, to drive millions of our
> kith and kin in coffin-ships across the seven seas to dwell in
> an alien clime with the naked savage, who have destroyed
> our industries and our crafts and our right to develop our
> national resources, who have not hesitated to violate the
> sacred tabernacle of our nation to steal therefrom, defile
> and destroy our melodious and kingly language — THE
> IRISH LANGUAGE — our sole badge of nationhood, our
> only historic link with the giants of our national past — Niall
> of the Nine Hostages, who penetrated to the Alps in his
> efforts to spread the Gospel, King Cormac of Cashel,
> Confessor, Saint and lawgiver, heroic St Laurence O'Toole
> who is the Patron Saint of Ireland's greatest city, and
> Patrick Sarsfield, who rode by night to destroy, no matter at
> what risk to himself, the hated foreigner's powder-train at
> Ballyneety! With what appalling and frightening curse,
> Captain Shaw, will I invoke the righteous anger of the
> Almighty against these wicked men who live in gilded
> palaces in England, cradled in luxury and licentious
> extravagance, knowing nothing and caring nothing for
> either the English masses, the historic and indefeasible Irish
> nation, the naked negro in distant and distressed India or
> the New Zealand pigmy on his native shore? With what
> stern word will I invoke the righteous anger of Almighty
> God upon their heads, Captain Shaw?   (p.60; *SP.* 158-9)

This kind of speech shows O'Brien at his extravagant,
fantastic best. It is not, however, a speech which really fits well
into the rest of the play, and O'Brien had not enough
dramatic experience to achieve on stage the superb blend of

fantasy and realism which provides the basic structure of his novels.

In fact, O'Brien never became a really successful dramatist, although he wrote a good deal for stage and television. His great comic creations, Myles, the uncle, the brother, were dramatic but their qualities needed the expansiveness of prose or the continuity of a long-term column in which to develop. Within the more rigid confines of dramatic structure, O'Brien did not develop the discipline and the compression needed to create successful dramatic characters. His genius was expansive, so when he turned to drama his speeches were too long, his essentially linguistic humour ignored the need for action on stage, and, while many of the *Cruiskeen Lawn* articles or separate passages from the novels can be successfully dramatised as incidents or dramatic monologues, O'Brien himself never acquired that sensitivity to dramatic effect which is an essential quality in a playwright.

Nevertheless, O'Brien was to continue to experiment with dramatic forms, and his next venture, written before *Faustus Kelly* was produced, was an adaptation of the Capek brothers' play *The Life of the Insects*. At the end of March 1943, when the Abbey production of *Faustus Kelly* was drawing to a close, O'Brien's *The Insect Play* opened at the Gaiety.

The Capek play consists of a prologue, three acts, and an epilogue. The insects are butterflies, ants, moths and various kind of 'marauders', an ichneumon fly, dung beetles, and their victims, the crickets. The play draws a consistent parallel between the life of man and the life of the insects. Aspects of the life of the insects are disgusting, violent, pointless or beautiful. But the life-span of the insects is so short that man's life, when it is seen to follow the same pattern, seems insignificant, his claims mere pretensions.

It has so far proved impossible to trace a complete script of O'Brien's adaptation. All that is now available is the prologue and Act I, 'The Wasps'. From these fragments it is clear that O'Brien was intending to parallel the original quite closely. However, the fact that he was dealing with wasps rather than butterflies might be seen as an indication of his increasingly satiric and sunless outlook. People who remember the play say that one act was entitled 'The Ants' and that a dung-beetle appears intermittently. It was to be a political satire, with the insects representing various Irish political figures. From what remains it is impossible to ascertain this.

The prologue, which is somewhat different to the original, allows for a confrontation between the park keeper and an irate visitor who objects to being turned out of St Stephen's Green. The visitor is annoyed by the familiarity of the keeper, who is trying to impress upon him that if he were the civil servant actually in charge of parks and gardens he would be treated no differently from any other visitor. As it happens, the man *is* in charge of parks and gardens and, on discovering this, the keeper becomes all abject humility. The scene allows O'Brien to indulge his love of dialect and to make an oblique comment on the officiousness of public servants and the vast system of patronage which prevails in Ireland.

In Act I, instead of the Capeks' trivial but beautiful butterflies, O'Brien has a number of fatalistic wasps, unutterably bored with the pointlessness of their lives. They all speak with English accents very similar to that used by Captain Shaw in *Faustus Kelly*. Chance rules the world. All that enables the wasps to continue from day to day is the hope of mating with the queen. But there is only one queen and millions of wasps. Realising that the odds are impossible, two of the wasps make a death pact, sting each other and die. They had hoped that death, at least, would be an excitement, an event, a beautiful sensation. They die in agony as the queen enters, looking for a wasp with which to mate. In fury that they are all dead and that only an old drone, half-asleep and advising chastity in one of a series of quotations from Shakespeare, is left alive, she too resigns herself to death after stinging the helpless tramp who is merely an innocent bystander.

The world of the wasps is absurd. They themselves represent various human types. The drone is the 'peppery colonel' type. The young wasps are effeminate and discouraged, their speech a series of clichés, well illustrated in their farewells to each other before they die.

CYRIL. Well . . . old boy . . . eet has been nice knowing you.

CECIL. Pleasure all mine, old chap.

CYRIL. Sorry to part and all that.

CECIL. It does frightfully depress one, I mean, Fearful grey shaow.

CYRIL. But we will meet again in better land and all that, don't you think.[20]

The queen, O'Brien said, 'must be a superlatively erotic job' in appearance. In temperament she is imperious, petulant and bad-tempered. However, the characterisation in this play is not very well developed. The dialogue is quite tedious, the incessant quoting from Shakespeare is not comic and the stage-setting not very effective. O'Brien's note for the appearance of the queen read: 'For glitter and majesty she must exceed even Meriel Moore as the courtesan in "Jack-in-the-Box".' Of this Joseph Holloway was to comment: 'I heard that his adaptation of *The Insect Play* was a flop . . . His stage effects are distinctly vulgar and common, and not suitable in the Gaiety, the Abbey, or the Gate.'[21]

The play had, in fact, a very short run, but if Acts II and III continued with the same deficiencies in dialogue, this is not surprising. It may, of course, have improved and been drawn together by the succeeding acts but, as it stands, it is a good example of how O'Brien's humour could flag and his inventive powers become quite retarded.

O'Brien sent his sketch *Thirst* to Hilton Edwards soon after the production of *The Insect Play*. Although it was never put on in the Gate, it was performed with great success by Dublin University Players. It is a slight sketch about a gárda sergeant discovering after-hours drinking in a public house, entering, intending to make a report, and being drawn into drinking himself by the publican's long story of terrible heat and thirst in the desert during the war. The story, casually begun, builds up to such an intense climax that the three men listening to it are physically affected. As the publican describes his reactions, their throats tighten, they swallow nervously, they experience a drying of the mouth and an intense desire to reach out for the pint of Guinness placed before them. The publican who is a superb story-teller builds up his story with repetition and carefully selected detail. His imagination is extensive and he has a fine awareness of the refinements of physical distress: the agony of hot sand under the finger-nails, the parched throat, the swelling tongue, the flayed skin of the

feet, the sensation of inflamed eyeballs, and eyebrows and
lashes scorched off by the sun. When he has his audience
wincing, he begins to remind them of all the 'nice long cool
drinks' that could be had to assuage this overwhelming thirst.
Watching the reactions of the almost impassive Sergeant, 'the
large solemn country type', very carefully, he concludes his
story with a fine flight of sensuousness.

> I could see in me mind's eye the big vat above in Guinness's
> and myself divin' into it with me mouth open and
> swallyin' . . . swallyin' . . . swallyin' away for hours, lettin'
> the brown porter run down me neck until I was fit to
> burst . . . Until I was nearly dead from drinkin' the lovely,
> wet, cold, brown, lovely porter! (Here the Sergeant makes a
> loud incoherent noise, turns slowly and deliberately, lifts
> the glass of stout that is beside him and drinks it off in one
> long appreciative draught).[22]

This sketch shows all the skill in creating dialogue which
had been absent from *The Insect Play*. There is no action in it,
nor any need for it. The men barely move from their positions
at the bar; all the plot's development derives from the
language, which is both vivid and natural. The publican has
ample scope for his monologue; he is interrupted only by the
clearing of a throat or the odd interjection. Setting and plot
are, however, suitable for long speeches, and so the play,
though slight in content, works well and has been repeated
more often than any other of O'Brien's dramatic works.

For the moment, there were no more experiments with
drama. Not until 1955 did O'Brien try to write another play,
when he composed the first draft of *The Boy from
Ballytearim* as a television play, intending to offer it to the
newly-formed BBC station in Northern Ireland. They did not
accept it and it was not produced until 1962, when Hilton
Edwards, then head of drama in RTE, produced its revised
version.

Since it was originally written for Ulster television, the play
was consciously Northern in outlook. O'Brien specified
Northern accents, suggested that Belfast actors might be used,
and said that the play was based on a poem of the same name
which was written by Moira O'Neill in about 1900. 'The Boy
from Ballytearim', a poem from the Glens of Antrim, was a

fairly traditional ballad about a young man who leaves the poverty of his home to seek his fortune in America. He leaves behind him his ageing parents and his sweetheart. He returns rich and successful to marry his girl but finds that she has been dead for many years. The poem is sentimental and O'Brien's intention in the play was to modify 'the pathos' and to turn the sentiment 'upside down'.[23]

In both versions of the play, the pathos is modified by making the son a very disagreeable young man both before and after his trip to America, and by having his parents dislike and object to the girl. The versions are slightly different in that there is rather more sentiment in the first than the second. The young man's grandfather smokes and is always out of matches. When the grandson comes back from America he has brought with him a large package of matches, but his grandfather, like his sweetheart, is dead. In the second version the man who arrives after an absence of fifteen years is less sympathetic because he is fat, speaks with an American drawl, boasts more about his car and his dollars, and is very gaudily dressed. Yet in the first version the parents, who do not discover his attachment until after he has emigrated, are far more violent about the girl than they are in the second version.

One of O'Brien's main aims in this play was to attack the sentimentality attaching to the returned emigrant. The son was driven away by poverty, hard work, lack of opportunity and the nagging of his parents. He was himself ill-mannered and rude. He did not leave an idyllic little cottage and mourning parents. When he is gone, it is the neighbours who defend him while his parents accuse him of laziness, failure, and sins of the flesh. When he returns, his parents are old and worn out. His father has been left, like many a man, unable to run his farm without the hitherto unappreciated efforts of the son. The son is now out of place in the community and can manage only the bare bones of communications with his parents who have stayed in a place where nothing has changed for fifteen years. The son, while away, had built up a romantic dream about the warmth of home and the little girl waiting for him. He returns to find that that dream is a mirage, though his parents have more respect for a rich son than they had for a poor one. In the second version the mother, trying to console her son for the death of the girl, tells him that 'she never forgot

you', but the mood of the play is anti-sentimental and pro-
realistic, and this conventional reassurance seems out of place.
The anti-sentimental bias of the play is exaggerated by the
reading of the poem and the playing of a plaintive violin,
which act as an ironic contrast to the events taking place in the
house in Ballytearim. The second version, revised in 1962, has
only two acts, the conversation and the characters having been
slightly changed and the play, as a whole, made more
compact. O'Brien made an attempt, in the second version, to
describe the setting and to place the action more in its time. As
Act I opens, the father is discussing the Boer War. In Act II he
is talking about the Kaiser. It was probably more easy to
televise the later version because of its more ordered
development, but it is in some ways less interesting because the
characters are more sketchily drawn and the son is more
unpleasant.

It is interesting to note O'Brien's attitude to returning
Americans at this stage because this theme was to emerge
again in *Slattery's Sago Saga. The Boy from Ballytearim* was
not a particularly good play but it was the first of that long
series of television plays which were to be one of O'Brien's
major interest in the years from 1960 to 1966. It is, perhaps,
doubly interesting in that it is the only piece in which O'Brien
writes about the place of his birth, though it must be said that,
apart from the accents used, the conversation of the characters
follows very closely the lines of the conversation in the
Furriskey household.

O'Brien also experimented in these years with the writing of
short stories. Apart from the stories for the detective magazine
on the adventures of Sexton Blake, the famous detective
(which an admirer wrote to say were the best things he had
produced!), O'Brien wrote five short stories. The first of these,
Old Iron, was sent to William Saroyan's agents in New York
who acknowledged receipt of it. No trace of it has yet been
found. Of the stories available to us, *John Duffy's Brother* was
written in 1938 and published through the efforts of Matson &
Duggan (who did not think it funny) in *Story* magazine in
1941. *The Martyr's Crown* was published in 1950, *Two in One*
in 1952, while *Donabate* may be the same story as that
published in 1958 under the title *A Perfect Gentleman. Two*

in One was later dramatised as a television play called *The Dead Spit of Kelly.*

None of these stories is good. *The Martyr's Crown* is marginally better than the others though they are interesting only in that they shed some light on O'Brien's interests. *John Duffy's Brother* is the story of a day in the life of a civil servant who suddenly thinks he is a train.[24] O'Brien was always fascinated by trains and in this story takes joy in describing their complicated shunting operations, precise timing and the number and specifications of wheels possessed by the various types of engine. The story exists in two versions, one twice as long as the other. The longer version[25] provides an introduction and a conclusion and attempts to fill in more background to the strange occurrence. The story is interesting for some of its images, for O'Brien's periphrastic prose, and because it illustrates O'Brien's 'through the looking glass' notion of causality and is thus a step on the way to *The Third Policeman.* After all, a man thinking he is a train is not far removed from a man becoming a bicycle. In the introduction, O'Brien admits that he is entering an absurd world.

> We must admit that handicap at the beginning — that it is absurd for us to tell the story, absurd for anybody to listen to it and unthinkable that anybody should believe it. (*SP.* 91)

Nevertheless, he goes on to tell it, and it is not particularly amusing, though it does indicate that O'Brien's sense of eccentricity was ever-present. If his tendency to find insanity comic is not convincing here, it was a very important attitude in his novels.

The story *Two in One* is also close to the spirit of *The Third Policeman* and to parts of *The Hard Life.* It illustrates O'Brien's fascination with what is horrible and gruesome. It is the story of a taxidermist who murders his obnoxious employer and then disposes of the body in pieces, retaining only the skin which he fits on to his own body. He thus becomes literally 'the dead spit of Kelly' (the title of the dramatised version) and goes about pretending to be him so that the murdered man's absence will not be noticed. Unfortunately, things go wrong: he is unable to remove the skin and is eventually arrested and found guilty of murdering himself. It is the kind of story that

Alfred Hitchcock might have chosen to film, but it is difficult
to see how it is comic.

In the process of writing it, O'Brien gave a typically
pedantic history of taxidermy, and then manifests the same
kind of mentality which described the murder of Philip
Mathers in such sensuous detail.

> The loathsome creature had his back to me, bending down
> to put on his bicycle clips. Just to my hand on the bench was
> one of the long, flat, steel instruments we use for certain
> operations with plaster. I picked it up and hit him a blow
> with it on the back of the head. He gave a cry and slumped
> forward. I hit him again. I rained blow after blow on him.
> Then I threw the tool away.[26]

O'Brien himself, speaking as the murderer, explains
something of the atmosphere of the story.

> Once one enters a climate of horror, distinction of degree as
> between one infamy and another seems slight, sometimes
> undetectable.[27]

He is therefore able to make jokes about 'committing the
remains of, so to speak, the remains, to the furnace', as he
carves up the body.

Donabate is an even more trivial story about the drinking
and deterioration of Sir Sefton Fleetwood-Crawshaye, a
retired architect who, once introduced to the delights of Irish
whiskey, seeks opportunity to drink it all day. In the holy hour
he goes to the nearby railway station, buys a ticket to
Donabate in north County Dublin and, as a 'bona fide'
traveller, drinks in the station until the pubs reopen. But no
matter how degenerate he may become, he is always 'the
perfect gentleman'. He buys *first-class* tickets to Donabate.
This story is unenlivened by any real conclusion or by a felicity
of prose or subtlety of description.

The Martyr's Crown, the story of a brave woman, a martyr,
who seduced a British soldier to save the rebels hidden in her
house, and of her son, a proud man because, instead of dying
for Ireland, he was *born* for it, is the best of the four.

The story is told by Mr Toole to Mr O'Hickey. Mr O'Hickey,
while being well aware that the whole thing is a fabrication,

feels impelled to bribe Mr Toole with bottles of stout to tell the story. Mr Toole possesses the true story-teller's art. He is a modern shanachee in that he has the power of stimulating his listener's curiosity and then building up the story carefully, with much convincing detail, to a suitable conclusion. Mr Toole can always suggest mystery and excitement without revealing anything, and even if the listener know it is a fiction, it is a good one, and they appreciate the art of the telling.

In the telling, O'Brien manages to overturn many sacred nationalistic prejudices. The woman in question, almost Cathleen Ni Houlihan herself, is a 'very good woman', 'very strict'. She shelters men on the run when they have carried out a raid on the British soldiers. The story of the raid is narrated with the full orchestration of blood and mass murder. Mrs Clougherty, however, will allow no drink in the house and makes all the men say the rosary with her before retiring. Her moment of bravery comes when she turns abruptly into a trollop, speaking with a 'gutty' accent and loosening the buttons of her blouse before she faces the soldiers; Cathleen Ni Houlihan becomes a strumpet for the sake of Ireland. The son who is born as a result of her endeavours has a right to be proud, insists Mr Toole; his mother was a martyr, and he was born for Ireland!

All O'Brien's stories deal with the Dublin lower middle classes and find their main purpose in revealing the inflections of Dublin speech. In none of them are the characters well drawn and, like the plays, their literary form forbids that expansiveness which was essential to O'Brien. He did not manage to utilise the short story form to its greatest extent, and his achievements in this genre are, in effect, little more than extended anecdotes, very close, in some respects, to some of his newspaper articles.

Apart from *An Béal Bocht,* the writing of these years, was, in the main, ephemeral and inconsequential. It was, then, with a great sense of excitement that the publication of O'Brien's new novel, his first for over twenty years, was awaited by his friends and admirers.

7
'An Exegesis of Squalor':
The Hard Life

The Hard Life, O'Brien's second published novel, appeared
over twenty years after *At Swim*. The reissue of *At Swim* seems
to have inspired O'Brien to try again with a full-length work,[1]
and by August 1960 he was busy with the book. It took him, he
said, only about two months to complete, and was instantly
accepted by Timothy O'Keeffe at MacGibbon & Kee who
described it as 'funny and distinguished throughout'.[2] The
proofs were ready in July 1961, and Pantheon in America had
sent a large advance and an offer to publish it in the United
States.

Publication was delayed until November at O'Keeffe's
suggestion. O'Brien raised no objection for he was by now
obsessed with the question of censorship. He felt that the
anticlericalism of the book might cause it to be banned, and
he was girding his loins for legal battle in that event. O'Brien
was, and remained, a sincere Catholic, but he was often bitter
about the practices of the Church and its ministers and he
expressed this bitterness in fairly strong terms. Even so, the
attack on the Church in *The Hard Life* is innocent enough
and reflects as much on Mr Collopy's ignorance as on the
subject of his diatribes. O'Brien was at this time involved in a
number of legal battles, and with increasing skill prepared his
ground for the fully-expected attack on his book. He may even
have been disappointed when it did not materialise. A
favourite saying about literary success in Ireland is that the
best way to make a best-seller is to have the book
banned—then everybody wants to read it. O'Brien was fully
aware of this; he wrote to Tim O'Keeffe:

> Any intelligent person can get any book he wants. Two
> reputable bookshops keep banned books under the counter

like cigarettes in wartime. If the assistant knows you, you can have anything under the sun, including (for students) continental magazines full of pictures of women without a stitch on them.[3]

He went on to outline the statutory grounds on which a book could be banned, namely, obscenity and the advocation of artificial methods of birth control. Neither of these categories covers *The Hard Life*; indeed, O'Brien never mentions sexual relations in his books, with the exception of a passage in *Slattery's Sago Saga,* Mary's announcement at the end of *The Dalkey Archive,* and the rape of his beautiful heroine by Trellis in *At Swim.* On this subject O'Brien was unusually reticent. Nevertheless, he felt that *The Hard Life* would be banned and regaled Tim O'Keeffe with stories of books which had been unjustifiably and ludicrously banned, and went on:

> For those reasons *I know The Hard Life* will be banned here. True, the book doesn't offend under heads (a) or (b) above, but the mere name of Father Kurt Fahrt, S J will justify the thunderclap. The ban will be improper and illegal and when it comes, I will challenge it in the High Courts here. I will seek not only a declaration that the book is one to be properly on sale but claim damages from those who imposed the ban and who will be shown in court to be incapable of quoting a line that contravenes . . . the Acts.[4]

He requested that the jacket of the book should be designed so that it could not afford 'ammunition to those most reverend spivs'. He thought that it should be 'utterly colourless, anonymous (pseudonymous), neutral',[5] and desired that absolutely no biographical information should appear on it. O'Keeffe tried to reassure him that the comedy of the book would defend it from censorship, but in November he was still obsessed with the idea. He had, at the same time, been getting advance judgments from friends and acquaintances.

> I lent the book to two persons who hadn't heard of it, deliberately chosen for what we will call their incongruity of temperament and judgment. The first found it very, very funny—uproarious. The second (a lady) handed it back to me sadly. She said she did not understand me and now doubted whether she ever had.[6]

It was not banned; indeed, it sold out in Dublin within forty-eight hours. The reviewers received it very kindly, even with exaggerated praise. From their point of view this was O'Brien's second book. *The Third Policeman* had never appeared, *An Béal Bocht* and *Faustus Kelly* were published in Ireland in very small editions. This, then, was the first full-length work to appear after *At Swim*. Its reception showed that anything by O'Brien was now eagerly awaited and would be acclaimed. Graham Greene, to whom *The Hard Life* had been dedicated, wrote to O'Brien in October to tell him that he was delighted with the dedication. Many of the reviewers, while praising the book found themselves mentioning Joyce in the same breath.

> Mr O'Brien employs a rich sub-Joycean language.
>
> (Maurice Edelman)[7]
>
> Mr O'Brien is less a disciple of Joyce than a drinker of the same hallucinatory, word-loving logomachic brew.
>
> (Anthony Burgess)[8]

O'Brien protested vigorously at this association of names, yet the book does bear a close resemblance in certain of its aspects to the work of Joyce, and it seems clear that certain parts are intended as a parody of *Dubliners* and *A Portrait of the Artist*.

There is no doubt that O'Brien was pleased with the book. He wrote to Tim O'Keeffe and told him:

> I believe *The Hard Life* is a very funny book but at this stage my belief can be disregarded, for it's a poor crow who isn't proud of it's own dirt.[9]

Later, at the time when he dismissed *At Swim* as 'adolescent trifling', he re-emphasised this opinion.

> What must be realised, is it will ultimately be established by sales, [is] that *The Hard Life* is a very important book and very funny. Its apparently pedestrian style is delusive.[10]

In spite of his confidence in it, however, *The Hard Life* is probably the least successful of O'Brien's books. It is hilarious in outline, sad and disjointed in execution. It appears to be the result of a hasty patching together of a number of separate, previously effective, elements. The 'brother' comes from *Cruiskeen Lawn* along with the attack on Dublin Corporation.

O'Brien has an increasing tendency to use pedantry as a comic device and to 'pad out' his books with a large amount of factual detail. Added to these familiar elements are a new attack on the Church and an exposition of squalid situations and characters. None of these elements are finally made to cohere within a unified and consistent whole. They remain separate and distinguishable parts within a book which gives the impression of trying to be *too* funny, *too* pedantic. In so doing it shows no important underlying theme or purpose. Laughter is, of course, its own justification, but after the complexity within order .of *At Swim* and the impressive overriding vision of *The Third Policeman,* the almost hysteria-reaching after-effect in *The Hard Life* becomes wearisome, especially since O'Brien relies on a small number of comic devices which become overworked and ineffective as the book progresses.

The Hard Life, set in Dublin at the turn of the century, presents O'Brien's most normal picture of reality. Some of the events which take place in the course of the book are ludicrous, some are horrible, most are sordid, all are feasible. The Dublin in which Finbarr and the 'brother', Manus, grow up is the city of Joyce's youth. It is full of decaying houses which reflect a past glory. Mr Collopy lives in Warrington Place, a continuation of the once 'lordly' Herbert Place. Dublin Castle is still staffed by the British, though there is agitation for Home Rule.

> And then you have all this talk about Home Rule, Mr Collopy asserted. Well how are you! We're as fit for Home Rule here as the blue men in Africa if we are to judge by those Bull Island looderamawns. (p.19)

The GAA and the Gaelic League are beginning to be big cultural forces.

> That's good. The native games for the native people. By dad and I see young thullabawns of fellows got out in their baggy drawers playing this new golf out beyond the Bull Island. For pity's sake sure that isn't a game at all. (p.19)

It is a time in which one defines one's Irishness by opposing all things British and by using as many Irish words as possible.

even if one cannot actually speak the language. Mr Collopy
admits that he does not know Irish, but he interlards his
speech with expressions like 'pishrogues', 'thullabawns',
'looderamawns', 'bosthoons', 'gorawars', 'smahan', and
'shaughraun'. The Church is respected and the Christian
Brothers, the chief educators, look for many of their boys to
join the Order. Much of this is presented by O'Brien, not
merely to establish the scene, to evoke the physical and
cultural environs of Dublin, but (as in *At Swim*) to mock those
things which James Joyce had also mocked.

The chief reference to Joyce comes, however, in the subtitle,
An Exegesis of Squalor. The book is an attempt to sum up the
atmosphere of *Dubliners* and *A Portrait of the Artist,* with sly
digs on the way at *Ulysses.* The satire of Joyce and his works
which began in *Comhthrom Féinne* and is present throughout
At Swim and *Cruiskeen Lawn,* culminates in *The Dalkey
Archive* where, as well as the malicious portrait of Joyce, there
is also a statement about his greatness. In this book there is no
direct reference to Joyce but, as the subtitle suggests, an
overwhelming evocation of squalor, both mental and physical.
O'Brien isolated this element from Joyce's book and made it
the overriding vision of his own. It is a vision which is
essentially depressing were it not for the ludicrous antics of the
brother, the mysterious work of Mr Collopy which culminates
in his strange interview with the pope, and the pedantic
quibbling about distorted views of the Church and Irish
history which take place in the big kitchen. These things
relieve the atmosphere of the book which begins with death
and with the smell of damp washing and ends in a 'tidal surge
of vomit'.

The idea of squalor is presented throughout and is
reinforced in every detail. It is seen as an attribute of
environment, character and event in the book. Joyce had
presented a vivid picture of an Ireland that was squalid, but he
had done it primarily through a repeated pattern of image,
word and phrase. O'Brien's method is different and works by
direct presentation and comment. The narrator, Finbarr, is
aged five at the beginning of the book and sixteen at the end.
There is no attempt, as there is in *A Portrait of the Artist,* to
illustrate the developing consciousness and linguistic power of
the child. Finbarr is telling the story when he is much older

and makes no attempt to think back to the kind of perception and language he would have had as a boy of five. He uses words like 'lacuna', 'hiatus', and 'interregnum' and stresses the fact that his original impressions must have altered in the passage of years.

> There is something misleading but not dishonest in this portrait of Mr Collopy. It cannot be truly my impression of him when I first saw him but rather a synthesis of all the thoughts and experiences I had of him over the years, a long look backwards.   (p.16)[11]

Finbarr is thus a highly conscious narrator who is telling his story not, like Stephen Dedalus, experiencing his life. As a conscious narrator he can describe, judge and comment upon things from an emotionally uninvolved distance. This accounts for the finished nature of the judgments, for the clarity of the synthesis of experience, for the coherence of the pattern. This type of narrator is necessary in an exegesis, a detailed examination, to clarify the difficulties of the subject. However, it might be said that the distancing of the emotional involvement here lessens the impact of some of the events — especially the concluding one — where the bare statement 'There, everything inside me came up in a tidal surge of vomit' does not convey with any great force the horror and repulsion felt by Finbarr. It is clear that O'Brien is not specifically concerned with the character of Finbarr but with the events and characters Finbarr observes in the world around him. In this sense, at least, *The Hard Life* is O'Brien's most traditional novel, though it has little of the moral comment found in other novels of its type.

Finbarr describes the details of his and his brother's life, beginning with the death of their mother and their deliverance into the household of Mr Collopy. Their whole environment is squalid, not merely in the house itself but in the outside world as well. Before they move to Warrington Place they live in a house which has a poor water supply, so that Annie must spend most of her time washing. When Mrs Crotty arrives the first thing she mentions is dirt, and the references to dirt are to continue throughout the book. A permanent layer of grease and grime seems to lie over all the places described in the book. The food given to the boys is unappetising, an unvarying diet of 'boxty, kalecannon . . . and mince balls covered in a greasy paste'. The house in Warrington Place, though larger, better equipped, and owned by a man of some means is epitomised by its kitchen where the inhabitants spend most of their time. We know little about the house since it is not described in detail but it takes on many of the characteristics of its inhabitants and several passing references give the impression of an untidy, uncomfortable, dimly lit kitchen smelling of whiskey, washing and meat balls and dominated by a sprawling range. Every item of furniture mentioned in the course of the book is broken. The rest of the house seems to suffer from its lack of adequate lavatory facilities, and at least two rooms are associated with unpleasant smells. Mr Collopy's bedroom smells because he leaves his dirty socks on the floor for Annie to pick up and wash, and Mrs Crotty's bedroom smells because her illness included nocturnal bed-wetting and the mattress and springs of her bed are rotting and sodden. The atmosphere in this house is seen as a 'dead' one (a reference to Joyce's *Dubliners*) which is relieved only by the pedantic bickering of Mr Collopy and Father Fahrt and the shady business deals of the brother.

As the book progresses the dead atmosphere in the house becomes reality with the death of Mrs Crotty. Her illness is long and depressing, though aspects of it are comic, but the description of her fevered face and her weak voice calling from the other room create a gloom which builds to its ultimate in the description of her funeral which takes place on a very wet day.

A burial on a wet day, with the rain lashing down on the mourners, is a matter simply of squalor.   (p.59)

The mourners meet, including the tall emaciated ladies of Mr Collopy's committee, the hearse goes the long way along the sea-front, the 'sodden turgid clay' is dropped on the coffin while the brother curses and drinks from a hip-flask all the way through the service. Everyone is drenched and bad-tempered. The whole affair is pointless and miserable, very unlike the funeral in *Ulysses,* which is similar in detail if not in mood. In this instance the lack of emotion on the part of the narrator adds to the misery of the scene. After the funeral the brother returns drunk and begins a quarrel with Mr Collopy which increases the tension within the house.

The other house encountered by Finbarr is the Christian Brothers' school in Synge Street. Mr Collopy and Finbarr arrive there early in the morning. The door is opened by 'a slatternly young man in black' and they are ushered into a cold bare room which is ironically described as having an 'odour of sanctity'. Finbarr, with a child's quick intuition, compares the place with a prison and his feelings are reinforced by the man who comes to interview them. He is sad, prim and has several odd mannerisms. He laughs without meaning it, and Finbarr describes him as 'greasy'. Synge Street itself is 'sinister', a place of compulsion and corporal punishment. The account of this presents a good example of O'Brien's method of description which leaves the reader to supply the emotional and imaginative power from their own experience.

> That is how I entered the sinister portals of Synge Street school. Soon I was to get to know the instrument known as 'the leather'. It is not, as one would imagine, a strap of the kind used on bags. It is a number of such straps sewn together to form a thing of great thickness that is nearly as rigid as a club but just sufficiently flexible to prevent the breaking of the bones of the hand. Blows of it, particularly if directed (as often they deliberately were) to the top of the thumb or wrist, conferred immediate paralysis followed by agony as the blood tried to get back to the afflicted part. Later I was to learn from the brother a certain routine of prophylaxis he had devised but it worked only partly. (p.25)

If this passage is compared to the incident of the pandybat in *A Portrait of the Artist,* it is clear that Joyce's method of 'showing' is more effective than O'Brien's method of 'telling'. O'Brien's description indicates the extent to which he now relied for his comic effect on the reader's memory of incidents in Joyce which O'Brien simply had to recall. Here, however, the account of the miseries of Synge Street proves that misery is a condition of life and that unpleasant happenings are not confined to the Collopy establishment.

Warrington Place is near the canal, and the canal too is seen as a source of squalor. Annie is caught by Finbarr loitering with a group of lads near the canal, and from this point the book concentrates on the possible results of such loitering in terms of disease. The brother's letter emphasises this danger in graphic terms.

> There remains, of course, the Main Act. This disease is caused by a virus known as *spirochaeta pallida* or *treponema pallidum*. We can have skin rash, lesions of the mouth, enlargement of lymph glands, loss of scalp hair, inflammation of the eyes, jaundice from liver damage, convulsions, deafness, meningitis and sometimes coma.
>
> (p.114)[12]

Mr Collopy, with his terror of disease, which prevents him from sending his clothes to the laundry, makes syphilis seem like an everyday occurrence. The idea of disease becomes one of the underlying elements of a story whose whole environment is seen as dirty, disease-ridden, and depressing. In such circumstances, life and death become meaningless.

The characters in the book are equally depressing. Very few of them are likeable or attractive either in mind or in body. Mr Collopy is introduced to the reader in the most unflattering terms.

> He was sitting there at the range in a cracked, collapsed sort of chair, small reddish eyes looking up at us over the rims of steel spectacles, the head bent forward for closer scrutiny. Over an ample crown, long grey hair was plastered in a tatty way. The whole mouth region was concealed by the great untidy dark brush of a moustache, discoloured at the edges, and a fading chin was joined to a stringy neck which disappeared into a white celluloid collar with no tie. Nondescript clothes contained a meagre frame of low stature and the feet wore large boots with the laces undone.
>
> (pp. 16-17)

By giving this description of Mr Collopy in the passive voice, O'Brien makes him more like an object, a biological specimen to be regarded with curiosity, than a personality. Collopy is a man who dresses like a tramp, drinks a lot, is self-opinionated, quarrelsome, a nuisance about his food and his washing, full of strange fads and old wives' tales, and utterly selfish. His appearance is ugly and his manner worse; he spends a lot of his

time expressing himself forcibly on subjects about which he
knows very little, and he is a complete humbug.

His daughter Annie is 'a streel of a girl with long lank fair
hair'. She is not very good-looking but has a good heart and
works hard. She is unfavourably compared to Penelope,
Finbarr's ideal. The contrast between Annie, the reality, and
Penelope, the ideal, corresponds to the contrast in *A Portrait
of the Artist,* between the whore and Stephen's dream-woman.
Like Stephen, Finbarr experiences doubts about his real
intentions towards Penelope. Penelope, says Finbarr,

> was what was known as a good hoult, with auburn hair,
> blue eyes and a very nice smile . . . I remember being
> puzzled to think that she and Annie belonged to the same
> sex. Annie was a horrible, limp, lank streel of a creature.
>
> (p.89)

Later, when he hears Annie's voice from a dark corner of the
canal, he is worried.

> I paused involuntarily, deeply shocked, but I soon walked
> on. I had, in fact, been thinking of Penelope, and that one
> word threw my mind into a whirl. What was the meaning of
> this thing sex? What was the nature of sexual attraction?
> Was it all bad and dangerous? What was Annie doing late
> at night, standing in a dark place with young blackguards?
> Was I any better myself in conduct, whispering sly things
> into the ear of lovely and innocent Penelope? Had I, in fact,
> at the bottom of my heart dirty intentions, some dark deed
> postponed because the opportunity had not yet presented
> itself?   (p.111)

Mrs Crotty, Collopy's second wife, is eccentric, old, cross
and eventually very ill. Finbarr catches sight of her on one
occasion.

> This was when she was coming down the stairs leaning on
> Mr Collopy and clutching the banister with one frail hand,
> her robe or nightdress of fantastic shape and colour and a
> frightening pallor on her spent face.   (p.27)

The brother, inexhaustibly resourceful, is made to represent
the self-made man. He knows what people want and intends to

give it to them without any scruples. He is, however, capable of making a gesture — when he has the money and when it does not seriously upset him. He is a drinker, a womaniser and a hypocrite. He aims to make money, to be comfortable, and he has little concern about how this end is to be achieved. Even when faced with the result of some of his schemes he shows no apparent worry. The brother is openly criticised by Finbarr and is the only character in the book to be subjected to such treatment. However, even while he criticises him, Finbarr still admires him for his cleverness and his ability to circumvent the possible consequences of some of his more hair-brained schemes. Manus makes money primarily by marketing information gained from other people's books. It is this aspect of his activities which is most criticised. O'Brien, always contemptuous of false learning, makes the brother reveal himself, in his letter to Finbarr, as a complete charlatan.

> Do not pay too much attention to the list of subjects in the margin. I don't see why we shouldn't deal with them and plenty more as well, e.g. Religious Vocations, but I am not yet publicly using this notepaper. You could regard the list in the margin as a manifesto, a statement of what we intend to do. We really aim at the mass-production of knowledge, human accomplishment and civilisation. We plan the world of the future, a world of sophisticated and genial people, all well-to-do, impatient with snivellers, sneaks and politicians on the make; not really a Utopia but a society in which all *unnecessary* wrongs, failures, and misbehaviours are removed. The simplest way to attack this problem is to strike at the cause, which is ignorance and non-education or miseducation. (pp. 101-2)

In his characterisation of the brother O'Brien introduces his idea of moral squalor whereas before he had concentrated more on physical dirt and misery. O'Brien's art is the art of distortion. In the brother's letter he presents what could be a typical educational manifesto, a prospectus of studies to be completed, but he has exaggerated it and put it into the mouth of a character whom we know to be unworthy. He then relies on the disparity between the reader's ex-pectations — about education, culture and the like — and their knowledge of the brother's character to turn parody into satire. The brother intends to teach Boxing, Foreign Languages, Poultry Farming, Fretwork, Astronomy, Music, Ju-Jitsu, A Cure for Cancer, Bridge, Prevention and Treatment of Boils, The Ancient Classics and many other subjects, all mutually incompatible. The comic device used here is the placing of the sublime — The Ancient Classics — beside what, in association with it, becomes ridiculous — the Prevention and Treatment of Boils. The brother promises what is possible — the teaching of Bridge by correspondence — with what is impossible — A Cure for Cancer and the teaching of religious vocations by correspondence. At the same time as he is proposing to teach all these things by taking extracts from other people's books, he talks about the miseducation of the masses. In this letter parody, irony and satire are interchangeable, and the extract becomes an attack on quacks and charlatans, of whom the brother is a supreme example.

Father Kurt Fahrt, S J, is another main character in the book. O'Brien was very pleased with himself when he invented this character for he was both mocking the Jesuits (a favourite occupation of his own and a way of emulating Joyce) and continuing the theme of squalor with the presentation of another unsavoury character. He was later to describe *The Hard Life* as 'a treatise on piss and vomit' and Father Fahrt's name fits very appropriately into this. To a great extent the comedy of *The Hard Life* stems from its concentration on the basic functions of man set side by side with his intellectual pretensions. In the book O'Brien illustrates the same view of man as an ugly and ludicrous animal as had Swift. This is clear in the presentation of Father Fahrt, the subtle Jesuit, a casuist, a philosopher who bears (in English, at least) a ridiculous name and who is first seen scratching wildly at various sections of his anatomy. He is described as

> a very tall man, thin, ascetic, grey-haired, blue about the jaws with a neck so slender that there would be room, so to speak, for two of them inside his priestly collar.   (p.31)

Father Fahrt, although he thinks of himself as an educated, subtle man, is, in fact, quite stupid and misinformed about many things. Of all the characters in the novel he is the one whose thinking should be most precise, most trained, yet he proves himself to be incapable of clearly distinguishing subtleties of theology and as liable to trot out clichéd generalisations as any one else in the book.

The last character, Finbarr, with his saint's name, is the 'eye' of the book. He is a perceptive child who has the valuable quality, as has Manus, of being able to see through all the humbug surrounding them. This faculty does not make him as cynical as his brother, and it is important for the balance of the book that he retain some values, for it is through his eyes that false values are revealed. He has some patience with human failings and is able to respond to what good qualities can be discerned in the people he knows. At the same time he dislikes distortions of situations for the sake of sentimentality. This is clear in his final conversation with the brother.

> Yes, [said the brother] I'm very pleased that Annie is turning out like that. She is a good-hearted girl.
> But what are you talking about, I said rather puzzled. Hasn't she been looking after a whole houseful all her life? Poor Mrs Crotty in her day never did a hand's turn. She was nearly always sick and, God rest the dead, but Mr Collopy was a handful in himself, always asking whether there was starch in his food, no matter what you gave him. He even suspected the water in the tap.   (p.155)

But in spite of these good qualities, Finbarr too must be morally lacking to re-emphasise the squalor resulting from the lack of care and cultivation.

The events of the book are as squalid as the characters and their environment, but they are also comic, and the comedy is inseparable from the squalor. It is this mixture of the horrible and the comic which is the most characteristic element of O'Brien's vision here.

The early chapters are concerned with the creation of the mood and atmosphere of the book, with the setting of the scene and the introduction of the characters. The first thing of any importance that happens is the mention of Mr Collopy's 'work'. He is engaged in a great mission of some urgency for the women in Ireland. Apart from the members of his committee, who are all dedicated and persevering, his only confidant about his work is Father Fahrt. He and Father Fahrt discuss it at great length in the kitchen. However, the nature of the work is so delicate that they never mention precisely what it is, and even at the end of the book it has never been explicitly described. At first we only know that Mr Collopy is very angry about the progress of his plan. Since we do not know of what this plan consists, the discussion about it leaves the imagination free to devise the wildest ideas about the terrible situation that Mr Collopy is seeking to remedy.

> Father, said Mr Collopy at last, you would go off your bloody head if you had the same situation in your own house. You would make a show of yourself. You would tell Father Superior to go to hell, leap out the front door and bugger off down to Stephen's Green. Oh, I'm well up to ye saints. (p.33)

The most astonishing things can be imagined as a possible cause for Father Fahrt behaving in such an uncontrolled way. We know that this mysterious situation is in the hands of the Dublin Corporation; the solution lies with them, but they will not move to do anything about it. Father Fahrt suggests dropping them a hint, and this causes Collopy to explode with indignation.

> *If a hint were dropped,* Mr Collopy exploded. *If a hint were dropped!* Well the dear knows I think you are trying to destroy my temper, Father, and put me out of my wits and make an unfortunate shaughraun out of me. If a hint were dropped, my hat and parsley! Right well you know I have the trotters wore off me going up the stairs of that filthy Corporation begging them, telling them, ordering them to do something. I have shown you copies of the letter I have sent to that booby the Lord Mayor. That's one man knows all about chains, anyhow. What results have I got? Nothing at all but abuse from cornerboys and jacks in office. (p.34)

Gradually from hints, like the mention of chains and the measuring done for Mrs Crotty's room, the reader begins to comprehend the subject of Mr Collopy's representations to the corporation. From this point it becomes more and more clear as to what they are talking about, and the suspicion is clinched by the hydrometer which is passed round all the ladies of the committee to collect evidence to support their case, and maybe to establish a new scientific record. As it becomes evident that Collopy is involved in a scheme to establish lavatories for women in Dublin, the focus of the comedy shifts from the imagination of the reader to the disparity between the subject under discussion and the terms in which it is discussed, and to the ludicrous and inappropriate suggestions for the problem's solution. Collopy at all times speaks of suffering, and of saintly women being condemned to death by the apathy of the corporation. Various suggestions are advanced for the alleviation of their difficulties. Father Fahrt suggests prayer, Mr Collopy suggests that the 'scandalous situation' be denounced from the pulpits, Mrs Flaherty, a member of the committee, suggests that they blow up the corporation. Collopy advocates the provision of black trams circling Dublin. Each tram would have 'WOMEN' painted on it and a penny fare would be charged for each journey. Mr Collopy becomes quite lyrical about his scheme.

> I would like you to think this thing over, Father. Let us say that a lady and gentleman are walking down the street and have a mind to go for a stroll in the Phoenix Park. Fair enough. But first one thing has to be attended to. They wait at a tram stop. Lo and behold, along comes the Black Tram. The lady steps on board and away she goes on her own. And the whole beauty of the plan is this: *she can get an ordinary tram back* to rejoin her waiting friend. Do you twig? (p.42)[13]

If Collopy manages to achieve his life's work and successfully conclude his constant struggle, a great peace will descend upon him. In the meantime he labours on, devising cumbersome and ludicrous schemes, and eventually contracting rheumatism from standing in the rain heckling at a meeting. It is only after his death that he can accomplish anything practical as a solution. This practical solution is outlined in the terms of the Collopy Trust.

> After all that has been done, Mr Sproule went on, we have to set up the Collopy Trust . . . The Trust will erect and maintain three establishments which the testator calls rest rooms. There will be a rest room at Irishtown, Sandymount, at Harold's Cross, and at Phibsborough. Each

will bear the word PEACE very prominently on the door
and each will be under the patronage of a saint — Saint Patrick, Saint Jerome and Saint Ignatius. Each of these
establishments will bear a plaque reading, for instance,
'THE COLLOPY TRUST — Rest Room of Saint Jerome'. You
will notice that they are very well dispersed, geographically.
                                                      (pp.152-3)

Collopy sees no incongruity in associating such a basic
function with the idea of peace and with the names of saints.
The comedy of the situation arises from this incongruity and
from the embarrassment relating to the subject in the first
place. In *At Swim,* during the tea-party at Furriskey's, there is
an illustration of the same embarrassment and evasion. It is
funny there just because the attempt to evade the issue only
makes it clearer. Here, another layer of comedy is added in
that Collopy too is embarrassed — too embarrassed to mention
the subject in front of the boys — yet nevertheless earnest to the
point of absurdity about the importance of his mission. All
these elements are summed up in the interview with the pope.
Collopy has an audience with the pope. This is reported, in a
letter to Finbarr, by Manus, who, although present at the
audience, was sitting too far away to hear Collopy's mumbled
intercessions on behalf of his favourite topic. All that can be
gathered is the pope's horrified reaction at being asked to
intercede in such a personal matter. At first the pope thinks
that Collopy is mad, but when he realises that he is merely
sincere he blames Father Fahrt for having allowed Collopy to
go to such lengths. The comedy here depends on the subject
never being specified but on the reader knowing what it is, so
that the pope's replies have a specific point.

> But this is monstrous. Nor should our office be confused
> with that of a city council.   (p.136)
> We are deeply troubled by such a strange supplication for
> our intervention on such a question. It is improper that such
> a matter should be mentioned within these walls. This is a
> sacred place.   (p.137)

The interview with the pope takes to its ultimate the
association between basic functions and the Holy Office
(which is also brought out in the naming of Father Fahrt) and

continues the satire of certain aspects of the Church which has been noticeable throughout the book. The prudery of a society that will not discuss such matters or pretend that they exist is merely a single example of the tendency of that society to deceive itself in other matters. At times, therefore, the comic devices develop into a comment on Irish society as a whole.

The other main event of the book, the death of Collopy, has little comedy attached to it, except that arising from cruelty. O'Brien has already illustrated his capacity for this kind of cruel comedy in *At Swim* in the description of the punishment of Trellis. An essential part of his habit of observation and his method of description is his ability to concentrate on ugly, brutal or distorted elements in man. The killing of Philip Mathers is vividly described ('I felt and almost heard the fabric of his skull crumple up crisply like an empty eggshell') and there are many instances where people are described as if they were distorted. The description of Teresa, Trellis's servant, falls into this category.

> The figure of Teresa was visible at the stove, her thick thighs presented to the penetration of the fire. She was a stout girl of high colour, attired in grey and divided at the centre by the terminal ridge of a corset of inferior design.
>
> (*AS2B*.43)

The same distortion or exaggeration of one particular characteristic occurs in the description of Sergeant Pluck in *The Third Policeman*.

> Over the tight collar of his tunic he wore a red ring of fat that looked fresh and decorative as if it had come directly from the laundry.   (*TP*.120)

This habit of vivid description coupled with a delight in humour that springs from an apprehension of violence[14] combines to give the description of the death of Collopy, ludicrous and violent as it is. Collopy goes to Rome on the brother's invitation because the brother hopes that an audience with the pope will cure him of the excessive weight which is the result of an overdose of Gravid Water, the brother's patent cure for rheumatoid arthritis. Instead, Collopy uses his audience to intercede with the pope on behalf of his work. The result, far from being a miraculous reduction in his weight, is a papal threat to silence Father Fahrt. Collopy is left, then, in Rome with his hopes in disarray, and with a weight so excessive as to make it impossible to move him. This fact, which had been comic in the description of the attempt to get Collopy on the train, does not remain so for long, and when he climbs up a wooden staircase and collapses through it, the effect is no longer comic but horrifying.

> When I arrived the scene was grotesque. There was apparently no access to the space under the stairs and two carpenters using hatchets, saws and chisels were carefully breaking down the woodwork in the hallway below the landing. About a dozen lighted candles were in readiness on one of the steps, casting a ghastly light on the very shaken Father Fahrt, two gendarmes, a man with a bag who was evidently a doctor and a whole mob of sundry characters, many of them no doubt onlookers who had no business there.
>
> The carpenters eventually broke through and pulled away several boards as ambulance men arrived with a stretcher. The doctor and Father Fahrt, pushed their way to the aperture. Apparently Collopy was lying on his back covered with broken timbers and plastering, one leg doubled under him and blood pouring from one of his ears. He was semi-conscious and groaning pitifully.   (pp.143-4)

The episode becomes even more distressing when, after Collopy's death, instant decomposition sets in so that the body must be buried immediately. This whole scene best illustrates O'Brien's ability to create the grotesque and the horrifying. Here he adds to the squalor of the scene by making the brother's account totally devoid of emotion or guilt. Immediately after he has reported Collopy's terrible state, he says he will change the label on the Gravid Water, and then comments on the difficulties of the ambulance men in lifting Collopy. He feels a little glum but is able to express interest in the onset of immediate decomposition.

> I was interested in that mention of premature and rapid decomposition of the body. I am not sure but I would say that here was the Gravid Water again. I said nothing, of course.   (p.145)

The brother with his customary despatch arranges for Collopy's funeral and even provides an inscription for his headstone, a pun on the cause of his death: 'Here lies one whose name is writ in water.' This is a slight variation on the inscription on Keats's grave. Again it is the extra detail, the linking of Keats and Collopy, which provides the ultimate irony, which, even while it would seem to make Collopy's death in Rome romantic, only makes it the ultimate in squalor.

The final event in the book is the return of the brother to Ireland for a flying visit to sort out the legal details and to advise Finbarr about his future. Annie is now left fairly well off with an annual allowance and the house in Warrington Place. She works hard and looks after Finbarr quite well. The brother's suggestion is, therefore, that Finbarr should marry her and be comfortable for the rest of his life without having to do any work. This is the final revolting suggestion of the book and evokes an instant reaction from Finbarr.

> The slam of the door told me he was gone. In a daze I lifted my own glass and without knowing what I was doing did exactly what the brother did, drained the glass in one vast swallow. Then I walked quickly but did not run to the lavatory. There, everything inside me came up in a tidal surge of vomit.   (p.157)

O'Brien's view of reality in *The Hard Life* is a jaundiced one. With the exception of Penelope, who appears only briefly, and Finbarr, who can reprimand the brother for his irresponsibility ('Occasionally decent people get a right dose of Gravid Water!'), only the cab-driver is a likeable person. All the characters live a depressing existence. If any event occurs to lift them from their dead surroundings, it is grotesque or unpleasant. Their only purposes in life are ludicrous and embarrassing or unscrupulous and amoral. Sometimes this vision of reality as the 'hard life' becomes satirical. The brother is revealed for what he is. His sentiments about the scarcity of decent people are well repudiated and are shown to be hypocrisy. All the characters are shown to be humbugs. O'Brien presents us with his unflattering description of Mr Collopy and then has Hanafin praise him for looking so well. The brothers see through this straight away, but it nevertheless influences Manus to the extent that, as he knows everyone around him is lying, he sill simply lie better, and to more effect. The habit of speaking in meaningless clichés is shown by O'Brien to be not merely an intriguing habit but also a disquieting reflection of the mental and moral sloppiness which is a characteristic of the society as a whole and which can be harmful. Mr Collopy churns out an enormous number of assorted clichés which he really believes to be true. Later, when he stands in the rain believing that his early training as a hurler will stand him in good stead, he is proved to be mistaken. His empty phraseology even extends to the subject of hurling.

> From the winding banks of Nore, ah? Many a good puck I had myself in the quondam days of my nonage. I could draw on a ball in those days and clatter in a goal from midfield, man.   (p.18)

The brother takes refuge in sentimentality and Father Fahrt in accepted judgments which prevent him having to make any decisions of his own.

> Well, Collopy, what are we for in this world? We are here to suffer. We must sanctify ourselves. That's what suffering is for.   (p.32)

A great deal of the comedy in the conversations between Father Fahrt and Mr Collopy derives from the confrontation of the priest's accepted judgments and Mr Collopy's view of history which closely resembles the type of judgment found in *1066 and All That,* containing the same simplification, personalisation, overstatement and understatement.

> Father Fahrt, Mr Collopy said earnestly, you don't like the Reformation. Maybe I'm not too fond of it myself, either. But it was our own crowd, those ruffians in Spain and all, who provoked it. They called decent men heretics and the remedy was to put a match to them. To say nothing of a lot of crooked Popes with their armies and their papal states, putting duchesses and nuns up the pole and having all Italy littered with their bastards, and up to nothing but backstairs work and corruption at the courts of God knows how many decent foreign kings. Isn't that a fact?

It is not a fact, Collopy. The Reformation was a doctrinal revolt, inspired I have no doubt by Satan. It had nothing to do with human temporal weakness in the Papacy or elsewhere.   (p.37)

The satire-parody of accounts of Church history is maintained throughout and gives added point to the idea that *The Hard Life* is an exegesis in the original meaning of the word: a detailed examination and clarification of difficult points in the Bible. However, the long discussions between Father Fahrt and Mr Collopy, usually on Church history and the part played by the Church, or rather the Jesuits, in various affairs, political and economic, is more properly a constituent of the device of pedantry used throughout the book. The brother's letter and pamphlets wallow in a plethora of polysyllabic language (the facts contained in them are true), and he delights in giving as many details as possible in as roundabout a way as possible.

It were folly to asseverate that periastral peripatesis on the *aes ductile,* or wire, is destitute of profound peril not only to sundry *membra,* or limbs, but to the back and veriest life itself. Wherefore is the reader most graciously implored to abstain from *le risque majeur* by first submitting himself to the most perspicacious scrutiny by highly-qualified physician or surgeon for, in addition to anatomical verifications, evidence of Ménière's Disease, caused by haemorrhage into the equilibristic labyrinth of the ears, causing serious nystagmous and insecurity of gait. (pp.46-7)

This is seen as part of his total attitude to education, which he sees as a way of blinding the unwary with science to his own benefit. His use of such language is regarded as a moral, not merely as a linguistic, failing, and is commented upon by Finbarr.

I found that conscientiously reading that sort of material required considerable concentration. I do not know what it means and I have no doubt whatever that the brother's 'clients' will not know either.   (pp.47-8)

The satire of all kinds of jargon in *Cruiskeen Lawn* had revealed clearly enough that O'Brien was intolerant of any

language which tended to obscure rather than reveal its
subject. He was equally intolerant about mental sloppiness of
any kind, and the prejudiced arguments of Father Fahrt and
Mr Collopy are therefore satirised as essentially the squalid
products of untrained mentalities. Yet, that said, it is still
necessary to point out that there are a large number of these
conversations and an equally large number of letters from the
brother full of pedantic detail. The result is that the devices
fail to hold the attention for very long. Pedantry is apt
material for satire, yet it does not remain amusing in itself.
Misuse of information does appear amusing at times. Mr
Collopy's account of Mose Art and Pagan Neeny becomes
hilarious, as does his marvellous tendency to mix metaphors.

> By God's will, he explained, Manus's foot has been placed
> today on the first rung of the ladder of learning and
> achievement, and on yonder pinnacle beckons the lone star.
> (p.21)
> You might consider, Mrs Crotty, that the Lord would
> provide, even as He does for the birds of the air. I gave the
> bosthoon a tuppence. (p.21)

However, *The Hard Life* is ultimately unsatisfying to read
because it lacks coherence and is too one-sided a vision of
squalid reality. *The Dalkey Archive* while retaining many of
the positive aspects of *The Hard Life,* the characteristic
stylistic devices, the love of language and linguistic jokes, does
not suffer from the same lack of coherence and the same
striving after effect as seems apparent in *The Hard Life.*

8
The DMP and Miracles:
The Dalkey Archive

O'BRIEN'S LAST completed novel, *The Dalkey Archive*, was
written during a time when he was subjected to great physical
stress. He had many accidents and illnesses both during and
after the composition of the book and seems to have believed,
with perhaps a degree of seriousness, that St Augustine was
persecuting him for the rather cavalier treatment he had
received in the novel.[1] In spite of this, however, more care was
exercised in the writing of *The Dalkey Archive* than was
afforded to some of the other books, to the extent that O'Brien
revised it considerably before it reached publication.

The book, though not published until 1964, was begun
about September 1962. Early in that month O'Brien wrote to
Gerald Gross at Pantheon Books, New York, and outlined the
plot.

> I have just started on a new book to which the word extra-
> ordinary would be considerable understatement, though it
> will be very readable indeed and in parts quite funny,
> though time and the physical universe will get scant respect.
> As a clue, I may say that one of the characters is Saint
> Augustine. Ignorant reviewers have messed me up with
> another man, to my intense embarrassment and disgust,
> and he will be another character. I mean James Joyce. I'm
> going to get my own back on that bugger. (I suppose you
> know that, like Hitler, Joyce isn't dead at all. He is living in
> retirement and a sort of disguise at Skerries, a small
> watering place 21 miles N. of Dublin. He has been trying to
> screw up enough courage to join the Jesuits).[2]

It is clear from this letter that some elements of the plot were
fixed from the moment of conception. It is also evident that

the book carried on O'Brien's obsession with scientific
concepts and with the literary domination of James Joyce,
whose ghost he determined to lay for once and all. When he
wrote a little later to Tim O'Keeffe he elaborated on the
licentious character of St Augustine who, if he existed at all,
was a 'wonderful man' for becoming one of the Fathers of the
Church in spite of his licentious career and his angry assertion
that 'there was no such place as purgatory'. The letter also
reiterated the Joyce plot and amplified O'Brien's ideas about
science.

> You may remember Dunne's two books *An Experiment with
> Time* and *The Serial Universe,* also the views of Einstein
> and others. The idea is that time is as a great flat motionless
> sea. Time does not pass; it is we who pass. With this concept
> as basic, fantastic but coherent situations can easily be
> devised, and in effect the whole universe torn up in a
> monstrous comic debauch. Such obsessions as nuclear
> energy, space travel and landing men on the moon can be
> made to look as childish and insignificant as they probably
> are. Anything can be brought in, including the long-
> overdue rehabilitation of Judas Iscariot.[3]

O'Brien is still thinking along the lines of *The Third
Policeman* in his desire to satirise Dunne and to tear the
universe apart in a monstrous comic debauch. He intends to
use for the purpose a combination of unassociated subjects,
Joyce, St Augustine and scientific concepts. To this extent, the
scope of the book will be broader than that of *The Third
Policeman,* where the other elements are strictly subordinated
to the main theme and never gain the status of sub-plots, as
they are clearly intended to do here. He is aware, however,
that this conception may be difficult to execute.

> These rough glances at my project may seem to disclose a
> mass of portentous material that looks unmanageable. Not
> so. There is a pedestrian sub-theme that keeps the majestic
> major concepts in order as in a vice. Undue length is the
> only risk I see.[4]

The pedestrian sub-theme was to be a satire of the
Censorship of Publications Board which had recently banned

a number of books for reasons which O'Brien found indefensible (although it had not banned his own *The Hard Life*). This theme was not, however, included at all in the final draft.

Although O'Brien had told Gerald Gross that the book was started, he reported to Tim O'Keeffe in November that he was still checking details on St Augustine and had not actually started the writing. One of his comments on St Augustine deserves record, partly because it is a good pun and partly because it reveals one of O'Brien's continuing obsessions.

> There is no doubt that St Augustine was one of the greatest comics of the Christian era. He was preposterously conceited and, Bishop of Hippo, achieved astonishing feats in the sphere of hippocracy.[5]

By 1 March 1963 he was ready with the first 10,000 words and was satisfied enough with the quality of the material. He feared, however, that some critic, recognising the parody of science, would dub him a writer of science fiction. His fiction, though mainly fantasy, embraces more aspects than the scientific, and in this book, in particular, science comes off second best to more all-inclusive considerations, as O'Brien himself implies when he says: 'Thank God the climate is about to change, and the scene to the vestibule of heaven.'[6] On 15 November he reported that the book was finished but that he was dissatisfied, not with the plot and the base-material, but with the treatment of it. There was, he said, a surfeit of talk and booze, but he attributed this to his need to get things down on paper in no matter how incomplete or unpolished a form and then work on what was in front of him. He was disappointed in Tim O'Keeffe's reaction to the book and accused him of misjudging its intent. His previous reference to the scene taking place in the vestibule of heaven reveals what his intention was, and he states this quite clearly in another letter.

> In its final shape I believe this will be an important and scalding book, and one that will not be ignored. The book is not meant to be a novel or anything of the kind but a study in derision, various writers with their styles, and sundry modes, attitudes and cults being the rats in the cage. The MS is all bleary for want of definition and emphasis but I

regard the MS as something worthwhile to chew on . . .

There is, for instance, no intention to jeer at God or religion; the idea is to roast the people who seriously do so, and also to chide the Church in certain of its aspects. I seem to be wholly at one with Vatican Council II.[7]

O'Brien's principal intentions in *The Dalkey Archive* were thus perfectly clear in his own mind, but even in the final draft he could not find a technique by which they would be made equally clear to the reader. Tim O'Keeffe's comments were very unambiguous in pointing to the main areas of weakness. His observations indicate that the faults which marred *The Hard Life* were still evident and that O'Brien had not yet developed to the full his best qualities—his ability to make a satirical comment on his own world by placing his character in a situation of fantasy which, to some extent, and in a distorted fashion, parallels observable reality. Perhaps the main defect of *The Hard Life* was that it was too close a picture of reality. In *The Dalkey Archive* the plot provided scope for fantasy, but it seems that this element was not sufficiently emphasised. O'Keeffe told him:

> There are great things in it, without doubt. At the risk of seeming impertinent, I shan't dwell on them but on things which strike me as being less than the best. The opening—on Killiney—is slightly sentimental. Page 7, the discussion of music, is uneasy. The joke about the 'lawnmower' and the references to Teague as Leonardo stick out.
>
> The Augustine interview may be cruder than you intend, and I think should be cut. Your jokes against religiosity are not quite so good as you may think they are: a phrase like a 'dummy mummy' is not up to your own high standards . . . The plot is rich and must be developed and fantasticated but I think you ought to be careful with phrases like the one you put in Joyce's mouth—'well, I have an interest in words as you know'—because they may be too obvious.
>
> On balance, I think that you are definitely going in the right direction but that you ought to re-think the set dialogues and make the book move more than it does.

The scenes with Mary are great but I feel a bit uneasy about the tone — which strikes me as hating rather than one of development. You ought to be working towards more of a comically classic *reductio* than you are yet achieving. You don't, as yet, make me want to dissolve into laughter and I think that unless you do you have not succeeded.[8]

O'Brien's reply to this letter, a curiously humble one, reveals, nevertheless, that he was still thinking along lines different to those which formed the final version of the book. His comments indicate that the mood, mode of narration and general intention of the book must have undergone a radical revision to produce the version we have now. We know even from Tim O'Keeffe's comments that the discussion on music was reduced to a few sentences. O'Brien, however, retained the 'lawnmower' joke (he could never resist a bad pun, especially if it was directed at bad Irish). The conversations with Mary are not 'hating' in the published work, and some of the phrases that O'Keeffe objected to were also cut. What is clear from O'Brien's letter is that the original draft had a first-person narrator who was intended to be an unpleasant character, and that the attack on Joyce was rather personal.

I'm very glad you take a better view of the A R C H I V E but your criticisms were very well-founded and it would be a pity to release material that is ruinously flawed, particularly where the repair job might be comparatively easy and in parts very obvious . . . My ultimate plan is to excoriate the M S ruthlessly, cutting short here and rebuilding there, giving the book precision and occasionally the beauty of jewelled ulcers. It must above all be bitterly funny. The first person sing. must be made into a more awful toad than now. I know some of the writing is deplorable for a man of my pretences, and I'm not happy at all about the treatment of Joyce: a very greater mess must be made of him. Would one of his secret crosses be that he is an incurable bed-wetter?[9]

O'Brien goes on to say that he expects the book to be banned on grounds of blasphemy even though there is 'no blasphemy whatever' in it.

In fact, O'Brien did not carry out the changes that he had intended. He did rebuild the manuscript, but the impression conveyed by the final draft is not that of 'jewelled ulcers'. The narrator is not made into a worse toad; instead the narration is made third-person and the main character, Mick, is sometimes sympathetic. The section on Joyce, far from being more violently antagonistic contains a favourable assessment of Joyce's work in fairly balanced language, even though it continues the original idea of Joyce wanting to join the Jesuits. The final or, as O'Brien called it, the 'Authorised Version' was finished at the end of January 1964, and when he sent it off to Tim O'Keeffe, O'Brien, who had been laid up for several weeks after he had broken his leg, was relatively cheerful about its prospects. 'I have to say it sternly, but this will probably be the most important book in 1964.' He was contemptuous about the previous efforts and condemned them as

> a farrago of miswriting, slop, mistypes, repetition, with many passages quite meaningless.[10]

He went on to say that he did not believe he could have written it because 'the stuff about Joyce is withering in its ineptitude'.

The book as it stands continues many of what were, by then, firmly established main preoccupations. The parody of Joyce and of intellectual abstraction are as typical as the continued use of pedantry as a comic mode. The book is not, however, like *The Hard Life,* merely a variation on an already familiar theme. It represents a change, or development, in O'Brien's attitude to reality. To some extent its resolution was intended to be a resolution of problems and questions raised in the other books, but it is in many ways a sadly confused book, formless and without a single focus. In spite of this, a sympathetic reading can make O'Brien's intentions clear, even though they are not sufficiently worked out in the text.

The Dalkey Archive is essentially a rewriting of what O'Brien could remember of *The Third Policeman.* Just after he had finished the latter book he had remarked that the only thing good about it was the plot. It was not the plot, however, which reappeared in *The Dalkey Archive* but certain characters, attitudes and ideas. De Selby (now spelt with a capital D) appears in person, not just as a reported voice, and his conclusions about the nature of the universe seem just as chaotic as ever, except that he has gained sufficient power to manipulate its workings. The most obvious parallel to *The Third Policeman* comes in the scene where Mick meets Sergeant Fottrell in the Metropole and has explained to him the intricacies of the 'mollycule theory'. The discussion of De Selby on time and the nature of the universe, and of Sergeant Fottrell on the mollycule theory serve O'Brien's constant purpose of mocking the conclusions of science. At one point De Selby says:

> Call me a theologian or a physicist as you will, he said at last rather earnestly, but I am serious and truthful.   (p.18)

This implies that theologians and physicists are usually neither serious nor truthful, a conclusion which is borne out by the rest of the book.

The discussion of the mollycule theory on pp.86–97 of the *Dalkey Archive* parallels almost word for word the explanation of the atomic theory given to the narrator by Sergeant Pluck on pp.82–91 and 104–5 of *The Third Policeman*. Indeed, the situation in the police barracks is much the same since a policeman called Pluck spends most of his time repairing punctures deliberately made in his bicycle-tyres by Sergeant Fottrell. The characters of the two sergeants and their particular mode of convoluted speech is the same from book to book. The Sergeant explains to Mick:

> Everything is composed of small mollycules of itself and they are flying round in concentric circles and arcs and segments and innumerable various other routes too numerous to mention collectively, never standing still or resting but spinning away and darting hither and thither and back again, all the time on the go.   (p.87)

> The gross and net result of it is that people who spend most of their natural lives riding iron bicycles over the rocky roadsteads of the parish get their personalities mixed up with the personalities of their bicycles as a result of the interchanging of the mollycules of each of them, and you

would be surprised at the number of people in country parts
who are nearly half people and half bicycle.   (p.88)

This is, quite obviously, the same as Sergeant Pluck's account
but there are some variations in the two episodes. The
discussion in *The Dalkey Archive* is, in some cases, slightly
reduced. For example, compare the two accounts of the effects
of striking an iron bar with a hammer. In *The Third
Policeman* this reads:

> 'When the wallop falls, the atoms are bashed away down
> to the bottom of the bar and compressed and crowded there
> like eggs under a good clucker. After a while in the course
> of time they swim around and get back at last to where they
> were. But if you keep hitting the bar long enough and hard
> enough they do not get a chance to do this and what
> happens then?'
> 'That is a hard question.'
> 'Ask a blacksmith for the true answer and he will tell you
> that the bar will dissipate itself away by degrees if you
> persevere with the hard wallops. Some of the atoms of the
> bar will go into the hammer and the other half into the
> table or the stone or the particular article that is
> underneath the bottom of the bar.'   (p.85)

In *The Dalkey Archive* this account is much compressed.

> If you hit a rock hard enough and often enough with an
> iron hammer, some mollycules of the rock will go into the
> hammer and contrariwise likewise.   (p.88)

The real differences in the two episodes lie, however, not in
the compression or extension of elements of the explanation
but in the attitude of the speakers. Mick, at first, has the same
reaction to the Sergeant's words as the hero in *The Third
Policeman*. He calls to mind a scene — exactly similar to that
surrounding the narrator of *The Third Policeman* as he is told
about the atomic theory — of 'brown bogs and black bogs'
arranged with reassuring familiarity and remarks:

> The scene was real and incontrovertible but at variance
> with the talk of the sergeant.   (p.90)

There the similarity ends, for Mick, unlike the narrator of *The Third Policeman,* goes on to assert:

> Was it not monstrous to allege that the little people winning turf far away were partly bicycles.   (p.90)

After a while Mick enters into the spirit of the Sergeant's speculations with an extension of the theory not found in *The Third Policeman.*

> Well, Sergeant, I am delighted that we are quite agreed on one thing at least. Human metamorphosis vis-à-vis an iron bicycle is quite another matter. And there is more to it than the monstrous exchange of tissue for metal.
> And what would that be? the sergeant asked curiously.
> All decent Irishmen should have a proper national outlook. Practically any bike you have in Ireland was made in either Birmingham or Coventry.   (p.95)

Mick, then, though bewildered for a moment, is quick to assert that the Sergeant's words and conclusions are an example of eccentricity. He is not forced to see, as is the narrator of *The Third Policeman,* that they are a proper manifestation of a topsy-turvy world which he cannot understand or believe yet must accept. Mick does accept that the Sergeant is 'a poor man's De Selby' (thus pointing to the connection in O'Brien's mind between the two characters and their respective *weltanschaungen* in *The Third Policeman).* Mick is, however, as inclined to disregard the Sergeant's ideas as he is to oppose De Selby. His view, not theirs, is the dominating one in *The Dalkey Archive.* Because the interview with the Sergeant takes place, to some extent, in isolation from the other events of the book, and is not the culminating revelation of an anarchic universe, it does appear to be merely eccentric and purely comic. The description of the hanging of McDadd's bicycle for murder, for example, occurs in *The Third Policeman* just before the proposed hanging of the narrator himself. It has, therefore, all the horror and effect of yet another example of the illogic of the events which have brought him to this pass. There is none of this horror in *The Dalkey Archive.* The description of the hanging of McDadd's bicycle comes straight after the other descriptions of strange and wonderful events and takes up accumulated impressions of comic fantasy. Viewed in the context of the whole book, Sergeant Fottrell's endearing fancies are a comic extension of De Selby's not more grandiose but certainly more destructive ideas. Fottrell sees the physical universe through a distorted lens. He has a 'hobby-horse' about mollycules, but he does not intend to try and manipulate the universe in conformity with his ideas. To this extent he is meant to be a kindly contrast to De Selby, even while resembling him in other ways.

It can be pointed out, however, that the actual account of the mollycule theory contains some anomalous details. Sergeant Fottrell's discussion of the people of the locality is precisely similar to Sergeant Pluck's, but in *The Third Policeman* the Sergeant is talking about a rural community existing at a time a little earlier than that implied in *The Dalkey Archive*. The complete transference of the scene (and even of the mention of the postman's twenty-nine-mile round on the 'rocky roads of the parish') to an urban community at a time after the outbreak of the Second World War creates doubt in the reader's mind about the precision and appropriateness of some of the references.

There are other portions of the novel which, like the Sergeant Fottrell episode, are taken almost direct from other books. It seems that O'Brien wished to call to mind all his major concerns and themes in order to see them in the context of the pattern he apprehended in this work. Previous books had, in the main, dealt with chaotic situations. This one deals with universal order.

One of these episodes is Mick's discussion of the fine living habits of the Jesuits, which recalls one of Mr Collopy's fulminations in *The Hard Life*. Mr Collopy had said:

> There's no pinning a Jesuit down. Then we're told its a mendicant order. Sure there isn't a better-got collection of men on the face of the earth, churches and palaces all over the world. I know a thing or two. I've read books. I'll tell you something about 35 Leeson Street, the poor cave you hide yourself in . . . The emaciated friars in that place have red wine with their dinners. That's more than Saint Peter himself had. But Saint Peter got himself into a sort of a

divarsion with a cock. The holy fathers below in Clongowes Wood know all about cocks too. They have them roasted and they eat them at dinner. And they are great men for scoffing claret.

Such talk is most unworthy [said Father Fahrt]. We eat and drink according to our means.   (*HL*.76)

Allowing for the change in idiom and the more ironic tone of *The Dalkey Archive,* Mick's musings on the subject are substantially the same.

Mick was a bit surprised. The internal mechanics of the Jesuit Order (or Society, as they called themselves) was to him a mystery. It was one of the mendicant orders but he thought this term had a technical meaning. How could mendicants live in the grandiose palaces and colleges which the Jesuits customarily inhabit? The answer seemed to be that every Jesuit Father — and postulant for that matter — is personally a mendicant inasmuch as he is forbidden to have any means or goods whatsoever. If his duties call for him to make a journey across the town or across the world, he has to go to some superior or bursar and ask for his fare. It appeared that the Order was very wealthy, its members utterly indigent. He had heard that the Fathers lived and ate well in their princely abodes. Good luck to them! (p.120)

Mick's comments are part of the treatment of religion at the level at which it is mocked in *The Dalkey Archive.* This mockery takes two forms. It consists of an evocation, similar to that in *The Hard Life,* of the essential squalor of the religious life.

To my surprise, Mr Collopy next morning led me at a smart pace up the bank of the canal, penetrated to Synge Street and rang the bell at the residential part of the Christian Brothers' establishment there. When a slatternly young man in black answered, Mr Collopy said he wanted to see the Superior, Brother Gaskett. We were shown into a gaunt little room which had on the wall a steel engraving of the head of Brother Rice, founder of the Order, a few chairs and a table — nothing more.

They say piety has a smell, Mr Collopy mused, half to

himself. It's a perverse notion. What they mean is only the absence of the smell of women.   (*HL*.23)

In *The Dalkey Archive* the description applies to the house of the Jesuits which Mick and Joyce visit with a view to Joyce's joining the Order.

> They were respectable enough when they knocked on the large, discreet door of the big house at 35, Lower Leeson Street. An unkempt and ill-spoken youth opened it and showed them off the hall into a waiting room which was (Mick thought) tawdry, gloomy and indeed a bit dirty. Saintliness and cleanliness were not always kin, he reflected, but there was no reason why that boy, who had now departed in search of Father Cobble, had not washed himself that day and cleaned himself up.
>
> I discern the authentic note of austerity here, Joyce remarked pleasantly.   (p.208)

In the interview with Father Cobble, it emerges that the Fathers' greatest problem is the maintenance of their underwear. The priest suggests that Joyce should be employed to keep it in good repair.

> If we only knew, Father Cobble observed, why sweat is so corrosive, we would be perhaps getting somewhere. Upon my word my semmet is *rotted*.   (p.212)

This explicit connection between Joyce and squalor culminates the implied connection which existed throughout *The Hard Life*.

The second device used for mocking religion is that of pedantry. The subjects included within its scope extend the mockery far beyond the Jesuits themselves to the Fathers of the Church and the nature of religious speculation. Within this aspect is subsumed the discussion with Augustine and the reported discussions with Old Testament characters, like that with Jonas on the 'big fish'; New Testament characters like John the Baptist, who is very like a Jesuit; the place of the Holy Spirit, the Nicene Creed and the Manichaean heresies; and the rehabilitation of Judas Iscariot. The various discourses are given by different characters in the story but primarily by

Joyce and De Selby. Each of these two characters has an
obsession of his own. Joyce's is with the word *pneuma,* which
has been completely misinterpreted. This misinterpretation
has led to grave errors of doctrine.

> The Holy Spirit was the invention of the more reckless of the
> early Fathers. We have here a confusion of thought and
> language. Those poor ignorant men associated *pneuma*
> with what they call the working of the Holy Spirit, whereas
> it is merely an exudation of God the Father. It is an activity
> of the existing God, and it is a woeful and shameful error to
> identify in it a hypostatic Third Person.   (p.198)

De Selby's obsession is to discover the truth of the Jonas
episode. Mick asks him: 'Does it matter much whether it was a
whale or a shark?' and De Selby replies:

> It does to me in my office as theologian. The references in
> the Bible, in Testaments Old and New, are consistently to a
> 'great fish'. The whale as such is never mentioned, and in
> any event the whale is not a fish. Scientists hold, with ample
> documentation in support, that the whale was formerly a
> land animal, its organs now modified for sea-living. It is a
> mammal, suckles its young, is warm-blooded and must
> come to the surface for breath, like man himself. It is most
> unlikely that there were any whales in the sea in the time of
> Jonas.   (p.76)

Even Hackett develops an obsession of his own. He intends to
reclaim the reputation of Judas Iscariot.

> For a learned and enlightened man, [he tells Mick] you are
> surely a buck ignoramus. The Roman Church's Bible has a
> great lot of material named Apocrypha. There have been
> apocryphal Gospels according to Peter, Thomas, Barnabas,
> John, Judas Iscariot and many others. My task would be to
> retrieve, clarify and establish the Iscariot Gospel.   (p.71)

As well as these personal obsessions, the reader is presented
with a scene in which Mick, Hackett and De Selby meet St
Augustine in a cave under the sea at Dalkey. St Augustine has
an Irish accent and a plethora of prejudices which are
reminiscent of Mr Collopy's account of Church history in *The*

Hard Life. At one point he is questioned about the inhabitants of heaven and is asked 'Are there any other strange denizens?' He replies:

> Far too many if you ask me. Look at that gobhawk they call Francis Xavier. Hobnobbing and womanising in the slums of Paris with Calvin and Ignatius Loyola in warrens full of rats, vermin, sycophants and syphilis. Xavier was a great travelling man, messing about in Ethiopia and Japan, consorting with Buddhist monkeys and planning to convert China single-handed. And Loyola? You talk about me but a lot of that chap's early saintliness was next to bedliness. He made himself the field-marshal of a holy army of mendicants but maybe merchandisers would be more like it. Didn't Pope Clement XIV suppress the Order for its addiction to commerce, and for political wire-pulling? Jesuits are the wiliest, cutest and most mendacious ruffians who ever lay in wait for simple Christians. The Inquisition was on the track of Ignatius. Did you know that? Pity they didn't get him. But one party who wouldn't hear of the Pope's Brief of Suppression was the Empress of Rooshia. Look at that now!   (pp.37–8)

One of the purposes of presenting this great mass of facts is comic effect. The interview with Augustine is comic in that Augustine speaks with an Irish accent and his idiom and conversation is ludicrously at odds with our expectations of him. He is cheerfully irreverent on many subjects which are usually discussed with great seriousness. Talking about one of the Fathers of the Church, Origen of Alexandria, who castrated himself to prevent the recurrence of lustful thoughts, he says:

> How could Origen be the Father of Anything and he with no knackers on him? Answer me that one.   (p.37)

Augustine is presented as crude, vulgar, afraid of his mother, and prejudiced. The comedy is thus produced by the disparity between the character as presented by O'Brien and the reader's usual conception of Augustine. The interview with him is full of memorable images and puns, like the 'mendacious' Jesuits and *Origen* the *Father* of the Church, and

these add to the comedy. On the other hand certain of
Augustine's statements are serious when seen in the overall
context of the book, and this element of seriousness adds to the
confusion of the presentation of his character. It could,
however, be asserted that the interview with Augustine is too
long and the recitals of Church history and dogma grow
tedious. The material in itself is not intrinsically funny (as is,
for example, Sterne's long digression on noses) and cannot
hold the attention for very long even if used for the purpose of
ironic juxtaposition or to reveal hypocrisy of character.

Another, and indeed more important, purpose of all the
discussion of religious characters, incidents and problems is to
illustrate the pettiness, the casuistry of all such discussion.
Most debates on religious themes descend to the completely
trivial or the minute and end up as mere 'flannel', as De Selby
says. De Selby had himself admitted that the theologian, like
the physicist, was not always either truthful or serious. Here in
these long harangues the futility of such mental processes is
satirised by O'Brien. All the characters who engage in such
disputation are hair-splitting. They are 'subject to the
persistent hallucination that [they are] thinking'. (p.42). It is
Joyce who, despite the fact that he is one of the participants in
theological discussions, makes the point clear.

> I am not [said Mick] much experienced in Biblical
> studies . . .
> Of course you're not, because you were reared a Catholic.
> Neither are the Catholic clergy. Those ancient disputants,
> rhetoricians, theologisers who are collectively called the
> Early Fathers were buggers for getting ideas into their heads
> and then assuming that God directly inspired those ideas. In
> trying to wind up the Arian controversy, the Council of
> Alexandria in 362, having asserted the equality in nature of
> the Son with the Father, went on to announce the transfer
> of a third hypostasis to the Holy Spirit. Without saying boo,
> or debating the matter at all! Holy pokey but wouldn't you
> think they'd have a little sense!   (pp.198-9)

The point O'Brien is making is that all this discussion is, in a
sense, holy pokey, and that this particular form of
senselessness is not confined to the Early Fathers. All the

characters in the book, even while condemning it, are guilty of
it. All thought, whether religious (*The Dalkey Archive*),
scientific (*The Third Policeman*) or historical (*The Hard
Life*), is subject to abuses in the hands of man who misuses his
language and his intellect in the pursuit of objectives which
are outside his cognisance and which become nonsense when
subjected to the scrutiny of his pathetic intellect. Casuistry
provides no answers and is, O'Brien seems to think, a positive
evil.

The parody of Joyce, which was very evident in *At Swim* and
The Hard Life, reaches its climax in *The Dalkey Archive.* In
At Swim the parody was centred mainly round the character
of Stephen Dedalus, modelled in the student narrator, with his
artistic pretensions and body-lice. *The Hard Life* isolated the
atmosphere of squalor in Joyce's works and attacked that. In
The Dalkey Archive the parody is twofold and attacks both the
character of Joyce himself and the works he produced. The
attack on the character of Joyce is explicit, involving as it does
the direct confrontation between Mick and Joyce on three
separate occasions. The attack on Joyce's work is both explicit
(he discusses his own intentions) and implicit in the verbal
reference to *Ulysses* and the creation of the characters of Mick
(Stephen Dedalus) and Hackett (Gogarty).
The character of Joyce himself, like that of St Augustine, is
presented in such a way as to invert all the reader's
expectations. Sufficient is told about his background to
indicate that he is the real Joyce.

Our family was preoccupied with politics, God help them,
and with a little bit of music sometimes.   (p.147)

Joyce speaks French, has a knowledge of the root meanings of
Greek and Hebrew words, can describe the circumstances of
his escape from the continent, admits to knowing Sylvia Beach
and to having written (in collaboration with Gogarty)
Dubliners. He is also deeply concerned with the problem of
translating ineffable and epistemological concepts into
linguistic terms. There, however, the similarity with the
accepted picture of Joyce stops. Even Mick who meets him face
to face is so amazed by the revelations of the man he confronts

that he thinks this must be either an impostor, or a Joyce who
has become deranged with the passage of time. The Joyce he
meets is a rather shy, unassuming man — at first glance — who
drinks little and goes to daily mass. His acquaintances consider
him to be a bit of a humbug, a 'Holy Mary Ann'. He is very
angry about certain allegations which have been made about
him but which are entirely without foundation. At first he
does not reveal what these allegations are, but merely
expresses his anger at the way his character and background
have been maligned.

> I am a man who is much misunderstood — I will say
> maligned, traduced, libelled and slandered. From what I've
> heard, certain ignorant men in America have made a laugh
> of me. Even my poor father wasn't safe. A fellow named
> Gorman wrote that 'he always wore a monocle in one eye'.
> Fancy!   (p.149)

At first this seems like a perfectly justifiable fulmination
against bad American critics and biographers, but later it
becomes clear that what Joyce is complaining about is the
accrediting to his name of any part in the writing of *Ulysses*.
The book, he says, was the idea of Sylvia Beach and the
production of a company of

> Various low, dirty-minded ruffians . . . Muck-rakers,
> obscene poets, carnal pimps, sodomous sycophants, pedlars
> of the coloured lusts of fallen humanity.   (p.193)

Joyce himself has written only *Dubliners*. Far from having
created the character of the immoral Molly Bloom, he has
written a Catholic Truth Society pamphlet on marriage.
Neither could he have created rebellious, proud, drunken
Stephen Dedalus, for he has also written pamphlets on 'the
sacrament of penance, humility, the dangers of alcohol'.

However, in spite of his disclaimer about *Ulysses* and
Finnegans Wake Joyce is anxious to indicate that he is engaged
on a *magnum opus,* his 'real work'. He is careful to add,
however, that it would not be correct to say that he is 'writing'
a book.

> Writing is not quite the word. Assembly, perhaps, is
> better — or accretion.   (p.145)

Flann O'Brien: a critical introduction

We are reminded of the student narrator's dictum in *At Swim* that 'the modern novel should be largely a work of reference' (p.33). Joyce's new work seems to have something to do with the interpretation of three words: *ruach* (Hebrew), *pneuma* (Greek) and *spiritus* (Latin). These words are, Joyce asserts, usually, and falsely, defined in terms of one another. O'Brien's presentation of Joyce is at this point very effective, since even as Joyce disclaims those books which have made him famous, his conversation proves him to have retained those interests and attitudes which largely determine the form of those books.

> No, I'm rather at sea as to *language*. I have a firm grip of my thoughts, my argument . . .but communicating the ideas clearly in English is my difficulty. You see, there has been considerable variation as between English on the one hand, and Hebrew and Greek as vehicles of epistemology.
> I know, of course, [said Mick] that you're interested in languages as such . . .   (p.147)

Joyce's literary concerns are, then, closely associated with his religious views, so much so that he cherishes a secret desire to become a Jesuit and eventually, perhaps, rector of Clongowes. Mick's reaction to this revelation is one of shock.

> Into his mind came that other book, *Portrait of the Artist*. There had been renunciation of family, faith even birthland, and that promise of silence, exile and cunning. What did there seem to be here? The garrulous, the repatriate, the ingenuous?   (p.195)

But though Joyce's intentions are totally at odds with his reputation, they are, nevertheless, in harmony with his personality and interests as represented by himself to Mick. It is consistent, therefore, to find that he has grandiose ideas of a literary and religious nature. His literary plans, which he will defer till he is safe in the seclusion of the Order, are centred round a scheme to

> translate and decontaminate great French literature so that it could be an inspiration to the Irish, besotted with Dickens, Cardinal Newman, Walter Scott and Kickham.
>   (pp.192-3)

His religious views include a plan to reform, not just the
Society of Jesus, but the whole Church; to save it from its
distorted belief in 'shameless superstitions' and 'rash
presumptions' such as the doctrine of the Holy Spirit, which
springs from a basic misunderstanding which only Joyce, with
his acute semantic ability, is able to correct.

When Mick eventually takes Joyce to see Father Cobble, the
Jesuit, with final irony, suggests that the only place for Joyce in
the Society of Jesus is in the laundry repairing the Society's
underwear.

The presentation of Joyce, at first glance, seems simple. It is
obvious that Joyce was obsessed by the Jesuits; accordingly
O'Brien, in his usual fashion, renders a simple fact comic by
exaggeration and inversion. However, some of the
presentation of Joyce shows an awareness of the problems he
was trying to face and of his particular qualities as a writer,
and this awareness acts in contradistinction to the attack on
Joyce's person. Mick's summation of Joyce's achievements, as
Mick himself points out, is 'not bad at all'.

> Anybody's reasons for wishing to know the man should be
> obvious enough, Mick said coldly. In my own case, the first
> reason is curiosity. I believe the picture of himself he has
> conveyed in his writings is fallacious. I believe he must be a
> far better man or a far worse. I think I have read all his
> works, though I admit I did not properly persevere with his
> play-writing. I consider his poetry meretricious and
> mannered. But I have an admiration for all his other work,
> for his dexterity and resource in handling language, for his
> precision, for his subtlety in conveying the image of Dublin
> and her people, for his accuracy in setting down speech
> authentically, and for his enormous humour.   (p.111)

Mick's 'spontaneous appraisal' of Joyce's work is close to
O'Brien's. In *A Bash in the Tunnel*, an article on Joyce written
some years before the composition of *The Dalkey Archive*, he
had said:

> The number of people invited to contribute to this issue has
> necessarily been limited. Yet it is curious that none makes
> mention of Joyce's superber quality: his capacity for
> humour. Humour, the handmaid of sorrow and fear, creeps

out endlessly in all Joyce's works. He uses the thing, in the
same way as Shakespeare does but less formally, to
attenuate the fear of those who have belief and who
genuinely think that they will be in hell or in heaven shortly,
and possibly very shortly. With laughs he palliates the sense
of doom that is the heritage of the Irish Catholic. True
humour needs this background urgency: Rabelais is funny,
but his stuff cloys. His stuff lacks tragedy.   (*SP.*208)

The qualities which O'Brien discovers in Joyce are qualities
which are paramount in his own work. O'Brien, just as much
as Joyce, was fascinated by the intricacies of language, and he
therefore appreciates Joyce's 'dexterity and resource in
handling language'. When he points to Joyce's 'subtlety in
conveying the image of Dublin and her people' we are
reminded of his own memorable Dublin characters, the
brother, Shanahan, Lamont and Furriskey, Mr Collopy, the
uncle, characters whom he said could 'be examined phrase by
phrase'. O'Brien's own 'accuracy in setting down speech
authentically' is particularly evident in the vast amount of
different kinds of idiom in *At Swim* and in *Cruiskeen Lawn;*
and, just as in Joyce's works, 'enormous humour' is everywhere
evident, quite often associated with death, hell or physical
injury.

Yet in spite of this recognition of their similarity of
approach, at least in technical matters, it appears that
O'Brien did dislike, if not Joyce himself, then certainly the
idea of Joyce. This dislike was not a literary pose adopted for
the sake of a laugh in his books. Among his friends O'Brien
often attacked Joyce. Samuel Beckett recalls meeting O'Brien
at Niall Montgomery's house and having a conversation with
him about Joyce. He remarked that what O'Brien said on that
occasion 'is better forgotten'.[11] O'Brien saw the artist as
craftsman, yet he constantly parodied Joyce's character and
writings. He used, it is true, this parody as a springboard for
his own ideas, so that his response to Joyce was a complicated
one. Some of his attitude can be explained by reference to the
article *A Bash in the Tunnel* where he talks explicitly about
Joyce. Some of his comments there, about Joyce's claims for
the artist and his attitude to religion, explain both O'Brien's

presentation of him in *The Dalkey Archive* and his general
impression of him.

James Joyce was an artist. He has said so himself. His was
a case of Ars gratia Artist. He declared that he would
pursue his artistic mission even if the penalty was as long as
eternity itself. This appears to be an affirmation of belief in
Hell, therefore of belief in Heaven and God.

A better title for this article might be: *Was Joyce Mad?* by
Hamlet, Prince of Denmark . . .

Some thinkers — all Irish, all Catholic, some unlay — have
confessed to discerning a resemblance between Joyce and
Satan. True, resemblances there are. Both had other
names, the one Stephen Dedalus, the other Lucifer; the
latter name, meaning 'Maker of Light', was to attract later
the ironical gloss 'Prince of Darkness'! Both started off very
well under unfaultable teachers, both were very proud,
both had a fall. But they differed on one big, critical issue.
Satan never denied the existence of the Almighty; indeed he
acknowledged it by challenging merely His primacy. Joyce
said there was no God, proving this by uttering various
blasphemies and obscenities and not being instantly struck
dead.   (*SP.*201-2)

It seems to me that Joyce emerges, through curtains of
salacity and blasphemy, as a truly fear-shaken Irish
Catholic, rebelling not so much against the Church but
against its near-schism Irish eccentricities, its pretence that
there is only one Commandment, the vulgarity of its
edifices, the shallowness and stupidity of many of its
ministers. His revolt, noble in itself, carried him away. He
could not see the tree for the woods. But I think he meant
well. We all do, anyway.   (*SP.*207)

In *The Dalkey Archive* Joyce is presented primarily in terms
of this last paragraph. He is, however, also presented as a man
who oversteps his prerogatives, who makes too great a claim
for his intellect and blasphemes in the process. This is not
made very clear in the actual presentation of Joyce but only
emerges as an issue in the book when seen in a total context
that includes the characters of Mick, De Selby and Sergeant
Fottrell as well as the general parody of scientific and religious

modes of thought. One of Joyce's difficulties is the problem of translating abstruse speculations on the nature of God into terms accessible to the intellect of the ordinary man.

> The task I have set myself could probably be properly termed the translation into language of raw spiritual concepts. I stress here *translation* as distinct from *exposition*. It is a question of conveying one thing in terms of another thing which is . . . em . . . quite incongrous.
>
> (p.145)

This is not immediately seen as a criticism of Joyce until it is placed side by side with a similar speech of De Selby's. De Selby and Joyce are both theologians, both concerned with minute problems of interpretation. Although they criticise the stupidity of other theologians, they are as culpable in their own way, and it is O'Brien's purpose to point this out. De Selby, in his conversation with St Augustine, tells him dogmatically that the saliencies of existence are illusions and that man's reason cannot prove them to be other. It is again a case of abstraction gone mad, of 'thinking too closely', leading to a denial of common sense, a *reductio ad absurdum*. De Selby tells Augustine:

> The prime things — existence, time, the godhead, death, paradise and the satanic pit, these are abstractions. Your pronouncements on them are meaningless, and within itself the meaninglessness does not cohere.   (p.42)

De Selby accuses Augustine, then, not only of talking about things for which there is no immediate empirical evidence, but also of talking about these things within a framework which is not logical. Joyce's condemnation of the Church for inventing the Holy Spirit with no proof and then discussing it in terms whose meaning has been misinterpreted is, in essence, the same charge as De Selby's. St Augustine's answer is, in part, O'Brien's answer, and represents a profound change from the speculations of *The Third Policeman*.

> Discourse must be in words, and it is possible to give a name to that which is not understood nor cognoscible by human reason. It is our duty to strive towards God by thought and

word. But it is our final duty to believe, to have and to
nourish faith.   (p.42)

So it is clear that both De Selby and Joyce, while seeming to
fulfil their duty to God by striving towards him by 'thought
and word', are failing in their final duty, 'to have and to
nourish faith', by denying the pronouncements of faith and
setting up in its place the empirical method, the search for
concrete proof. Thus Mick remarks to Father Cobble about De
Selby:

> . . . the word 'pagan' would not occur to me in connection
> with him. In fact he believes in God and claims to have
> verified the divine existence by experiment. I think you
> could say he lacks the faith because he is in no need of it. He
> *knows.*   (p.119)

Again, Sergeant Fottrell, with one of his casual remarks,
points to O'Brien's attitude to the scientist. He describes De
Selby, the scientist as 'piercing insentiently the dim secrets of
the holy world' (p.99).

In their rejection of faith, both De Selby and Joyce are
therefore, in a sense, blasphemers, and their attitude leads
them to assume the prerogatives of God. They are, however,
not alone in this, and O'Brien emphasises his point by creating
two further characters, Mick and Sergeant Fottrell, who also
suffer from an overdose of intellectual pride and a messianic
compulsion. That overweening pride O'Brien associates with
Satan, but here he shows all his hubristic characters recreating
the sin of Satan in the name of God. Joyce has ideas of purging
the Church. He says:

> I must be candid here, and careful. You might say that I
> have more than one good reason for wishing to become a
> Jesuit Father. I wish to reform, first the Society and then
> through the Society the Church. Error has crept in . . .
> corrupt beliefs . . . certain shameless superstitions . . . rash
> presumptions which have no sanction within the word of the
> Scriptures . . .
> Straightforward attention to the word of God . . . will
> confound all Satanic quibble.   (p.197)

Flann O'Brien: a critical introduction

His aims are thus shown to be grandiose, and he is clearly
setting himself up as the final authority on what should be
believed and denying the possibility of divine revelation to the
Early Fathers of the existence of the Holy Spirit. Nevertheless,
he still seems, as O'Brien says, to 'mean well' until his designs
are seen as the first step on the way to De Selby's, which are
also for the benefit of God and the discomfiture of false
churches. De Selby, however, intends to go one stage further
than Joyce, and destroy the whole earth.

> No, this globe only was in question and the destruction he
> planned was a prescribed doom, terrible but ineluctable,
> and a duty before God so far as he personally was
> concerned. The whole world was corrupt, human society an
> insufferable abomination. God had founded his own true
> Church but contemplated benevolently the cults of even
> capricious daemons provided they were intrinsically good.
> Christianity is God's religion but Judaism, Buddhism,
> Hinduism and Islam are tolerable manifestations of God;
> the Old and New Testaments, the Veda, Koran and Avesta
> are all sacred documents but in fact every one of these
> organised religions were in decomposition and atrophy.
> The Almighty had led De Selby to the DMP substance so the
> Supreme Truth could be protected finally and irrevocably
> from all the Churches of today.
> In fact, Mick asked, is this a second divine plan for the
> salvation of mankind?
> You could call it that.
> Salvation by way of complete destruction?
> There is no other way. All will be called home and
> judged.
> Mick did not feel like pursuing such colloquoy . . . his
> mind felt sickeningly clouded by the modest claim of De
> Selby—for it was nothing less—that he was in fact a new
> Messiah. Mick thought: what blasphemous drollery!   (p.80)

However ambitious De Selby's plans are, they too, are
eventually superseded by Mick's own, for he considers not
merely the salvation of earth but of heaven too. The process by
which he reaches this state is gradual. Early on he decides that
he wants both explanation and action on the strange events

that he has witnessed in the underwater cave. He exhibits, in this, the same empirical attitude as De Selby and Joyce, and explains to Hackett that 'even complication would be preferable to permanent mystery with no bottom to it' (p.73). This is the attitude which leads to the casuistry which O'Brien detested. At this stage Hackett warns Mick:

> You magnify what are mere impressions and you give yourself a status of grandeur. You know what happened to one Redeemer of humanity. Do you want to be another.
>
> (p.73)

Mick, it seems, does want to be another. He is determined to save the world from the De Selby menace, and in the process his attitude to himself changes radically.

> 7. Was he losing sight of the increase and significance of his own personal majesty? Well, it seemed that he had been, probably out of the force of habit in his lowly way of life theretofore. Nobody, possibly not even Mary, seemed to think that he mattered very much. But his present situation was that he was on the point of rescuing everybody from obliteration, somewhat as it was claimed that Jesus had redeemed all mankind. Was he not himself a god-figure of some sort?
>
> 8. Did not the Saint Augustine apparition mean that all was not well in heaven? Had there been some sublime slip-up? If he now carried out his plan to rescue all God's creatures, was there not a sort of concomitant obligation on him to try at least to save the Almighty as well as his terrestrial brood from all his corrupt Churches—Catholic, Greek, Mohammedan, Buddhist, Hindu and the innumerable manifestations of the witch doctorate?
>
> 9. Was it his long-term duty to overturn the whole Jesuit Order, with all its clowns of the like of Father Cobble, or persuade the Holy Father to overturn it once again—or was it his duty to overturn the Holy Father himself? (pp.129-30)

In this way Mick takes to himself all the aims of De Selby and Joyce and goes even further. In *A Bash in the Tunnel* O'Brien had said that Stephen Dedalus was not a separate character but another name for James Joyce. Here, Mick in his intellectual arrogance is meant to represent Stephen. This association is made clear in the verbal reference to *Ulysses,* which makes Hackett represent Gogarty. Hackett and Mary sit in the Colza Hotel. Mick is greeted as he comes in.

> Enter the Prince of Denmark! Hackett said, a thickness in his loud voice.   (p.217)

Later Hackett makes a remark about Mick's mother to which he takes exception and replies:

> If you mention my mother again, he snarled, I'll smash your dirty mouth.   (p.220)

When we first meet Mick and Hackett they are swimming, like Stephen and Buck Mulligan in the first episode in *Ulysses.* Mick drinks a good deal as Stephen does, and he intends to join the Church but is deflected by a woman. To some extent this is also true of Stephen. Mick, as his intellectual pretensions grow, turns away from people and begins to despise all those around him, but at the same time, in a hypocritical fashion, he reminds himself of the virtues of compassion. As the book progresses his character becomes more and more reprehensible, his remarks carrying the impression of pompous humbug. This is only alleviated by his kindness to his friend and his concern for his mother.

The comic part in this collection of characters all suffering from delusions of grandeur is taken by Sergeant Fottrell, who also claims to be directly inspired by God. His voices, however, tell him not to destroy the world or to reform the Church in order to save the Almighty, but to puncture bicycles in order to save their owners from the worst excesses of the mollycule theory. The presentation of Sergeant Fottrell adds another ironic perspective to the satire of the three main characters. Their pretensions seem ludicrous when placed beside his.

> There are times, he said, when I must take my superior officer to be the Man Above. It is my plain duty to guard members of the human race, sometimes from themselves. Not everybody understands the far from scrutable periculums of the intricate world.   (p.99)

All the four main characters, therefore, share a common

belief that they, whether through divine inspiration or by a knowledge of the mollycule theory, the root meanings of words or pneumatic chemistry, understand the 'periculums of the intricate world'. Indeed, De Selby mocks those who, once possessed of this kind of knowledge, rejected it in favour of something else.

> You men, he said, should read all the works of Descartes, having first thoroughly learnt Latin. He is an excellent example of blind faith corrupting the intellect. He knew Galileo, of course, accepted the latter's support of the Copernican theory that the earth moves round the sun and had in fact been busy on a treatise affirming this. But when he heard that the Inquisition had condemned Galileo as a heretic, he hastily put away his manuscript. In our modern slang he was yellow.   (p.16)

Mick is still uncorrupted at this stage and puts another view about Descartes.

> That man's work, Mick interjected, may have been mistaken in some conclusions but was guided by his absolute belief in Almighty God.   (p.15)

And this is not an insignificant point, for De Selby's disclaimer of Descartes' ideas on time is associated with his intention to destroy the world with DMP. De Selby had asserted that God had led him to discover the DMP substance and, in the process, to find out that Descartes had been wrong. The question is thus: was God against Descartes who had such absolute trust in him? It seems not, for De Selby denounced Descartes' (and others') thoughts about time in harsh terms, refuting, in the process, such abstract concepts as eternity and infinity.

> Consideration of time, he said, from intellectual, philosophic or even mathematical criteria is fatuity, and the preoccupation of slovens. In such unseemly brawls some priestly fop is bound to induce a sort of cerebral catalepsy by bringing forward terms such as infinity and eternity.
>   (p.14)

Later, however, St Augustine discusses the nature of time by reference to those very terms.

If you would know God, you must know time. God is time.
God is the substance of eternity. God is not distinct from
what we regard as years. God has no past, no future, no
presence in the sense of man's fugitive tenure.   (p.43)

This is not, however, the kind of discussion which De Selby
finds acceptable. He describes it as 'flannel' and continues
to point out the inconsistencies and anomalies in man's
definition of time. His own conclusion, that time is an illusion,
denies the commonsense awareness that time does, in fact,
pass.

In *The Third Policeman* such speculations had been taken
to their logical conclusion, and the resultant chaos proved how
far man is dependent on such concepts for his sanity. The
revelation that this chaos was, in fact, hell, did not remove the
question which had been posed about the logical extension of
such speculations in the real world. In *The Dalkey Archive* this
question is answered only after the confusion has been cleared
up regarding the source of De Selby's power. If it is really God
who has led him to the DMP which seems to negate time, then
his conclusions are right and St Augustine is wrong. St
Augustine would be, then, the representative of the devil De
Selby suspects him to be (p.47). Later, however, it is revealed
that De Selby was, in fact, wrong. Hackett tells Mick:

He said he knew you had certain suspicions about his
intentions with that chemical he used in the Saint Augustine
episode. He does not blame you but wanted you to know
that he has completely changed his mind. He now admits
that he had been under bad influence, pretty well subject to
an exterior power. But by a miracle — or a series of
them — his mind was cleared.   (p.175)

With this admission on De Selby's part it becomes clear that he
has been wrong all along the line. By means of a miracle the
immaterial world has stepped in to prevent harm coming to
the material world. Heaven is intact and powerful and Mick's
doubts were unnecessary. In fact, by doubting the power of
heaven to look after its own domain he had interfered too
much and has been responsible for *saving* the container of
DMP from the disastrous fire, presumably also sent from
heaven, which gutted De Selby's house. Mick, then, has not

saved the world; he has salvaged the one substance which can utterly destroy it. When the book was finished and was adapted for the stage by Hugh Leonard, the end was changed to allow Mick and Sergeant Fottrell to dispose of the container, not by placing it in the Bank of Ireland, but by throwing it into the sea. They return to the Colza Hotel only to discover that the agent which activated the DMP is sea-water. O'Brien wrote that this ending would have much improved the book, presumably because it would have made Mick's mistake all the more disastrous.

Mick has been mistaken in believing his understanding of the situation to be complete. He has not had sufficient faith in miracles, and it is the idea of miracles, which prove the existence of a benevolent and watchful God, that provides the particular atmosphere of this book and attempts to answer the questions raised in O'Brien's other books. In *At Swim* O'Brien had seemed to distrust the merely factual and the purely abstract. Instead he presented a world in which reality and fantasy were constantly interconnecting. In *The Dalkey Archive* he presents a world where reality and the miraculous — the unexpected and the supernatural — can merge into one another at any moment. In *The Third Policeman* and *The Hard Life* he had seemed to concentrate only on the conceptual and material worlds and on the difficulties which resulted when man tried to understand them. The narrator in *The Third Policeman* is in hell because he constantly tries to explain what is beyond his cognisance and to explain it in terms which deny the evidence of the physical world around him. O'Brien's answer is the simple one of faith. Believe that the real world is there because the eye of God is always on it, and believe that even if there does not seem to be an adequate logical explanation, or if that explanation will lead to negation (as it seems to do in the work of Beckett) if it is followed very far, then cease to look for any explanation, and trust instead that, in God, there is one. This is O'Brien's solution, and it is a solution that leads him to an acceptance of life which has been evident before only in parts of *At Swim*. This acceptance is seen in passages like that in which Mick thinks about his mother.

His mother? It might be thought odd that his poor mother,

with whom he lived alone, so little occupied his thoughts. She was simple and devout in the manner of Mrs Laverty but much older. She was indeed an old woman and to talk to her even in the mildest and most superficial way about the like of De Selby was unthinkable; the very idea itself was almost funny. If she understood a word, she would charitably conclude that he had 'a sup taken', for, having loved his father and accepted that he had died from drink, she well knew that he was no stranger to the taverns. Yes, it is strange and sad to live so close to one so dear and yet have no real point of contact outside banal and trivial smalltalk, no access to exchanges of the mind. Did he not notice the state nearly all his shirts were getting into? How often must he be reminded to buy at least four pairs of socks? Ah, but it was a sweet dead-end.   (p.68)

This, and the presentation of Mary early in the book (the only female character presented in any depth in O'Brien's novels) show a new spirit of compassion and emotional involvement that is lacking in his other novels.

In *The Dalkey Archive* this interchange of reality and miracle, each, O'Brien thought, part of a more inclusive vision of reality (the one not sufficient without the other), is only possible within the confines of Dalkey, a place that is rather like the Garden of Eden.

> . . . a dazzle of mildly moving leaves, a farrago of light, colour, haze and copious air, a wonder that is quite vert, verdant, vertical, verticillate, vertiginous, in the shade of branches even vespertine.   (p.7)

Dalkey is an 'unlikely' town, a place where nothing is as it seems to be, where appearances are deceptive. It is the 'vestibule of a heavenly conspection', the one place where the material and immaterial worlds are closely connected. It is only fitting, therefore, that such a place should be rich in miracles. As well as the actual supernatural occurrences which take place during the story, many references are made to other miracles in order to extend the scope of this aspect of the book. One of these miracles is that of Jonas and the whale; this story is included to illustrate De Selby's contempt for the explanation of such experiences. He is forced to admit, however, that 'We can't expect the victims of miracles to explain the miracles.' (p. 78) He, however, tries to explain the miracle, to solve its mystery, even if the result is, as Mick says about a different matter, to replace mystery with complication.

> They drank in silence, pondering this strange occurrence, the dark mystery infixed in it, unresolved even by a consultation between De Selby and Jonas himself.   (p.78)

O'Brien himself would be more content to leave the mystery unresolved, to leave unpierced the 'secrets of the holy world', because the presence of such secrets adds to the beauty of the visible world.

> They paused in their talk from these two sacred conferences to a general survey of De Selby's ghastly plan for world catastrophe. Mick asked him did he not find the known world of the common man lit up and shot through with the magic of the preternatural world to which he had access, far too absorbing and wonderful an organised creation to be destroyed summarily and utterly.   (p.79)

In *The Third Policeman* the horror experienced by the narrator, had been alleviated from time to time by his belief in 'the known world of the common man' but, as he was in hell, this belief was found to be invalid. If *The Third Policeman* was about hell, *The Dalkey Archive,* to some extent, is about heaven, or at least about the world seen, not as chaotic, but as an 'organised creation'. The first few pages stress that the idea of order is to be predominant, and that the order is to be associated with 'true reality'. Near Dalkey is the Vico Road, a place where it seems that 'a curtain had been miraculously whisked away' (p.7). Perhaps that curtain is phenomenal reality, the 'painted veil' that masks, in a platonic sense, the true design of the world. Having presented the place, O'Brien speculates as to its significance.

> But why this name Vico Road? Is there to be recalled in this magnificence a certain philosopher's pattern of man's lot on earth — thesis, antithesis, synthesis, chaos?   (p.8)

He answers his own questions by saying simply: 'Hardly.' The outcome of the events in Dalkey will not be chaos, but order. In rejecting chaos he is rejecting the vision of *The Third Policeman* and, to some extent, of *The Hard Life;* he is also rejecting De Selby, whose music is chaotic and inchoate, and Joyce, who is, through his espousal of the ideas of Vico, associated with the idea of chaos. Concerning this aspect of Joyce's thought, O'Brien had written in *A Bash in the Tunnel:*

> In *Finnegans Wake,* Joyce appears to favour the Vico theory of inevitable human and recurring evolution — theocracy: aristocracy: democracy: chaos . . .
> What was really abnormal about Joyce? At Clongowes he had his dose of Jesuit casuistry. Why did he substitute his home-made chaosistry?   (*SP*.207)

The Dalkey Archive, whatever O'Brien's afterthoughts about the appropriateness of the final scene in Hugh Leonard's dramatisation, ends with chaos averted and with the resumption of the relationship between Mick and Mary as it had been in the beginning. In order for this to happen, however, Mick must gain sufficient self-knowledge to admit that he has been 'a bloody fool', neglecting life in the pursuit of his grandiose schemes. His intention of joining the Trappists must be abandoned since it was a manifestation of the delusion of grandeur which resulted in him completely misunderstanding the nature of his real feeling and thinking about Mary in harsh terms.

> He would simply tell Mary firmly, even crudely, that he had no further time for her, and that that was that finally. Memories, or recollections of tenderness long past, was just sentimentality, silly schoolboy inadequacy, like having a dirty nose. He was a grown man, and should behave like one.   (p.215)

All this bravado collapses when Mary announces that she is to marry Hackett. Eventually Mick and Mary are reunited, but Mick must pay a price. The book does not end on this quiet note telling of resumed relations, but on Mary's mysterious statement, 'I'm certain I'm going to have a baby.' (p.222) This is the final mystery and, perhaps, the final miracle. Are we to search for an explanation of this statement in the events of the book, or are we to follow the dictates of the book and accept the presence of mystery and miracle without question? Is this the final culmination of the references to Mick's 'pious Mary' and the pun on Hackett's 'divine thought' when he mentions her? (p.8). Has heaven recognised man's need, indicated by the messianic compulsions of Sergeant Fottrell, De Selby, Joyce and Mick, and decided to provide a messiah of its own choosing? O'Brien chooses to end his book on a comic question.

On this reading it is easy to see why O'Brien was upset by Tim O'Keeffe's reading of the book as a skit on religion. In it O'Brien emerges as a deeply religious man, trusting that the questions which are unanswerable will one day be answered completely, that they will not remain half-believed bits or doubts 'hurting you like when you lose the stud of your shirt in the middle of the bed' (p.88). In O'Brien's view, all men who separate faith and intellect and who try to solve the mysteries of the universe without recourse to faith can be described as 'idiot-savants'. This is the real point of his comment to Tim O'Keeffe:

> There is, for instance, no intention to jeer at God or religion; the idea is to roast the people who seriously do so, and also to chide the Church in certain of its aspects. I seem to be wholly at one with Vatican Council II.

It is also the point of the dedication to the book, which, like everything he wrote in comic form, can be taken more or less seriously. In any case it seems to sum up completely the mixture of fantasy, serious purpose, love of weird situations, and, as he said of Joyce, laughter that 'palliates the sense of doom that is the heritage of the Irish Catholic'.

> I dedicate these pages to my Guardian Angel, impressing upon him that I'm only fooling and warning him to see to it that there is no misunderstanding when I go home.

9
Any Other Business:
Slattery's Sago Saga
and Plays for Television

AT THE time of his death O'Brien had completed seven chapters of a new novel which came to be known as *Slattery's Sago Saga*. It is possible that this might not have been a final choice, for O'Brien had already rejected six other titles. The book had been called *The Great Sago Saga*, *The Savage Sago Saga*, *The Sad Sago Saga*, *Sago's Savage Saga*, *Sarsfield's Sago Saga* and *The MacPherson Sago Saga*. The existing fragment reveals that the book was intended to be a fantasy and a political satire.

The idea for the book germinated throughout 1964 and on 23 October O'Brien wrote to Tim O'Keeffe and told him:

> I have a hell of a book in my head, by no means of the sophisticated or pseudo-intellectual kind, but a thing that links western Europe and the USA in a monstrous picture.[1]

Six days later he sent a detailed outline of the plot to O'Keeffe.[2] Emphasising that both names and title were still tentative, O'Brien said that the story would be set in the 'immediate future'. In itself this was something of a departure since his other novels, even if set in the present, often had a deliberate air of antiquity about them. The events of the novel were to cover a long time-span so it would, of necessity, be episodic in structure.

One of the main characters was to be Tim Clery (Hartigan in the final version), a young man who is caretaker of a castle in Ireland. The wealthy owner of the castle, Ned Holohan (Hoolihan in the final version), has emigrated to America following the rejection of his revolutionary agricultural methods by the local peasants. In Texas he buys thousands of acres and begins 'scientific' farming. His farm is found to lie over an immensely rich oil field and Holohan becomes even richer than he had been before. While in America, he has married 'a fearful virago' named MacIntosh (later changed to MacPherson) who hates the Irish and resents the way in which the potato-famine had driven so many of them to America where they had instilled, in her opinion, 'syphilis, gangsterdom, Roman Catholicism, monopolies, kidnapping and other blights'.[3] She is determined to prevent the possibility of another mass emigration by outlawing the potato in Ireland and replacing it with sago, a substance equally rich in starch but infinitely more resistant to disease. She intends to bring this about by buying up all the agricultural land in Ireland and letting it back to the original owners at a nominal rent on the condition that they grow sago instead of potatoes. She succeeds in her plan. Ireland becomes covered with sago forests, and sago becomes the staple food of the country. Meanwhile in America, Holohan has become a politician, 'manipulator of votes and money, and a near-hoodlum'. Tim Clery is sent for and made Governor of Texas. All is not well, however.

> Something goes wrong nationally. There is small but continuous Irish immigration and eventually throughout North America there are complaints of sago stomach, sago-leg and dread sagosis, an infectious and lethal disease. There is an atmosphere of nationwide catastrophe, and a Congressional Committee is set up to investigate. MacIntosh, back from Ireland, dies of sagosis. Several Congressional Committee meetings are abortive for want of a quorum, as a result of sago-stomach. Sago is rumoured to be an ingredient of the hydrogen bomb. CRISIS![4]

Holohan is a very resourceful man and he manages to stave off the crisis by buying radio stations and newspaper chains and having Tim elected as President of the United States. O'Brien intended this to be the climax of the book for he said that

> Clery's maiden speech on sago to the combined Houses of Congress, in effect rehabilitating the potato, will be one of the great moments of literature and history.[5]

This was, of course, only the roughest outline. There were

to be many supporting characters rejoicing in such appropriate names as Cactus Mike Broadfeet, Harry Poland, Senator Hovis Oxter, Katie ('The Dote') Bombstairs, George ('The Girder') Shagge, steelman, Congressman Theodore Hedge, Pogueen O'Rahilly, Governor Orelsile Ryder, M. Paul, detective, Mr Scheisemacher, American Ambassador to Ireland and Dr the Hon. Eustace Baggeley, who lives on a combined diet of morphia, cocaine and mescalin. The novel's setting was to alternate between Ireland and America, the scenes in Ireland taking place mainly in Shaughraun Castle (which in the final version was changed to Poguemahone Hall).

In the summary of the plot, O'Brien had expressed the intention of including 'persistent but not offensive political satire' and of producing a book which would be straightforward, with 'no "literary" complications', and which would sell well in the USA. The letter which accompanied the summary told Tim O'Keeffe that the book would be a 'masterpiece based on the cosmic substance known as SAGO' and he explained some of the possibilities of the central idea.

> Countless things are omitted, e.g. compulsion by the state of the manufacture and use of furniture made from sago-tree bark, distillation of sago-whiskey, burial in sago coffins, and so on.[6]

It is clear that this kind of plot satisfied two of O'Brien's basic needs. It gave him scope for his satirical viewpoint and it allowed for fanciful and detailed elaboration of a basic idea.

In January 1965 he was able to report:

> I have made a hesitant start on what has now come to be called MacPherson's Sago Saga. There will be so much in it about US hoodlums and politicians (and what's the difference?) that publication there is pretty certain.[7]

He was, however, being over-optimistic in expecting an easy acceptance in the USA. Cecil Scott of Macmillan, New York, wrote to him expressing doubts about the proposed book. O'Brien wrote back, obviously full of confidence:

> Forgive me for saying that it is rather supererogatory to

declare that a book not yet written would be an almost
hopeless gamble for the American market. It is almost like
saying that a child yet unborn is certain to go to hell. (And
that attitude, apart from being irrational, is sinful.) Far
from being a hopeless gamble, this book will be no gamble
at all; its US rights will be eagerly sought and it will almost
certainly be made into a film, very likely by my pal John
Huston [*sic*], who now lives in these parts . . . Four chapters
have been written since mid-January, and this is an
American book to the extent that 2/3rds of the action will
be sited there.[8]

At the same time he wrote to O'Keeffe expressing satisfaction
with the possibilities of his plot and amplifying the elements of
political satire which could be included in the novel. He was
again in a world where everything was possible and even
thought that he had another opportunity to score a point
against de Valera.

The central SAGO idea is so magnificent that sub-ideas
proliferate. There is sago furniture, made from the bark of
the trees, and the same trees are by no means so immune
from disease as the Scoto-American hawsie imagines. This
necessitates the appearance of a new profession or sect — the
sago vet . . . At the top of p.2 of Chapter one of SAGO it is
revealed that the baby destined for the Presidency was born
in Chicago and, as an orphan, adopted and brought to
Ireland when he was about 3. No accident that there is an
obvious parallel here with the de Valera case, and that that
murderous reptile is fully qualified to be President of the
United States.[9]

O'Brien must have changed his mind to some extent about
this aspect of the plot, for in the passage where Tim Hartigan's
birth is dealt with (his name was by now changed from Clery)
he is described as having been born in Ireland and it is
Sarsfield Slattery, a neighbour, who was born in Chicago. If
O'Brien was intending to drop the de Valera parallel (and he
would have been wise to do so, as such obvious bitterness rarely
elicits good writing), it may have been because he intended to
dwell more on a parallel between the history of the Hoolihans

and the Kennedys. In May 1965 he wrote to Miss Connolly at MacGibbon & Kee and revealed that this element was now foremost in his mind.

> Meditation on the crazy idea behind this book has made it grow strange horns [?] and the finished book will turn out to be a comic but unmistakeable attack on the Kennedy family. Dead President Jack will be let off lightly for undoubtedly he had some fine qualities, but the Pop is a crook and the surviving brothers contemptible hangers-on. No names will be mentioned . . . but the general idea will escape no reader over 8.[10]

None of this element of the book was ever developed and it is difficult to see how O'Brien could have escaped a law suit, even if he mentioned no names, if it had been completed and published.

In November he wrote to Tim O'Keeffe telling him that he expected to finish the Sago Saga within six months. He also wrote to Cecil Scott, with whom his differences had apparently been reconciled, and his letter, which repeats much of what he had said to Miss Connolly about the Kennedy implications, revealed that the book had progressed as far as it would ever go. He had completed seven chapters in which the scene was set, the great sago plan outlined and the 'characters established for the main paroxysms of bedlam, which [are] planned to take place in the US and culminate in the election of a president'.[11] The characters of Tim Hartigan, Crawford MacPherson, Dr the Hon. Eustace Baggeley and Sarsfield Slattery had been introduced. Although he appears only briefly in the completed portion, one feels that as he was born in Chicago and as two of the novel's variant titles bears his name, Sarsfield Slattery must be destined to play a very important part. He is

> of smallish structure, thin, with moppy fair hair; sharp, perky features were lit up with narrow navy-blue eyes, and his peculiar way of speaking with jerky accent and intonation was permanent evidence that he had been born in the northern part of Ireland and was to that extent a sort of disguise, for he had been born in Chicago. The air he

carried with him, whether he liked it or not, was one of ineffable cuteness and circumspection. Strangers knew that they had to be very wary with Sarsfield. (*SP.* 41)

Sarsfield is a much better candidate for the man who is to become President of the United States than Tim Hartigan who is a quiet, thoughtful sort of character like Mick in *The Dalkey Archive*. In fact, the mood of *Slattery's Sago Saga* is quite similar to that of *The Hard Life* and *The Dalkey Archive*. Dr Baggeley is the equivalent of De Selby. This eccentric scientist injects himself with weird combinations of drugs, plies his guests with whiskey, acts as a source of information on the oddest subjects and calls his house Sarawad Castle, which is Gaelic (he says) for 'before long' — a joke which reminds one of 'Lawnmower', the name of De Selby's house. Dr Baggeley's workman is treated with a mysterious drug for his 'rheumatism' and promptly disappears. This is similar to the Gravid Water which has such odd effects on Mr Collopy. Crawford MacPherson, who requests Tim to bring in her clothes-horse from the horse-box, is thereafter suspected of being a bed-wetter like Mrs Crotty, and Mr Scheisemacher is a worthy successor to Father Fahrt.

In one respect, however, *Slattery's Sago Saga* is noticeably different to all O'Brien's previous books. In all of these, with the possible exception of Mary's mysterious pronouncement at the end of *The Dalkey Archive*, there is no mention of sex. This seems to have been a subject which O'Brien always steered clear of. In *Slattery's Sago Saga* it is mentioned explicitly for the first time. In his conversation with Sarsfield Slattery, Tim worries about the strange behaviour of Crawford MacPherson, Ned Hoolihan's wife, who has just arrived at Poguemahone Hall.

'I'm not a windy sort of fellow as you know, Sarsfield,' he said, 'but I don't like the idea of being by myself with *her* in that house. God knows what she'd turn around and do.'

'You can lock the kitchen at night, can't you?'

'At night? Couldn't she get funny ideas during the day?'

'What sort of funny ideas?'

'Couldn't she walk down the stairs without a stitch on her?'

'Ah, I wouldn't say she's that sort.'

'Or write and tell Ned that I came up with her tray in the evening and me ballock-naked?'   (*SP*.42)

This is surprising in an O'Brien novel, although it is primarily comic. Crawford has already been introduced as an elderly and rather ugly woman, dressed in hairy tweeds and with an intense hatred of the Irish for what she considers to be their sexual immorality. Tim is a typical Irishman in the way he imagines the most improbable situations and is terrified of the prospect of being trapped in a compromising situation. This marks his great difference from the doctor, an Anglo-Irishman, who is amused by Tim's innocent confession that he has a woman living with him. The doctor's response is something of a surprise and an embarrassment to Tim.

'Dear Boy! Well well well. *Living* with you . . .?

He rose and paced delightedly to the hearth rug.

'Living with you in mortal sin, in the opprobrious bondage of the flesh?'   (*SP*.47)

As it stands there is very little scope in the seven chapters of the novel for this element to be developed. Indeed, none of the elements could be developed in such a small space, and one is left with a frustrated sense of the potential which never came to fruition. It is only just possible to see where the novel might have gone.

There are only a few references to the subject of Irish-American relations and the political corruption occasioned by the spread of Irish influence in the United States, though Ned Hoolihan's letter at the end gives some indication of what was to come. O'Brien had indicated in *The Boy from Ballytearim* that he disliked the Irish-American 'thing'. He reiterates this attitude very early in *Slattery's Sago Saga* when he shows Tim speculating about the character of Crawford MacPherson who has not yet arrived and whom he assumes to be male.

Would this damn Scotchman wear kilts, maybe play the bagpipes and demand his own sort of whiskey? But that was bogus, music-hall stuff, like Americans calling an Irishman

a boiled dinner and having him wear his pipe in the ribbon
of his hat. (*SP.*26)

Crawford, when she arrives, is seen to represent the puritan
element of America. She has a passion to protect her 'adopted
country' from the evils which are so obviously there and which
she attributes to the agency of the Irish 'tinkers' and
'superstitious thieves' who

> very nearly ruined America. They bred and multiplied and
> infested the whole continent, saturating it with crime,
> drunkenness, illegal corn liquor, bank robbery, murder,
> prostitution, syphilis, mob rule, crooked politics and
> Roman Catholic Popery . . . Adultery, salacious dancing,
> blackmail, drug peddling, pimping, organising brothels,
> consorting with niggers and getting absolution for all their
> crimes from Roman Catholic priests . . . (*SP.*33–4)

Tim has demonstrated his willingness to dispense with 'bogus'
attributions of national characteristics, but Crawford is not so
willing and piles upon the 'dirty' Irish all those crimes of which
they have so often been accused and a few that they have never
heard of. Tim is somewhat taken aback by such an attack and
protests that lots of other foreigners emigrated to America too.
But Crawford is not to be reasoned with; it is her contention
that 'People from the European mainland are princes
compared with the dirty Irish.' (*SP.*34)

The odd thing is that Crawford had to become a Catholic
in order to marry Ned Hoolihan and they had a full nuptial
mass celebrated by Cardinal Cushing. If her motives are
a little suspect, and Ned's ingenuousness a little difficult to
credit in such a wealthy and successful businessman, his letter
to Tim reveals that there is a large kernel of truth in
Crawford's jaundiced view of Irish-Americans. Ned talks
incessantly about money and about his wife's attitude to his
money. He has set up 'HP' (Hoolihan Petroleum) and has over
three hundred derricks in operation. There is, however, the
possibility that great quantities of uranium have now been
discovered under his land. The possession of money
necessitates the constant presence of a squad of private guards.
Ned himself carries a gun and 'knows how to use it'. He has
been instructed in its use by 'the Marshal of Fort Worth, a

Clareman named O'Grady'. The net of Irish Catholic influence spreads far, and Ned is anxious that Tim should join him in America for he feels that he can trust only a real Irishman. At times, dedication to the Irish connection and the Catholic Church can have its disadvantages, as Ned explains.

> A Jesuit Father, Michael Peter Connors, managed to get himself invited up to breakfast with me on the pretext of getting a sub for a new convent of the Little Sisters of the Stainless Eucharist in Dallas (of course I'm still as much of a sucker for the old Church as ever I was as a simple farmer at Poguemahone) and when he pulled out some sort of an illuminated book for me to sign so that I would be remembered in 10,000 Masses that are to be offered in the convent chapel for benefactors over twenty-five years from the opening date, a little box of .357 Smith and Wesson slugs fell out into his damn plate of bacon.   (*SP.*71-2)

Hoolihan's letter to Tim continues with a description of the political situation in Texas and the neighbouring state of New Mexico. In New Mexico two men, Cactus Mike Broadfeet and Harry Poland, are running for the governorship of the state. Ned supports both of them but suspects that Cactus Mike will make it, for, even though Harry Poland seems to be a good Catholic, he is suspected of being a Lithuanian Jew. (In an article written in the 1950s O'Brien had castigated the journalists of *The United Irishman* for their anti-semitism in thinking that to brand a man a Jew was sufficient for his life and opinions to be ignored as worthless.)[12] It is also thought that Harry Poland is a mobster, a drug-pusher and might even be prepared to condone the assassination of a political rival. The most horrifying thing about Ned's letter is the matter-of-fact and quite cheerful and guileless manner in which he relates these facts. It is clear that politics, money and religion are inextricably bound up with one another in America.

> This whole State is alive with hoodlums and politicians, and when was there any difference between those two classes? . . . I play the Kennedy RC ticket and I'll be just another brave US Catholic as soon as my citizenship comes through — Cactus Mike says I'm perfectly right and that this great state of over seven million souls is entitled to a

Cardinal and if he is elected Governor in New Mexico he
intends to park some fixers and use money (mine, I
presume) in Rome. By God, if he wants to serve the Cross
that way, why wouldn't he since he serves or used to serve
the fiery cross with the KKK outfit — and now with an
election next door there's no shortage of those gunboys in
nightshirts putting the fear of Jesus into the niggers. (*SP.*73)

Even if O'Brien's contempt for Ned's hypocritical amorality
were not evident in the rather heavy-handed irony of such
passages, it would be clear in the contrast between Ned's idea
of religion and O'Brien's. He had become increasingly
concerned with religion in his novels, but nowhere does he
make it more evident that he thought a religious concern was a
proper function for the artist — taking religion in the broadest
sense of the word — than in the few pages of *Slattery's Sago
Saga.* In an unusually warm phrase he referred to the
countryside as 'god's opulent extemporising' (*SP.*24). Later, in
a seemingly unconnected passage, Tim meditates about the
qualities of Thomas Hardy, whose *Jude the Obscure* he has
been reading.

Some people, Tim reflected as he finished his food, thought
Hardy a rather repressed and dismal writer, more taken
with groans than lightness of the heart. Well, he was long-
winded all right but the problems he faced were serious,
they were human questions, deep and difficult, and the
great Wessex novelist had brought to them wisdom, solace,
illumination, a reconciliation with God's great design.
(*SP.*27-8)

This passage is very similar to that in *The Dalkey Archive*
where Mick meditates on the qualities of James Joyce. It is
possible that Thomas Hardy was to be the submerged novelist
of *Slattery's Sago Saga,* the qualities ascribed to him by Tim
acting as an implied criticism of the 'serious' concerns of its
characters.

As O'Brien grew older he turned more and more to direct
satire, finding hypocrisy and corruption intolerable and
unable any more to laugh at it or expose it by exaggeration
and parody. There is no parody in the seven chapters of this
book, but there is irony, and it is fairly bitter. There is, too, a

lot of direct statement which is never as artistically successful as a more indirect, comic approach. Ned's letter attempts an ironic juxtaposition between the facts as they have been presented in the book and the facts as seen through the mists of Ned's self-deception. His seeming innocence about his wife's character and motives, his vision of the hard-headed resourceful elderly woman as a 'decent young married woman', his concern to be philanthrophic, are all nonsensical when they are seen in the light of his true motives and of Crawford's effect on other people. Having seen her in action, it comes as a great surprise to find her described sentimentally as a saint and cast in the role of a heroine of old Ireland. If nothing else, it shows O'Brien's keen sense of the ridiculous.

> . . . my dear wife is finding happiness in the fulfilment of philanthropic yearnings far from home. It is a great pleasure and consolation to me that she should decide to see the bigger world from the resolve, God willing, to improve it and in doing so to help me to discharge honourably the burdens of the great wealth which has flowed to me, and that keeps flowing in an ever-rising tide, from the Texas soil. There are not many dedicated persons in this shabby old world, and Crawford Hoolihan is one of them. Ireland may yet salute her, with holy Saint Brigid and Queen Maeve and the other great ladies of our storied past, not forgetting Graunya Wayl.   (*SP*. 77-8)

If *Slattery's Sago Saga* had been completed, it is not its political aspect, I think, which would have made it a fine novel. If it had been a success, that success would probably have been the result of those elements of the plot which would have allowed O'Brien to free his imagination, to create, as he had done in *At Swim* and *The Third Policeman,* alternative worlds which were logically consistent within the terms of their own imaginative construction. It is possible, however, that he might have been unable to unite the two elements of the book in a consistent whole, that the semi-realism of the political sub-theme might have defied fusion with the fantasy and refused to be subsumed under some more encompassing unity. As it is, the sago saga and its interesting ramifications are only very loosely connected to the rest of the book, but it is clear that it might have provided the kind of detailed foundation on which most of O'Brien's best fantasy had been based.

The basic facts about the sago tree are carefully set out in quotations from various books which Tim reads in Dr Baggeley's library, and O'Brien assured Tim O'Keeffe of their authenticity.

You'll find everything I said about the sago tree is genuine. You'll find amusing but fairly accurate notes on it by Marco Polo when he visited Tanganyika where lived, he mentions, the ugliest women in the whole world. There was no suggestion, however, that this condition was attributed to a diet of sago.[13]

O'Brien usually treated information in any kind of precise detail as something to use for comic effect either as a mockery of pedantry which he saw as being one of the chief foolishnesses of the world (although he was quite capable of being at times unutterably pedantic himself) or as the basis of a fantastical view of reality which could be achieved by accumulating and associating enough odd or even commonplace facts. The picture which emerged would always be based on reality, but it would be, at the same time, wildly improbable. It is clear that O'Brien was preparing for this kind of fantasy when he wrote a sentence like 'What untold things might not result from the collision of the drug-charged doctor and a foreigner with no right command of her wits?' (*SP*.61). The only thing which does result is the vision of the Ireland of the future, an unrecognisable place covered with vast sago forests and with, naturally, a radically different kind of wild life. The doctor and MacPherson allow their imaginations to run riot, picturing Ireland as the image of the Far East where they had spent so many exciting hunting-trips. The doctor reveals that he had never enjoyed having to shoot at people, even if they were niggers or coolies, but that he had always loved a tiger-shoot. MacPherson is reminded of her own experiences with Asiatic elephants, bison, rhinoceri, and several types of bear. She does not think that Ireland will be able to provide a home for such animals.

'But these large mammals would scarcely find sustenance in Ireland, even if they were allowed to kill and eat the people. But the smaller wild animals can be deadlier. The sago rat is indigenous in any territory where the pine grows. The tapir, the sambhur and the siamang, a strange sort of anthropoid ape, will probably appear here. Also the crab-eating macaque, I can see that flourish in Connemara. I would not be sure of the Asiatic tiger and black panther coming here, for they are very wide-ranging and predatory creatures, but many smaller jungle cats and wild boars may be expected. There would be no counting the breeds of alien birds which would roost in the sago pines . . .'

'Ah, my dear lady — blue partridge, argus pheasant and the cotton teal, I sampled them in the eating-houses of Hong Kong.'

'Yes, Doctor, but a thing not to be ignored will be the swarms of new insects house-monkeys and quadruped snakes and, glory be to God, the din will be something new to this country, particularly at night.   (*SP.*69)

Too little of the book was written (and the existing text might have been further revised) to say whether it would have been as successful as *At Swim* and *The Third Policeman*. It is quite clear that O'Brien was not attempting to strike out in any significantly new directions, and possibly his last novel would have been marred by the faults of both *The Hard Life* and *The Dalkey Archive*.

It is possible, however, that O'Brien might have learnt something from one of the significant events of these years, the extremely successful adaptation for the stage of *The Dalkey Archive* which was carried out by Hugh Leonard. Leonard's playscript recast certain parts of the book and, in the process, sorted out the disorder of the original and provided a dramatic conclusion. O'Brien had, in fact, consulted closely with Leonard during the rewriting and, though he does not seem to have had much of a hand in the actual structuring of the play, he was able to comment on the spirit of the book. One of his remarks about *The Dalkey Archive* might almost serve as an illustration of the peculiar vision of O'Brien's work as a whole: 'You must remember that the most crackpot invention must be subject to its own stern logic.'[14] O'Brien thought that Leonard's ending, where the dangerous box of DMP is thrown into the sea before Mick and the Sergeant realise that sea-water is the activating element, was far better than his own inconclusive finish.[15] He wrote to Ian Sainsbury of the *Sheffield Telegraph* and said:

> I have just received the typescript copy of Hugh Leonard's play based on The Dalkey Archive and I must say I am very pleased with it. He seems to have pulled together what may in parts [have] seemed like a rather rumpled mattress and produced something solid that has cohesion, coherence and pace without losing any of the original funny business. He has made several ingenious alterations . . . in the plot, and produced a smashing final curtain.[16]

O'Brien was able to produce the 'funny business' to order but what seemed to have failed was his ability to structure it. It might have been expected that his efforts to write plays would have taught him something about climax and effect, but this does not seem to have been the case. However, his awareness of the improvements Leonard had made in his play might have prompted him to look with more care at the structuring of *Slattery's Sago Saga.* It is just possible that, if finished, it might have been the better book as a result of its author's experience with the dramatisation of *The Dalkey Archive.*

O'Brien himself made one more effort to write a play for the stage in this period. This was *The Handsome Carvers,* a very brief two-act sketch of which the first act is really a mime. It was never performed or published. O'Brien described it as 'A Tragedy in Two Acts' and it is, in effect, an attempt at a moral sketch on the dangers of alcohol. The curtain rises on a marital row. The scene is a meanly furnished room from which everything of worth has been pawned. The husband is drunk, wild-eyed, prowling round like an animal; the wife is weeping and hysterical; the stage direction reads: 'There is terrific tension.' The wife speaks once, taunting her husband: 'There's a couple of wedding presents left — why don't you pawn them too?' This is, somehow, the final straw for the husband, who emits a wild-animal roar, rushes to the sideboard and takes from it a handsome black cutlery case. From that he takes out a large gleaming carving knife, pursues his terrified wife and, as the stage blacks out to the sound of a

terrible scream, poises the knife to strike. Act II is a flashback
to the presentation of the carving knife, a wedding gift from
the man's colleagues. A group of civil servants are gathered
together in an hotel room. They are celebrating the man's
marriage, drinking, smoking and making speeches of
congratulation. The speeches are made by two men, one with
a refined accent, one with a very flat Dublin accent, both of
them laden with clichés. The young husband is generally
described as a very decent man with a prim 'cultured' voice. It
is a great day for him, for not only has he been presented with
the 'handsome carvers' which he promises to cherish as long as
he lives, but he has also just had his first glass of whiskey.
Ominously he says: 'I fear I have missed a lot in life up to now.
I propose to have another one right now.' The scene fades out
to the singing of 'For He's a Jolly Good Fellow'.

O'Brien thought briefly of moving into radio and wrote a
sample script for what he hoped would be a weekly radio
series. The script, entitled *The Lurch of Time,* was to be
spoken by Myles na Gopaleen, who was envisioned as having a
voice, 'loud, hectoring and a bit americanised', which would
be uniformly strident irrespective of the subject of its
conversation. Myles, in this guise, undertook to explain the
news, in language they could understand, to the Plain People
of Ireland. It is probably a good thing that this radio series
never got on the air, for it would almost certainly have
destroyed in many a faithful reader's mind the image of Myles
which they had created for themselves.

Experiments with the theatre or radio were, however, really
abberations in this period, which was given over mainly to
writing for television. Apart from two completed series of
sketches, O'Brien wrote four full-length plays for television.
These plays are, however, largely inconsequential, and it is
clear that O'Brien had no very clear idea of the resources of
the television camera.

Flight is a thirty-minute play whose action takes place in an
aeroplane on a flight from Dublin to London. The plane
carries a motley collection of passengers, including a beautiful
young woman, a seemingly placid old lady, a couple of
aggressive young Dubliners, a Northerner, and an Englishman
who gradually becomes the butt of everyone's animosity. As

the flight proceeds, engine-trouble develops and the captain, also a Dubliner, is very nonchalant as the plane sheds pieces of its engine into the Atlantic. The Englishman wishes to reach London, the others are content to turn back. Eventually the plane crashes, but all its passengers are unharmed. The Englishman departs, sure that he is in London. The final line is the captain's remark that he will be very surprised to find himself in Wexford. To the laughter of all the remaining passengers, the screen fades out.

The Time Freddie Retired is a fifty-minute play in three acts. Its main theme is the difficulty of retirement. Freddie, who has been a civil servant all his life, finally retires. He has wonderful plans about what to do with his new leisure. He will write a book and grow grapes, fix everything about the house, improve his golf and his snooker, attend properly to the St Vincent de Paul conference, and perhaps even learn the violin. Act I finds him outlining all these plans to his neighbours. Act II, however, finds him in a stupor of in-activity, complaining of imaginary rheumatism and sliding quickly into a decadent round of heavy smoking, drinking and gambling. His wife is furious with him and tells him that he can look after himself in future. Act III brings a visitor to the house, in the shape of a Mr Hackett, a zoo keeper. He suggests that Freddie take on the job of curry-combing kangaroos to rid them of their dandruff. The play ends with a dumbfounded Freddie trapped unknowingly into accepting this curious job which will have to be kept secret from his friends at the golf club.

The Man with Four Legs tells of the misadventures which befall a busy young office worker when he wins a donkey in a twopenny raffle. First he is forced to pay for its feed and its transport to his house in Blackrock. The man who brings it has also managed to acquire an old cart which he leaves behind him when he goes. The donkey is found to be suffering from anthrax and mange and to be completely blind. After paying the vet for his advice, the young man has to take out his gun, shoot the donkey, and pay a man to bury it deep in the ground. Just as he thinks he has escaped from further consequences a garda sergeant arrives, sees the gun and asks for its licence. It is unlicensed, so the young man faces the prospect of a fine, possible confiscation of the valuable gun, and a fat fee to a solicitor. But the sergeant has other matters on his mind. The cart is stolen property, and the play ends with the young man going off to the police station to be charged with receiving stolen goods.

The Dead Spit of Kelly is an adaptation for television of the short story *Two in One*. The young taxidermist kills his boss, adopts his skin and takes up his life. He has difficulties, however, because he smokes and Kelly did not and he plays snooker while Kelly was a billiards player. For a time he gets away with it, but eventually the detectives arrive and arrest him for the murder of himself.

The first instalment of the television series *The Ideas of O'Dea* appeared in September 1963. Each episode lasted about fifteen minutes and appeared once a week. There were two characters in each episode, and the series starred the ageing but very popular comic Jimmy O'Dea. He played the part of a railroad watchman and carried on lengthy and supposedly erudite conversations with his companion Ignatius who was, O'Brien said, 'a stupid, vacant gawm who has little to say, the little being stupid and meaningless'.[17] All the burden of the conversation fell upon Jimmy and this presented problems, for Jimmy O'Dea was too ill to memorise long speeches and O'Brien was producing scripts which were remarkably similar to some of the brother's lengthier effusions in *Cruiskeen Lawn*. Conversation was everything in these scripts, and O'Brien was content to let speech reveal comic misconceptions or odd quirks of personality. He sometimes ended a conversation with a pun, and the subjects were those which had become familiar through long usage. There were some eighteen scripts dealing with such subjects as the joys of alcohol and the dangers of public houses, the antics at the Dublin Horse Show, hallucinations brought on by over-indulgence, politics, the budget, the stupidity of travel, the arrival of supermarkets, the dangers of marriage and the complications of naming children, mixed sports, the Irish language, the effects of television, the advantages of being in prison, physical fitness, Christmas celebrations, and the American way of celebrating St Patrick's Day.

The second series, *Th' Oul Lad of Kilsalaher,* was created on substantially the same pattern. The two characters in this

series were Uncle Andy and his niece Marie-Thérèse. Uncle
Andy is a Mr Collopy figure. He always wears odd and badly
fitting clothes and is always to be found sitting in a ragged
cane chair draped with old cushions and blankets. He
'repeatedly shows that he not only knows everything that is
going on but more than appears on the surface and the proper
remedy for big snags when they arrive'.[18] Apart from Mary in
The Dalkey Archive, the niece is probably O'Brien's only extensive female character. She is 'young, witty, flighty, and in
dress and manner could be called a tart. There is a never-ending
private war going on between her and Uncle Andy, but usually
Puddiner (Uncle Andy's name for her) manages to give as
good as she gets.'[19] They have Dublin accents but live in the
country as 'exiles'. 'Country customs and situations
obtrude . . . The scene is always a comic kitchen.'[20] O'Brien
later changed Andy's name and he became Hughie. There is
less stress in this series on arguments over controversial
subjects. Most of the conversations are based on the struggle
for superiority between the two characters. Puddiner manages
to get money from Hughie in one of the episodes to go to the
dogs. In another she tries to have a party in the house, much to
his chagrin. The conversations are, as a result, on more
homely topics like sales, houses, drink, the increasing
popularity of Irish ballads, old Hallowe'en customs, card
tricks, and ways of celebrating Christmas. The fourteenth
script, in which Puddiner decides that she wants to be an air
hostess, was never produced. The controller of programmes
had decided that the series was not worth continuing. The
director of the series thought that the material of the last
episode might be suitable for *Cruiskeen Lawn.* O'Brien agreed
that the 'show never really got going'.[21] He praised the
performance of Máire Hastings as Puddiner but was unhappy
with Danny Cummins's personality as Hughie. He had already
planned his third television series, *The Detectional
Fastidiosities of Sergeant Fottrell,* which he felt would be a
very great success since the Sergeant had been so popular a
character in *The Saints Go Cycling In.* He wanted the
Sergeant to be played by Martin Dempsey. Sergeant Fottrell's
companion, Policeman Pluck, was to be 'an appalling slob
who occasionally stumbles on brilliance'.

In his work for television O'Brien was aiming for a performance of 'convincing idiosyncrasy, dialogue and action'.[22] His scripts did sometimes achieve idiosyncrasy, as when Jimmy in *The Ideas of O'Dea* suggested that a lot of revenue in taxation could be gained from imposing a levy on all the fat rats in publicans' cellars. The dialogue in the plays and the series was always convincing, if sometimes tedious. O'Brien found the speech habits of the Dubliner an unending source of amusement and was very concerned to portray them accurately. He forgot, however, that speech which is repetitious, misinformed and trivial will eventually bore if the content is not significant. As for action, this was quite obviously lacking. In only one play, *The Man with Four Legs,* was there any provision for movement and outside shots. Apart from this, O'Brien designed his television plays with a fixed set and made them rely almost completely on dialogue. Some of the subjects are interesting. It is quite clear that O'Brien kept up a quite high level of political satire. Civil servants are often to be found in several of his plays, and it is tempting to speculate that *The Time Freddie Retired* is partly autobiographical in that it represented what might have happened to O'Brien on his retirement from the civil service if he had not actually written the kind of book Freddie is thinking of—'something important and substantial, it will be in part autobiographical. There will be plain speaking on certain political matters.' Of course Freddie, being a cross between the uncle in *At Swim* and Faustus Kelly, has not got quite the same attitudes as O'Brien. His idea of importance is revealed when he says:

> There are some things that require to be said. And said very bluntly . . . Unmask all our political and business chancers, denounce humbug . . . cheating . . . immoral films . . . suggestive books . . . contempt for marriage in high places.

O'Brien's failure as a dramatist is most evident where action and tension are demanded by the script. When, therefore, a murder is committed, as in *The Dead Spit of Kelly,* O'Brien should have built up the tension and the emotion so that what occurs is, at least, explicable. Instead he shows us Kelly

grumbling in a surly fashion about Burke's habit of smoking in
the workshop.

KELLY. Yes I might as well be playing blind man's buff
here. I can't see what I'm doing. Do you know what it
is, Burke. You have made the air in this room taste like
a sewer.
BURKE. I don't know what sewers taste like.
KELLY. And do you know why?
BURKE. Do I know why what?
KELLY. Do you know why? Because you are only a slob.
BURKE. What was that you called me?
KELLY. Because you're only a slob. A *slob*.
    KELLY *is stooped at his table, his back towards* BURKE
    *The latter picks up a heavy metal bar and smashes him
    over the back of the head with it.* KELLY *collapses face
    down behind the table. In a frenzy* BURKE *continues to
    bash him on the head. He stops and looks towards the
    camera, aghast.*
BURKE *(hand to head)*. Good Lord! *Great* Lord! I've killed
the bastard. Heavens Almighty.
Camera forward to show close up BURKE *rolling* KELLY *on
his back, and checking pulse at wrist.*
BURKE *(as if talking to self)*. He's dead all right. Gone
for his tea. Dead. Stone dead. I suppose I smashed the
skull. Smashed it up like an egg-shell. Well, well, WELL.
*Goes to back of door and struggles into raincoat and hat.
He is very frightened.*
BURKE. Me a murderer, ah? Lord save us! I must do some
thinking. Maybe a drink might help.
Fade out. End of Part 1.

As in *The Handsome Carvers,* where O'Brien had said that the
tension in the room was tremendous, so here he is more able to
say that Burke is 'very frightened' than he is to *show* how he
manifests that fear. In the second act, as in much of *The Man
with Four Legs,* the actor mimes movement on the screen
while his voice comes out on the sound-track superimposed as
a monologue.

The basic material for *The Detectional Fastidiosties of
Sergeant Fottrell* was so good and so much in line with
O'Brien's central idea of 'sane madness' that it is likely that a

good producer could have overcome a large number of the difficulties occasioned by his lack of feeling for a moving and visual element. Unfortunately only one page of the sample script, *The Case of the Unspeakable Spokes,* was written before O'Brien died. The notes ('Rave-Raw') for the series show that O'Brien was thinking of leaving the world of direct satire and returning to his true *milieu.*

> The period of the plays is timeless, and the feeling of fantasy can be encouraged by having the barrack walls decorated with portraits of President Kennedy, Queen Victoria, Joe Louis and St Patrick.

But the Sergeant never had the chance to wander in his timeless fantasy-world, for O'Brien did not live to elaborate the character who might have become as great a comic creation as Brother Barnabas or Myles na gCopaleen.

It is very difficult to attempt a summation of O'Brien's unique qualities. The unevenness of his output and the extensiveness of his interests precluded that discipline and obsessiveness which often make the truly great writer. O'Brien is not in the first rank of creative artists, yet he could at times meet their measure.

His main creative urge came originally from the desire to deflate and mock the pretensions of writers, scientists, respectable men, Gaeilgeoirí and intellectuals of all sorts. His characteristic turn of mind demanded that the form chosen to effect this deflation should be exaggeration and complication. By exaggerating a particular tendency he showed how ridiculous it was. To this extent, he was a secret moralist, and parody and satire are inextricably mixed in his work. The satiric purpose was, however, often an artistic side-track for O'Brien, for it seems clear that he is best when his vision becomes most fantastical. The fine display of erudition, the close and loving accumulation of all the styles of English and Irish literature, the encyclopaedia-like enumeration of facts proved to be a key to the realm of the imagination where fancy could run riot, piling detail upon detail, dwelling upon the comic, the frightening and the merely stupid with equal attention and making them all elements of a world which was newly apprehended with a kind of wild joy. O'Brien delighted

in the limitless creativity of the human mind, where there were
no limits to supposition, where everything was possible, where
all combinations of experience were valid. Yet he was aware
that this wild imagination could not exist without the
touchstone of reality and without the unceasing realisation
that it was imagination. O'Brien feared man when, in his role
as scientist or writer, he lost the awareness that his creations
were more than half illusion and thought that his vision of the
universe was an ultimate reality. When man thinks that his
concepts, his logic, his scientific explanations are the
undeniable truth and not another fantasy, then, O'Brien
thought, he steps outside the scope of his prerogative and loses
hold on reality.

That reality, as O'Brien shows it in his writing, is a
combination of material and spiritual. A denial of either part
leads to the horror of *The Third Policeman* or the moral
squalor of *The Hard Life*. It leads, too, to the sophistic
confusions of *The Dalkey Archive*. O'Brien's vision shows man
in many lights. It reveals him as a pitiful creature, pathetic
and disconnected in appearance, in thrall to a corrupted
consciousness which would persuade him, in the interest of
'higher' faculties, to deny all the sureties it needs. These
sureties, 'the firmness of the abiding earth', 'God's opulent
extemporising', the soul which defines man and makes him all
that he is, the belief and faith in the beauty of the world which
is saturated with hints of another world, are the only things
which preserve man from hell and insanity. O'Brien's vision is
always close to horror and despair, to maniacal laughter.
Because he held these things so precious he was forced to laugh
at them, to cover his essential seriousness behind a fool's mask,
to play the iconoclast in order to defend basic beliefs. However
close 'sane madness' may come to the edge of real bitterness
and negation, there is always fantasy or 'hallucination' to draw
it back. The stress of Sweeny making his lay in the trees, or
Mick's moment of love for his mother, save the novels (with the
possible exception of *The Hard Life*) from toppling over into
darkness. What emerges instead is a combination of
cleverness, mockery, arrogance and humility, complete
conviction and yet an unwillingness to 'know' anything, but to
believe it is there all the same, and to take delight in the
sweetness and variety of it all.

Notes

CHAPTER 1. BIOGRAPHY: BRIAN, FLANN, MYLES
(pp. 1-37)

1. Quoted in Thomas Hogan, 'Myles na gCopaleen', *The Bell* XIII, 2 (Nov. 1946), 129.

2. 'Éire's Columnist' (anon.), *Time* XLII, 8 (23 Aug. 1943), 90, 92.

3. Myles na gCopaleen, 'De Me', *New Ireland* (Mar. 1964), 41.

4. Ciarán O'Nolan to Anne Clissmann, 4 Dec. 1972.

5. Note by Brian O'Nolan for *Twentieth Century Authors* (unpublished).

6. Ciarán O'Nolan to Anne Clissmann, 4 Dec. 1972.

7. James Meenan, ed., *A Centenary History of the Literary and Historical Society of University College, Dublin, 1855-1955*, Tralee 1957, 241.

8. *Ibid.*, 241. 9. *Ibid.*, 241.

10. *The National Student* I, 1 (New Series) (Mar. 1930), 1.

11. *Ibid.*

12. Niall Montgomery, 'An Aristophanic Sorcerer', *Irish Times*, 2 Apr. 1966.

13. Niall Sheridan to David Powell, 27 Nov. 1969.

14. Niall Sheridan, 'Brian, Flann and Myles', *Irish Times*, 2 Apr. 1966.

15. *Comhthrom Féinne* IV, 1 (23 Apr. 1932), 205.

16. *Ibid.* III, 3 (17 Mar. 1932), 188.

17. *Ibid.* I, 3 (Summer 1931), 55.

18. *Ibid.* III, 3 (17 Mar. 1932), 193.

19. *Ibid.* VII, 3 (Jan. 1934), 46.

20. *Ibid.* III, 1 (29 Jan. 1932), 140.

21. James Meenan, *History of the Literary and Historical Society of UCD, 1855-1955*, 242.

22. *Ibid.*, 242. 23. *Ibid.*, 242. 24. *Ibid.*, 242.

25. *Ibid.*, 243. 26. *Ibid.*, 243. 27. *Ibid.*, 249-50.

28. *Ibid.*, 262. (The comment was made by Patrick Purcell.)

29. *Ibid.*, 245. 30. *Ibid.*, 246.
31. 'What is Wrong with the L. and H.?', *Comhthrom Féinne* X, 3 (Mar. 1935), 58.
32. *Ibid.*, 59.
33. 'The L and H Controversy', *Ibid.* XI, 1 (Apr. 1935), 12.
34. 'Tidying the Garden', *Ibid.* XI, 2 (May 1935), 43.
35. 'These Names Make College News', *Ibid.* XII, 1 (Jul. 1935), 23.
36. William Burne to BON, 8 Feb. 1939.
37. Jack White to David Powell, 15 Jan. 1970.
38. *Ibid.*
39. TOK to BON, 7 May 1959.
40. BON to Brian Inglis, 17 Aug. 1960.
41. *Ibid.*
42. BON to Miss Green at A. M. Heath & Co, 27 Aug. 1964.
43. Graham Greene to BON, 25 Oct. 1961.
44. BON to TOK, 10 Jan. 1963.
45. BON to TOK, 3 Jun. 1963.
46. BON to Hugh Leonard, 3 Jul. 1965.
47. Ian Sainsbury to David Powell, 14 Nov. 1969.
48. Gunnar Rugheimer to BON, 9 Mar. 1966.
49. BON to Gunnar Rugheimer, 15 Mar. 1966.
50. *Ibid.*
51. Donald S. Connery, *The Irish*, London 1968, 82.
52. BON to Alan Montgomery, chief PRO for Guinness & Co., 4 May, 1965.
53. *Cruiskeen Lawn*, 30. Nov. 1943.
54. *Ibid.*, 4–6 Nov. 1953.
55. Brian Nolan, 'A Bash in the Tunnel', *Envoy* V, 17 (May 1951), 11; repr. *Stories and Plays*, 208.

CHAPTER 2. EARLY WRITINGS: BROTHER BARNA BAS AND OTHER CELEBRITIES (pp. 38–75)
1. Niall Sheridan, 'Brian, Flann and Myles', *Irish Times, 2 Apr.* 1966.
2. *Comhthrom Féinne* IV, 2 (30 Apr. 1932), 228.
3. *Ibid.* IV, 1 (23 Apr. 1932), 200.
4. *Ibid.* IV, 2 (30 Apr. 1932), 229.
5. *Ibid.* II, 3 (Christmas 1931), 116.
6. *Ibid.* III, 1 (29 Jan. 1932), 146. 7. *Ibid.*
8. *Ibid.* III, 3 (17 Mar. 1932), 186.
9. *Ibid.* IV, 1 (23 Apr. 1933), 207. 10. *Ibid.*, 206.
11 *Ibid.* IV, 1 (23 Apr. 1933), 208.
12. *Ibid.* IV, 2 (30 Apr. 1932), 226.

348 Flann O'Brien: a critical introduction

13. *Ibid.* VI, 3 (Dec. 1933), 47.   14. *Ibid.* VII, 1 (Jan. 1934), 12.
15. *Ibid.* VI, 3 (Dec. 1933), 65.   16. *Ibid.* VIII, 2 (May 1934),
17. *Ibid.* 30.
18. *Ibid.* IX, 1 (Oct. 1934), 12-13.
19. *Ibid.* I, 2. (15 May 1931), 31.
20. *Ibid.* I, 3 (Summer 1931), 55.
21. *Ibid.* II, (1 (13 Nov. 1931), 78.
22. *Ibid.* II, 3 (Christmas 1931), 116.
23. *Ibid.* III, 1 (29 Jan. 1932), 146-7.
24. *Ibid.* III, 2 (4 Mar. 1932), 166-7.
25. *Ibid.* III, 3 (17 Mar. 1932), 186-7.
26. *Ibid.* IV, 2 (30 Apr. 1932), 227.
27. *Ibid.* II, 2 (9 Dec. 1931), 103.
28. *Ibid.* IV, 3 (Summer 1932), 248.
29. *Ibid.*, 249.   30. *Ibid.* V, 3 (Mar. 1933), 48.
31. *Ibid.*, 48.   32. *Ibid.*, 48.
33. *Ibid.* V, 4 (May 1933), 70.
34. *Ibid.* VI, 3 (Dec. 1933), 47.
35. *Blather* (Aug. 1934), 1.   36. *Ibid.*   37. *Ibid.*
38. *Ibid.*, 4.   39. *Ibid.* (Jan. 1935), 92.
40. *Ibid.* (Aug. 1934), 16.   41. *Ibid.* (Jan. 1935), 90.
42. *Ibid.*   43. *Ibid.* (Christmas 1934), 68.
44. *Ibid.* (Nov. 1934), 58.   45. *Ibid.* (Aug. 1934), 12.
46. *Ibid.* (Nov. 1934), 49.   47. *Ibid.* (Oct. 1934), 27.
48. *Ibid.*, 31.   49. *Ibid.* (Christmas 1934), 67.
50. *Ibid.* (Jan. 1935), 96.   51. *Ibid.*
52. 'Our Contributors' (editorial), *Comhthrom Féinne* IV, 2 (30 Apr. 1932).
53. *Ibid.* XII, 2 (Aug. 1935), 23.
54. *Ibid.* V, 3 (Mar. 1933), 46.
55. *Ibid.* V, 4 (May 1933), 66.
56. *Ibid.* I, 3 (Summer 1931), 52.
57. *Ibid.* VI, 3 (Dec. 1933), 54.
58. *Ibid.* I, 1 (1 May 1931), 21.
59. *Ibid.* V, 2 (Feb. 1933), 20.
60. *Ibid.* V, 3 (Mar. 1933), 40.
61. *Ibid.*, 40-1.

CHAPTER 3. 'THE STORY-TELLER'S BOOK-WEB': *AT SWIM-TWO-BIRDS* (pp. 76-150)
1. *Comhthrom Féinne* (now called *The National Student*) XI, 3 (Jun. 1935), 62-3.
2. Niall Sheridan, 'Brian, Flann and Myles', *Irish Times*, 2 Apr. 1966.

Notes

349

3. BON to C. H. Brooks, 31 Jan. 1938.
4. A. M. Heath to BON, 22 Sep. 1938.
5. BON to A. M. Heath, 19 Oct. 1938.
6. BON to Longmans, 15 Jan. 1939.
7. Eóghan Ó Tuairisc in *The Encyclopaedia of Ireland*, 122.
8. Niall Sheridan to TOK, 4 Mar. 1960.
9. A. M. Heath to BON, 14 Apr. 1939.
10. Richard Watts, Jnr to Anne Clissmann, 12 Mar. 1968.
11. BON to TOK, 25 Nov. 1961.
12. BON to TOK, 1 Sep. 1959.
13. BON to TOK, 15 Oct. 1965.
14. BON to TOK, 18 Dec. 1965.
15. John Wain, 'To Write for My Own Race', *Encounter* XXIX, 1 (Jul. 1967), 71 ff.
16. Richard Harrity, 'A Comic Masterpiece of Irish Fantasy', *New York Herald Tribune,* 11 Mar. 1951.
17. Vivian Mercier, 'At Swim-Two-Birds', *Commonweal,* Liv. 3 (27. Apr. 1951), 68, 70.
18. Mary Ellmann, 'Unreal City', *New Statesman,* 9 Feb. 1973. 206.
19. Vivian Mercier, *The Irish Comic Tradition,* Oxford 1962, 40.
20. M. H. Abrams, *A Glossary of Literary Terms,* 3rd ed., New York 1971, 114.
21. Northrop Frye in *The Anatomy of Criticism* defines the Anatomy or 'Menippean Satire' as a form characterised by a 'creative treatment of exhaustive erudition', normally using a 'loose jointed narrative form often confused with the romance', and dealing 'less with people as such than with mental attitudes. Pedants, bigots, cranks, parvenus, virtuosi, enthusiasts, rapacious and incompetent professional men of all kinds, are handled in terms of their occupational approach to life as distinct from their social behaviour.' (*Anatomy of Criticism,* Princeton 1957, 309)
22. E. M. Forster, *Aspects of the Novel* (1927), Harmondsworth 1963, 74.
23. Joseph Conrad in *A Personal Record* recounts feeling much the same way about the 'reality' of imagined characters. Characters, he said, visited him in much the same way as Finn visits the narrator: 'Unknown to my respectable landlady, it was my practice directly after breakfast to hold animated receptions of Malays, Arabs and half-castes. They did not clamour for my attention. They came with silent and irresistible appeal.'
24. James Branch Cabell, *The Cream of the Jest* (1917), London 1972, 39.
25. Aldous Huxley, *Point Counter Point,* Harmondsworth 1969,

298. The narrator says: ' . . . my small collection contained works ranging from those of Mr Joyce to the widely read books of Mr A. Huxley, the eminent English writer.' (p.12)

26. In 'The Artist-Novelist in Transition', Gerald J. Goldberg writes: 'By putting such a premium on process, the contemporary artist asserts the relevance of the creative act itself to the final meaning of his work.' *English Fiction in Transition* IV, (1961), LV, 39, 25.

27. N.J.S., 'Contemporary Fiction', *The National Student* II, 2 (Jun. 1931), 76.

28. This problem had also been posed by Aldous Huxley. 'The novelist can assume the god-like creative privilege and simply elect to consider the events of the story in their various aspects. But perhaps this is a tyrranical imposition of the author's will. Some people would think so. But need the author be so retiring? I think we're a bit too squeamish about these personal appearances nowadays.' (*Point Counter Point*, 298).

29. Laurence Sterne, *The Life and Opinions of Tristram Shandy*, Routledge edition of *The Works of Laurence Sterne*, n.d., 241.

30. Forster had commented in *Aspects of the Novel* that 'The people of a novel come into the world more like parcels than human beings.' O'Brien's method of character description would seem to bear him out in this opinion.

31. Sterne, *Tristram Shandy*, 3.

32. Sheridan in *The National Student* II, 2 (Jun. 1931), 76.

33. James Joyce, *A Portrait of the Artist as a Young Man* (1916), Harmondsworth 1960. 215.

34. James Meenan, ed., *A Centenary History of the Literary and Historical Society of University College, Dublin, 1855-1955.* Tralee 1957, 240-1.

35. The uncle is undoubtedly based on the uncle in Joyce's *Dubliners*. In *Araby* he is the fictive counterpart for Joyce's father; he disappoints the young ˙boy and then becomes complacent and clichéd.

My uncle said he was very sorry he had forgotten. He said he believed in the old saying: 'All work and no play makes Jack a dull boy.' He asked me where I was going and, when I told him a second time, he asked me did I know *The Arab's Farewell to his Steed.* When I left the kitchen he was about to recite the opening lines of the piece to my aunt. (*Dubliners*, 31).

The uncle also appears in *The Sisters*, but here O'Brien seems to be basing the narrator's response to his uncle on the boy's response to Mr Cotter rather than to his uncle.

'It's bad for children,' said old Cotter, 'because their minds are so impressionable. When children see things like that, you know, it has an effect`. . .' I crammed my mouth with a stirabout for fear I might give utterance to my anger. Tiresome old red-nosed imbecile. (*Dubliners*, 9).

36. The committee's discussion on this point is probably based on a row in UCD in 1934 which developed when the SRC decided to hold a céilí on St Patrick's Day. There was bitter opposition to the scheme on the grounds that Irish dances were 'primitive'. The Gaelic League often overreacted to such statements by banning all dances other than reels and sets, etc. as non-Irish and, therefore, harmful to Irish purity. O'Brien was to return to this kind of topic in *An Béal Bocht*.

37. Joyce, *A Portrait*, 100.

38. *Ibid.*, 67.   39. *Ibid.*, 214-15.   40. *Ibid.*, 204.

41. There are several other places, notably in the section where the 'learned' discussion between Shanahan, Lamont and Furriskey takes place in Orlick's manuscript, that the 'Ithaca' episode is parodied. The parody of legalistic language is very prevalent in O'Brien's work. It is this that leads one to label it an 'Anatomy' even as a distrust of 'abstract' talk can be seen to be an aspect of Celtic literature.

42. The influence of *Dubliners* may, possibly, be discerned also in the Circle N episode of the book where the idea of associating the Dublin environment and the 'wild west' may have been inspired by *An Encounter*. 'The adventures related in the literature of the Wild West were remote from my nature but, at least, they opened doors of escape.' (*Dubliners*, 17) 'We walked along the North Strand Road till we came to the Vitriol Works and then turned to the right along the Wharf Road, Mahony began to play the Indian as soon as we were out of public sight.' (*Dubliners*, 20)

43. *A Portrait*, 203.

44. In an article in *Dublin Doings* (Christmas 1940) O'Brien, while criticising the cultural pretensions of the Irish speaker, also speaks of the Irish language as 'an instrument of beauty and precision'.

45. 'A Bash in the Tunnel', *Envoy* V, 17 (May 1951), 5-11. (This is discussed in Chapter 8.)

46. From *Cruiskeen Lawn*, quoted in a television documentary, 'The World of Flann O'Brien', RTE, summer 1971.

47. Standish James O'Grady, *Finn and His Companions*, Dublin 1921, 13-14.

48. In T. P. Cross and C. H. Slover, ed., *Ancient Irish Tales*, Chicago, 1936, 432.

49. Quoted by Douglas Hyde in *A Literary History of Ireland*,

352   *Flann O'Brien: a critical introduction*
London, 1967, 379.
    50. *Ibid.*, 373-4.   51. *Ibid.*, 368.
    52. Quoted in the Introduction to *Buile Shuibhne (The Frenzy of Suibhne): being The Adventures of Suibhne Geilt, a Middle Irish Romance*, edited and translated by J. G. O'Keeffe (Irish Texts Society) London, 1913, xvi-xvii.
    53. *Ibid.*, 13.   54. *Ibid.*, 137.   55. *Ibid.*, Introduction, xxxvi.
    56. *Ibid.*, Introduction, xxxvii.
    57. The Pooka is mentioned in Padraic Colum's *The King of Ireland's Son*, in Olcott's *Wonder Tales from the Fairy Isles*, Yeats's *Irish Fairy Tales*. T. C. Croker in *Fairy Legends* (1825) says: 'Irish superstition makes the Pooka palpable to the touch. To its agency the peasantry usually ascribe accidental falls.'
    58. Again, this passage may be derived from a statement in *Aspects of the Novel* where Forster says: 'Well, in what sense do the nations of Fiction differ from those of the earth? . . . They have nothing in common in the scientific sense. They need not have glands, for example, whereas all human beings have glands.'
    59. K. H. Jackson, *A Celtic Miscellany*, London 1967, 153 (note on Celtic magic).
    60 Alwyn and Brinley Rees, *Celtic Heritage*, London 1961, 342.
    61. Lecture given by Proinsias Mac Cana at the conference for the International Association for the Study of Anglo-Irish Literature (IASAIL) in Cork, 1973.
    62. Ciarán O'Nolan, 'The Return of Finn', *Comhthrom Féinne* XI, 1 (Apr. 1935), 8.

CHAPTER 4. BICYCLES AND ETERNITY: *THE THIRD POLICEMAN* (pp. 151-81)
    1. BON to William Saroyan, 14 Feb. 1940; repr. in *The Third Policeman*, 200.
    2. Donagh MacDonagh, 'The Great Lost Novel', unpublished MS. at MacGibbon & Kee, London.
    3. A.M. Heath to BON, 11 Mar. 1940.
    4. *The Third Policeman* can be seen to have derived, in part, from the ideas of the Celtic other-world expressed in such texts as the Voyage of Bran, the Voyage of Maeldune and the story of Oisin in Tír na nÓg. The world to which the narrator goes has some of the qualities of this other world. Time has no meaning in it, so that what seems like a day's sojourn can be really a hundred years.
    5. De Selby is modelled on Des Esseintes, hero of Huysmans' *Á Rebours* (Against Nature) and possibly on Slawkenbergius, the savant whose works are the lifelong obsession of Walter Shandy in Sterne's *Tristram Shandy*. Indeed, the extensive footnotes in which

most of the references to de Selby and his commentators are found
are a great parody of 'learned argument' similar to that which is
pervasive in *Tristram Shandy* as a whole. (See J. K. Huysmans,
Against Nature, translated by R. Baldick, Harmondsworth 1959
(Niall Sheridan remembers encouraging O'Brian to read this), and
L. Sterne, *The Life and Opinions of Tristram Shandy,* in the
Routledge edition of *The Works of Laurence Sterne,* especially
pp. 109–21.)

6. This idea seems to be derived from the work of the philosopher
Anaximander.

7. J. W. Dunne, *An Experiment with Time,* London 1927 and
The Serial Universe, London 1934.

8. BON to TOK, 21 Sep. 1962.

9. J. W. Dunne, *Nothing Dies* (a condensed version of the ideas
from the previous two books), London 1940, 70-1.

10. As well as the 'voyages' on which saints and heroes witness very
strange places and beings, there are many folk-tales in which people
stray, without noticing it, into odd corners of the world, ruled by
magic, or cross the sea to America in small boats, or visit their
friends, and then return to find that they have been absent only half
an hour. See Seán O'Sullivan, *Folktales of Ireland,* London 1966.
The motif used is a common one in Irish literature.

11. All O'Brien's policemen were of the large, solemn country
type. They were undoubtedly inspired by his own experiences in
Dublin, where most policemen were from the country, and probably
by the policemen in James Stephen's novels *The Crock of Gold* and
The Charwoman's Daughter.

12. The same image reoccurs on p. 118 with the narrator's
speculations as to whether Joe, his soul, had a body: 'What if he *had*
a body? a body with another body inside it in turn, thousands of such
bodies within each other like the skins of an onion, receding to some
unimaginable ultimatum?' The image may bear some relationship to
the discussion about homunculi in *Tristram Shandy.*

13. See Huysmans, *Against Nature,* 38, for a similar discussion of
the environment.

14. There seems to be a direct reference to voyage literature here.
'They went forward after that all through the wood nearest to them,
and found an orchard with lovely purple-crested apple-trees and
leafy oaks of beautiful colour and hazels with yellow-clustered nuts.
"It is wonderful to me, my men," said Tadhg, "what I have
noticed — it is winter with us in our land now, and it is summer here
in this land," said Tadhg.' (K. H. Jackson, *A Celtic Miscellany,* 190,
quoting an unknown author, probably of the fourteenth or fifteenth
century.)

15. Des Esseintes, too, believes that journeys are hallucinations. (Huysmans, 35-6).

16. Des Esseintes has a room full of parallel mirrors which he uses for scientific experiments. (Huysmans, 25)

17. The narrator later remarks: 'As in many other of de Selby's concepts, it is difficult to get to grips with his process of reasoning or to refute his curious conclusions.' (p.117)

18. This idea is, surely, based on the 'hobby-horses' of the characters in *Tristram Shandy* of which Sterne says: 'By long journeys and much friction, it so happens that the body of the rider is at length filled as full of HOBBY-HORSICAL matter as it can hold: so that if you are able to give but a clear description of the nature of one, you may form a pretty exact notion of the genius and character of the other.'

19. In 1945 O'Brien wrote: 'Is it not time that you Irish woke up to the unsuspected frailty of the human intellect.'

20. The description of the death of Mathers is verbally similar to the description of the slaying of his father which Christy Mahon gives in *The Playboy of the Western World:* 'I just riz the loy and let fall the edge of it on the ridge of his skull, and he went down at my feet like an empty sack, and never let a grunt or groan from him at all.' The punishment of the narrator for the murder of Mathers may have been intended as a criticism of Synge's apparent lack of moral comment.

21. The image was, perhaps, derived from Aldous Huxley's *Point Counter Point*, with its image of a Quaker holding a packet which has on it a picture of a Quaker holding a packet, and so on *ad infinitum*, and from Dunne's attempt in *Nothing Dies* to illustrate the idea of serialism by describing an artist painting a picture of an artist painting a picture *ad infinitum*. (*Point Counter Point*, 298; *Nothing Dies*, Chapters 1 and 2 *passim*).

22. The 'hoppy men', led by Martin Finnucane are parallels of the narrator himself. Not only are they alike in that they have only one leg, they are also thieves and murderers. The meeting with Martin Finnucane at the beginning of the narrator's journey may be the first stage in a process of self-recognition which is aided by Joe's remark on Finnucane: 'A droll character'.

23. The circular nature of the hell which the hero endures is similar to that envisioned by Sartre in his play *Huis Clos*. The similarity points to an affinity between *The Third Policeman* and the Drama of the Absurd. Martin Esslin in *The Theatre of the Absurd*, Harmondsworth 1968, has said: 'Many of the plays of the Theatre of the Absurd have a circular structure, ending exactly as they began', and Arnold P. Hinchcliffe provides a definition of the Absurd that

makes it clear how close to it was O'Brien's vision: 'It challenges the audience to make sense of nonsense, to face the situation consciously rather than feel it vaguely, and perceive, with laughter, the fundamental absurdity.' (*The Absurd*, London 1969, 12).

CHAPTER 5. 'OUR GAELIC SATIRIST': *CRUISKEEN LAWN* (pp.182-227)
  1. 'More Extracts from a Diary of Dreams' in Austin Clarke, *Old-Fashioned Pilgrimage*, Dublin 1967, 220.
  2. Letter to the Editor, *Irish Times*, 17 Oct. 1940.
  3. Letter to the Editor, *Irish Times*, 19 Oct. 1940.
  4. Benedict Kiely, 'An Ear for Dublin Talk', *New York Times* LXXIII, 46 (17 Nov. 1968), 32.
  5. Note in the O'Brien collection in the Morris Library, University of Southern Illinois.
  6. Letter to the Editor, *Irish Times*, 17 Oct. 1940.
  7. Letter to the Editor, *Irish Times*, 18 Oct. 1940.
  8. Letter to the Editor, *Irish Times*, 18 Oct. 1940.
  9. Myles na Gopaleen, 'De Me', *New Ireland* (Mar. 1964), 41.
  10. Gerald Griffin, *The Collegians*, Dublin 1963, 82.
  11. *Man Bites Dog* appears regularly in the *Irish Times*.
  12. BON to Mark Hamilton, 27 Nov. 1962.

CHAPTER 6. GAEILGEOIRÍ, POLITICIANS AND THE DEVIL: *AN BÉAL BOCHT* AND OTHER WRITINGS 1940-60 (pp.228-68)
  1. Myles na gCopaleen, 'Baudelaire and Kavanagh', *Envoy* III, 12 (Dec. 1950), 79.
  2. Note on the title page of the unpublished typescript of *The Boy from Ballytearim*, 1962.
  3. First published, under the name Brian Nolan, in *Envoy* V, 17 (May 1951), 9.
  4. BON to TOK, 27 Feb. 1960.
  5. Flann O'Brien, 'Standish Hayes O'Grady', *Irish Times*, 16 Oct. 1940.
  6. *Ibid.*
  7. Tomás Ó Crohan, *The Islandman*, Dublin 1934, 227.
  8. Seán O'Casey to BON, 2 Aor. 1942.
  9. BON to Seán O'Casey, 13 Apr. 1942.
  10. 'I don't think there is any point about translating stuff I have written in Irish into English. The significance of most of it is verbal or linguistic or tied up with a pseudo-Gaelic mystique and this would be quite lost in translation.' BON to TOK, 27 Feb. 1960.
  11. Ó Crohan, *The Islandman*, 2.

12. *Ibid.*, 1.

13. Niall Montgomery to BON, 26 Mar. 1937.

14. BON to William Saroyan, 14 Feb. 1940.

15. BON to Michael Walsh, 31 May 1942.

16. BON to Hilton Edwards, 20 Jun. 1942.

17. *Ibid.*

18. Myles na Gopaleen, 'The Fausticity of Kelly', *Radio-TV Guide*, 25 Jan. 1963.

19. BON to Ernest Blythe, 21 Jun. 1942.

20. *Journal of Irish Literature* (Newark, Del.) III, 1 (Jan. 1974), 35.

21. Joseph Holloway's diary, 30 Mar. 1943, in R. Hogan and M. J. O'Neill, ed., *Joseph Holloway's Irish Theatre*, III (1938-44), Carbondale & Edwardsville [USA], 1967, 86. See also p.83 for Holloway's comments on *Faustus Kelly.*

22. This passage does not appear in the abridged version of the text published in *Stories and Plays*, 101-13.

23. Notes on the title page of *The Boy from Ballytearim*, 1962.

24. The story was probably inspired by Joyce's 'A Painful Case' in *Dubliners;* there are many similarities between the two tales.

25. *Stories and Plays*, 91-7.

26. Myles na Gopaleen, 'Two in One', *The Bell* XIX, 8 (July 1954), 31; repr. in *Journal of Irish Literature* (Newark, Del.) III, 1 (Jan. 1974), 57.

27. *Ibid.*

CHAPTER 7. 'AN EXEGESIS OF SQUALOR': *THE HARD LIFE* (pp.269-90)

1. In *Cruiskeen Lawn* on 10 February 1953 Myles wrote that he was busy on a new book called *The Hard Life* and written under the pseudonym 'Felix Kulpa'. It seems clear from the article that the theme and atmosphere of the novel were already fixed in O'Brien's mind, even at this early date.

2. Telegramme, TOK to BON, 14 Feb. 1961.

3. BON to TOK, 1 Sep. 1961.

4. *Ibid.*   5. *Ibid.*

6. BON to TOK, 25 Nov. 1961.

7. Maurice Edelman, review of *The Hard Life* in the *Sunday Times* (Manchester), 12 Nov. 1961.

8. Anthony Burgess, review of *The Hard Life* entitled 'Misterpiece' in *Yorkshire Post,* 16 Nov. 1961.

9. BON to TOK, 16 Dec. 1960.

10. BON to TOK, 7 Jun. 1961.

11. It is possible that O'Brien was intending to use this mode to

parody some of the stories of Frank O'Connor, such as *My Oedipus Complex*, where the first person narrative of the child is belied by the maturity of many of his insights.

12. Most of these passages were taken, almost verbatim, from the *Encyclopaedia Britannica*, which was used more for *The Hard Life* than for any of the other novels.

13. O'Brien was delighted to learn that a scheme very similar to this had been used in Belfast during a public holiday.

14. This tendency is also evident in the short story *Two in One* but it can be traced as far back as the Brother Barnabas article describing the death of Mr Bewley Box.

CHAPTER 8. THE DMP AND MIRACLES: *THE DALKEY ARCHIVE* (pp. 291-323)

1. There is an article in *The Guardian* which continues this theme. Called 'Can a Saint Hit Back?', it appeared on 19 January 1966.
2. BON to Gerald Gross, 10. Sep. 1962.
3. BON to TOK, 21 Sep. 1962.
4. *Ibid.*
5. BON to TOK, 4 Nov. 1962.
6. BON to TOK, 1 Mar. 1963.
7. BON to TOK, 15 Nov. 1963.
8. TOK to BON, 22 Nov. 1963.
9. BON to TOK, 27 Nov. 1963.
10. BON to TOK, 22 Jan. 1964.
11. Samuel Beckett to Anne Clissmann, 27 Dec. 1967.

CHAPTER 9. ANY OTHER BUSINESS: *SLATTERY'S SAGO SAGA* AND PLAYS FOR TELEVISION (pp.324-45)

1. BON to TOK, 23 Oct. 1964.
2. BON to TOK, 29 Oct. 1964.
3. *Ibid.* 4. *Ibid.* 5. *Ibid.*
6. BON to TOK, 29 Oct. 1964 (covering letter).
7. BON to TOK, 2 Jan. 1965.
8. BON to Cecil Scott, 9 Mar. 1965.
9. BON to TOK, 9-10 Mar. 1965.
10. BON to Miss Connolly, 8 May 1965.
11. BON to Cecil Scott, 22 Nov. 1965.
12. Myles na gCopaleen, 'Baudelaire and Kavanagh', *Envoy* III, 12 (Dec. 1950), 80.
13. BON to TOK, 9 Nov. 1964.
14. BON to Hugh Leonard, 14 Nov. 1964.

15. Hugh Leonard, *The Saints Go Cycling In* (unpublished typescript).

16. BON to Ian Sainsbury, 6 Aug. 1964.

17. Note on the first script of *The Ideas of O'Dea* (unpublished typescripts).

18. Note for the first script of *Th' Oul Lad of Kilsalaher* (unpublished typescripts).

19. *Ibid.*   20. *Ibid.*

21. BON to Jim Fitzgerald, 15 Dec. 1965.

22. Brian O'Nolan, 'Rave Raw' (note on the projected series *The Detectional Fastidiosities of Sergant Fottrell*), 2 pp., undated.

Select Bibliography

The following bibliography lists only those works which have been relevant to this book. A complete list of articles on the work of Flann O'Brien, and reviews of his books, is contained in David Powell, 'The English Writings of Flann O'Brien' (unpublished doctoral thesis, University of Southern Illinois, 1971). This list is reprinted in *Journal of Irish Literature* (Newark, Del.) III, 1 (Jan. 1974), 104–12.

The Morris Library, University of Southern Illinois, holds a large collection of original and unpublished material comprising typescripts of novels, plays and short stories, articles, letters and television scripts.

For convenience, the title of a work by Brian O'Nolan will be followed by the pseudonym under which it was written.

Works by Brian O'Nolan

PUBLISHED WORKS

At Swim-Two-Birds by Flann O'Brien. London 1939, 1960. New York, 1951, 1967.

An Béal Bocht by Myles na gCopaleen, Dublin 1941; trans. by Patrick C. Power as *The Poor Mouth*, London 1973.

Cruiskeen Lawn (extracts from the *Cruiskeen Lawn* column in the *Irish Times*) by Myles na gCopaleen, Dublin 1943.

Faustus Kelly by Myles na gCopaleen, Dublin 1943.

Máiréad Gillan by Brian Ó Nualláin (trans. from Brinsley MacNamara's play in English, *Margaret Gillan*), Dublin 1953.

The Hard Life by Flann O'Brien, London 1961.

The Dalkey Archive by Flann O'Brien, London 1964.

The Third Policeman by Flann O'Brien, London 1967.

The Best of Myles (selections from *Cruiskeen Lawn* by Myles na gCopaleen), ed. with an introduction by Kevin O'Nolan, London 1968.

Stories and Plays by Flann O'Brien, London 1973.

Contents: *Slattery's Sago Saga*
The Martyr's Crown
John Duffy's Brother
Thirst
Faustus Kelly
A Bash in the Tunnel

WORK CONTAINED IN PERIODICALS AND NEWSPAPERS

'Going to the Dogs!' by Flann O'Brien, *The Bell* I, 1 (Oct. 1940), 19-24.

'Standish Hayes O'Grady' by Flann O'Brien, *Irish Times*, 16 Oct. 1940

'The Trade in Dublin' by Flann O'Brien, *The Bell* I, 2 (Nov. 1940), 6-15.

'The Dance Halls' by Flann O'Brien, *The Bell* I, 6 (1940), 44-52.

Cruiskeen Lawn by Myles na gCopaleen, *Irish Times*, 4 Nov. 1940-1 Apr. 1966.

John Duffy's Brother by Flann O'Brien, *Story* XIX:90 (Jul.-Aug. 1941), 65-68.

'The Insect Play' by Myles na gCopaleen (1943), *Journal of Irish Literature* (Newark, Del.) III, 1 (Jan. 1974), 24-39.

'Drink and Time in Dublin' by Myles na gCopaleen, *Irish Writing* 1 (1946), 71-77.

'The Martyr's Crown' by Brian Nolan, *Envoy* I, 3 (Feb. 1950), 57-62.

'Baudelaire and Kavanagh' by Myles na gCopaleen, *Envoy* III, 12 (Dec. 1950), 78-81.

'A Bash in the Tunnel' by Brian Nolan, *Envoy* V, 17 (May 1951), 5-11.

'Two in One' by Myles na Gopaleen, *The Bell* XIX, 8 (July 1954), 30-34; *Journal of Irish Literature* (Newark, Del.) III, 1 (Jan. 1974), 56-61.

A Weekly Look Around by John James Doe, *Southern Star* (Skibbereen), 15 Jan. 1955-27 Oct. 1956.

'Donabate' by Brian Nolan (1958), *Journal of Irish Literature* (Newark, Del.) III, 1 (Jan. 1974), 62-64.

'Cruiskeen lawn' by Myles na gCopaleen (a selection from the *Irish Times*), *Nonplus* 1-4 (1959).

'Words by Flann O'Brien, *Development* 9. (Spring 1959), 1.

'National Gallery: Sean O'Sullivan' by Flann O'Brien, *Development* 16 (Dec. 1959), 1.

George Knowall's Peepshow by George Knowall, *Nationalist and Leinster Times* (Carlow). (Early to mid-1960s).

'Public Taste and Decorum' by Myles na gCopaleen, *Hibernia* XXIV (9 Sept. 1960), 3.

'Small Men and Black Dogs' by Brian Nolan, *Manchester Guardian,* 14 Oct. 1960.

'This Job of Work' by Myles na gCopaleen, *Evening Mail* (Dublin), 12 oct. 1961.

'1961' by Myles na gCopaleen. *The Harp* (Winter 1961), 18.

'Old Hat Re-blocked' by Flann O'Brien, *Irish Times,* 14 Mar. 1962.

'Enigma' by Flann O'Brien, *Irish Times,* 16 Jun. 1962.

'The Man with Four Legs' by Brian Nolan (1962), *Journal of Irish Literature* (Newark, Del.) III, 1 (Jan. 1974), 40-55.

'The Fausticity of Kelly' by Myles na Gopaleen, *RTE Guide,* 25 Jan. 1963.

'Pots and Pains' by Myles na gCopaleen, *Irish Housewife Annual* XIV (1963-64), 70-1.

'De Me' by Myles na Gopaleen, *New Ireland* (Mar. 1964), 41-42.

'Behan, Master of Language' by Flann O'Brien, *Sunday Telegraph,* 22 Mar. 1964.

'Gael Days' by Flann O'Brien, *Manchester Guardian,* 6 May 1964.

'George Bernard Shaw on Language' by Flann O'Brien, *Irish Times.* 23 Jan. 1965.

'At the Crossroads' by Flann O'Brien, *Irish Times,* 20 Feb. 1965.

'A Pint of Plain' by Myles na gCopaleen, *The Harp* (Summer 1965), 21, 27.

'The Cud of Memory' by Flann O'Brien, *Manchester Guardian,* 15 Oct. 1965.

'Can a Saint Hit Back?' by Flann O'Brien. *Manchester Guardian,* 19 Jan. 1966.

UNPUBLISHED MATERIAL

Much of this material consists of typescripts for television plays. The originals of these are held at the University of Southern Illinois and are undated. RTE, for whom most of them were written, also hold copies and would know the dates on which the sketches were presented. Unfortunately they are unable to make this information available. The dates given below are, as a result, only approximate.

The Boy from Ballytearim by Brian Nolan. 1955; revised version, 1962. Televison play.

The Dead Spit of Kelly by Brian Nolan. 1962. Television play. (Dramatised version of the story *Two in One.)*

Flight by Brian Nolan. 1962 Television play.

The Time Freddie Retired by Brian Nolan. 1962. Television play.
The Handsome Carvers by Myles na gCopaleen. Stage play.
The Lurch of Time by Myles na gCopaleen. Radio script.
The Ideas of O'Dea by Brian Nolan, Sep. 1963–Mar. 1964.

    Television series.
1. The Meaning of Malt.
2. Places to Keep Out Of.
3. The Horse Show.
4. Getting the Creeps.
5. A New Party.
6. The Presidential Stakes.
7. A Sensible Budget, Now.
8. Flying High.
9. Supermarkets.
10. Wedding Bells.
11. The Nuptial Knot.
12. The New Arrival.
13. Playing the Game.
14. The Language Question.
15. Th' Electric.
16. Is TV a Good Thing?
17. Jail's Not so Bad.
18. The Holliers.
19. Keeping Fit.
20. Hullaballoons at Christmas.
21. Present Problems.
22. The March of Time.
23. The Stampede.
24. Boots and Saddle.
25. St Patrick's Day.
26. Sales Talk.

Th' Oul Lad of Kilsalaher by Brian Nolan, Sep.–Dec. 1965.
Television series.
1. Trouble About Names.
2. Animals of Erin.
3. Party Warfare.
4. Danger at the Sales.
5. When Dublin's Falling Down.
6. The Crown is Tops.
7. The Ballad Wave.
8. Apples and Nuts.

9. Beirt Eile.
10. Hughie For Pres!
11. Jiggery Pokery.
12. A Novel Party.
13. The New Abbey Theatre.
14. Flying High.

The Detectional Fastidiosities of Sergeant Fottrell by Brian Nolan, 1966.
  1. Rave-Raw. (This is a note outlining the scope of the series.)
  2. The Case of the Unspeakable Spokes. (1 page of uncompleted first script.)

There are some poems translated from Irish published in *The Oxford Book of Irish Verse*, ed. Donagh MacDonagh and Lennox Robinson, Oxford 1958, 315-16, and in *The Lace Curtain* 4 (Summer 1971), 46-7. There are a few manuscripts of poems among the papers at Illinois, but these are usually of poems which appeared in *Cruiskeen Lawn*.

There is an, as yet, untraced short story called *Old Iron* and there may be two other newspaper columns *The Column Bawn*, by Myles na gCopaleen which may have appeared in the *Sunday Despatch* and *Matt Duffy's Column* by Matt Duffy which may have appeared in the *Sunday Review*.

WORKS RELATING TO BRIAN O'NOLAN, AND SOURCE MATERIAL
J. B. Cabell, *The Cream of the Jest*, London 1930.
A. Clissmann, 'Parody and Fantasy in the English Novels of Flann O'Brien'. (Unpublished M Litt thesis, University of Dublin, 1971.)
T. P. Cross and C. H. Slover, ed., *Ancient Irish Tales*, Chicago 1936.
J. W. Dunne, *An Experiment with Time*, London 1927.
  The Serial Universe, London 1934.
  The New Immortality, London 1938.
  Nothing Dies, London 1940.
E. M. Forster, *Aspects of the Novel*, London 1927.
D. Hyde, *A Literary History of Ireland*, London 1967.
A. Huxley, *Point Counter point*, London 1928.
J. K. Huysmans, *A Rebours*, Paris 1884; trans. By R. Baldick as *Against Nature*, Harmondsworth 1958.
K. H. Jackson, *A Celtic Miscellany*, London 1967.

364   *Flann O'Brien: a critical introduction*

J. Joyce, *Dubliners*, Paris 1914.
    A Portrait of the Artist as a Young Man, paris 1916.
    Ulysses, Paris 1922.
B. Kiely, *Modern Irish Fiction: A Critique*, Dublin 1950.
J. Mays in *Myles*, ed. T. O'Keeffe, London 1973.
V. Mercier, *The Irish Comic Tradition*, Oxford 1962
T. O. Crohan, *The Islandman*, Dublin 1937. (Transl. of *An tÓileánach* by Tomás Ó Criomthain.)
S. H. O'Grady, *Silva Gadelica*, London 1892.
S. J. O'Grady, *Finn and His Companions*, Dublin 1921.
M. O'Sullivan, *Twenty Years a-Growing*, London 1933.
J. G. O'Keeffe, trans. and ed., *Buile Shuibhne* (Irish Texts Society), London 1913.
Myles Orvell, 'Entirely Fictitious: The Fiction of Flann O'Brien', *Journal of Irish Literature* (Newark, Del.) III, 1 (Jan. 1974), 93-103.
A. and B. Rees, *Celtic Heritage,* London 1961.
J. Stephens, *The Crock of Gold,* London 1912.
    The Charwoman's Daughter, London 1912.
L. Sterne, *The Life and Opinions of Tristram Shandy*, New York and London 1760-67.
The Oxford Book of Irish Verse, ed. Donagh MacDonagh and Lennox Robinson, Oxford 1958.
Comhthrom Féinne. Published by the SRC of UCD.
The National Student. Published in UCD.
Blather. Published in UCD.

REVIEWS, ARTICLES, OBITUARY NOTICES

Reviews of O'Brien's books appeared in all the major journals in England, Ireland and the United States. Only those found to be of particular interest have been listed here.
Brendan Behan, *Irish Times*, 30 Jul. 1960.
Bernard Benstock, 'Flann O'Brien in Hell: *The Third Policeman'*, *Bucknell Review* XVII, 2 (May 1969), 67-8.
Bernard Benstock. 'The Three Faces of Brian O'Nolan', *Eire-Ireland* III, 3 (Autumn 1968), 51-65.
Austin Clarke, *Dublin Magazine* (Sept. 1939).
John Colemen, *The Spectator,* 22 Jul. 1960.
Thomas Hogan, 'Myles na gCopaleen', *The Bell* XIII, 2 (1946), 120-40.
Ivan del Janik, 'Flann O'Brien: The Novelist as Critic', *Éire-Ireland* IV, 4 (Winter 1969), 64-72.
Benedict Kiely, 'Fun After Death', *New York Times*, 12 Nov. 1967.

John V. Kelleher, 'Dublin's Joyce and Others', *Virginia Quarterly Review* XXXIII, 1 (Winter 1957), 132-5.

L. L. Lee, 'The Dublin Cowboys of Flann O'Brien', *Western American Literature* IV, 3 (Fall 1969), 219-25.

John Montague, *Hibernia*, 12 Aug. 1960.

Niall Montgomery, 'An Aristophanic Sorcerer', *Irish Times*, 2 Apr. 1966.

V. S. Prichett, *New Statesman*, 20 Aug. 1960.

Niall Sheridan, 'Brian, Flann and Myles', *Irish Times*, 2 Apr. 1966.

John Wain, 'To Write for My Own Race', *Encounter* XXIX, 1 (Jul. 1967), 71ff.

Mervyn Wall, 'Mylestones', *Irish Times*, 14 Sep. 1968.

Index